THE NATIONAL INTERI

To Richard,

Remembering many stimulating discussions in our Merton years.

Chris

26 July 2024

The National Interest in Question: Foreign Policy in Multicultural Societies

CHRISTOPHER HILL

Great Clarendon Street, Oxford, OX2 6DP,
United Kingdom

Oxford University Press is a department of the University of Oxford.
It furthers the University's objective of excellence in research, scholarship,
and education by publishing worldwide. Oxford is a registered trade mark of
Oxford University Press in the UK and in certain other countries

First published 2013
First published in paperback 2015

Published in the United States of America by Oxford University Press
198 Madison Avenue, New York, NY 10016, United States of America

British Library Cataloguing in Publication Data
Data available

Library of Congress Cataloging in Publication Data
Data available

ISBN 978–0–19–965276–1 (Hbk.)
ISBN 978–0–19–874535–8 (Pbk.)

To the memory of Andreas Papadopoulos, 1977–2010

Contents

List of Figures and Tables

Glossary of Abbreviations

AFSJ	Area of Freedom, Security and Justice (of the EU)
ANA-MPA	Athens News Agency/Macedonian Press Agency
BBC	British Broadcasting Corporation
BRIC	Brazil, Russia, India, and China
CEECs	Central and Eastern European Countries
CEPOL	Collège européen de police (European Police College)
CFSP	Common Foreign and Security Policy
CIA	Central Intelligence Agency
CIDOB	Centre d'Estudis i Documentació Internacionals a Barcelona (Centre for International Studies and Documentation, Barcelona)
COSI	Standing Committee on Operational Cooperation on Internal Security (EU)
CSDP	Common Security and Defence Policy
DCRI	Direction centrale du renseignement intérieur (French security service)
DDR	Deutsche Demokratische Republik (German Democratic Republic)
DPP	Danish People's Party
DRC	Democratic Republic of the Congo
EC	European Commission/European Community
EU-15	The 15 Member States of the European Union as of 31.12.2003
EFPU	European Foreign Policy Unit (LSE)
EFTA	European Free Trade Association
ENI	Encuesta Nacional de Inmigrantes (The National Survey of Immigrants)
ETA	Euskadi Ta Askatasuna (Basque Homeland and Freedom)
EU	European Union
EUNAVFOR	European Union Naval Force Somalia
Eurojust	European Judicial Cooperation Unit
Europol	European Police Office
Eurosur	Eurosurveillance
FLN	Front de libération nationale Algeria)
FRG	Federal Republic of Germany
FRIDE	Fundación para las relaciones internacionales y el diálogo (Foundation for International Relations and Dialogue, Madrid)
FPA	Foreign Policy Analysis
Frontex	European Agency for the Management of Operational Cooperation at the External Borders of the Member States of the European Union
FYROM	Former Yugoslav Republic of Macedonia
GB	Great Britain
GDP	Gross Domestic Product
GIA	Groupe Islamique Armé (Armed Islamic Group)
GMFUS	German Marshall Fund of the United States
GNI	Gross National Income

GOP	Grand Old Party (US Republicans)
ICC	International Criminal Court
IISS	International Institute for Strategic Studies
INGO	International Nongovernmental Organisation
IR	International Relations
IRA	Irish Republican Army
ISAF	International Security Assistance Force
ISTAT	Istituto nazionale di statistica (National Institute of Statistics, Italy)
JHA	Justice and Home Affairs
K4 Committee	Coordinating committee of senior officials preparing JHA work
LAOS	Popular Orthodox Rally (Greek political party)
LSE	London School of Economics and Political Science
LI	Liberal intergovernmentalism
LPF	List Pim Fortuyn
MEP	Member of the European Parliament
MI5	Military Intelligence, Section 5
MIPEX	Migrants Integration Policy Index
MIREM	Migration de Retour au Maghreb (EU research programme)
MITI	Migrants Information Territorial Index
NATO	North Atlantic Treaty Organisation
NGO	Nongovernmental Organisation
ODA	Overseas Development Assistance
OECD	Organisation for Economic Cooperation and Development
OSCE	Organisation for Security and Cooperation in Europe
PACA	Provence-Alpes-Côtes-d'Azur (region of France)
PNR	Passenger Name Record
PP	People's Party
PSC	Political and Security Committee
PSOE	Partido Socialista Obrero Español (Spanish Socialist Workers Party)
PVV	Partij voor de Vrijheid (Party for Freedom, Netherlands)
RAF	Red Army Faction
SPD	Sozialdemokratische Partei Deutschlands (Social Democratic Party of Germany)
SVP	Schweizerische Volkspartei (Swiss People's Party)
SWIFT	Society for Worldwide Interbank Financial Telecommunications
TREVI	Counter-terrorism working group
UK	United Kingdom
UN	United Nations
US/USA	United States/United States of America
WASP	White Anglo-Saxon Protestant
WMD	Weapons of Mass Destruction
WTO	World Trade Organisation

Preface

Academic books, no less than novels, have personal origins. This one is no exception. It comes out of two aspects of my life.

The first is the fact that I am a Londoner. I have enjoyed living in the Borough of Haringey—one of the city's most diverse, and also most deprived—for nearly all of my adult life, although as a south Londoner by birth I had risked serious cultural estrangement by settling north of the river. I have watched London change dramatically over my sixty years of recall, from the bomb-damaged, drab, but quite cohesive place of the mid-1950s to the glamorous cosmopolitan environment of today where it is quite possible to take a journey on the Tube and think English a minority language. This transformation has resulted from London engaging with the outside world, as it was bound to do given Britain's history as a great power and multi-ethnic empire. The world has come to London in many ways, whether through young French bankers, with a local polling station for their presidential election, global plutocrats buying up football clubs and the best residential areas, or the mass of low-paid workers who do the jobs in hospitals, bars, and cleaning firms which keep the capital going. And London has also gone out to the world, so that it no longer seems bizarre—as it did when Ken Livingstone started the practice—for Mayor Johnson to behave like a municipal foreign minister by staging well-publicized visits to major cities like New York and Mumbai.

London is not the only UK city to have become cosmopolitan. To lesser degrees the same process is also visible in Birmingham, Bradford, Bristol, and Manchester, while Liverpool has always stood for a particular kind of openness to the world, through its maritime trade, and connections to Ireland. Moreover, if the UK's cities are the most diverse in Europe, other countries are following the same path. Amsterdam, Barcelona, Berlin, Brussels, Dublin, Marseilles, Milan, and Paris are becoming ever more multicultural in their populations and atmospheres.

As a citizen who has watched this fascinating historical process at close hand, I am interested in how and why it has happened, which historians and sociologists have already thrown light on. But I am most concerned with the nature of the relationships which it entails between a particular society and the outside world with which it is now engaged to a far greater extent than in the past, even allowing for the open borders of nineteenth-century Europe, and the fact that migration is a permanent feature of all societies. What we loosely call 'multiculturalism' implies a reworking of the notion of foreignness, for it suggests both the co-existence of very different ways of life within the one national society, and the way the groups which live in them connect across borders with their equivalents in other countries. The key question which then arises is about the significance of the political dimension of these relationships, both inside a society and transnationally. What are the consequences of the new diversity for a given society in terms of how it manages its connections to the world, and of its conception of common interests?

The second personal factor which is at the root of this book is that by profession I am a political scientist with a special interest in international relations, and in particular in foreign policy and its making. I have always taken a comparative approach to my subject, concentrating empirically on the region which used to be called western Europe, but since the end of the Cold War now extends to Poland's border with the Ukraine, and into the Balkans. A central part of this focus has been on the 'domestic sources of foreign policy' and indeed on the international sources of domestic policy and politics. It has always seemed to me axiomatic that if you want to understand a given country, you need to know about its external context and relationships, while to explain a foreign policy only in terms of the 'great game' of international politics is to provide thin gruel indeed. Each country's ability to cope with the international situation it finds itself in is a product of its distinctive traditions, values, demography, constitution, infrastructure, and many other things which mark it out from other states.

These assumptions, on top of my personal experiences, have led me to enquire into the nature of the interplay between changing societies and changing foreign policies. For the countries of western Europe (by which I broadly mean the Member States of the European Union (EU) before the enlargement of 2004–7) have also been in the process of adapting their attitudes and strategies in a world which itself has moved on. European empires disappeared in the 1960s, though the mental habits associated with them have taken longer to fade. The Cold War and the division of Europe disappeared with the collapse of communism. The international economy displayed breathtaking signs of growth and integration, until the western half of it ran into a major financial crisis which is still with us. New powers have emerged, putting the old Eurocentric order into a very different perspective.

In response to these challenges and opportunities the European states have reinvented themselves through foreign policy, focusing on human rights, conflict prevention, development aid, and other forms of soft power.

Yet some have taken this new orientation further, into 'humanitarian intervention', which brings me to the last key issue lying behind this book, the all too familiar one of war. For it turned out that the West's self-regarding notion of benevolent stewardship in international relations was not only not accepted in many other parts of the world, but was violently opposed. The rise of Islamist terrorism which caught the United States so unawares in 2001 was rapidly countered by US–European attacks in Afghanistan and Iraq. This sequence of events darkened the whole climate of international politics, and in terms of the present theme it had a particularly devastating consequence. For the changing societies of Europe found that war was not after all so distant; it reverberated at home through some terrorist attacks, the fear of more, and a spiral of insecurity expressed in tensions over inter-communal differences, particularly in relation to Islam.

This is where the element of autobiography in this account comes full circle, because London became an epicentre of fear and tension. The bomb attacks of 7 July 2005, and those two weeks later which killed no one but could easily have been as lethal, were carried out by British citizens against British citizens, for reasons which went well beyond any domestic grievance. And this in a city which had not only been lauded for its cosmopolitanism, but where, as I knew from my own daily life in Haringey, ordinary people from very different cultures managed to rub along surprisingly well, even if they did not much mix. How had it come to this?

It is this question more than any other which has motivated my enquiry. I want to use my professional knowledge of foreign policy, of European politics, and of transnational relations to disentangle the complex tangle of domestic and international factors which have been shaping developments in the United Kingdom and its EU partners over the last decade, with a view to understanding better both the impact of civil society on foreign policy (indeed on external relations more generally), and the converse—the way in which our very civil societies are being affected by international politics and how we engage with them.

In the pursuit of this goal I have attempted to pull together a wide range of sources, ideas, and scholarly literatures, including those dealing with migration, terrorism, foreign policy, comparative politics, European integration, international relations, and multiculturalism—to say nothing of specialized works on at least nine individual European countries. I cannot hope to have done justice to the vast materials I have delved into, but one has to stop somewhere. I have done my best to avoid stereotypes and simplifications on these many complex issues, respecting the fact that specialists have devoted careers to matters which I have only touched on. But it seems to me of great importance that someone should start the work of trying to put the whole picture together, which means risking a cross-disciplinary approach and a single-authored interpretation.

Although I alone am responsible for the contents of this book, very many people have helped me during the work which has gone into it over the last six years. I am particularly grateful to the friends and colleagues who took the time to read draft chapters and to correct some of my exuberances. They were: Filippo Andreatta, Elisabetta Brighi, Fraser Cameron, Helen Drake, Pavlos Efthymiou, Catherine Gegout, Roy Ginsberg, Ulf Hedetoft, Mark Gilbert,

Peter Mandaville, Anand Menon, Roger Morgan, Hans Mouritzen, Rick Stanwood, and Bertjan Verbeek. Mike Smith advised me with his usual perceptiveness on the original design of the project, while Ken Booth had encouraged me at the outset by inviting me to give the E. H. Carr lecture at Aberystwyth, which was the first stimulus for my thinking on the subject.[1] Lisbeth Aggestam then persuaded me to take part in her interesting Chatham House project, leading to our joint article on the European dimension of multiculturalism.[2] I have also been grateful for the opportunity to present papers on the theme at CERI in Paris, IBEI in Barcelona, Johns Hopkins in Bologna, St Antony's College, Oxford, Rider University, New Jersey, the Royal Institute of International Affairs, Chatham House, the Brookings Institution, Washington DC, St John's University, York (in conjunction with York Minster), the Department of Government at the University of Essex, the Department of Politics and International Relations at the University of Edinburgh, and of course to the talented students of my own Department of Politics and International Studies at Cambridge.

Others have also helped me in various ways, whether by advising on particular issues, answering sometimes arcane queries, providing encouragement, or (as practitioners) by providing interviews. Not all of the latter can be included in the following list of people to whom I owe a debt: Massimo Ambrosetti, Nasira Ashraf, Esther Barbé, Duncan Bell, Sven Biscop, Gianni Bonvicini, Sophie Briquetti, Chris Brown, General Mini Camparini, Irena Caquet, Edward Chaplin, Devon Curtis, Marta Dassù, Sir Richard Dearlove, Geoffrey Edwards, Mette Eilstrup-Sangiovanni, Luca Einaudi, Georgios Evangelopoulos, Timothy Garton Ash, Andrew Geddes, Eda Gemi, Bastian Giegerich, Robert Gordon, Pierre Hassner, Simon Hix, Ted Hopf, George Joffé, Michael Kenny, Henrik Larsen, Christian Lequesne, Margot Light, Andrew Linklater, Dzuliana Luksa, Raffaele Marchetti, James Mayall, Miguel Medina Abellan, Nicola Minasi, Pervaiz Nazir, Kerem Öktem, Sir David Omand, Inderjeet Parmar, John Peterson, Annalisa Poli, Mario Poli, Luca Ratti, Olivier Roy, Tom Ryan, Paul Scheffer, Alessandro Silj, Sara Silvestri, Brendan Simms, Julie Smith, Karen Smith, Dimitri Sotiropoulos, David Spence, Bernhard Stahl, Fouzia Younis-Suleman, Andreas Takis, Natalie Tocci, Asle Toje, Robert Tombs, Anna Triandafyllidou, Charalambos Tsardanidis, Loukas Tsoukalis, Thanos Veremis, Wolfgang Wessels, Richard Whitman, Anders Wivel, William Vlcek.

I apologize if I have missed anyone out, and remain deeply grateful to all for the help I have received, including to the British Academy for the original

[1] Leading to: Christopher Hill, 'Bringing War Home: Foreign Policy-making in Multicultural Societies', *International Relations*, 21/3 (2007), pp. 259–83.

[2] Lisbeth Aggestam and Christopher Hill, 'The Challenge of Multiculturalism in European Foreign Policy', *International Affairs*, 84/1 (2008), pp. 97–114.

small grant on public opinion in Europe which enabled me to start down a road whose end I did not then foresee.

Intellectually two people have been of particular importance to me, from very different starting-points. Fred Halliday was an expert on more subjects than most of us have even dipped into. His robust but nuanced understandings of ethnicity, culture, and international politics acted as a touchstone at many of the earlier stages of my thinking. I enjoyed a number of helpful discussions with him on the theme of this book, including one in Barcelona in 2009 which ensured that I did not miss out the sub-national dimension of the diversity issue. The second person, even more of a personal friend as well as colleague, was David Allen. His expertise on the European Union and on British foreign policy mapped closely onto my own interests. Dave advised me on many technical points, but he was also a constant source of generous support and confidence in the project, especially when things were not going so well. Like Fred, and at much the same age, he died before having the chance to enjoy the freedom from university duties which they had both more than earned. Like so many others, I miss their friendship and their stimulus.

Some people have helped a great deal with logistics and encouragement. Among them are Wendy Cooke, Lottie Garrett, Angela Pollentine, Jenny Barnett, and Victoria Jones on the administrative staff of my department, and Dominic Byatt, my OUP editor. I am only one in a long line of authors to be grateful not only for his cheerful and crisp efficiency, but for his real interest in and knowledge of the subjects he deals with. Andrew Gamble has been a comrade-in-arms at POLIS. As Head of Department he made it possible to continue with this project when circumstances brought it to a halt. I much appreciate his understated generosity. Björn Siebert was a terrific research assistant at a crucial stage. His ability to cover both security and multiculturalism is unusual in a PhD student, and was a major asset. His successor in the last stages of the work, Tom Barker, was equally indispensable. His commitment, eagle eye, and excellent judgment have helped me at innumerable points as we have pulled the text together. Sarah Beadle has rescued me over the index.

My wife, Maria McKay, has read most of my drafts and has invariably improved them. She has given up a lot of time to enable me to finish this book, which is for her as much as for anyone. She understands its personal as well as intellectual roots, not least as a migrant in childhood herself. But the book is dedicated to our son-in-law Andreas, who, to the distress of all who knew him, succumbed to a fulminating brain tumour at the age of 32. He was a brilliant and loveable man who changed my ideas about migration, Greece, England, and (most of all) courage.

Christopher Hill

Cambridge
14 April 2013

1

The social context of foreign policy

Fact is always judgement.[1]

Foreign policy has domestic sources, it is commonly agreed. But what does that statement mean? Such sources are usually identified in terms of either an aggregated public opinion or the nature of a regime. The diversity of civil society is rarely seen as relevant to foreign policy, even in multinational states such as Spain and the UK. This is understandable for part of the history of modern democracies, but it is an approach which has gradually become anachronistic. The changes brought about in recent decades by economic globalization, information technology, the waning of the Cold War and its associated security ethos, and most importantly by migration, have become increasingly significant for foreign policy.

The fundamental aim of this book is to explore the impact of these changes by examining how foreign policy is shaped and constrained in modern European democracies with increasingly heterogeneous civil societies, and how it in turn reverberates within society, with potentially serious effects. Its concern sits at the intersection of three broad areas of research, foreign policy-making, domestic politics, and multiculturalism, which have not yet been systematically brought together.

At the highest level a focus on the social context might lead to a belief that states make war because of domestic imperatives, as with Serbian nationalism in the 1990s. More prosaically, it can refer to the way riots might disrupt a diplomatic strategy or a fishing lobby might persuade a government to take up its cause in an international negotiation. Historians and area studies specialists have few problems with incorporating such observations into their accounts together with external factors like the changing balance of power. But social scientists, which in this context means specialists in International Relations (IR), are not usually content with such idiographic treatment. They search for generalizations, usually at the level of the international system as a whole,

[1] Michael Oakeshott, *Experience and its Modes* (Cambridge: Cambridge University Press, 1933; repr. 1966), p. 112.

trying to confirm or discredit theories such as neorealism, to establish whether phenomena like regimes exist, or to explore key concepts such as sovereignty. While these are perfectly valid, indeed important, exercises they do not do justice to the messy, multidimensional realities of international politics, or say much about agency—in the sense of the key actors in international relations and the forces which shape their choices.

There are two main exceptions to this rule. On the one hand Foreign Policy Analysis (FPA) has as its rationale the study of how states formulate and execute their strategies. It also pays considerable attention to the influence of domestic factors. But it relies on middle-range theory to generate a limited set of generalizations about behaviour, on the basis of types of state or types of policy problems. These have to compete with the apparently more powerful theories at the systemic level, whether realism, English School liberalism, or globalization, in comparison to which, it seems to some, FPA merely provides embroidering detail.

The other main avenue by which the hegemony of generalization is challenged without retreating into a reverence for detail, is constructivism. In its variants this approach—for it is too unspecified to be a theory—directs us towards how the positions of international actors come to be as they are, while taking an eclectic view as to which influences might be most important: ideas, language, history, memory, institutions, norms, interests.[2] It assumes that nothing is fixed and that positions taken or criteria used will always be open to reshaping, not least because any given policy has to be the product of 'intersubjective agreement'.[3] Constructivism starts to fall short when it comes up against problems of implementation, and the ability of ideas, through the mediation of human actors, to change the logic of international politics. But it does have the great advantage of accepting that both international and domestic influences shape attitudes and behaviour, while there is nothing predetermined about the balance to be struck in any account between material and ideational forces. It also brings to the fore the importance of 'social' processes, by which is meant the interaction of human beings in their myriad contexts, from the UN Security Council to the Arab Street. This sometimes socializes, by recruiting actors over time to a culture or way of behaving, but at other points will have less predictable outcomes, opening up new possibilities and contesting any notion of 'iron laws' in international politics.[4]

[2] For a sophisticated assessment of the now extensive literature on constructivism see Emmanuel Adler, 'Constructivism and International Relations' in Walter Carlsnaes, Thomas Risse, and Beth A. Simmons (eds), *Handbook of International Relations* (London: Sage, 2005), pp. 95–118.

[3] Alexander Wendt, *Social Theory of International Politics* (Cambridge: Cambridge University Press, 1999), pp. 160–1.

[4] Underlying constructivism, and indeed other voluntarist or agency-centred approaches in the social sciences, is the assumption that hindsight overdetermines and that history did not have

The relevance of society to foreign policy can have a more straightforward dimension, in terms of the way class, interest groups, and public opinion may affect decision-makers' calculations, through their own leverage or via their place in the values of the political system. Any nation-state, particularly of a democratic and capitalist character, is in a perpetual state of tension between the need for a cohesive identity and diverging definitions of the 'national interest' on a whole range of issues. Surprisingly little research has been conducted on such matters even in relation to the most active and well-documented states. Although in recent decades FPA has undergone a welcome revival, after a decade or more of neglect during the heyday of globalization theory and the presumed demise of the state, this has not generally extended to studies of individual countries and the relationship between their internal and external activities.[5] The rise of China has led to much discussion of the links between its rapidly changing socio-economic life, and its international behaviour, while in Europe work has finally started to appear on the foreign policies of Germany and Italy now that those two states have become more confident about acting independently in world affairs. But there is a paucity of recent studies of the diplomacy of Britain, France, and Spain, especially compared to the ever-rising tide of literature on the European Union's (EU) role in the world. For its part the United States naturally generates much interest in its foreign relations, but there is much less specialist work on the domestic dimension, for example on economic interests or on the role of its churches, than one might expect.

The immense growth of transnationalism since 1945 complicates the issue of domestic sources further. Corporate firms which acknowledge no patriotism, ideas and information which flow freely across borders, and migratory movements which create a complex web of diasporas, have all blurred the boundary between inside and outside. By the same token they have made it easier for governments to influence each other's domestic environments, while non-state actors are less confined in their activities by official gate-keeping and the concept of frontiers.[6]

to turn out as it in fact did. For a lively discussion of this issue see Philip E. Tetlock, Richard Ned Lebow, and Geoffrey Parker (eds), *Unmaking the West: 'What-if?' Scenarios that Rewrite World History* (Ann Arbor: University of Michigan Press, 2006).

[5] The recent wave has generally been comparative and analytical. See Chris Alden and Amnon Aran, *Foreign Policy Analysis: New Approaches* (Abingdon: Routledge, 2012); Christopher Hill, *The Changing Politics of Foreign Policy* (Houndmills: Palgrave Macmillan, 2003); Valerie M. Hudson, *Foreign Policy Analysis: Classic and Contemporary Theory* (Lanham, MD: Rowman & Littlefield, 2007); Steve Smith, Amelia Hadfield, and Tim Dunne (eds), *Foreign Policy: Theories, Actors, Cases* (2nd edn, Oxford: Oxford University Press, 2012).

[6] The standard works on transnationalism did not see diasporas, migration, and religion as at the forefront of the process. This is a more recent development, noted by the literature on IR theory, globalization, and social movements. For the first wave, see Robert O. Keohane and Joseph S. Nye (eds), *Transnational Relations and World Politics* (Cambridge, MA: Harvard

This is the context from which the current book begins. The focus is on the changing domestic environments of European states, with special reference to the issue of social diversity and its relationship with foreign policy, broadly conceived. The presumption is that there will be a two-way flow between international events and domestic politics, with a third dimension being added by the practices of transnationalism. 'Social diversity' is not interpreted to mean the full range of difference which exists in a modern society, from gender and age cohorts, through regional variations, and contrasts in wealth and lifestyle. Rather, it is used to refer to the particular set of issues associated with what is popularly termed 'multiculturalism'. The definitional problems arising from this notion are addressed later in this chapter. For the moment it may stand as short-hand for the existence of a substantial number of ethno-cultural minorities in society, a phenomenon which is new to European states in varying degrees. If it is clearly a significant development at the level of society, as indicated by the high level of debate and controversy attached to it, does it also have relevance for the international relations of the states concerned? Given the transnational links inherent in the arrival of new groups in a society, with ties to home countries and other cultures, there is a strong *prima facie* case for thinking so.

THE NATIONAL INTEREST IN QUESTION

The very existence of the nation-state as a way of fixing the boundaries—arbitrary, historical, but nonetheless real—around territorial agglomerations of human beings, means that when it comes to acting in the world it faces the issue (in principle) of how to sum the wide range of interests and beliefs of its citizens. Since even in Switzerland it is only occasionally feasible to involve direct democracy, this entails the transfer of powers to government on an even more extensive basis than with domestic policy areas such as education or health, where a good deal of delegation and devolution is possible. It then becomes inevitable that political argument over the criteria for decision revolves around a simplistic idea like 'the' national interest. Yet it is evident that every state has multiple interests, meaning that on a given issue the real

University Press, 1973); Thomas Risse-Kappen (ed.), *Bringing Transnational Relations Back In: Non-State Actors, Domestic Structures and International Institutions* (Cambridge: Cambridge University Press, 1995). For the second, see Jan Aart Scholte, *International Relations of Social Change* (Milton Keynes: Open University Press, 1993); Daphne Josselin and William Wallace (eds), *Non-State Actors in World Politics* (Houndmills: Palgrave Macmillan, 2001); Steven Vertovec, *Transnationalism* (London: Routledge, 2009); Rainer Bauböck (ed.), *Diasporas and Transnationalism: Concepts, Theories and Methods* (Amsterdam: University of Amsterdam Press, 2012).

question is, 'what is the nation's interest in this particular context?' This is an understandable way to proceed, up to a point. If genuine debate on foreign policy were to be a regular occurrence then the concept of the national interest would have traction, because there would be some chance of forging consensus on an overall strategy, linking issues and plural inputs together. In practice, however, this is rare even in mature democracies, which opens the door to abuse and scepticism.

As a result, academic students of IR have mounted three broad kinds of critique of the concept of national interest and of its uses.[7] Firstly, it can be seen as a mere screen for the self-interests of a governing elite, which imposes in top-down style a set of prescriptions which purport to serve the national community as a whole, and/or to represent its historic concerns.[8] This fits with many empirical studies of foreign policy-making, which show that the executive tends to dominate and that it is difficult for public opinion in its various guises to influence decisions. According to one's point of view this can be seen as a natural consequence of complexity in modern democracies, a desirable form of responsible leadership, or a hypocritical disregard of the populace, who end up making sacrifices from which the already powerful benefit. It should be noted, however, that it is not necessary to believe in the cynicism of elites in order to assert that they control definitions of the national interest. Indeed, it is now common to accept that policy-makers genuinely believe the narratives they articulate, which in a democracy must include notions of service and accountability, however little they are lived up to.[9]

This last point leads naturally to the second key critique of the 'national interest', from the constructivist perspective (summarized earlier). In this context, an attempt is made to *de*construct the claims made about the national interest to see what sets of ideas, preferences, and prejudices they might contain.[10] There tends to be an assumption that dominant ideas are 'embedded', and therefore change relatively slowly, but it is also possible to envisage quite sharp changes of tack as the result of learning through

[7] The first powerful critique, especially on 'objectivist' accounts of the national interest, came from behavioural FPA. See James N. Rosenau, 'The National Interest' in his *The Scientific Study of Foreign Policy* (New York: Free Press, 1971), pp. 239–49, first published in David L. Sills (ed.), *International Encyclopedia of the Social Sciences* (New York: Macmillan and The Free Press, 1968), pp. 34–40; see also George Modelski, *A Theory of Foreign Policy* (New York: Praeger, 1962), pp. 70–2.

[8] See for example: Jack Snyder, *Myths of Empire: Domestic Politics and International Ambition* (Ithaca: Cornell University Press, 1991), pp. 14–20; John J. Mearsheimer, *Why Leaders Lie: The Truth about Lying in International Politics* (New York: Oxford University Press, 2011), e.g. p. 7; also Mark Curtis, *Web of Deceit: Britain's Real Role in the World* (London: Vintage, 2003), pp. 285–94.

[9] Peter J. Katzenstein (ed.), *The Culture of National Security: Norms and Identity in World Politics* (New York: Columbia University Press, 1996), p. 27.

[10] Martha Finnemore, *National Interests in International Society* (Ithaca: Cornell University Press, 1996).

argument, reasoned and otherwise, or of changes in dominant ideologies.[11] As Wendt says, 'Actors do not have a "portfolio" of interests that they carry round independent of social context; instead they define their interests in the process of defining situations.'[12] On this view there is nothing objective about the national interest; even if there are some 'rules of the game' in international politics, which if ignored can have damaging consequences, actors always *interpret* the world and are far more than desiccated machines for calculating advantage. Rather, they inhabit cultures, which often stretch beyond the confines of their own state, and which are manifest in distinctive languages of politics, identities, and ethics. On this basis the national interest may well be understood in fundamentally different ways according not only to geographical site, but also to historical period, and to who holds power. From an analytical perspective it then becomes an important starting-point for understanding the dominant ideas and assumptions underlying policy.

The third critique of the idea of the national interest is less sophisticated. It consists in the view that it is a political football, to be kicked in different directions according to whoever wins a particular policy battle. The assumption here is not that of a stable power elite driving forward its own interpretation of the country's external needs, but rather of a pluralist political system of competing groups, some more effective and better-organized than others, but none with a monopoly of influence. Each needs to be able to claim it is acting in the national interest so as to legitimize itself before the national community as a whole, forestalling accusations of partiality, but also pre-empting others from wrapping themselves in the flag.[13] The tactic is essentially short term, which diminishes the credibility of future claims, and of the concept as such. It is also inherently difficult for minorities, such as ethnic groups, to use such an approach.

An important consideration when analysing any concept is the issue of binary opposites—that is, defining something in part on the basis of its logical

[11] Thomas Risse, '"Let's Argue!": Communicative Action in World Politics', *International Organization*, 54/1 (2000), pp. 1–39. Risse here follows Jürgen Habermas, *The Theory of Communicative Action* (London: Heinemann, 1984). See also Andrew Linklater, *The Transformation of Political Community: Ethical Foundations of the Post-Westphalian Era* (Cambridge: Polity, 1998), and, from a different starting-point, Karen E. Smith and Margot Light (eds), *Ethics of Foreign Policy* (Cambridge: Cambridge University Press, 2001).

[12] Alexander Wendt, 'Anarchy is what states make of it: The Social Construction of Power Politics', *International Organization*, 46/2 (1992), p. 398.

[13] This model can apply at the level of bureaucratic/governmental politics, where decisions end up as the sub-optimal outcomes of turf battles, or at that of interest-groups acting on government. For the former, see Graham T. Allison and Philip Zelikow, *Essence of Decision: Explaining the Cuban Missile Crisis* (2nd edn, Harlow: Longman, 1999); for the latter, David Skidmore and Valerie M. Hudson (eds), *The Limits of State Autonomy: Society Groups and Foreign Policy* (Boulder, CO: Westview Press, 1992), and Thomas Risse-Kappen, 'Public Opinion, Domestic Structure and Liberal Democracies', *World Politics*, 43/4 (1991), pp. 491–517.

opposite.[14] This becomes more complex when the concept itself represents a combination of features. In the case of the national interest we therefore need to think about the opposites of both 'national' and 'interest' in order to assess what is meant, and what is being excluded. In the case of the national, there is more than one plausible opposite. 'International' is one candidate, but that term can refer either to more than one nation, or to the whole world of nations. 'Universal' is another, with its connotation of all humanity, free from the divisions of the state-system. Finally, the opposite of one national view might be that of a particular antagonist, as so often in relations between pairs such as Greece and Turkey or India and Pakistan.

Turning to the idea of 'interest', central to so much debate across the social sciences, the first thing to say is that while the direct opposite of being interested is being actively 'uninterested', there is also the possibility of 'disinterest', that is, having no view or stake in a given issue.[15] On this score an interest refers to the possession of something which it would be undesirable to lose or have damaged. Yet in the discourse of IR it is more common to counterpoise interests with ideals, morals, or norms—even if this sets up some artificial dichotomies. Liberalism, for example, has a long heritage of belief in the possibility of ideals and interests coinciding, while realism, in its sophisticated form, accepts that an interest will be more effectively protected if it can be shown to have taken into account the needs of others.[16]

The fact that neither 'national' nor 'interest' has a single or clear binary opposite undermines their own usefulness as precise guides to decision-making. This problem is exacerbated when one bears in mind that states do not coincide with nations, despite the US tendency to talk about 'relations between nations'.[17] This is why the French and German terms of *raison d'état* and *Staatsraison* (both meaning reason of state) are more satisfactory—if still not sufficient. This is partly because 'state' is more accurate than 'nation', complying as it does with political and legal realities; but also because where 'reason' refers descriptively at a minimum to the purpose or justification of a

[14] A philosophical problem, particularly common in Western thought and deconstructed by such writers as Jacques Derrida and Ferdinand de Saussure. See Duncan Bell (ed.), *Ethics and World Politics* (Oxford: Oxford University Press, 2010), pp. 62–4. It can be argued that the human condition itself leads us down this path, given the binaries of male/female, right/left, day/night, etc.

[15] The misuse of 'disinterested' is one of the most common blunders in modern English.

[16] As in the classical realism of Hans J. Morgenthau and Stanley Hoffmann, notwithstanding popular stereotypes. See Michael C. Williams, *The Realist Tradition and the Limits of International Relations* (Cambridge: Cambridge University Press, 2005), pp. 170–210; Michael C. Williams (ed.), *Realism Reconsidered: The Legacy of Hans J. Morgenthau in International Relations* (Oxford: Oxford University Press, 2007). Also Jonathan Haslam, *No Virtue like Necessity: Realist Thought in International Relations since Machiavelli* (New Haven: Yale University Press, 2001), pp. 204–46, which illustrates the vacillations and quasi-liberal instincts of some leading realists.

[17] Frederick H. Hartmann, *The Relations of Nations* (6th edn, New York: Macmillan, 1983).

policy, and at a maximum to its underlying rationale, 'interest' denotes who or what is served by or benefits from it—a much more difficult claim to substantiate. On the other hand, the continental European tradition does also talk of national interests, sometimes interchangeably with 'reason of state'.[18] The latter term, however, raises the opposite set of difficulties by setting the state up over and above society, with the implication that international relations requires rational and unitary actorness.

However terms like 'national interest' are used, the combination of two contestable ideas into one compounds any inherent problems. But in foreign policy there are always difficult circles to square—nation v. state, state v. society, cohesion v. democracy, interests v. values, nation-state v. international society. There are no easy rules of thumb to be found. Furthermore, in the new context being explored here, the development of a more heterogeneous society with complex links to the external environment will increasingly expose any set of criteria to questioning.

Nonetheless, it is hoped that the analysis of the real-world dilemmas facing the governments and variegated peoples of Europe will lead us towards some ideas about how the criteria for external action might be reformulated. That issue will be returned to explicitly in Chapter 9. For the moment the aim is to show how the idea of the 'national interest' is both inherently unsatisfactory and rendered ever more difficult in contemporary conditions. The next section explains why this last claim is made.

MULTICULTURALISM AND MULTICULTURALITY

The experience of daily life in the countries of western Europe has changed visibly over the last few decades, especially in the big cities: there is more variety among the people on the streets, with a wider range of nationalities, ethnicities, languages, and cultural practices. This phenomenon is usually described as 'multiculturalism'. Here again, however, there is an unfortunate divergence between popular usage and specialist vocabulary. For multiculturalism as a general term covers some divergent practices. The *Oxford English Dictionary* first included the term in 1976, defining it as, 'the characteristics of a multicultural society; (also) the policy or process whereby the distinctive identities of the cultural groups within such a society are maintained or supported'.[19] As Brian Barry saw, this elides three things: (*1*) multicultura*lity*,

[18] As for example in a special issue of the leading Italian review *Aspenia, L'interesse dell'Italia. Chi siamo, cosa vogliamo*, 34 (2006).

[19] 'Multiculturalism', *Oxford English Dictionary* [online] (June 2012), <http://www.oed.com/view/Entry/234921> accessed 15 August 2012.

which refers to the *fact* of cultural diversity, with many groups defining themselves separately from the nation-state—perhaps asserting their right to autonomy and other loyalties, but not necessarily having that right recognized; (2) multicultural*ism*, which is an *ideology-cum-project* about the acceptance of diversity and group rights; (3) *ethnicity*, which strictly refers to racial distinctiveness but is often wrongly used to denote national, linguistic, or religious communities.[20] A multi-ethnic society may or may not be a multicultural one, and vice versa, although there is always likely to be a significant overlap between the two sources of difference. A fourth category may be added—that of multi*nationality*, referring to the fact that some states (like the United Kingdom or Spain) are made up of regionally distinct nations enjoying a formal status and varying degrees of devolution. Taken together, these distinctions enable us to identify the contrasts which exist between the different societies of the EU.[21]

Multiculturality is the basic condition of most of the states of the EU-15.[22] It derives largely from the immigration which started in the 1950s, as the post-war economic revival gained pace, bringing with it the need for cheap labour, satisfied in the United Kingdom from the Caribbean, in Germany from Turkey, and in France from the Maghreb. Migrants were likely initially to come from past colonies or zones of influence, which meant that a small and densely populated country like the Netherlands, through its close connections with ex-colonies such as Indonesia and Suriname, also experienced early changes in its social composition.[23] Conversely, those European countries

[20] Brian Barry, *Culture and Equality: An Egalitarian Critique of Multiculturalism* (Cambridge: Polity, 2001), pp. 22–3. Barry abhors the linguistic ugliness of 'multiculturality', but notes the term, and takes the underlying distinction, from Charles Westin, 'Temporal and Spatial Aspects of Multiculturality', in Rainer Bauböck and John Rundell (eds), *Blurred Boundaries: Migration, Ethnicity, Citizenship* (Aldershot: Ashgate, 1998).

[21] For further discussion, see Christopher Hill, 'Bringing War Home: Foreign Policy-making in Multicultural Societies', *International Relations*, 21/3 (2007), pp. 259–83. A further problem, for which there is no space here, is that of defining 'culture', which is a highly contested notion. See Anne Phillips, *Multiculturalism without Culture* (Princeton: Princeton University Press, 2007), especially pp. 8–10 and pp. 42–72.

[22] For an explanation of why the EU-15 is the chosen group for analysis, see the 'Disciplinary silos' sub-section later in this chapter.

[23] The numbers were relatively small in the early years for the Netherlands, with *c.*200,000 immigrants in 1975, mostly from what is now Indonesia, including a small proportion of South Moluccan exiles, and from Suriname, both ex-colonies. Numbers rose, with guest-workers from Morocco and Turkey in the next decade, to *c.*600,000 or nearly 4 per cent of the population of about 15 million. Melissa Siegel and Chris de Neubourg, *A Historical Perspective on Immigration and Social Protection in the Netherlands,* UNU-MERIT Working Paper 2011-014 (Maastricht: Maastricht University and United Nations University, 2011), p. 5, <http://www.merit.unu.edu/publications/wppdf/2011/wp2011-014.pdf> accessed 11 December 2012. Also Hans van Amersfoort, How the Dutch Government Stimulated the Unwanted Immigration from Suriname, IMI Working Paper 47 (Oxford: Oxford University International Migration Institute, 2011), p. 4, <http://www.imi.ox.ac.uk/pdfs/imi-working-papers/wp-11-47-how-the-dutch-government-stimulated-the-unwanted-immigration-from-suriname> accessed 11 December 2012.

for which the imperial experience was more remote or problematic, like Greece, Spain, and Italy, remained countries of net emigration until the 1990s. For all, however, the needs of the labour market were in due course to suck in guest workers, largely from the poorer countries in what we now call Europe's 'Neighbourhood'. The consequent pressure for family reunions, together with the requests of many refugees from the world's trouble-spots (often with close ties to particular European states) then increased numbers further.

Immigration brought forth different reactions in public policy according to the state concerned, although in the first waves few newcomers experienced a warm welcome, while those who were both poor and non-white often encountered suspicion, resentment, and outright racism. This led to the archetypal reaction by first generation arrivals of attempting not to draw attention to their differences, least of all as a group with special claims. Over the longer term the Member States responded to the changes immigration brought in a variety of ways. Some were relatively homogeneous societies for whom the new diversity represented an obvious challenge. Others, being more plural in the first place, saw the process as a natural extension of the social mosaic. Thus within the EU we find some states which explicitly adopted what I have termed, following Barry, the 'multiculturalist project'. These are Britain, the Netherlands, and Sweden. Others have resisted, or simply ignored the possibility, among whom the most prominent cases are France, Denmark, and Greece. The rest mostly muddle through, evading an explicit choice. Almost all tend to blur the linguistic issues. The term 'integration', for example, is widely used both by those who do not want to admit that their preference is for 'assimilation'—in other words, hoping that immigrants will conform to an existing way of life without adding their own tastes to the *smørrebrød*—and those who fear a commitment to multiculturalism as an ideology. The confusing reality is that most of these terms will be used in any given country in the course of debate which, given the dual use of the adjective 'multicultural' for both the fact of diversity and the project, too often produces a dialogue of the deaf.

What is clear is that the societies of western Europe are in a condition of social flux due to growing ethnocultural diversity, and that this is intimately connected to their relationships with the outside world, through a range of dilemmas from migration, identity, and religion, to human rights, security, and the fear of terrorism. Quite apart from each individual state's domestic sources of foreign policy, or the internal feedback that policy generates, transnational linkages increasingly complicate the picture. These may be categorized, following James Rosenau's typology, as emulative, penetrative, and reactive.[24] An emulative linkage is what the economists call a

[24] James N. Rosenau, *Linkage Politics* (New York: Free Press, 1969). See also Hill, *The Changing Politics of Foreign Policy*, pp. 208–14.

demonstration effect, or a form of imitation. An example from a multicultural society might be the Belgian debate on the Islamic veil echoing that in France.[25] A penetrative linkage is when actors in one society deliberately attempt to influence events in another—as when the Dutch anti-Islamic politician Geert Wilders sought entry to Britain in 2009 to show his propaganda film.[26] Lastly, a reactive linkage is when elements in one society react—positively or negatively—to events in another. An example in this context is the strong reactions of solidarity with the United States shown by Europeans in the immediate aftermath of the atrocities of 11 September 2001, epitomized by *Le Monde*'s headline: 'Nous sommes tous Américains'.[27]

In fact the events of 9/11 finally threw a searchlight onto the possibility that there might be a relationship between high politics in foreign policy, and the evolving character of civil society. Previously, few had seen much connection between the lively debates on multicultural practices and international affairs—despite the uproar in 1989 over the Iranian fatwa issued against the author Salman Rushdie over his book *The Satanic Verses*.[28] The presence of minority groups with foreign origins within a dominant culture was suddenly deemed the source of a potential threat to security, especially within the United States. That apprehension was to be reinforced, and extended to Europe, by a number of dramatic events over the ensuing decade. Increasingly sharp, even hysterical debates over multiculturalism developed in many countries, affecting foreign policy, while actions like the invasion of Iraq fed back into domestic politics, exacerbating existing tensions and fostering new ones. Suddenly, instead of foreign policy having a few, intermittent, 'domestic sources' or constraints, it had become intimately connected to the very nature of the society which it ostensibly served, with a plethora of confusing interactions involving both official and non-state actors. The diverse approaches states took to the phenomenon of multiculturality, and the muddled language in which it was discussed, compounded these new problems.

[25] 'A Local Saying Goes: It Drizzles in Brussels when it Rains in Paris'. See Hassan Bousetta and Dirk Jacobs, 'Multiculturalism, Citizenship and Islam in Problematic Encounters in Belgium', in Tariq Modood, Anna Triandafyllidou, and Ricard Zapata-Barrero (eds), *Multiculturalism, Muslims and Citizenship: A European Approach* (London: Routledge, 2006), p. 30.

[26] He was refused entry by the British government, but an Asylum and Immigration Tribunal ruled in his favour eight months later.

[27] *Le Monde*, 13 September 2001. The editorial which followed, by Jean-Paul Colombani, was more nuanced, but it was the headline's sentiment which caught the attention of the world.

[28] Daniel Pipes, *The Rushdie Affair: The Novel, the Ayatollah, and the West* (2nd rev. edn, New Brunswick: Transaction Press, 2004).

KEY QUESTIONS

The issues of social context, multiculturality, and a contested national interest in foreign policy provide the main themes of this book. But they also provide the platform for five specific, although interrelated, sets of questions:

1. To what extent does ethnocultural diversity within a European society affect the conduct of a country's foreign policy? Here 'ethnocultural' is an important qualifier, for any society will have many different manifestations of diversity. It corresponds to 'multicultural' in the sense of multiculturality. For its part 'foreign policy' is to be understood broadly, to include the full range of a state's relationships with the outside world, not just those formally expressed by a foreign ministry.
2. In what ways, and with what significant consequences, have foreign policy actions and events impacted upon civil society in the multicultural societies of western Europe? How far have they complicated relations between different groups in society, and the maintenance of social peace?
3. What difference does the particular approach taken by a society towards multiculturality make to the interaction between the domestic environment and foreign policy? Does an acceptance of multicultural*ism* go hand in hand with a more cosmopolitan and less sovereignty-obsessed approach to international relations? Or does it, by contrast, open up divisions which make agreement on national positions more difficult, and compromise the country's image in the world? Alternatively, does a full-blooded integrationist approach tend to discipline domestic society so that foreign policy-makers have a freer hand—albeit at the risk of stirring up resentment among minorities and diasporas?
4. What difference is made to the interaction between the internal and the external by the nature and scope of the foreign policy which a government pursues, or indeed by the fact or perception of external threats?[29] Are there policies which are particularly likely to cause tensions in multicultural societies? Are European governments becoming more sensitive to ethnocultural lobbies on international matters?
5. How do the various developments entailed in the interplay between civil society and foreign policy affect the concept of the national interest, and its use as the fundamental criterion for states' external actions? Already rendered problematic by democratic pluralism, particularly in

[29] As Huntington points out, involvement in war makes it more difficult for minorities to assert their distinctive identities, but if 'the external threats to America are modest, intermittent, and ambiguous, Americans may well remain divided over the appropriate roles of their Creed, language, and core culture in their national identity'. Samuel P. Huntington, *Who Are We? America's Great Debate* (London: Simon & Schuster, 2004), p. 177.

multinational states, has it now become an irrelevance in the age of ethnocultural minorities with variable levels of identification with the home country? If so, can it be reconfigured, or are there other criteria or ways of thinking about foreign policy which might be more viable? From a normative point of view, how is the balance best struck between the needs of the state as a whole and the concerns of particular minorities, which might be strongly held?

DISCIPLINARY SILOS

This book is essentially a study in European FPA, meaning both that its subject is the foreign policies of European states, and that it reflects the characteristic methodology of European scholarship. The time-frame consists of the post-Cold War period, with particular emphasis on the period since 9/11.

On the first count, the focus is the EU-15—the states which joined the Union before 2004, when a further ten states acceded, followed by two more in 2007. The twelve states which joined the Union in 2004 and 2007 are excluded from the discussion in this book, less for reasons of manageability or because of their recent accession, than because ten of the twelve are relatively poor ex-Warsaw Pact countries. For the most part they have not yet had the experience of significant multiculturality, while the remaining two (Cyprus and Malta), as small island states, are special cases. Even among the fifteen, as will become clear, the main focus is on ten states. While Austria, Ireland, Luxembourg, Finland, and Portugal all have some experience of multiculturality, and at times have been internationally active, their situations do not justify inclusion here, given space constraints.

On the second count, the approach is 'European' because it employs a qualitative and comparative methodology, but without attempting to set up formal hypotheses which may then be tested against a clearly identified data-set. There are American scholars who also prefer this approach, notably Stanley Hoffmann and Joseph Nye, just as there are Europeans who follow a more scientific path, but broadly speaking the generalization holds. My own choice is founded in epistemological beliefs about the impossibility of explaining much of significance through 'if-then' statements, given the multifactoral and normatively charged nature of world politics (as the democratic peace debate illustrates). I thus prefer to combine an historical and analytical understanding of the interplay between the forces of change and continuity in human affairs with a rigorous treatment of the key concepts at issue. The result cannot avoid some degree of subjectivity, but the assumptions being made and the evidence used should be transparent and open to refutation. The approach to the problems raised is also systematic, in the sense that the problems under review are analysed using a consistent taxonomy and regular reference back to the fundamental questions. The aim is to make possible a sophisticated conversation about the key issues at stake, in the full awareness, as Michael Oakeshott said, that '[p]olitics offers the most difficult of all "literatures" . . . with which to learn to handle and manage the languages of explanation: the idiom of the material to be studied is ever ready to impose itself upon the manner in which it is studied'.[30] That view led Oakeshott to be satirical about the wish to '"analyse" (blessed word)', but since the alternative in this important but so far barely researched area is the blinkered vehemence of so much of public discussion, it is important to analyse the issues in as considered and neutral a manner as possible.[31]

There are other reasons than pure epistemology for taking a less than formal approach to the comparative foreign policy/comparative politics theme of this book. The nature and scope of the problem requires it. The domestic and foreign politics of at least ten diverse nation-states represent a large canvas, with multiple groups (ethnic, religious, regional, party political) and issue-areas (war, human rights, culture, identity) at work. The problems can only be addressed through a combination of multifaceted empirical knowledge and conceptual clarity. The sources for the empirical side of the work have been many and various: official documents, immigration statistics, opinion poll data, interviews, and a wealth of secondary literature from the multiple relevant specialisms. As is common across the social sciences the English language dominates these materials, but where possible relevant writings have also been consulted in French, Italian, Spanish, and (to a lesser extent) German. The huge extent of writing on each individual country, however, means this is still the work of a generalist, with part of the claim to originality resting on the synthesis of diverse debates.

The conceptual and the empirical aspects of the project have involved drawing together material from the three broad areas of FPA, domestic politics, and multiculturalism, involving six specialist literatures, which thus far have largely developed in self-contained academic silos. The first is that of *multiculturalism itself*. From the 1980s on there has been a growing tide of writing, particularly from political philosophers and sociologists, about the issues arising over ethnocultural diversity and minority rights. According to

30 Michael Oakeshott, 'The Study of Politics in a University', in his *Rationalism in Politics and Other Essays* (London: Methuen, 1962), p. 333.

31 Oakeshott, 'The Study of Politics in a University', p. 326. On his powerful but admittedly romantic view of the benefits of conversation rather than a search for truth or fixed conclusions see his essay in the same volume, 'The Voice of Poetry in the Conversation of Mankind', pp. 197–247. The value of a conversation is, however, also relevant to the debate over rationalism and constructivism. See James Fearon and Alexander Wendt, 'Rationalism v. Constructivism: A Skeptical View', in Carlsnaes, Risse, and Simmons (eds), *Handbook of International Relations*, pp. 52–72.

Paul Kelly, the first standard works were written as the Cold War came to an end.[32] Discussion arose from many quite specific issues to do with claims by groups for autonomy on certain issues—whether dress, religious practices, language, or military service.[33] Various dramatic events stimulated particular waves of interest, notably the Rushdie affair and the terrorist attacks of 9/11, which added a security dimension to the debates about social cohesion and human rights. These gave political urgency to the arguments about whether multiculturalism was desirable or not, and indeed put its supporters very much on the defensive.

From an intellectual point of view a particular (and welcome) characteristic of multiculturalism as a subject is the way it brings together empiricists and philosophers. For it is impossible to analyse the issues in a wholly abstract way without reference to the particular contexts in which they have arisen. Thus the major critique of multiculturalism by the political theorist Brian Barry is replete with examples, as is the collection of essays engaging with Barry's views.[34] Similarly, Will Kymlicka, the world's leading scholar on multiculturalism, is both a professor of philosophy and an authority on nationalisms and the practice of minority rights.[35] His cooperation with the public policy expert Keith Banting has produced one of the most useful websites in terms of empirical data on multiculturalism.[36] Nonetheless, the ultimate preoccupation of this increasingly rich literature, augmented by migration and country experts, has mostly been the classical issue of the nature of the good life within a given polity, connecting up with the great traditions of thought about liberalism, egalitarianism, and human rights.[37]

[32] These were Will Kymlicka, *Liberalism, Community and Culture* (Oxford: The Clarendon Press, 1989), and Iris M. Young, *Justice and the Politics of Difference* (Princeton: Princeton University Press, 1990). See Paul Kelly (ed.), *Multiculturalism Reconsidered* (Cambridge: Polity, 2002), p. 1. Young was concerned with 'social groups', by which she meant people sharing the same 'way of life', and particularly those 'oppressed or disadvantaged', p. 187. She did not, however, talk much about ethnicity or even use the term 'multiculturalism'.

[33] For a full list of the kinds of exemption sought see Table 3.1 in Chapter 3. These issues are also found in many societies outside Europe, as the clashes in 2012 over military service between Ultra-Orthodox Jews and the Israeli state illustrate.

[34] Barry, *Culture and Equality*; Kelly (ed.), *Multiculturalism Reconsidered.*

[35] As in Will Kymlicka, *Politics in the Vernacular: Nationalism, Multiculturalism and Citizenship* (Oxford: Oxford University Press, 2001).

[36] 'Multiculturalism Policy Index' [online index] (Queen's University, Canada), <http://www.queensu.ca/mcp/index.html> accessed 16 December 2012; see also the 'Migrant Integration Policy Index', 'MIPEX' [online tool and reference guide] (British Council and Migration Policy Group), <http://www.mipex.eu/> accessed 16 December 2012.

[37] For example: Michael Walzer, *Politics and Passion: Towards a More Egalitarian Liberalism* (New Haven: Yale University Press, 2004); Anthony Simon Laden and David Owen (eds), *Multiculturalism and Political Theory* (Cambridge: Cambridge University Press, 2007); Phillips, *Multiculturalism without Culture*; Tariq Modood, *Multiculturalism: A Civic Idea* (Cambridge: Polity, 2007); Cécile Laborde, *Critical Republicanism: The Hijab Controversy and Political Philosophy* (Oxford: Oxford University Press, 2008).

The international dimension has not however been wholly neglected. John Rawls opened the door to serious philosophical interest with his emphasis on 'peoples', as opposed to states, nations, and nation-states.[38] Rawls' attempt to define a people (especially in contrast to a nation) was not notably successful, but in asserting the moral primacy of a 'law of peoples' over state sovereignty, and in talking so much of toleration, and of 'reasonable pluralism', he began to imply a kind of isomorphism between the peaceful co-existence of groups (or 'peoples') within a state and the requirements of international society. In doing so he was coming close to Andrew Linklater's more coherent account of what might be called a 'pragmatic cosmopolitanism' being worked out at much the same time, if not to the post-state 'cosmopolitan democracy' view of Archibugi and Held.[39] Linklater is in effect a supporter of multiculturalism within the state and of cosmopolitanism globally, but recognizes that the state and citizenship are the platforms on which these have to be built. Rawls also sees the state as fundamental, but does not take the extra step of linking his preference for pluralism at all levels to the rights of groups/peoples within the state. Indeed, in *The Law of Peoples* he does not explicitly discuss multiculturalism.

Will Kymlicka, for his part, has always been more explicitly focused on multiculturalism and indeed is committed to the normative project of diffusing its principles. This has led him to be aware of the power of example in such cases as that of the United States, leading to emulative linkages. He notes how 'English-speaking Canadians have been heavily influenced by American debates'.[40] Canada itself has been the most notable case of multiculturalism, influential in both Europe and Australasia. By 2007 Kymlicka was acknowledging 'the new international politics of diversity', by which he meant the increasing role of international organizations in supporting the principle of multiculturalism and the way in which it and minority rights have come to constitute a global political discourse.[41] What he did not choose to do, however, was to follow up his own earlier brief discussion of the possible

[38] This idea was first developed in 1993, in the Amnesty Lecture at Oxford. See Stephen Shute and Susan Hurley, *On Human Rights: The Oxford Amnesty Lectures* (New York: Basic Books, 1993). It was given much fuller treatment in John Rawls, *The Law of Peoples* (Cambridge, MA: Harvard University Press, 1999). For an analysis, see Peter Jones, 'The Ethics of International Society', in Bell (ed.), *Ethics and World Politics*, pp. 121–4.

[39] Linklater, *The Transformation of Political Community*. It is interesting that Linklater too makes no explicit mention of multiculturalism, although at various points (e.g. pp. 82–5) he effectively discusses it. Daniele Archibugi, *The Global Commonwealth of Citizens: Towards Cosmopolitan Democracy* (Princeton: Princeton University Press, 2008); David Held, *Democracy and Global Order: From the Modern State to Cosmopolitan Governance* (Cambridge: Polity, 1995).

[40] Kymlicka, *Politics in the Vernacular*, p. 272.

[41] Will Kymlicka, *Multicultural Odysseys: Navigating the New International Politics of Diversity* (Oxford: Oxford University Press, 2007).

connection between internal debates on group rights and foreign policy problems—in that case the tension between US resistance to minority claims at home and support for them in Kosovo.[42]

This is the missing link in multicultural studies: how ethnocultural diversity relates to states' foreign policies, both empirically and normatively. The literature on multiculturalism has opened up to internationalism, in the form of international law, international organizations, and the relationship with globalization, but it has not been interested in the possible connections with states' external strategies. Bhikhu Parekh observes that 'while immigration has long been part of European history, hardly any political theorist has systematically theorised it'—and now immigration has become part of foreign policy for most European states.[43] For example, readmission agreements with various Neighbourhood countries, especially in sub-Saharan Africa, have become a common way by which Member States try to handle irregular immigration.[44]

Migration studies thus represent the second specialist area of importance to the current work. This is a specialized and growing field whose exponents rightly focus on issues such as border controls, visa regimes, legal versus 'irregular' population movements, the treatment of asylum seekers, integration, diasporas, and people trafficking. Through burgeoning research centres it has produced invaluable data and analysis for anyone whose work carries them in this direction—and migration is increasingly important for sociology, political economy, globalization, political science, International Relations, and European Studies, aspects of all of which it incorporates.[45] Although under-theorized by political philosophy, and indeed by political science more generally, for the researcher in a related area it represents a rich resource base. In the European context the trail has been blazed by such figures as Robin Cohen, Zig Layton-Henry, Martin Baldwin-Edwards and Martin Schain, Steven Vertovec, and Catherine Wihtol de Wenden.[46] The

[42] Kymlicka, *Politics in the Vernacular*, pp. 273–4. There are some references to foreign policy implications in the 2007 book, notably in the chapter on the EU (pp. 173–246), but by far the main concern is with international norms and regimes.

[43] Bhikhu Parekh, *A New Politics of Identity: Political Principles for an Interdependent World* (Houndmills: Palgrave Macmillan, 2008), p. 286.

[44] For a significant example, see Emmanuela Paoletti, *The Migration of Power and North–South Inequalities: The Case of Italy and Libya* (Houndmills: Palgrave Macmillan, 2010), pp. 107–83.

[45] In Europe key research centres currently exist at the Universities of Amsterdam, Bamberg, Belfast, Berlin, Lille (2), Oxford, Sussex, University College London, and the London School of Economics and Political Science.

[46] Important sources are: Martin Baldwin-Edwards and Martin A. Schain (eds), *The Politics of Immigration in Western Europe* (Ilford: Frank Cass, 1994); Robin Cohen (ed.), *Cambridge Survey of World Migration* (Cambridge: Cambridge University Press, 1995); Zig Layton-Henry (ed.), *The Political Rights of Migrant Workers in Western Europe* (London: Sage, 1990); Martin A. Schain, *The Politics of Immigration in France, Britain and the United States: A Comparative*

newer generation is led by Andrew Geddes, Sandra Lavenex, and Anna Triandafyllidou.[47]

The IR community was relatively slow to take interest in migration. It found no place in the otherwise path-breaking study of transnational relations by Keohane and Nye in 1971.[48] The end of the Cold War, however, produced a wave of people movements both within and towards Europe to rival that of 1945, leading the Copenhagen School to include it in their 'new security agenda', while three of the best-known UK analysts of foreign policy were also quick to see its importance.[49] Little has been built on these foundations, however, in terms of either integrating the problem of migration (whether into or out of a state) into the study of foreign policy, or even using the data generated by specialists.[50]

The third area of literature on which this book draws is the most obvious, namely that of *comparative European foreign policy*. The rationale for the current work is the fact that the subject of domestic diversity has hardly been explored so far by analysts of foreign policies in Europe, whether focusing on the EU or individual Member States.[51] Diplomacy in most of its forms has been given extensive treatment, with much attention given to decision-making and some (if rather less, as we have seen) to its domestic sources. But the role of social factors, whether ethnicity, culture, class, gender, or religion, is strangely neglected. The majority of the work (some of it by this author) has

Study (Houndmills: Palgrave Macmillan, 2008); Steven Vertovec and Robin Cohen (eds), *Migration, Diasporas and Transnationalism* (Cheltenham: Edward Elgar, 1999); Steven Vertovec (ed.), *Migration*, 5 vols (Abingdon: Routledge, 2009); Catherine Wihtol de Wenden, *Les immigrés et la politique. Cent cinquante ans d'évolution* (Paris: Presses de la Fondation nationale des sciences politique, 1988).

47 Representative works are: Andrew Geddes, *The Politics of Migration and Immigration in Europe* (London: Sage, 2003); Andrew Geddes, *Immigration and European Integration: Beyond Fortress Europe* (2nd edn, Manchester: Manchester University Press, 2008); Sandra Lavenex, *The Europeanisation of Refugee Policies: Between Human Rights and Internal Security* (Aldershot: Ashgate, 2001); Anna Triandafyllidou, *Immigrants and National Identity in Europe* (London: Routledge, 2001). A superb country study is Luca Einaudi, *Le politiche dell'immigrazione in Italia dall'Unità a oggi* (Roma-Bari: Editori Laterza, 2007).

48 Keohane and Nye, *Transnational Relations and World Politics*.

49 Ole Wæver et al., *Identity, Migration and the New Security Agenda in Europe* (London: Pinter, 1993); Brian White, Richard Little, and Michael Smith (eds), *Issues in World Politics* (Houndmills: Macmillan, 1997).

50 With the growth of digitization and online resources, governmental statistical offices are now much more accessible to researchers and citizens. As with Europe's railway timetables, the German authorities are far and away the best starting-point, and not just for German data: 'Area and Population' [online database] (Statistische Ämter: Des Bundes und der Länder), <http://www.statistik-portal.de/Statistik-Portal/en/en_inhalt01.asp> accessed 16 December 2012.

51 Apart from incidental discussions the only treatments of the European issues so far are: Shane Brighton, 'British Muslims, Multiculturalism and UK Foreign Policy: "Integration" and "Cohesion" In and Beyond the State', *International Affairs*, 83/1 (2007), pp. 1–17; Hill, 'Bringing War Home', pp. 259–83; Lisbeth Aggestam and Christopher Hill, 'The Challenge of Multiculturalism in European Foreign Policy', *International Affairs*, 84/1 (2008), pp. 97–114.

dealt with the interplay between national foreign policy and the attempt to create an effective common European foreign and security policy, with its ever-growing ambitions and intermittent successes.[52] All of these books in their different ways attempt to do justice to the importance of the domestic dimension, but their priority is in surveying the actual content and direction of policy, with particular reference to the problem of convergence within the EU. Thus no single factor, let alone that of social groups, can get more than passing attention. Where domestic sources are the focus it is usually in relation to a specific case, as with the Falklands War.[53] The only work which comes near to providing a comparative foreign policy treatment of issues relating to multiculturalism focuses on the radical right, which is an important but partial perspective.[54]

By contrast there is a literature which takes social diversity as its focus while also comparing the different Member States. This, our fourth source of material, may be labelled *comparative multiculturalism studies*. Scholarship under this heading is developing rapidly, as specialists in migration, political theory, and sociology come together to work in a genuinely interdisciplinary way on what has become one of the most important issues facing European societies. These authors are often also politically committed to multiculturalism as a normative project, and to that end sometimes join forces with the more reflective activists. The work is almost always collective, because of the difficulty in achieving expertise in the politics of so many states. It has three separate strands: one, a form of comparative politics, explores the differential experiences of minorities, and the varying approaches taken to multiculturalism across the EU, using country-studies appropriate to the issue under discussion.[55] Another focuses on Islam in its different national contexts, sometimes being more concerned with the

[52] The relevant works here are: Christopher Hill (ed.), *National Foreign Policies and European Political Cooperation* (London: Allen & Unwin for the Royal Institute of International Affairs, 1983); Christopher Hill (ed.), *The Actors in Europe's Foreign Policy* (London: Routledge, 1996); Ian Manners and Richard Whitman (eds), *The Foreign Policies of European Union Member States* (Manchester: Manchester University Press, 2000); Eva Gross, *The Europeanization of National Foreign Policy: Continuity and Change in European Crisis Management* (Houndmills: Palgrave Macmillan, 2009); Reuben Wong and Christopher Hill (eds), *National and European Foreign Policies: Towards Europeanization* (London: Routledge, 2011).

[53] Stelios Stavridis and Christopher Hill (eds), *Domestic Sources of Foreign Policy: Western European Reactions to the Falklands Conflict* (Oxford: Berg, 1996).

[54] Christina Schori Liang (ed.), *Europe for the Europeans: The Foreign and Security Policy of the Populist Radical Right* (Aldershot: Ashgate, 2007).

[55] For example: Gideon Calder and Emanuela Ceva (eds), *Diversity in Europe: Dilemmas of Differential Treatment in Theory and Practice* (London: Routledge, 2011); Alessandro Silj (ed.), *European Multiculturalism Revisited* (London: Zed Books, 2010); Anna Triandafyllidou (ed.), *Irregular Migration in Europe: Myths and Realities* (Aldershot: Ashgate, 2010); Steven Vertovec and Susanne Wessendorf (eds), *The Multiculturalism Backlash: European Discourses, Policies and Practices* (London: Routledge, 2010).

impact of European culture on Muslim minorities, and sometimes the reverse.[56] Lastly there is a strand which compares states and their changing social composition in terms of the identity questions which arise. Here immigrants, and Islam, are important but variable factors according to the state in question, for some have significant identity problems already—deriving from past traumas or sub-national pressures—with which newcomers then interact.[57] The work in all these three strands has added immeasurably to our knowledge, but despite extensive collaborative work few have so far engaged with the foreign policy dimension, leaving an important gap to be filled.[58]

A fifth research area which needs to be drawn upon for the current project is that of *terrorism*. This emerged as a new theme in IR in the 1970s, as domestic terrorism plagued a number of European countries—Britain, Germany, and Italy in particular—at the same time as various Palestinian groups and their sympathizers were attacking Israeli targets wherever they were vulnerable. The wave of interest died down as the Cold War came to an end, and only began to revive towards the end of the 1990s. The attacks on the United States in 2001 then catapulted the subject to the top of the agenda for many students of international politics. It remains an active research area, encouraged by official funding, with a huge technical literature. Its main concerns are identifying the causes of terrorism, the consequences, and the best means of combating it, to which end there is a distinction to be made between counter-terrorism (combative) and anti-terrorism (preventive, including addressing the root causes).[59] Terrorism can be seen both as having been made easier by globalization, with its instant communications and increased human mobility, and as a violent reaction against it.[60] In its

[56] Good examples are: Jocelyne Cesari and Seán McLoughlin (eds), *European Muslims and the Secular State* (Aldershot: Ashgate, 2005); Christian Joppke, *Veil: Mirror of Identity* (Cambridge: Polity, 2009); Ayhan Kaya, *Islam, Migration and Integration: The Age of Securitization* (Houndmills: Palgrave Macmillan, 2009); Modood, Triandafyllidou, and Zapata-Barrero, *Multiculturalism, Muslims and Citizenship*; Jan Rath et al., *Western Europe and its Islam* (Leiden: Brill, 2001).

[57] For instance: Heidi Armbruster and Ulrike Hanna Meinhof, *Negotiating Multicultural Europe: Borders, Networks, Neighbourhoods* (Houndmills: Palgrave Macmillan, 2011); Lene Hansen and Ole Wæver (eds), *European Integration and National Identity: The Challenge of the Nordic States* (London: Routledge, 2002).

[58] Sjursen is an exception, linking the identity issues of a number of different European states to their policies on enlargement. Helene Sjursen (ed.), *Questioning EU Enlargement: Europe in Search of Identity* (London: Routledge, 2006).

[59] In a literature where quantity tends to outweigh quantity, clear-thinking is provided by: Bruce Hoffman, *Inside Terrorism* (New York: Columbia University Press, 2006); Charles Townshend, *Terrorism: A Very Short Introduction* (Oxford: Oxford University Press, 2011).

[60] James D. Kiras, 'Terrorism and Globalization', in John Baylis, Steve Smith, and Patricia Owens (eds), *The Globalization of World Politics* (4th edn, Oxford: Oxford University Press, 2008), pp. 370–85; Christopher Coker, *War in an Age of Risk* (Cambridge: Polity, 2009), p. 150.

different manifestations it can accept the legitimacy of states and the states-system, or seek violently to undermine it.[61]

The last decade or so has witnessed a preoccupation with Islamic jihadism, at the level of the international system but also right down to the profiling of individual psychologies.[62] In this kind of writing there is at least a willingness to allow that the behaviour of Western states in world politics might engender bitter feelings among Muslims inside their own countries, as well as world-wide.[63] Although much of the terrorism literature is applied to the point of being ephemeral, and driven by simple counter-insurgency motives, there is also a structural awareness of the interpenetration of the domestic and the external—a notion other subject areas pay lip-service to, but rarely pursue. The public policy orientation of the sub-field, however, needs balancing with a knowledge of Islam and historical perspective, as evident in the work of scholars like Fred Halliday.[64] It is equally important to have an understanding of the situations in individual countries, on which there are surprisingly few studies.[65] Studies of the EU level of combating terrorism, otherwise helpful, tend only to discuss the Member States in terms of intergovernmentalism, and do not drill down into their civil societies.[66] And yet terrorism's aim is to reach the heart of a society by creating fear. As Ulrich Beck has said, it 'undermines the trust in fellow citizens, foreigners and governments . . . [it] triggers a self-multiplication of risks by the de-bounding of risk perceptions and fantasies'.[67]

[61] Ayşe Zarakol, 'What Makes Terrorism Modern? Terrorism, Legitimacy, and the International System', *Review of International Studies*, 37/5 (2010), pp. 2311–36.

[62] For examples of the systemic perspective, see Benjamin Barber, 'Democracy and Terror in the Era of Jihad vs. McWorld' and Bhikhu Parekh, 'Terrorism or Intercultural Dialogue', both in Ken Booth and Tim Dunne (eds), *Worlds in Collision: Terror and the Future of Global Order* (Houndmills: Palgrave Macmillan, 2002), pp. 245–62 and 270–83; also Lawrence Freedman, *Superterrorism: Policy Responses* (Oxford: Blackwell, 2002); for detailed micro research, see Angel Rabasa et al., *Beyond al-Qaeda. Part 1: The Global Jihadist Movement* (Santa Monica, CA: RAND, 2006), e-book available at <http://www.rand.org/pubs/monographs/2006/RAND_MG429.pdf> accessed 16 December 2012.

[63] Rabasa et al. analyse the case of European converts to Islam, and the dangers they represent. Rabasa et al., *Beyond al-Qaeda*. pp. 51–5.

[64] Halliday was also concerned to put terrorism into the context of normal politics, and not to demonize Islam. Fred Halliday, *Two Hours that Shook the World: 11 September 2001: Causes and Consequences* (London: Saqi Books, 2002), and *The Middle East in International Relations: Power, Politics and Ideology* (Cambridge: Cambridge University Press, 2005).

[65] But see Gary J. Schmitt (ed.), *Safety, Liberty and Islamist Terrorism: American and European Approaches to Domestic Counter-Terrorism* (Washington, DC: American Enterprise Institute, 2010), and Karen von Hippel (ed.), *Europe Confronts Terrorism* (Houndmills: Palgrave, 2005), both of which provide national case-studies. Also, on single states, see Christopher Andrew, *The Defence of the Realm: The Authorised History of MI5* (London: Penguin, 2010), pp. 816–40; and François Heisbourg and Jean-Luc Marret, *Le terrorisme en France aujourd'hui* (Sainte-Marguerite-sur-Mer: Éditions des Équateurs, 2006).

[66] Geoffrey Edwards and Christoph O. Meyer (eds), *Journal of Common Market Studies*, 46/1, Special Issue (2008), pp. 1–218.

[67] Ulrich Beck, *The Cosmopolitan Vision* (Cambridge: Polity, 2004), p. 44, cited in Coker, *War in an Age of Risk*, p. 76.

Furthermore, not all societies will prove equally vulnerable, whether through internal or external factors. For these reasons the study of terrorism needs linking to the study of both society and foreign policy, particularly when transnational in scope and purpose. It also needs placing in the context of differing national experiences.

The sixth and final specialism on which this investigation draws is that of the *European Union*—another vast field of literature. The EU dimension is present in every aspect of the relationships between the nation-states in question and the outside world, given that the experiment in regional integration has been transformative for every single European state, even those not members of the club. Accordingly, the relevance of the EU to the themes of this book is evident throughout the discussion, as well as being acknowledged in a separate chapter of its own. The most important areas of collective activity for our purposes are foreign policy, identity, internal security (what the EU calls the Area of Freedom, Security, and Justice—AFSJ), and human rights/ democratic governance.

The European foreign policy literature has been referred to earlier; it is drawn upon throughout the book, and in Chapter 8 in particular. European identity is a subject which has fascinated practitioners and academics, without there being much substance (of policy or popular behaviour) on which to draw. Nonetheless it is central to the issue of whether national societies are changing in terms of their internal cohesion, and of the role of the outside world as an external 'pull' factor. It is also instructive to consider the competing pulls in terms of identity of national, regional, and non-European points of reference. Accordingly, Chapter 5 specifically focuses on the problem of identity.

This leaves the inter-related areas of FSJ and human rights/democratic governance. From the Maastricht Treaty of 1993 the EU had a role in what it then termed Justice and Home Affairs (JHA), becoming the AFSJ after the Treaty of Amsterdam in 1999. It corresponds to what the USA termed 'homeland security' after 9/11, although in the EU one of the key issues is precisely what counts as a citizen's 'homeland'; there is the tension between the Union as a whole and the Member State, while for minorities there may well also be the pull of a third country. The very wording of 'freedom, security, and justice' epitomizes Europeans' struggle to reconcile two key priorities—ensuring citizens' daily security from crime and violence on the one hand without sacrificing their liberty on the other.[68] In principle the democratic process should act to restrain executive excess and to decide the appropriate trade-offs between emergency powers and fundamental values.

[68] For an overview of the development of the JHA into the AFSJ, see Valsamis Mitsilegas, Jörg Monar, and Wyn Rees, *The European Union and Internal Security: Guardian of the People?* (Houndmills: Palgrave, 2003).

For our purposes the key aspects of the AFSJ are the Schengen arrangement for open borders, the attempts to move towards common policies on asylum and migration, and the administrative scaling up involved in coordination over policing and counter-terrorism, with the development of institutions like Europol, and the agreement on a European Arrest Warrant.[69] All this represents the attempt by governments to mitigate the consequences of the Single European Market, which in creating a freer movement of trade, money, and people confronted Member States facing new security problems with a choice between trusting in the resilience of democracy and substituting new forms of surveillance for border controls. Given the bureaucratic and psychological pressures in favour of over-insuring on security, it is not surprising that the result has been a significant increment in the powers of government, at both national and European levels, with a rebound effect of alienating those perceiving themselves as scapegoated. Plenty of critics have pointed to the 'securitisation' of areas like immigration and normal policing, under the influence of concerns about terrorism and fundamentalist Islam.[70] There are indeed serious issues of human rights, legal and political, raised by the responses to concern about transnational security threats. Furthermore, what Coker has called the 'ethnic fault-lines running through Bradford, Birmingham and Berlin' can hardly have been weakened by a decade of suspicion and sometimes heavy-handed policies.[71]

Such measures have been the one area where even Eurosceptics have urged cooperation at the EU level. Yet internal security is now intimately connected with external relations. The United States is both a major partner in counter-terrorism and a source of persistent pressure on Europeans, shaping how they manage their own legal and law-enforcement systems. The notion of the 'War on Terror' may have been firmly rejected by Europeans, but events in such countries as Somalia, Yemen, and Pakistan can still have serious consequences within the EU, and are watched nervously by its governments. Thus, as Jörg Monar says, the Member States see the external dimension of internal security as inevitable, and 'making a substantial contribution to achieve AFSJ internal objectives which, especially in the case of the fight against crime and migration

[69] A full and up-to-date treatment of both legal and political aspects can be found in Sarah Wolff, Flora A. N. J. Goudappel, and Jaap W. de Zwaan (eds), *Freedom, Security and Justice after Lisbon and Stockholm* (The Hague: T. M. C. Asser Press, 2011).

[70] For a useful summary of these issues see Christina Boswell, 'Justice and Home Affairs', in Michelle Egan, Neill Nugent, and William E. Paterson, *Research Agendas in EU Studies: Stalking the Elephant* (Houndmills: Palgrave Macmillan, 2010), pp. 278–304. The key critics have been Didier Bigo and Jef Huysmans. See, for example, Didier Bigo, 'Security and Immigration: Toward a Critique of the Governmentality of Unease', *Alternatives*, 27/1, Supplement (2002), pp. 63–92; Jef Huysmans, *The Politics of Insecurity: Fear, Migration and Asylum in the EU* (Abingdon: Routledge, 2006).

[71] Coker, *War in an Age of Risk*, p. 83.

management, address major concerns of their citizens'.[72] Yet by the same token it creates differences of view both within and between the states.

STRUCTURE

The book is divided into two parts. Chapters 2–4 break down the generalization of 'multicultural societies' into three categories, each dealt with separately. Chapter 2 deals with the countries where the 'multiculturalist project' has been accepted over several decades as a desirable way of handling multiculturality. These are Britain, the Netherlands, and Sweden. The analysis starts by examining the principles underlying such a project, and what it means in practice, before examining the implications for foreign policy. It moves on to the problem of security, which is partly responsible for the backlash against multiculturalism. The chapter ends by examining the implications for the making of foreign policy in all three countries.

Chapter 3 goes to the opposite end of the spectrum by analysing the 'integrationist model' with its emphasis on civic nationalism and the refusal to grant groups any special status within society. It comes close to pure assimilationism, or the view that minorities should absorb a pre-existing set of norms so as to conform to a particular way of life. Yet no modern democracy wants to deny that society is in constant evolution or that newcomers might be able to contribute something valuable to the social mix. Hence the ambivalence and tensions over minorities on view in the three cases treated in this chapter—Denmark, France, and Greece.

As in the previous chapter, the model—if it deserves that status—is dissected theoretically, before its relationship with foreign policy and the outside world is discussed in relation to each of the three states in turn. The implications of an integrationist approach for foreign relations are potentially great. In an era of *de facto* increasing ethnic diversity one might expect considerable resistance to the centralizing impulse, perhaps supported by outsiders with transnational ties into a particular state. No action, whether the banning of the *hijab* or a change in the abortion laws, now exists in a vacuum, unaffected by the international environment.

[72] Jörg Monar, *The External Dimension of The EU's Area of Freedom, Security and Justice: Progress, Potential and Limitations after the Treaty of Lisbon* (Stockholm: Swedish Institute for European Policy Studies, SIEPS, 2012), p. 72, <http://www.sieps.se/sites/default/files/Rapport%202012_1_A5.pdf> accessed 16 December 2012. See also Wyn Rees, 'The External Face of Internal Security', in Christopher Hill and Michael Smith (eds), *International Relations and the European Union* (2nd edn, Oxford: Oxford University Press, 2011), pp. 226–45; and David Spence (ed.), *The European Union and Terrorism* (London: John Harper, 2007).

Chapter 4 follows this pattern, but does not identify a clear third way between multiculturalism and integrationism. Rather, it looks at the states which are engaged in a major encounter with immigration and diversity, but which have produced 'parallel societies' because they have no clear approach to its management. In these states the language of integration stands in contrast to the separation of lives on the ground between the majority and the sizeable minorities which have become established. The main cases are Germany, Italy, and Spain, countries which, perhaps by coincidence, also exhibit high degrees of devolution in their internal structures to regions, some of which regard themselves as autonomous nations. The chapter begins by examining the structural compromises thus required on both geographical and social levels, using the related examples of Belgium and Switzerland to establish the parameters. It then looks at the three main cases in more detail, showing how multiculturality has come to lie as an extra layer over the decentralized state, with the resulting dilemmas made more complex through the tentative emergence of distinctive national foreign policies in the countries concerned, all of which had found self-assertion difficult in the second half of the twentieth century.

After charting the three distinct approaches to multiculturality identified in Chapters 2–4, the book then turns to the most difficult political dilemmas which arise from these relationships. Of the four identified here two focus more on the domestic side of the equation—through the problems of identity on the one hand, and the uneasy relationships between loyalty, democracy, and transnationalism on the other—and two on the foreign policy dimension, through discussion first of the issues raised by debates over external interventions, and second of the impact of the framework of regional integration represented by the European Union. As all the issues focused on in Chapters 5–8 straddle the internal/external divide, they should be able to throw light on the issue of interaction between the two sides.

Chapter 5 takes as its starting-point the proposition that multiple identities have become one of the conditions of modernity, particularly in rapidly changing civil societies. Against this stands the argument of Samuel Huntington that a country's future is uncertain if it lacks a strong sense of shared identity. These arguments are considered here in the context of the notion of national identity, and of its relationship with the fundamental foreign policy concept of national interest. That leads on to the possible connections with ideas about a country's role in the world, and then to the more specific conceptions of outsiders, whether friends, enemies, partners, or rivals, and to the differences there might be on such matters within society.

Chapter 6 moves from the cultural level of analysis to the more classical issues of loyalty and democracy, considered in the context of the transnational issues of diaspora ties, and ethnic or religious communities beyond the state. The terrorist attacks in Spain and Britain in 2004–5 by insiders, in some cases fellow-citizens, raised the questions of how far some members of minority communities have become alienated from the majority, and of the role which foreign policy has played in bringing about that alienation. Even if only a tiny minority is willing to act subversively, that still raises major security issues for the state, in terms of surveillance, detention, profiling, and recruitment into key public services. The chapter surveys these issues while also addressing that of loyalty and what that means in an increasingly diverse democracy, including the impact on the concept of a loyal opposition. The further issue of how far foreign policy should be responsive to the pressures of committed and vocal minorities is the other side of this coin.

In Chapter 7 the most difficult foreign policy dilemma of recent times is considered: how far to intervene in the affairs of other states, and on what grounds. Debate in European democracies has become lively on this issue regardless of the multicultural dimension. But the competing narratives of human rights and neo-colonialism, together with the fact of a military presence inside Muslim countries, leading to the deaths of many innocents, has inevitably led to anger on the part of minorities. It is then plausible that there will be a 'blowback' onto civil society, whose nature will depend on the particular European state involved, and on the foreign policy it is conducting. The analysis here attempts to gauge the seriousness of this blowback, from discontent, through alienation and protest, to the extremes of subversion, and to disentangle the various factors which shape any given intervention (or lack of it)—for ethnocultural groups are far from being the only ones with concerns about such issues as Iraq or Libya. A typology is constructed of the different kinds of intervention in which the European states have been involved.

The last of the four cross-cutting issues dealt with in Chapters 5–8 is that of regional integration, the focus of Chapter 8. It is an interesting paradox that the European Union, which penetrates so deeply into the domestic environments of its Member States, on the face of it has little role to play in the important issues of multiculturalism and social cohesion. On the other hand, the EU does seek to promote a common European identity, which could conceivably relieve some of the tension associated with the pressures of nationality and patriotism. It also stands, with the Council of Europe, for the human rights and democratic values which are intended to provide the framework within which social differences may be safely expressed. This chapter therefore examines the extent to which the EU has any effect on the debates about multiculturalism and multiculturality, looking in particular at whether a European *demos* might conceivably resolve the problems arising from competing identities, and at whether the efforts to create a European foreign policy make the situations of individual Member States easier or more difficult in this regard.

The book ends with Chapter 9, which draws threads together by identifying some general conclusions. European states and their foreign policies are now embedded in a range of multilateral activity, rarely considering an action which does not involve some form of international cooperation. At the same time, their domestic base is more fragmented, symbolized by the idea of multiculturalism and complicated by the facts of multiculturality. Both trends call severely into question the idea of a coherent and consistent national interest. And yet: states and their civil societies vary; the state itself is evidently not withering away; and each state's sense of itself in relation to others remains sharp. What all governments are thus engaged in, to a greater or lesser extent, is a constant process of reconciling diverse inputs on foreign policy, just as they routinely do in other areas of public policy—a process complicated by the increased interpenetration of domestic and foreign policy and by the now extensive transnational links between civil societies. This produces a range of serious challenges for governments—political, ethical, and managerial—as foreign policy becomes at once more important to a multifaceted public opinion, less clear in its outlines, and more complex in its conduct. Governments have not found either the conceptual or political tools to come to terms with them.

Yet there are reasons to believe that society is more robust than it might seem, while it is important to distinguish between the kinds of approach taken by a state, both to multiculturality and to foreign policy. Each can make a big difference to outcomes. At the same time the 'models' presented here are only that—academic abstractions which enable us to discern broad trends and contrasts. They are fuzzy at the edges and subject to perpetual change. Although no society can reinvent itself at will, it is possible to adjust and change direction over time, as the Netherlands has done in its retreat from the philosophy of multiculturalism, and as Germany has been doing in its opposite attempt to come to terms with the meaning of integration. Nor is foreign policy set in fixed channels. It can and should evolve according not only to the changing nature of the international system, but also in response to the views and demands of citizens in a democratic society. How the balance is struck between minority and majority, between competing minorities, and between pressure-group politics and constitutional process, is another matter, and one for every polity to settle in its own way. These issues, normative and practical, always arise at the interface between public policy and a diverse society. Thus while the interplay between multiculturality and foreign policy has its distinctive features, it is also just the latest version of a familiar problem in political life.

2

Multiculturalist societies and foreign policy

It is the multiculturalist group of countries which is the focus of this chapter. In Europe this refers mainly to Britain, the Netherlands, and Sweden, all of which in their different ways have reacted to increasing diversity during the last decades of the twentieth century by pursuing policies which they were content to see labelled as 'multiculturalism'. In the technical definition of Banting and Kymlicka this meant policies which went beyond the protection of basic civil and political rights for individuals 'to also extend some level of public recognition and support for ethnocultural minorities to maintain and express their distinct identities and practices'.[1]

Facing significant demographic change from the 1960s on, through the increasingly open and globalized nature of economic life as well as the fall-out from empire and decolonization, some societies (in practice, meaning their agents in local and central governments) decided that there was no point in swimming against the tide of history. Rather, in their view, the state should accept both the limits on its ability to control social formations, and the anachronistic character of nationalism. This meant embracing cosmopolitanism as a fact and a virtue at the social level, while the state itself would retreat into a regulatory posture, holding the ring for a vibrant interplay between multiple communities and sources of identity, rather than attempting to uphold essentialist ideas of what a country should stand for. This was, strangely, consistent with Margaret Thatcher's famous view from the same period that 'there is no such thing as society'.[2] For if individuals are thrown

[1] Keith Banting and Will Kymlicka (eds), *Multiculturalism and the Welfare State: Recognition and Redistribution in Contemporary Democracies* (Oxford: Oxford University Press, 2006), p. 1.

[2] In her memoirs Thatcher later clarified her remark, which had been made in an interview with *Woman's Own* on 31 October 1987: 'My meaning, clear at the time but subsequently distorted beyond recognition, was that society was not an abstraction, separate from the men and women who composed it, but a living structure of individuals, families, neighbours and voluntary associations'. Margaret Thatcher, *The Downing Street Years* (London: HarperCollins, 1993), p. 626. Thatcher admired the enterprise of many in the ethnic minorities, but took a strong line

back on their own resources, without seeing their national community as the helper of first resort, they naturally turn not only to their own families, but to any other group which can provide extended kinship. And in due course this effectively creates multiculturalism, which Conservative individualists like Thatcher tended to deplore for other reasons.

At the global level the first examples of the explicitly multiculturalist approach were Canada and Australia, starting from a set of liberal preferences about the way to build a tolerant and stable society in an ever more mobile global environment. The former had the particular sub-national issue of Quebec to deal with, but through a positive immigration policy was steadily becoming more diverse in most of its provinces. Australia, by contrast, was gradually coming to terms with the discrimination which its aboriginal population had suffered, at the same time as it too began to open up to immigrants from first Europe and then Asia, thus accelerating the move away from its British-based homogeneity. These two countries, perhaps encouraged by their membership of the Commonwealth—one of the few international organizations to bridge the North–South divide—have held fairly fast to the multiculturalist project, even if Australia in particular has suffered some sharp internal conflicts as a result.

The spread to Europe of what Will Kymlicka calls 'immigrant multiculturalism' (as opposed to national minorities) took place largely in the era of full-blown globalization.[3] Although it took some time for debate to move on from immigration to coping with social diversity (in Britain, Enoch Powell's apocalyptic 1968 'Rivers of Blood' speech predicted nightmarish consequences for immigration), by the 1980s policy had crystallized sufficiently for 'multiculturalism' to have been identified as a possible model.[4] It was then more or less consciously adopted in three European countries—Britain, the Netherlands, and Sweden—even if the discourse was also used more loosely elsewhere. What follows discusses the implications of multiculturalism as a social and political experiment in these three states, before moving on to the implications for foreign policy. The chapter ends by reversing the direction of the analysis to look at the way foreign policy, and international affairs more generally, have impacted upon the politics of these three European societies.

on immigration (Thatcher, *The Downing Street Years*, p. 307). Her memoirs make no mention of multiculturalism as such.

[3] Will Kymlicka, *Politics in the Vernacular: Nationalism, Multiculturalism and Citizenship* (Oxford: Oxford University Press, 2001), pp. 152–76.

[4] Writing in 1985, John Rex said that multiculturalism was 'a new goal for British race relations' and that it had not been discussed much before 1968. John Rex, 'The Concept of a Multicultural Society', *Occasional Papers in Ethnic Relations No. 2* (CRER, 1985), reprinted in Montserrat Guibernau and John Rex (eds), *The Ethnicity Reader: Nationalism, Multiculturalism and Migration* (Cambridge: Polity Press, 1997), p. 206.

MULTICULTURALISM AS A PROJECT

The adjective 'multicultural', according to the *Oxford English Dictionary*, describes any society which consists of a number of cultural groups, 'especially in which the distinctive cultural identity of each group is maintained'. The first use of the word seems to have been in 1935, in the United States. 'Multicultural*ism*', however, does not appear until 1957, again in the United States, referring to 'the characteristics of a multicultural society', but also to the 'process whereby the distinctive identities of the cultural groups within such a society are maintained'. The first European reference (in the English language) was in Scotland, celebrating the 'new and promising challenge of Multiculturalism' for Gaelic speakers. By 1990 things had moved on to the extent that an English journal of the intellectual left could observe that 'the policy of multiculturalism has been widely adopted as a more tolerant way forward than full integration into a "British way of life"'.[5]

These definitions beg the questions of what is meant by 'culture' and 'cultural groups', but they do provide a good sense of the origins and evolution of thinking about multiculturalism. For multiculturalism as a project is something which has been almost wholly defined in its practice. There was no pre-existing political theory of a multiculturalist school which governments could attempt to implement. Gradually, with the models of Australia and (particularly) Canada before them, those European states inclined to go down the multiculturalist road began to work out in the 1980s what it would mean in their own distinctive contexts.

The multiculturalist project thus varies across nation-states, with a long list of possible characteristics, depending on the perception of the observer. For the purposes of this discussion, however, it is seen as depending on five central propositions. In due course their significance for the conduct of foreign policy in the states in question will emerge, but for the moment the focus is on the kind of domestic society which has been promoted under conscious policies of multiculturalism.

The first key tenet is that *communities below the level of the state exist and deserve protection*, even promotion, over and above that which is afforded to all individuals under the law. Thus Will Kymlicka, one of the world's leading authorities on the subject, sees multiculturalism as 'an umbrella term designed to provide some level of public recognition, support, or accommodation to non-dominant ethnocultural groups'.[6] The terms 'positive discrimination' and

[5] *Marxism Today*, 31 March 1990, p. 3. Cited in the *Oxford English Dictionary* (3rd edn, Oxford: Oxford University Press, 2003), available online, <http://www.oed.com/> accessed March 2010.

[6] Will Kymlicka, *Multicultural Odysseys: Navigating the New International Politics of Diversity* (Oxford: Oxford University Press, 2007), p. 16.

'affirmative action' have become such lightning conductors for polemics that they are best avoided, but a special status is essentially what is at stake. And to be supported, 'ethnocultural groups' have to exist, or rather, to be 'recognized', on the basis of their ability to organize themselves in the first place. Such recognition has two elements: first, the valuing of a plurality of groups as well as of individuals—the view that groups with an ethnic and cultural identity (as opposed to an interest-group, or a literary society, say) add something to society; and second, the recognition of particular groups whose claims have merit in the context of the specific state where they are made.

Together, these two acknowledgements amount to a form of communitarianism with cosmopolitan effects, as the protection of minority communities promotes diversity of habits, customs, even languages within a society. And it is *diversity* which is the second of the five key propositions of the multiculturalists. Diversity as such is characteristic of all human life, while post-Reformation Europe had generated loose congeries of different confessions and principalities.[7] In western Europe over the last 200 years the nation-states which succeeded them have remained diverse in terms of religion, albeit within Christianity, and through the increasing acceptance of atheism. Since 1945 they have added a growing ethnocultural diversity, largely through increased immigration. But it is not diversity in terms of the mere variety of habits, beliefs, and skin colours which is central to multiculturalism as a project. That goes beyond even the pluralism of ethnicities and religious groups, which is the consequence of human beings' innate wish to cluster together on the basis of shared characteristics and preferences. It entails the positive recognition of group rights to autonomy in significant areas of social life.

These rights will vary according to context, but the most important relate to education, especially through faith schools, to religion, and to morality, in terms of particular sets of believers keeping themselves to themselves and inculcating a set of values which may be at odds with those of wider society. Language, where a minority community makes retaining its own language a priority, is also an important source of group rights. They in turn derive from the external recognition of the group as having a strong historical, cultural, and possibly ethnic identity of its own, very often with kinship links to another society altogether. There may or may not be a distinct geographical identity in the sense of occupying one particular part of the state, but there is always a tendency for the culturally similar to cluster in the same places—whether

[7] Paul W. Schroeder, 'Not Even for the Seventeenth and Eighteenth Centuries: Power and Order in the Early Modern Era', in Ernest R. May, Richard Rosecrance, and Zara Steiner (eds), *History and Neorealism* (Cambridge: Cambridge University Press, 2010), pp. 78–102; also Andreas Osiander, *The States System of Europe, 1640–1990: Peacemaking and the Conditions of International Stability* (Oxford: The Clarendon Press, 1994), pp. 16–89.

Left Bank literati or Turkish migrants in Kreuzberg. Such characteristics are familiar to most European peoples. But what is distinctive about multiculturalist societies is that it is official policy to affirm these rights as desirable, even critical to the development of a civilized democracy. They then become interpenetrated with notions of human rights, albeit uneasily given that individuals are the basis of the latter and groups are the basis of the multiculturalist project. Great political battles were fought in European societies for centuries over the privileges of the church, with victory largely going in the end to the spirit of toleration. Even more blood was shed through nationalism and ethnic prejudices. As a result, most European societies accept diversity in principle as something of value. But some, notably Britain, the Netherlands, and Sweden, have gone further, to institutionalize diversity through the active promotion of the type of rights described.

The reasons that some states in particular have gone down this path bring us to the third tenet of multiculturalism as an idea and a project—*concerns about racism*. Of those European states which acquired significant numbers of different migrant groups as the post-war economy picked up, Germany was the most obviously anti-racist in its state ethos. But being preoccupied with its lost Jews, and with Israel, while taking in migrant labour mostly from one country (Turkey), it did not feel the need to adopt multiculturalism as a project, despite the term being in common use. For its part France, insofar as colonial guilt and anti-racism were on the agenda, dealt with the problem by asserting that those newcomers who were accepted had, by definition, become French, without need for group rights. In Belgium there is much talk of multiculturalism, but the country's real priority is the damaging Walloon/Flemish divide, managed through a federal and consociational political system in which the rights of only three communities—French, Flemish, and German—are recognized.[8] Others, including the large states of Italy and Spain, had simply not become societies of immigration, and were therefore more homogeneous in their social composition by the time the multiculturalist project took off in Britain and elsewhere in the 1980s.

In Britain, the Netherlands, and Sweden, however, the combination of the new social reality with an overt hostility to racism on the part of the liberal elites, was a significant factor in leading to official multiculturalism. In Britain, despite the Conservative government of Margaret Thatcher being in power throughout the 1980s, developments in education, social services, and local government led to multiculturalist values becoming embedded in civil society. The trend was reinforced by the decisive national victory of New Labour in 1997. In the Netherlands a new policy was laid down in 1983 by the

[8] See the indicators analysed on the website of Queen's University, Ottawa: 'Multiculturalism Policies in Contemporary Democracies: Belgium' [online index], <http://www.queensu.ca/mcp/minoritynations/evidence/Belgium.html> accessed 17 July 2012.

Minderhedennota (Minorities Document), which accepted the 'equality of cultures' (as stipulated in the Dutch Constitution of the same year which broke the existing ties between church and state) as well as the increasingly multicultural nature of society. Yet the new policy did not adopt multiculturalism on principle, as it also implicitly looked forward to a future in which immigrants, as they left poverty behind, would gradually integrate into mainstream Dutch society. Rather, the contested Article 23 of the Constitution allowed for the continuation of the 'pillar system' in Dutch society, whereby separate denominations (previously Protestant and Catholic, but now also Muslim) could set up their own schools and have the right to state funding to do so.[9] As a result Dutch civil society became characterized by many of the practices of multiculturalism, even if the reaction against them started earlier than almost anywhere else in Europe, in the 1990s.[10] The Netherlands is a notably tolerant, anti-racist society, but it also has a strong sense of its historical identity, centred on notions of individual freedoms, which set it on a collision course with some elements of Islam within its borders. As a result its multiculturalist project has been strongly contested over the last decade or more, with some observers concluding that it has been reversed.[11]

Sweden adopted a multiculturalist policy in the 1970s as a result of various factors, including the generous attitude of its people towards refugees and economic migrants from developing countries. Its wealth and extensive welfare provisions attracted even those for whom its climate and language were unfamiliar.[12] It swiftly gave immigrants permanence and labour rights, unlike the guest worker approaches of Germany and the Netherlands.[13] By 2009 around 14 per cent of the population was foreign-born, but the country remained—in stark contrast to its neighbour Denmark—committed to multiculturalism as a statement of its cosmopolitan and anti-racist value-system. Indeed, it declared 2006 to be 'The Year of Multiculturalism'.[14] Its corporatist policy culture reinforced the practice of consultation and dialogue between

[9] See Thijl Sunier, 'Assimilation by Conviction or Coercion? Integration Policies in the Netherlands', in Alessandro Silj (ed.), *European Multiculturalism Revisited* (London: Zed Books, 2010), pp. 217–22. Also Maarten P. Vink, 'Dutch "Multiculturalism": Beyond the Pillarisation Myth', *Political Studies*, 5/3 (2007), pp. 337–50.

[10] See Frank J. Lechner, *The Netherlands: Globalization and National Identity* (London: Routledge, 2008), pp. 158–70 and 282.

[11] New parties, the LPF (Pim Fortuyn List, 2003–8) and the PVV (Party for Freedom, 2005–), have risen on the back of criticism of the established parties which they have referred to as the 'multiculti elite'. See Cas Mudde, 'A Fortuynist Foreign Policy', in Christina Schori Liang (ed.), *Europe for the Europeans: The Foreign and Security Policy of the Populist Radical Right* (Aldershot: Ashgate, 2007), pp. 209–21.

[12] Harald Runblom, 'Swedish Multiculturalism in a Comparative European Perspective', *Sociological Forum*, 9/4 (1994), pp. 623–40.

[13] Andrew Geddes, *The Politics of Migration and Immigration in Europe* (London: Sage, 2003), pp. 118–22.

[14] Kymlicka, *Multicultural Odysseys*, p. 77.

social groups. Immigrant associations received subsidies.[15] Nonetheless, even here migration issues became steadily more politicized, which is inevitable given 'the seamless way in which the two concepts of "the people"—those of *demos* and *ethnos*—have been fused into one coherent whole'.[16]

The fourth tenet of the multiculturalist approach is the tendency to show *sensitivity towards religious belief and in particular towards the co-existence of different faiths.* Some European democracies have displayed an exaggerated respect for minority religions given the majority tendency to desert their traditional churches. Indeed Brian Barry has suggested that 'for many multiculturalists, culture has taken the place once assumed by religion'. They '. . . tend to have a warm feeling towards cultures simply by virtue of their being cultures'.[17] If true, this may derive from a sense that national and local cultures have been both diluted by globalization and reduced to ersatz spectacles by the mass media. The enthusiasm for multiculturalism in the 1980s can thus be explained in part through an envy of perceived authenticity, and a delayed reaction to a lost spiritual dimension in mass society. It might be thought that this factor applies across modernity as a whole, and therefore has little to contribute to an explanation of why only some states actively endorsed multiculturalism. Yet the states of southern and eastern Europe, where church-going remains relatively high, have not shown such enthusiasm for multiculturalism, while France, which on this indicator is the most secular country in Europe, has a strong, state-driven, sense of its national identity which is by definition opposed to group rights. Clearly there are multiple reasons for the three countries identified here with the multiculturalist project to have gone down that road, but a notable degree of tolerance, even respect, for minority faiths does seem to have been one common factor. The historical memory of the struggles of protestantism for recognition may have been another.

The corollary of respect for minority groups, their religions and their traditions, is regular embroilment in *debates over possible exemptions, de jure* or *de facto*, from the normal application of the law. This is the fifth of our multiculturalist tenets. In Britain this first came to notice with the refusal of Sikh motorcyclists to wear helmets, but problems of honour killings, clitoridectomy, and blasphemy have been more dramatic—and more widespread. They have occurred wherever minorities have settled in any numbers,

15 Geddes, *The Politics of Migration*, p. 119 and 121.

16 Lars Trägårdh (ed.), *State and Civil Society in Northern Europe: The Swedish Model Reconsidered* (Oxford: Berghahn Books, 2007), p. 27; see also Mikael Spång, 'Sweden: Europeanization of Policy, but not of Politics?', in Thomas Faist and Andreas Ette (eds), *The Europeanization of National Policies and Politics of Immigration: Between Autonomy and the European Union* (Houndmills: Palgrave Macmillan, 2007), pp. 127–33.

17 Brian Barry, 'Second Thoughts: Some First Thoughts Revived', in Paul Kelly (ed.), *Multiculturalism Reconsidered* (Cambridge: Polity, 2002), p. 235.

and do not apply only to Islam, as the joint Jewish–Muslim protests over a court ruling against male circumcision in Germany in 2012 demonstrate.[18] It is likely that this controversy will die down and be confined to Germany, whereas the debates over the *hijab* and the *burka* spread right across Europe, causing social tensions. France was willing to risk conflict by taking a clear legal position and the highest profile on such matters. By contrast the multiculturalist approach found itself inevitably attempting to reach a compromise between the principle of equality under the law, and the wish to accommodate the traditions and sincerely held beliefs of minorities. This produces particularly sharp dilemmas. Thus Salman Rushdie's life had to be protected by the state (at great cost) for two decades after the publication of his book *The Satanic Verses*. The British authorities had little choice but to defend the principle of free speech against threats of violence, at the same time as sympathizing with those offended by what they saw as blasphemy—which at the time still counted as an offence in the UK, if only in a Christian context.[19] Since then the law has been changed to ensure that Christianity no longer has privileged status. The offence of blasphemy has been replaced by the offence of intending to stir up hatred on religious grounds, whichever religion is at stake.[20]

The Netherlands suffered even more turmoil. This began with the arrival in politics of the charismatic anti-Islamic figure Pim Fortuyn, who transformed the debate on multiculturalism and immigration. After his murder in 2002, days before a likely electoral success (by an environmentalist activist who said that he had done it to protect Muslims), there were powerful reactions across society and in particular from figures such as Ayaan Hirsi Ali and the filmmaker Theo van Gogh against what they saw as the inappropriately protected place of Islam in Dutch society. Their opinions, provocatively expressed, culminated in the brutal and ritualistic murder of van Gogh, while cycling

[18] 'Circumcision Debate Goes Global', DW (*Deutsche Welle on-line*), 18 July 2012, <http://www.dw.de/dw/article/0,,16101977,00.html?maca=en-aa-pol-863-rdf> accessed 23 July 2012.

[19] On Rushdie, see Daniel Pipes, *The Rushdie Affair: The Novel, the Ayatollah, and the West* (2nd revised edn, New Brunswick: Transaction, 2004). Also Gilles Kepel, *Allah in the West: Islamic Movements in America and Europe* (Cambridge: Polity Press, 1997), pp. 126–46.

[20] In 2008 the blasphemy laws were repealed in the UK by the Criminal Justice and Immigration Act, having not been applied since the 1920s. Ironically this was at the time when pressures from non-Christian religious groups for protection against offensive publications were becoming stronger. The Labour Government had tried to fill the gap with the Racial and Religious Hatred Act of 2006, which made it an offence to incite hatred against people by virtue of their religion or skin colour. But it had been forced by the House of Lords to limit the offence to the *intention* to incite hatred, so as to protect freedom of comment, opinion, and satire. For a useful analysis, see Norman Doe and Russell Sandberg, 'The Changing Criminal Law on Religion', *Law and Justice*, vol. 161 (2008), pp. 88–97. As Doe and Sandberg point out, 'moral panics' over the clash between freedom of expression and freedom of religion are likely to occur regularly whatever the legal context.

to work in Amsterdam, this time by a Muslim fellow-citizen.[21] Evidently, freedom of expression and the multiculturalist ideal did not sit easily together. Indeed, their conjunction had produced dangerous hatreds across community lines, playing into what had become a general distrust of minorities on the part of the majority.[22]

Sweden has experienced fewer such dramas, but its support for Denmark over the cartoons of the Prophet Mohammed in 2005 led to difficult internal debates. In March 2006 the Swedish Foreign Minister, Laila Freivalds, was forced to resign when she tried to face both ways on the Cartoon Crisis, while her Danish counterpart held firm.[23] Although the attachment to anti-racism has inhibited the blunt discussion of immigration seen in Denmark and elsewhere, and by extension also of multiculturalism, there have been signs of growing tensions.[24] According to Ulf Hedetoft, despite the 'Year of Multiculturalism' in 2006, 'government reports . . . are less concerned with depicting and managing a multicultural polity than with combating "structural discrimination"'.[25] He goes on to argue that Sweden has evolved from 'paternalistic multiculturalism' to a position where demands for an integrationist approach are making for a more acrimonious debate, even if the consensus is still multiculturalist. '"The nation" is striking back by tightening the net of demands around immigrants and their descendants, often in populist forms'.[26]

IMPLICATIONS FOR FOREIGN POLICY

The foreign policies of the three European countries discussed earlier have attracted much comment, scholarly and otherwise, since the events of

[21] For these Dutch traumas, see the powerful accounts and analysis in Ian Buruma, *Murder in Amsterdam: The Death of Theo van Gogh and the Limits of Tolerance* (London: Penguin Books, 2006).

[22] As argued by Femke Bosman, 'Dutch Muslim Soldiers in the Dutch Armed Forces', in Iris Menke and Phil C. Langer (eds), *Muslim Service Members in Non-Muslim Countries: Experiences of Difference in the Armed Forces in Austria, Germany and The Netherlands, FORUM International*, 29 (Strausberg, Germany: Sozialwissenschaftliches Institut der Bundeswehr, 2011), pp. 45–8. In the Netherlands all those born abroad, or with one or both parents born abroad, are known by the same, rather negative, term—'allochtoon'—which tends to push all those from minority communities into a 'non-western' category.

[23] See Ulf Hedetoft, *Multiculturalism in Denmark and Sweden* (Copenhagen: Danish Institute for International Studies, December 2006), p. 6.

[24] Patrick Chabal and Jean-Pascal Daloz, *Culture Troubles: Politics and the Interpretation of Meaning* (London: Hurst, 2006), pp. 130–1.

[25] Ulf Hedetoft, 'Denmark versus Multiculturalism', in Steven Vertovec and Susanne Wessendorf (eds), *The Multiculturalism Backlash: European Discourses, Policies and Practices* (London: Routledge, 2010), pp. 111–29.

[26] Hedetoft, 'Denmark versus Multiculturalism', pp. 111–29.

11 September 2001. The same is true of their domestic politics, in terms of the place of Islam in society. Much less common are attempts to put the two sets of developments into a single analytical framework. But each has implications for the other, and indeed they exist in a condition of perpetual, if indirect, interaction. Some evidence of significant interplay already exists, with the potential for more in the future. While the later chapters look in detail at some of the specific issues, this section surveys the broad parameters of the relationship between foreign policy and the multiculturalist project.

The flow of impact runs both ways, from multiculturalism to foreign policy, and vice versa. To begin with the former, it is inevitable that social groups should try to harness national foreign policy to their own ends. This is legitimate and familiar to any democracy in the form of interest-group politics. But multiculturalism is based on communities, not economic interests or cause groups, and communities have distinctive histories and sets of values. They are also very likely to have transnational ties, as part of the diaspora of their country of origin.

In consequence there is a natural wish on the part of ethnocultural minorities to shape the foreign policy of their adoptive country to reflect their own partial concerns. They may attempt this in a variety of different ways, through lobbying, demonstrations, harnessing themselves to other groups or causes—or in extreme cases by violence, however counter-productive. This last was the tactic of those second generation members of the Moluccan community in Holland in 1975, and again in 1977, who decided that taking train passengers hostage was the best way to draw attention to the demands of the South Moluccan islands for independence from Indonesia, and to get support from the Dutch government. All too predictably both crises escalated, leading to the murder of some hostages. Yet this was before multiculturalism, as a philosophy, had taken root; the Moluccans had kept themselves separate, but without the benefits they had hoped for in terms of help with their aim of returning to their own country, independent of Indonesia.[27]

Such tactics were to be emulated by the young Muslims in Britain who were responsible for the atrocities of 7 July 2005. They too felt alienated from the country in which they lived, even if their agitation was stimulated by acts of official commission—in the form of British foreign policy in Iraq and Afghanistan—rather than omission, as in the Moluccan frustration at the lack of Dutch support for the homeland they sought. The two episodes, 30 years apart, were both rooted in feelings of rage which were purely atavistic, having no chance of producing support in the two countries concerned.

[27] Buruma, *Murder in Amsterdam*, pp. 11–13. The Indonesian Consulate in Amsterdam was occupied at the same time. The hostage-takers surrendered and received the lenient sentences of 14 years in prison, which may reflect official guilt over the persistent neglect of the Moluccan community in the Netherlands, largely housed in 'camps' across the country.

More typical of the activities of minorities were the attempts of the Gurkha and Chagos Islands communities to persuade the British government to change policies in their favour, the Gurkhas seeking the right of residence in the UK as reward for loyal military service to the crown, and the Chagos Islanders seeking the right of return to their homes in Diego Garcia and other small islands, from which they had been evicted in 1975. In the former case, which is an international issue if not strictly foreign policy, the Ghurka Justice Campaign secured the support of high-profile figures like the actress Joanna Lumley, finally securing a dramatic victory in the dying days of the Labour government in May 2009.

In the case of Diego Garcia and other Chagos islands, the small number of Chagossians able to live in the UK (the remainder are in Mauritius) have formed the UK Chagos Support Association, which keeps up steady pressure on the Government to allow the right of return. Still far from any likely success, it has the capacity to complicate UK–US relations, as when Wikileaks revealed the UK's floating of a proposal to set up a Marine Conservation Zone.[28] Richard Mills, the US diplomat from the London Embassy who was quoted in the leaked telegram, argued that:

> . . . the Chagossians and their advocates, including the 'All Party Parliamentary Group on Chagos Islands (APPG),' will continue to press their case in the court of public opinion. Their strategy is to publicize what they characterize as the plight of the so-called Chagossian diaspora, thereby galvanizing public opinion and, in their best case scenario, causing the government to change course and allow a 'right of return.' They would point to the government's recent retreat on the issue of Gurkha veterans' right to settle in the UK as a model.

Mills saw that despite the Foreign and Commonwealth Office's avowal that a Marine Zone would end the possibility of the Chagossians returning home, it was possible that in the long run it would have the reverse effect, of making the use of the archipelago for military purposes seem less defensible, thus getting the British government off the hook of domestic protest.

The methods employed by the Gurkha and Chagos lobbies are commonplace for any student of US foreign policy-making. They have been the subject of much analysis—and controversy—particularly with respect to the Israel lobby.[29] Yet while the *concept* of foreign policy lobbying is familiar enough to

[28] 'HMG FLOATS PROPOSAL FOR MARINE RESERVE COVERING THE CHAGOS ARCHIPELAGO (BRITISH INDIAN OCEAN TERRITORY)', leaked cable passed to the *Telegraph*, 4 February 2011, available online, <http://www.telegraph.co.uk/news/wikileaks-files/london-wikileaks/8305246/HMG-FLOATS-PROPOSAL-FOR-MARINE-RESERVE-COVERING-THE-CHAGOS-ARCHIPELAGO%20-BRITISH-INDIAN-OCEAN-TERRITORY.html> accessed 19 December 2012.

[29] For an important general survey, see Tony Smith, *Foreign Attachments: The Power of Ethnic Groups in the Making of US Foreign Policy* (Cambridge, MA: Harvard University Press,

European observers, there is surprisingly little systematic analysis of its impact.[30] Decision-makers in European states are highly sensitive to the operations of lobby-groups in economic and social fields, so that with the blurring of the domestic/foreign dividing-line, their foreign policies are likely to be increasingly subject to similar forces. It may be that because governments are used to taking the view that national security requires them to stand above what they see as the ephemeral currents of public opinion, they tend to play down the operations of foreign policy lobbies, and without the equivalent of a powerful, independent Congress in European states, they are able to do so. This is not true, however, in the area of development aid, where governments are so dependent on the expertise and resources of organizations like Oxfam and *Médecins sans Frontières* that they have sub-contracted activity to them, and accepted some of their agenda.[31] Human rights is another area where pressure-groups have acquired status and often advisory roles.

This kind of corporatist relationship is otherwise only seen in the external realm with defence contractors. On matters of classical foreign policy, especially those involving controversy, interested groups and communities face an uphill struggle to exert influence. Governments continue to play the card of 'the national interest', with the implication that opposition to official policy is unpatriotic, or even dangerous to national security. Furthermore, the very nature of foreign policy, which rarely involves legislation, and mostly relies on agreements with other governments, means that the normal practices of domestic politics, whereby deals can be cut, logs rolled, and pork barrels dipped into, apply less often. Groups have to transform their cause into high politics if they are to put pressure on decision-makers used to more freedom of action than on the home front. This is difficult, but if they succeed, the consequences can be momentous.

With such activism foreign policy has become, for those officially responsible, a more complex and unpredictable process in societies where the multicultural project has advanced. Domestic factors are an ever more significant part of the policy-making environment, especially in trade and investment, for a range of reasons—diversity being prominent amongst them. Depending on the condition of international politics at the time, and on the

2000). See also John J. Mearsheimer and Stephen M. Walt, *The Israel Lobby and US Foreign Policy* (London: Penguin Books, 2008).

[30] For a useful but populist account of one dimension, see Omer Taspinar, 'Europe's Muslim Street', *Foreign Policy*, 135 (March/April 2003), p. 76. Those analysing British foreign policy, led by William Wallace, have focused on pressure-groups since the 1970s, but few have followed. See William Wallace, 'The Role of Interest-groups', in Robert Boardman and A. J. R. Groom (eds), *The Management of Britain's External Relations* (London: Macmillan, 1973), pp. 263–88.

[31] Bertjan Verbeek and Philip Quarles van Ufford, 'Non-State Actors in Foreign Policy-Making: A Policy Sub-System Approach', in Bas Art, Math Noortmann, and Bob Reinalda (eds), *Non-State Actors in International Relations* (Farnham: Ashgate, 2001), pp. 127–44.

policy being pursued, the attitudes of minority groups can bring issues out of the shadows, where politicians might prefer to keep them, sharpen the moral climate in which they are discussed, and create linkages with other problems. In short, they may create a turbulence which forces decision-makers to look perpetually over their shoulder when dealing with other states. Not only is their claim to be speaking with one voice on behalf of a unified nation undermined, but a large amount of political energy has to be expended in attempting to secure the domestic base. They may even have to pay an electoral price for their foreign policy choices, a prospect which they have usually been able to discount. In the era of multiculturalism and globalization, domestic society cannot be taken for granted.

The other side of this coin is the impact of foreign policy on domestic society itself. In avowedly multiculturalist systems minority groups may be used to having a significant voice in domestic politics, especially in relation to their own affairs. When it then comes to a foreign policy issue in which they have a stake they may be stung by their sudden lack of access. The feeling of exclusion will be heightened by a sense of entitlement if the issue is literally 'close to home', that is, concerning their country of origin. The sense of 'our people' being affected may not even be geographical; the Muslim notion of the *umma* refers to the world-wide community of belief, which means that when Muslims are under threat, it is a matter of concern for their co-religionists wherever they may be located. This used to be true for Catholics and Protestants, but since the seventeenth century Europeans' criterion for concern has gradually moved away from religion, first to race, then to nationality, and now, arguably, to human rights.

It may be, however, that minority groups in European societies tend to care about international issues more ardently than does the majority. Apart from the issue of Islamic solidarity, which in any case only applies to some minorities, any diasporic group will have by definition strong links either to a homeland or to their fellow-dispersees elsewhere. Often they will share the longing for a state of their own. The best-known case of the latter is that of the exiled Palestinians, but they only inhabit European societies in small numbers. It is more obvious in the case of the Kurds, whose presence is most notable (proportional to population) in Austria, Germany, the Netherlands, and Sweden (see Table 2.1). In our three multiculturalist societies the most sizeable diaspora groups with links to particular states are, in Britain: the Pakistanis, Indians, Jamaicans, Bangladeshis, Chinese, and Nigerians;[32] in

[32] It should be noted that official statistics also tend to cluster those of 'Caribbean' and 'black African' origin. These categories have not been used here because of the number of different states and interests they subsume. See Ruth Lupton and Anne Power, *Minority Ethnic Groups in Britain* (London: London School of Economics and Political Science, November 2004). Only extra-EU countries have been listed.

Table 2.1. The principal Kurdish populations of EU Member States

Country	1995	2006	Approx. % of population in 2006
Austria	50–60,000	50–60,000	0.7
Belgium	50–60,000	10–15,000	0.1
France	100–120,000	120–150,000	0.2
Germany	600–650,000	700–800,000	1.0
Greece	20–25,000	20–25,000	0.2
Netherlands	70–80,000	70–80,000	0.5
Sweden	25–30,000	80–100,000	1.1
UK	20–25,000	80–100,000	0.2

Sources: The 1995 figures are from the Institut Kurd de Paris, the main European culture institute for Kurdish minorities, 'The Kurdish Disapora', <http://www.institutkurde.org/en/kurdorama> accessed 23 July 2012. Those for 2006 come from the Lord Russell-Johnston's Report of the Committee on Culture, Science, and Education of the Council of Europe's Parliamentary Assembly, 'The Cultural Situation of the Kurds' (7 July 2006), <http://www.assembly.coe.int/ASP/Doc/XrefViewHTML.asp?FileID=11316&Language=EN> accessed 17 March 2013. Both must be treated with caution, however, which will be evident from the strange decline of the Belgian numbers between 1995 and 2006. The Russell-Johnston Report admits that no reliable census has ever been possible.

the Netherlands: the Turks, Moroccans, Surinamese, Indonesians, and Antillean-Arubans; in Sweden: the Finns, ex-Yugoslavs, Iranians, Kurds, and Iraqis. These groups understandably keep a close eye on events in their homelands, many of which are in the eye of the storm of political conflict—which is precisely why they produced so many émigrés. Although concern tends to weaken with the passing of the generations, this may take considerable time. Indeed, expatriate communities often develop strong attachments through historical myths which have outrun personal experience. Of these the leading example is the romantic Irish-American support for the Provisional IRA, despite its proclivity for the terrorism abhorred by Americans in other contexts.[33]

Minority groups in all democratic societies are subject to these feelings of attachment and concern, which makes them a potential source of complications for those conducting their state's foreign policy. But in societies which aspire to the multicultural ideal, the difficulties are likely to be greater, because the groups will be stronger and are used to being taken seriously. The passions which then may develop over foreign policy, and the conflicts which result, can easily rebound onto civil society itself. Frustration over the inability to change national foreign policy on a deeply held concern, together with the sense of difference from majority opinion which can emerge, has the potential

[33] A 1992 study found that only 25 of the chairpersons of 200 Irish-American groups placed primary responsibility for the Northern Ireland conflict on the Provisional IRA. Nonetheless, the Irish diaspora in the USA contained competing trends, especially on the issue of violence. See Adrian Guelke, 'The United States, Irish Americans and the Northern Ireland Peace Process', *International Affairs*, 72/3 (1996), especially p. 532.

to strip away fragile feelings of belonging inside the wider community, and to throw members of the minority back on their own resources. Events like the London bombings of 2005 may be exceptional, but they are the fruit of a generalized if more law-abiding discontent, which in turn is a new development for societies which have previously prided themselves on managing social change progressively.

As the huge London demonstration of 15 February 2003 against the Iraq War showed, on a given foreign policy action many members of society may identify with the slogan 'not in my name'. Yet on most issues most people do not agitate in this way. Members of ethnocultural groups are also liable to apathy, but when they perceive that their religion and their homelands are under attack, especially from the very country in which they have chosen to live, their deepest values and feelings will be engaged. If the government then also seems to be immune to opinions expressed through normal democratic channels, and if it seems particularly deaf to the views of the minority community, reactions become unpredictable, and direct action a real possibility. This might take the form of public abuse of soldiers returning from war, as happened in Luton in the UK on 5 June 2009 with riotous consequences, or it might produce terrorism. At the least, it weakens the sense of integration into wider society felt by the minority group, and sharpens the prejudices of those already hostile to them. A vicious circle is set up between ferment over foreign policy, domestic unrest, and security concerns at home and abroad.

THE SECURITY DIMENSION

The burden of the argument in the previous section has been that foreign policy-making has become an arena in which domestic politics are increasingly being played out, while in multiculturalist societies this process is exacerbated. Indeed, to some degree the inherent problems of multiculturalism itself are finding expression through debates over international politics. Without the events which flowed first from the war over Bosnia, and then the invasions of Afghanistan and Iraq, who would have guessed that second and third generation British Muslims were so alienated from their home society? In the Netherlands, Mohammed Bouyeri, the murderer of Theo van Gogh, was filled with hate not only for blasphemers like his victim, but also for 'Zionists and Crusaders'.[34] In a letter pinned to van Gogh's body he predicted that Islam would destroy Holland, Europe, and the United States. Up to a point these can be dismissed as the ravings of a deranged individual. But Bouyeri was found

[34] Buruma, *Murder in Amsterdam*, pp. 2–6, 199, and 218–19.

sane by the court, and saw himself as a warrior against democracy. His language, both in the letter and at his trial, was a dark echo of Huntington's derided 'clash of civilisations'.[35] Such diatribes were unknown before the Rushdie crisis two decades ago. Now, spasms of hatred occur at both extremes of the argument.

When events of this kind occur it is not surprising that security concerns take centre stage. Foreign policy is itself geared to the goal of security policy, while those within society who challenge it, even legally, risk coming to the attention of the authorities, anxious about possible acts of disloyalty and ties to hostile foreign forces. At such times the democratic instinct gets all too easily suppressed. Since 9/11, for example, many Western governments have taken extra emergency powers to hold suspects without trial, and/or to stop and search people without a warrant, while Muslims in particular are more likely to suffer inconvenience, even humiliation, through airport checks and the like. Loyal citizens who happen to disagree with government policy may find themselves under surveillance—or worse, as we saw with the practice of 'rendition'. From its own perspective the state apparatus cannot take chances over the possibility of domestic terrorism, with the result that the security services have increased their surveillance over minority communities, while also attempting to penetrate and recruit from them. Security agencies regularly exaggerate threats, as they did over domestic communists during the Cold War, but in the current circumstances they know that even one serious underestimation could produce disaster on the scale of 9/11—or worse. They are therefore bound to err in the other direction.

It may be inevitable, but this tendency heightens distrust and stereotyping on all sides, with knock-on effects in terms of race and intercommunal relations. Issues such as that of the *hijab*, or the building of mosques, become far more difficult to resolve in such a securitized environment. Nor is the problem merely one of perceptions. The reality is that of genuine threats to the lives of fellow-citizens from small but dangerous groups of alienated young people, for whom the society in which they live is simply one site in the global battle between good and evil, and who can move undetected in the densely populated streets of their own community. There is a catch-22 at work here: while the international battle against al-Qaeda goes on, played out in states with Muslim communities and civilian casualties, there will always be discontent and the potential for violence within Western countries (regardless of the sensible move away from a generalized 'War on Terror'). Equally, in multicultural societies after 9/11, intercommunal disputes—for example, over matters of dress or free speech—soon reverberate around the world, acquiring a transnational and then a foreign policy dimension.

[35] Buruma, *Murder in Amsterdam*, pp. 187–95. Samuel P. Huntington, *The Clash of Civilizations and the Remaking of World Order* (New York: Simon and Schuster, 1996).

Governments are thus going to find it difficult to reach the point where they feel that they can reduce the state of alert over terrorism to 'low', and feel free from subversion by elements of their domestic minorities. This affects democracy. As Sir David Omand, the ex-Security and Intelligence Coordinator in the British Cabinet Office, has said of the giant iron gates which now prevent people from approaching Number 10 Downing Street, 'The day seems far away when the gates and barriers might come down. Can we ever return to what now seems an age of innocence?'[36]

But gates and barriers are only the visible parts of the dragnet which has been thrown around society as a result of the attacks of recent years. Immigration has moved firmly into the realm of foreign and security policy, away from the social and legal realm it used to occupy. Britain in particular is confirmed in its desire, for reasons of both security and social harmony, to stay out of the Schengen arrangements which abolished border controls in the European Union. Even France, Italy, and Denmark, which have been pillars of Schengen, demanded exemptions from it during the wave of migrants produced by the war in Libya during 2011. Such individuals were for the most part genuine refugees, but they added to the mass of 'sans papiers' in Europe, about whom security services get nervous.

Education, particularly in its religious context, is another area of social life which has become 'securitized' over the last decade, with anxieties over mosques and schools particularly heightened in the multiculturalist countries. The recognition has painfully dawned that schools, no more than society in general, have not turned out to be the hoped-for drivers of integration. Segregation on an ethnocultural/religious basis has continued to parallel that on geographical lines, as minority communities have clustered in certain locations—ghettoes is too strong a word—in all three states focused on here. The process is determined both by the natural desire of people to live close to those of a similar background and belief-system, and by the precipitate fears of those living in areas to which immigrants are drawn, many of whom choose to move out once a (rather low) tipping point has been reached. This means that many local state schools get dominated by one ethnic or religious group, raising the spectre of 'bussing' for local authorities concerned to pursue long-term social harmony by integration. Multiculturalism is thus caught on the horns of its own dilemma, in wanting to allow the freedom to be different at the same time as encouraging interaction and the 'rainbow effect' of mutual appreciation.

Accordingly, multiculturalism is seen, especially in the context of concerns about war and terrorism, to have the result of sharpening intercommunal tensions rather than reducing them. The identification of some mosques as

[36] David Omand, *Securing the State* (London: Hurst & Co., 2010), p. 85.

sources of extreme Islamism and hate-preaching has spread suspicion all too quickly to all places of Muslim worship and education. New building projects are viewed through the lens of encouraging an 'enemy within' rather than through that of the freedom of conscience which is in principle a key democratic value. There are also technical dilemmas which face governments in this respect. The famous Finsbury Park mosque in north London, where Abu Hamza preached his apocalypse, was probably allowed to function for as long as it was by the British authorities due to their desire to see whom it attracted and to monitor the traffic of radical Islamists through its doors.

Security concerns have impacted seriously on the everyday business of all European citizens as a result of terrorism—indirectly because of US demands for data on the movements of money and people, and directly through the concerns of European governments themselves after the bombings in Madrid and London, and the assassinations in the Netherlands. Sweden has not suffered so directly from intercommunal conflict, but the assassinations of its leading politicians Olaf Palme and Anna Lindh have made it deeply nervous about its long-held commitment to the openness of political society.[37] Technological developments have made it possible to introduce citizen monitoring, through iris-recognition, car number-plate recognition, and GPS systems embedded in mobile telephones, which only ten years ago would have been regarded as an Orwellian nightmare.[38] But such limits on liberty, justified by security and driven by the difficulties of infiltrating minority communities where religion and skin colour pose even greater obstacles than those which faced MI5 in Northern Ireland, have come to be accepted by the majority—on the implicit grounds that they are only applied to certain groups within society. Muslims in Britain, the Netherlands, and elsewhere thus feel singled out, as the subjects of excessive suspicion and discrimination. Another form of intrusion relates to personal banking, which used to be a matter of personal privacy, but is now the focus of intense governmental interest, given that international money-laundering is central to the survival of terrorist and criminal networks.[39] Lastly, the informal use of 'profiling' at border controls means that those of Asian or Middle Eastern appearance are more likely to be interrogated than white Anglo-Saxons—a predictable consequence of both the need to monitor a very large number of movements, and

[37] Chabal and Daloz, *Culture Troubles*, p. 293.

[38] See many relevant works by Didier Bigo and colleagues. It is Bigo who has done most to open up this subject, taking a 'critical security' perspective which emphasizes speech acts, bureaucratic routines, and the epistemic community of security professionals—and which is not simply the product of 9/11. See for example, Didier Bigo and Anastassia Tsoukala (eds), *Terror, Insecurity and Liberty: Illiberal Practices of Liberal Regimes after 9/11* (Abingdon and New York: Routledge, 2008).

[39] See for example, William Vlcek, 'Hitting the Right Target: EU and Security Council Pursuit of Terrorist Financing', *Critical Studies on Terrorism*, 2/2 (2009), pp. 275–91.

the increased diversity of modern European societies. It reflects a deep official ambivalence among Member States about the role of borders and controls, which seem redundant *within* the EU but turn out to be essential at the common EU frontier.

The perception of threat in all European countries has changed dramatically over the last decade, to focus more on possible internal dangers and less on the conventional concerns of defence policy. Ordinary people no less than governments have a palpable if intermittent sense of unease over the possibility of terrorist attacks, or simply public disorder. But there is little doubt that this feeling has been far less prevalent in countries like Poland or Norway, which are relatively homogeneous, than in countries which have experienced rapid changes in their social composition.[40] And among the latter, those which have actively fostered multiculturalism have had, in their blackest moments, to face suggestions that they were heading for the kind of tensions which plague life in the Lebanon. If a country's foreign policy then alienates one or other minority, and indeed divides the country as a whole, the existing divisions in society become even more vulnerable to fracture. We now turn back to the three particular states in view here, to see how their foreign policy has evolved since 2001, and with what effects on their domestic model.

MAKING FOREIGN POLICY IN A MULTICULTURALIST SOCIETY: THREE COUNTRY STUDIES

We saw in the second section of this chapter how foreign policy-making and domestic politics have become increasingly mutually entangled, particularly in multiculturalist societies. Groups want to capture elements of their state's foreign policy, while decision-makers adopt strategies both to evade influence and to anticipate it. But it is important to look at events themselves, and to identify the extent to which the substance of foreign policy has become the source of contention inside the Netherlands, Sweden, and the UK if we are to know the extent to which the relationship with multiculturalism is significant.

The Netherlands has a history of remarkable global engagement for a small country, and also one of welcoming strangers, given its role as a great trading nation and entrepôt. While the security provided by the American alliance has been critical, in the modern period its foreign policy has also been built around balanced multilateralism, stressing the importance of NATO, the UN, and

[40] The mass murder committed by Anders Breivik in Norway on 22 July 2011 is the exception that proves this rule, since his obsession with multiculturalism transforming the country was greeted with incredulity as well as outrage by most of his fellow-citizens.

European institutions, while it has also become known for its generosity as a donor of overseas aid. The country's own role-conception has evolved into that of an active promoter of human rights, at first associated with its support for a democratic and embattled Israel, but gradually moving towards a more even-handed position on the Middle East, and attempting to show no favour to any oppressive state, even one as powerful as China.[41]

Thus Dutch foreign policy has been broadly progressive, but not to the extent of abandoning the Atlantic alliance or of retreating into the pacifistic neutrality which had led it to disaster in 1940. It has also become notably more realist over the last fifteen years, as disillusion has set in with the hopes for a more harmonious post-Cold War world, and for a common European foreign policy. In this balance it reflects elements of its domestic environment, for the Netherlands has been the site both of some of the most liberal social experiments in the world, and elements of inward-looking resistance to change. That until recently it has also had a reputation for enviable equilibrium owes something to a shared belief in a form of governmental subsidiarity, whereby hierarchy defers to the autonomy of the units which are closest to the problem or area in question. Thus even at the highest level of the Cabinet, each ministry expects to be independent of any coordinating authority.[42] This can be seen as analogous to the acceptance of multiculturalism as a desirable model for society as a whole, building on the long-standing 'pillars' tradition of independence for the various Christian churches.

Over the last decade the Netherlands has been loyal to its multilateralist tradition, while suffering significant domestic consequences. Led from 2002–10 by the Christian Democratic prime minister Jan Peter Balkenende, the government gave strong political support to the US–UK invasion of Iraq in 2003; from 2006–10 the country made a major contribution to the international coalition's operations in Afghanistan; and in 2011 it helped to patrol the no-fly zone over Libya. However, the Iraq action led to increasing internal criticism, culminating in the authoritative Davids Report of January 2010, which concluded that, 'The Dutch government lent its political support to a war whose purpose was not consistent with Dutch government

[41] Keukeleire and MacNaughtan describe the Dutch role conception in this way. Stephan Keukeleire and Jennifer MacNaughtan, *The Foreign Policy of the European Union* (Houndmills: Palgrave Macmillan, 2008), p. 138. On human rights, and the willingness to challenge China, see Catherine Gegout, 'A Pure CFSP Case: The Condemnation of China's Human Rights Policy (1997–2005)', Chapter 3 of her *European Foreign and Security Policy: States, Power, Institutions and American Hegemony* (Toronto: University of Toronto Press, 2010), especially pp. 91–4, 99, 106, and 113.

[42] In 1995, for example, a major attempt was made to coordinate foreign policy by reorganizing the relevant ministries, but without notable success. See Duco Hellema, 'The Netherlands', in Brian Hocking and David Spence (eds), *Foreign Ministries in the European Union: Integrating Diplomats* (revd. edn, Houndmills: Palgrave Macmillan, 2005), pp. 184–7.

policy. It may therefore be said that the Dutch stance was to some extent disingenuous.'[43]

The report also accused the prime minister of having been distracted by domestic concerns, by which it meant the rise of populist parties in the previous twelve months, including the rise and death of Pim Fortuyn, all associated with arguments over new measures on crime and immigration. In the words of Jacques Pelkmans and Bas Limonard this was 'one of the most turbulent periods in Dutch domestic politics since the beginning of general suffrage'.[44] As for Afghanistan, the Netherlands was one of the few smaller countries willing to take on the burden of the hard, front-line, fighting in the south of the country, and hosting the NATO–ISAF Joint Force Command at Brunssum. In general it has not shied away from the use of force, being one of the five founder-members of the European Gendarmerie Force in 2004, but at home it has tended to play up its role in reconstruction, rather than war-fighting, for predictable reasons. After one renewal of a two-year parliamentary mandate in late 2007, the government fell when it attempted in February 2010 to back away from a commitment to a scheduled withdrawal. The final pull-out took place in August 2010.

This record shows that the Balkenende government gave priority to what it saw as its alliance commitments and the needs of international order, but that it paid an eventual price at home for so doing. Domestic opinion proved anything but indifferent to foreign policy. Yet it cannot be said that it was the multicultural character of society which had any particular effect here. Dissent was mobilized through traditional media and parliamentary channels, and was as much concerned with the rising number of casualties (24 Dutch soldiers died in total) and the justification of the war as such, as with the specifically Muslim dimension. In this the Netherlands was typical of trends across Europe.[45] Furthermore, much of Dutch foreign policy displays continuity, as with its high levels of Overseas Development Assistance (ODA), and its willingness from 2002 to host the new International Criminal Court (ICC) at The Hague, despite the risk of terrorism which that poses. Even on the Middle East, the Netherlands is careful to be even-handed, and when it comes

[43] *Rapport Commissie-Davids: Conclusions* (English summary), 12 January 2010, para 7, <http://vorige.nrc.nl/multimedia/archive/00267/rapport_commissieri_267285a.pdf> accessed 2 June 2013.

[44] Jacques Pelkmans and Bas Limonard, 'The Netherlands and the Future of Europe Convention', EPIN Briefing Note (European Policy Institutes Network, March 2003), p. 1, <http://www.epin.org/new/files/debate_netherlands.pdf> accessed 17 March 2013.

[45] Polls conducted in 2009–10 showed a general trend in Europe towards disillusionment with the war in Afghanistan, which is hardly surprising given its length. See the German Marshall Fund, Transatlantic Trends poll conducted in June 2010, <http://trends.gmfus.org/files/archived/doc/2010_English_Key.pdf> pp15-16 accessed 17 March 2013, p. 42.

under pressure from the country's pro-Palestinian NGOs they are rather more likely to be from Christian than Muslim communities.[46]

Yet if multiculturalism has not shaped Dutch foreign policy overtly, it has had some significant indirect effects. The sense of insecurity, from both external and internal threats, has palpably heightened over the last ten years, leading to a diminished trust in the benefits of interdependence, and a greater willingness to entertain realist prescriptions. If nationalism would be too strong a term for the contemporary Netherlands, the country has certainly concluded that it needs to protect its own interests more robustly, as seen, for example, in negotiations within the European Union. It has also introduced tough restrictions on immigration and asylum. From 1945 onwards the Netherlands' main historical traumas related first to the failure to save Dutch Jews from the Nazis (reinforced by the diary of Anne Frank), and subsequently to the way the Dutch UN Brigade had stood by while the forces of Ratko Mladic rounded up the 8,000 Bosnian men and boys whom they then murdered in Srebrenica in 1995. This created a culture in which human rights took an ever more important part in Dutch foreign policy. But after 9/11 the activities of Fortuyn, van Gogh, Hirsan Ali, and then Geert Wilders exacerbated existing concerns about multiculturalism in general, and increased the pressure on Islam in particular.[47] The associated episodes of violence have turned the country more inwards, to a debate over the competing needs and rights of groups within civil society, as opposed to notions of international obligation. This represents the other side of the coin from minorities' wish to influence foreign policy, or reactions against it when they cannot. The external–internal interplay also affects broader issues such as attitudes towards society and conceptions of national identity.

The most striking example of this is the change which has taken place in attitudes towards Turkish entry into the European Union. In 2006 a Eurobarometer report judged the Netherlands to be one of the 'relatively more enlargement-friendly' states, with 55 per cent of Dutch people in favour of Turkish accession, if Turkey met all the conditions of entry (compared to 39 per cent of the EU-25 population as a whole).[48] By 2009, however, the situation had changed, with 50 per cent against any further enlargement, and

[46] For example, Israel complained to the Dutch government that it was unwittingly funding those calling for a boycott of Israel, in the form of (established) NGOs such as IKV, Pax Christi, and the Interchurch Organization for Development Cooperation. *Jerusalem Post*, 15 May 2011.

[47] Geert Wilders is the leader of the PVV, an anti-Islam party which he founded in 2005. In the 2010 elections it became the third (equal) largest party in Parliament. On its origin, see Mudde, 'A Fortuynist Foreign Policy', pp. 213 and 219.

[48] Eurobarometer, 'Attitudes towards European Union Enlargement', Special Eurobarometer 255, fieldwork conducted March–May 2006 (for the European Commission, July 2006), p. 71, available online, <http://ec.europa.eu/enlargement/pdf/reportsp255enlargement20060612_en.pdf> accessed 19 December 2012.

the Netherlands being perceived in Ankara as one of the main obstacles to Turkey's entry.[49] This is almost certainly the product of a combination of concerns about the workings of multiculturalism, the fact that most Muslims in the Netherlands are from either Turkey or Morocco, and the sheer size of Turkey's population, which has the potential to make the influx of Poles and Romanians upon their states' EU entry look like small beer.[50] It would also change the costs of the Common Agricultural Policy much to the disadvantage of the Dutch. The absolute number of Turks in Holland is small, at 389,000, but they have grown from 1.95 per cent of the population in 2000 to 2.34 per cent in 2011, as part of a more general rise of the 'non-western background' segment of the population from 8.9 per cent to 11.4 per cent.[51] And in the febrile atmosphere of the last ten years it has been perceptions which count as much as cold facts. The density of population in the Netherlands, especially in the cities, which is one of the highest in the world, is also a factor. The comparison with sparsely populated Sweden may explain why the latter takes a different view on Turkish accession.[52]

In short, the Netherlands has become hyper-sensitized to the issue of Islam, in its external policy as well as in its social diversity. This is why, when the Ministry of Foreign Affairs announced cut-backs in its staff and overseas representation in 2011, the axe fell on missions in Latin America and in Africa. Those in the Middle East were spared.[53] Yet the Netherlands has other major international priorities like commerce and drug controls. As the letter to Parliament about the closure of missions asserted, 'this country is so

[49] Eurobarometer, 'Public Opinion in the European Union', Standard Eurobarometer 71, fieldwork conducted June–July 2009, p. 74. Dutch opinion was divided, with 50 per cent being 'Against', 44 per cent 'For', and 6 per cent 'Don't Know', <http://ec.europa.eu/public_opinion/archives/eb/eb71/eb713_annexes.pdf> accessed 19 December 2012. The common perception of the Netherlands as having become one of the main opponents of Turkish accession, together with Austria, Cyprus, France, Germany, and Greece, can be found in *A Very Special Relationship: Why Turkey's EU Accession Process will Continue*, Opinión Europa, No. 91 (Barcelona Centre for International Affairs, CIDOB, November 2010), <http://www.cidob.org/en/publications/opinion/europa/a_very_special_relationship_why_turkey_s_eu_accession_process_will_continue> accessed 19 December 2012.

[50] In 2011 Turkey's population was approximately 71.5 million and Holland's 16.7 million.

[51] Official Dutch statistics on the population, to be found online at Statistics Netherlands, 'Key Figures' [online database], <http://www.cbs.nl/en-GB/menu/cijfers/default.htm> accessed 19 December 2012.

[52] Carl Bildt from Sweden was one of the 16 Foreign Ministers who published an article in Turkey's *Hurriyet Daily News* on 28 June 2012 calling for a reinvigoration of the accession process. The eleven countries which did not sign were: Austria, Belgium, Czech Republic, Cyprus, Denmark, France, Greece, Ireland, Luxembourg, Malta, and the Netherlands. Sweden does not register ethnicity but most estimates have its Turkish-born population at about 0.5 per cent of the population, or less than 50,000.

[53] 'Reforming Diplomacy: Clear Choices, New Emphases', Announcement by Foreign Minister Uri Rosenthal, 8 April 2011 (Ministry of Foreign Affairs, the Netherlands), <http://www.government.nl/ministries/bz/about-the-ministry/missions-abroad/reforming-diplomacy-clear-choices-new-emphases> accessed 17 March 2013.

hard-wired into the wider world that we cannot shrug our shoulders when we see what is happening in other parts of it. The line between the foreign and the domestic blurs'.[54] In addition, the letter states that, 'The internet and social media are making it easier for people to share information and form opinions. Networks are widening. *If you want something, you have to look further, share, and connect*'.[55] But if policy is to proceed on this basis, it will need to recognize that the character of Dutch society and the nature of foreign policy are two sides of the same coin, with each having the potential to knock the other off course.

The case of Swedish foreign policy presents an interesting contrast to that of the Netherlands, in that its foreign policy has undergone a major shift over the last fifteen years. At the same time there have also been important changes in domestic politics. Like the Netherlands, Sweden looks back to a glorious seventeenth century from a tradition of independence. Unlike it, however, Sweden has also managed to preserve its independence from powerful neighbours, even during the Second World War and the Cold War. On this foundation it built a foreign policy during the second half of the twentieth century based on internationalism, openness, and progressive liberal values. European integration and the Atlantic alliance were developments held at arm's length in the interests of the policy of neutrality, adopted in 1815 and becoming the *leitmotif* not just of foreign policy, but of Swedish identity.

Against this backdrop the end of the Cold War precipitated change which over the course of twenty years proved to be revolutionary. Sweden entered the EU in 1995, and has become an active player in the Common Foreign and Security Policy. Its deepest values have not changed—which explains the 2001 initiative to commit the EU to a conflict prevention strategy, reflecting a desire to avoid war and build international cooperation—although the means and the partners certainly have.[56] Yet this in turn has meant abandoning, at least discursively, the cherished principle of neutrality. Membership of the EU and the CFSP themselves were seen by many in Sweden as a *de facto* repudiation of neutrality, so it was no surprise that that policy came then to be defined more in terms of non-alignment, and 'non-participation in military alliances'.[57]

[54] <http://www.minbuza.nl/en/appendices/news/newsflashes/2011/04/reforming-diplomacy-clear-choices-new-emphases/letter-to-the-house-of-representatives-modernising-dutch-diplomacy.html> accessed 2 June 2013. 'Executive Summary of a Letter to the House of Representatives Entitled "Modernising Dutch Diplomacy—A Timeless Profession Remodelled for Today".'

[55] <http://www.minbuza.nl/en/appendices/news/newsflashes/2011/04/reforming-diplomacy-clear-choices-new-emphases/letter-to-the-house-of-representatives-modernising-dutch-diplomacy.html> accessed 2 June 2013. Italics in the original.

[56] See Christopher Hill, 'The EU's Capacity for Conflict Prevention', *European Foreign Affairs Review*, 6/3 (2001), pp. 315–33; also Douglas Bromesson, 'Normative Europeanization: The Case of Swedish Foreign Policy Reorientation', *Cooperation and Conflict*, 45/2 (2010), pp. 224–44.

[57] Lee Miles, 'Sweden and Finland', in Ian Manners and Richard G. Whitman (eds), *The Foreign Policies of European Union Member States* (Manchester: Manchester University Press, 2000), pp. 181–7.

Indeed, while Sweden has kept out of NATO, it no longer sees itself, as it did in the era of the Vietnam War, as representing a form of third way between capitalism and communism.[58] Carl Bildt, a key figure in the evolution of Sweden's stance in the current century, acknowledged in an official statement of the country's foreign policy direction that, 'Membership of the European Union means that Sweden is part of a political alliance and takes its share of responsibility, in the spirit of solidarity, for Europe's security'.

He went on to say that 'The United States is the European Union's principal strategic partner'.[59] These statements could not have been made by Sweden's Foreign Minister even 15 years ago without raising a storm of protest. They reflect the reality that Sweden has entered fully into European crisis-management activities, albeit by developing (with the help of other ex-neutral Member States) its 'civilian' side.[60] It has participated in operations in both Afghanistan and Libya, proving itself a reliable and effective partner. In Afghanistan a cross-party agreement provides for the continuation of Sweden's 500-troop presence (in a 'reconstruction team') before withdrawal between 2012 and 2014, despite their being effectively under NATO command—a sensitive question domestically. In Libya in 2011 Sweden contributed to enforcing the no-fly zone virtually from the outset, although only by providing surveillance and support services, again the result of a party compromise. This was in the tradition of Sweden's long commitment to UN-authorized peacekeeping, and its policy of active humanitarianism—which saw it willing to envisage the overthrow of Saddam Hussein, until it transpired that a UN Resolution would not pass—and its massive practical contribution to the reconstruction of Iraq from 2004–9. It is also the case that Sweden has accepted a disproportionately large number of Iraqi refugees over the last two decades, many of them Kurds (see Table 2.1). 37,000 arrived in the 1990s (only 3,000 fewer than from the former Yugoslavia), and another 54,000 in the period 2003–10.[61]

One Swedish Iraqi, admitted to the country long before the 2003 war and subsequently domiciled in Britain, blew himself up in Stockholm in December 2010, apparently in protest against the Swedish presence in Afghanistan and against Swedes' silence over the Danish cartoons affair.[62] It was fortunate that his act did not wreak considerable havoc, and so far it remains an isolated

[58] Bromesson, 'Normative Europeanisation', p. 230.

[59] Carl Bildt, Minister of Foreign Affairs, *Statement of Government Policy in the Parliamentary Debate on Foreign Affairs* (Stockholm: Ministry of Foreign Affairs, 16 February 2011), pp. 3 and 6, <http://www.government.se/content/1/c6/16/11/48/dc78c337.pdf> accessed 21 November 2012.

[60] Keukeleire and MacNaughtan, *The Foreign Policy of the European Union*, pp. 181–2.

[61] Statistics compiled from data available on the website of Statistics Sweden (English version) at <http://www.scb.se/Pages/List____250611.aspx> accessed 17 March 2013.

[62] *Daily Telegraph*, 12 December 2010.

incident. Public opinion is more active on foreign policy questions in Sweden than in most European countries, with strong human rights and development lobbies, but ethnic minorities have not played an active part.[63] Their importance is more indirect, through the rise of the anti-immigration Sweden Democrats, who see government policy as having been too generous in admitting refugees, with the result that the country's stability and generous welfare provisions have come under pressure.[64] Thus foreign and domestic policy are brought together in a continuous loop—Sweden's internationalism leads it into external commitments, whose internal consequences may include jihadism and corresponding reactions. At the very least they shake up the established pattern of party politics, and thus the conventional assumptions of foreign policy. Furthermore, through the series of incremental steps which Swedish foreign policy has gone through since 1995, it has now become a committed member of the EU's 'political alliance' and security structures. Indeed, it faces choices as to whether to develop—or acknowledge the *de facto* existence of—a structured, intimate relationship with NATO, if not actual membership. A debate on this would touch the very foundations of Sweden's sense of itself, not least because Swedes see an inherent connection between their values and their international role.[65]

At one level there has been surprisingly little domestic upheaval as a result of foreign policy, given the changes which have occurred since EU entry.[66] This is partly the result of political maturity, as issues are thoroughly aired and major choices owned across the political spectrum, as over Afghanistan (with even the Greens in support) and Libya. But the increase in social diversity may complicate matters once ethnocultural groups have had time to settle and to organize their lobbies. On the other hand, there is genuine acknowledgement in the Iraqi community, for example, of Swedish generosity in terms of both aid and asylum. Furthermore, the multiculturalist perspective has enabled Foreign Minister Bildt to keep Sweden among the dwindling band of firm

[63] Indeed 'the absence of ethnic minorities is a remarkable feature' of associational life in Sweden more generally. Erik Amnå, 'Associational Life, Youth, and Political Capital Formation in Sweden: Historical Legacies and Contemporary Trends', in Trägårdh (ed.), *State and Civil Society in Northern Europe*, pp. 172 and 180.

[64] The Sweden Democrats were isolated by the other parties, unlike their equivalent in Denmark, the Danish People's Party. But their emergence certainly affected the balance of power.

[65] Lars Trägårdh, 'Sweden and the EU: Welfare State Nationalism and the Spectre of "Europe"', in Lene Hansen and Ole Wæver (eds), *European Integration and National Identity: The Challenge of the Nordic States* (London: Routledge, 2002), pp. 36 and 153. Also Lisbeth Aggestam, 'The European Internationalist: Sweden and European Security Cooperation', *Nação Difesa* (Lisbon), 118 (2007), pp. 203–18.

[66] For example the prime minister declared his gratitude for domestic support in preparing for the EU presidency of 2001. See Magnus Ekengren, 'National Foreign Policy Coordination: The Swedish EU Presidency', in Walter Carlsnaes, Helene Sjursen, and Brian White (eds), *Contemporary European Foreign Policy* (London: Sage, 2004), p. 218.

supporters of Turkish accession to the EU (as Britain has been), and to become a member of the EU core group on Somalia.[67] If times get harder, while at the same time Sweden is seen as a more orthodox partner in Western interventionism, the situation will become more unpredictable. But Sweden has the advantages of size, wealth, and a low density of population, which gives it a greater margin of manoeuvre in terms of domestic–foreign interactions than the Netherlands or Britain.

Turning finally to the case of the United Kingdom, we saw earlier in this chapter some examples of foreign policy having produced turbulent effects on the home front. Historically this is not new. Liberal causes as well as jingoism brought forth occasional expressions of popular feeling in the nineteenth century, while after the First World War a more critical response was in evidence, as with the pacifist demonstrations of the 1930s, and those against nuclear weapons from the 1960s onwards. But such episodes were intermittent, and did not disturb the confidence of the London elite in its ability to conduct foreign policy relatively undisturbed. It was the coincidence of two new factors, beginning in the 1990s, that changed their outlook.

The first was the emergence of a new phase of activism, indeed interventionism, in world affairs. After the decision to withdraw from East of Suez in 1968 the UK had seen a global role as too difficult to sustain, and, with the exception of the UN-authorized wars to resist the invasions of the Falklands in 1982, and Kuwait in 1991, had avoided sending troops 'out of area'. Such prudence had culminated in the unwillingness of the Conservative government under John Major to take a forward role in the Balkans during the breakup of Yugoslavia, despite the growing evidence of genocide and Serbian expansionism.[68] All this changed with the arrival in power of New Labour in 1997. Fused with a post-Thatcherite confidence in Britain's ability to lead the world, morally if not politically, and with concern for human rights sharpened by the disasters of Cambodia, Rwanda, and Bosnia, Foreign Secretary Robin Cook gave new emphasis to the 'ethical dimension' of foreign policy, by which he primarily meant help for the Third World, plus a more careful approach to arms sales. But prime minister Tony Blair took the idea forward in a rather different direction. He saw certain autocracies, notably those of Serbia and Iraq, as representing a danger to international peace as well as to their own people, and was willing to carry the fight to them. Within six years his government had intervened militarily on five occasions, in four different theatres. The first three were short-lived, and achieved their aims: Iraq, 1998; Kosovo, 1999; Sierra Leone, 2000–2. But the last two turned into

[67] The Somalia Core Group consists of the Commission, Britain, Italy, and Sweden. Keukeleire and MacNaughtan, *The Foreign Policy of the European Union*, p. 113.

[68] Brendan Simms, *Unfinest Hour: Britain and the Destruction of Bosnia* (London: Penguin Books, 2001).

running sores: Afghanistan, 2001–present and Iraq, 2003–11.[69] Britain thus once again became a global player and, furthermore, the one European state indelibly associated with the combative policies of the United States after 11 September 2001.

The second new factor affecting the politics of British foreign policy was the flowering of multiculturalism inside the country. By this is meant both the steady increase in social diversity, and the active promotion of the multiculturalist project by New Labour—although this had been effectively started in the late 1970s. Britain's particular version of cosmopolitanism had its origins in empire, and the reversal of migration patterns in the 1950s as poor people from the colonies sought better lives just as the metropole began to need more cheap labour. Other consequences of empire were the taking in of the Asian communities expelled from east Africa in the 1970s, and the sense of responsibility (if not guilt) which was particularly prevalent in the Labour party, whose internationalism was far more rooted in the Commonwealth and the United Nations than in the supranationalist experiments of continental Europe. Thus New Labour embraced with enthusiasm the idea of a multicultural Britain, where different traditions, faiths, and tastes could not only coincide but enrich each other, especially if they were not cramped by an old-fashioned, defensive, nationalism. This was the 'cool Britannia' which was artistically vibrant and so attractive to visitors as the twentieth century drew to a close.

At this point the fact that multiculturalism might not prove always progressive was not prominent in discussion, with the Rushdie affair seemingly confined to the past. Nor was there a sense that a foreign policy which was being driven (in the eyes of its makers) by humanitarian concerns could rebound onto domestic harmony. But all too soon Britain became the leading example of the interplay between the two spheres, due to its high-profile, pro-US, foreign policy, and a society which contained groups with the motives and ability to react against what was being done abroad in their name, often at the expense of their co-religionists. Bosnia alienated many British Muslims dismayed at the government's apparent indifference, leading to a disregard of the actions in Kosovo which did aim at protecting a Muslim community (against Serbian oppression). It was seen as evidence of cynical double standards more than genuine concern. Even the actions in Sierra Leone, which restored stability and a legitimate government, were criticized for the use of mercenaries to circumvent a UN arms embargo, and for neo-colonialism in a country rich in 'blood diamonds'. Yet both Kosovo and Sierra Leone encouraged Blair to think that humanitarian interventions could work in short order,

[69] See John Kampfner, *Blair's Wars* (London: The Free Press, 2003); also Christopher Hill, 'Putting the World to Rights: The Foreign Policy Mission of Tony Blair', in Anthony Seldon and Dennis Kavanagh (eds), *The Blair Effect, 2001–5* (Cambridge: Cambridge University Press, 2005), pp. 384–409.

even if changes of state borders or regimes might be required. And after 9/11 this in turn led to the forward policies in Afghanistan and Iraq which, whatever their justifications, led many British citizens (Muslim and non-Muslim) to be appalled at the 'collateral damage' inflicted on civilians through the invasion and occupation of sovereign states. These were literally explosive events, occurring in a compressed time-frame and commanding the attention of the world's media. Foreign policy had come to dominate British politics over an extended period and with far more domestic ramifications than had been anticipated.

With these precedents, it was not surprising that other foreign policy issues also stirred up interested minorities inside the UK, from sympathy for white Zimbabwean farmers to Tamils desperate for a cease-fire as the Sri Lankan government finally crushed the Tamil Tigers in the north of the country. Citizens of Indian and Pakistani origin watched events in the sub-continent vigilantly from their competing perspectives, which meant that ministers had to tread with particular care in their diplomacy over Kashmir, terrorism, and nuclear proliferation.[70] African, and pro-African, lobbies also found their voices in pressing for more aid to what remained the poorest of the world's continents—in this case finding an increasingly sympathetic official reaction.

It is true that foreign policy was never simply driven by such pressures—in Zimbabwe, for example, despite being excoriated by Robert Mugabe, Britain never placed his administration under seriously damaging pressure, while the huge numbers of Tamil demonstrators who intermittently occupied Parliament Square in April–June 2009, some on hunger strike, achieved little more than to draw attention to their case.[71] Yet those responsible for British foreign policy have had to take into account a more turbulent and less predictable domestic environment. Part of this is the consequence of world events themselves, but the emergence of active ethnic lobbies has interacted with them to heighten the general level of public interest in foreign policy, with the media picking up on the dramatic interplay between external crises and internal opposition to increase the pressures on decision-makers.

The British experience was most notable for the number and seriousness of the terrorist attacks suffered from the turn of the century on. These incidents were inflicted for the most part not by infiltrators or drifters, but by people living and working in society. Moreover, their target was not the apparatus and representatives of the state, but their fellow-citizens, going about everyday life. Tony Blair has denied that such acts had anything to do with the nature of

[70] On Kashmir, see Vernon Hewitt and Mark Wickham-Jones, 'New Labour and the Politics of Kashmir', in Richard Little and Mark Wickham-Jones (eds.), *New Labour's Foreign Policy: A New Moral Crusade* (Manchester: Manchester University Press, 2000), pp. 201–17.

[71] *The Times*, 7 April 2009; *The Guardian*, 20 April 2009; BBC News website, 25 November 2009, <http://news.bbc.co.uk/2/hi/uk_news/8377531.stm> accessed 19 December 2012. The prime minister did send a special representative to the UN, and Britain did call for a cease-fire—but this was in full awareness that no outsider could change the facts on the ground.

his foreign policy, but the evidence is against him. On balance it seems probable that the reason for Britain having been the principal target for terrorism lies in the combination of, on the one hand, a high-profile foreign policy entailing acts of war in Muslim countries and, on the other, a society in which a significant minority of second and third generation immigrants felt alienated—despite, or possibly because of, the autonomy their communities enjoyed. Individually, neither of these factors would probably have been enough to have precipitated insurgency; together, they produced an explosive mixture.

CONCLUSION

What, then, are we to make of the experience of these three multiculturalist societies in terms of the place of foreign policy in their politics? For all of them the last decade has brought new and testing challenges. The Netherlands and the UK have both suffered serious internal turmoil, to the point where multiculturalism has been brought into question. Some of the problems which they have suffered have resulted from, or at the very least been exacerbated by, their foreign policies. Yet it would be wrong to assume that economic and social issues have not been at least as important—especially in the Netherlands, where the conflicts surrounding Islam have been of a multifaceted nature, concerning social mores and problems of integration at least as much as hostility to the Dutch policy on Iraq or Afghanistan. Levels of immigration—actual and perceived—have been an important factor in both countries.

The foreign policies of the two states have, in turn, been significantly complicated by domestic tensions, not least because issues like immigration, and indeed multiculturalism itself, have come to span the divide between home and abroad. Yet they have not been directly shaped by domestic opposition, or the fear of future turmoil. Where foreign policy has changed, as in the Dutch withdrawal, it has been through setbacks in the field itself, and/or a general loss of political support at home. Ethnic minorities have become more vocal and assertive, but they have not reached anything like the level of organization or influence enjoyed by, say, those active on development questions. Indeed, it is politically unhealthy that they seem for the present to have few middle options, between a silent and sometimes resentful passivity on the one hand, and random violence on the other. Mere indifference is a luxury enjoyed by the majority who feel at one with their society and/or its foreign policy.

Sweden is a rather different case. Its progressive foreign policy tradition has made it less inclined to pursue policies which might enrage its Muslim minorities, while it does not suffer from the density of population which sharpens tensions in the UK and Holland. Recently, however, reactions against both immigration and immigrants themselves have produced significant changes in party politics, while Swedish foreign policy has moved closer to that of the bigger EU Member States, indeed closer to that of NATO in certain respects, with a willingness to engage more actively in a multilateral defence of the Western way of life. This could bring to an end the exception which jihadists seemed to grant to Sweden (Osama bin Laden is supposed to have asked the United States and others why Sweden had not been attacked) while also stirring up domestic controversy—but across the board, not simply with minorities.[72]

In sum, the multiculturalist project is in trouble in all three of the countries discussed here. At times foreign policy has been a catalyst for its difficulties, while at others social diversity has impinged on the conduct of foreign policy. But a project like multiculturalism is not created overnight, nor can it be wished away by fiat, as with David Cameron's statement to the Munich Security Conference in February 2011 that it had 'failed'.[73] In the three countries we have examined, multiculturalism, despite its problems, is embedded in social, legal, and political practices—and in mentalities. Thus, if polarization occurs at both domestic and international levels, it is difficult to prevent interaction between the two via the transnational linkages discussed in Chapter 1. Reaction, emulation, and penetration have all been fostered by the events of 9/11, but also by the very nature of multiculturalism, independent of governments. Accordingly, both the conduct of foreign policy and the maintenance of domestic order have been made that much more difficult. Any government which is attached both to the project of multiculturalism and to a foreign policy which disregards its diverse social base, risks opening Pandora's box.

[72] Bin Laden was reported to have said: 'Free people do not relinquish their security. This is contrary to Bush's claim that we hate freedom. Let him tell us why we did not strike Sweden, for example'. BBC News Transcript of videotape shown on al-Jazeera, 29 October 2004, <http://news.bbc.co.uk/1/hi/world/middle_east/3966817.stm> accessed 19 December 2012.

[73] 'David Cameron Sparks Fury from Critics Who Say Attack on Multiculturalism has Boosted English Defence League', *The Guardian*, 5 February 2011.

3

The Integrationist Model

The opposite of the multiculturalist approach to diversity is that which used to be called 'assimilation'. By this was meant the wish and ability of a society to absorb new arrivals by helping them to become like the existing citizenry, thus conforming to certain dominant civic norms and avoiding fragmentation. This would be achieved through a combination of sticks and carrots, but whichever instruments were in play the process was essentially top-down, and presupposed a certain national consensus (to a degree idealized, as with Benedict Anderson's 'imagined community') to begin with.[1] The notion of assimilation came, however, to seem paternalist at best, racist and colonialist at worst, and was gradually superseded in the late twentieth century—notably in France, where 'assimilation' had been most trumpeted—by that of 'integration'. This term implies an equality between the various elements which might be integrating, and a horizontal rather than vertical process by which it occurs. Like its opposite, multiculturalism, it contains elements of idealism—here in envisaging a shared journey towards a new vision of society made up by the merging of majority and minority characteristics. Yet it also represents a devious use of language, in the sense that it disguises a *de facto* continued belief in assimilation to the 'essence' of a country's character, despite the fact that the discourse of integration is also employed by many for whom assimilation would be abhorrent.[2]

What the two words have in common is the presupposition that a nation-state is best run on the basis of a high degree of social homogeneity, with as few concessions to the autonomy of groups—or even regions—as possible. In one sense all states are integrationist by definition, which is why they almost always resist attempts at secession and the concept of no-go areas within their borders. But some make particularly determined efforts to achieve a single, unifying, sense of nationhood to which their citizens must subscribe. Countries like this are clearly at the opposite end of the

[1] Benedict Anderson, *Imagined Communities: Reflections on the Origins and Spread of Nationalism* (London: Verso, 1983).

[2] See for example the MIPEX project—footnote 8.

spectrum from those like the UK examined in Chapter 2. This chapter will explore their experiences through a discussion first of what integrationism entails—both theoretically and empirically—and then of the particular histories of the three European states which conform most closely to the abstract model: France, Denmark, and Greece. The second half of the chapter draws out the implications of the strategy for external relations, and vice versa, concluding with some reflections on the degree to which the very process of domestic/external interaction is bringing about change in the model itself.

THE THEORETICAL DIMENSION OF INTEGRATIONISM

The attempt to achieve integration necessarily involves the relationship between the state and civil society, an issue which is at the heart of much political theory, and of economics. The debates which have arisen revolve for the most part around the place of the individual, and the extent to which his or her freedoms are compatible with the common weal. Any state has to be both integrationist and diverse in terms of how it relates to civil society and the myriad individuals it comprises—it is just a question of how far to go in each direction. Without any sense of common rules, institutions, and purposes, a state could not function at all; with too much emphasis on uniformity it becomes a mere device for oppression, denying that people have a right to any life outside the political realm. That way lies pure totalitarianism, which even the nightmare regimes of Hitler, Stalin, Mao, or Pol Pot never quite managed to impose fully.[3] Most states which retain legitimacy, whether democratic or not, survive on the basis of a balance between centralism and devolution, between unity and diversity. The issue at stake, then, becomes that of the appropriate balance between the rights and freedoms of the individual on the one hand, and the needs and vision of the state on the other. Depending on the nature of the state—in terms of size, location, history, conformation, ideology, and organizing principles—the degree of integration will vary.

[3] J. L. Talmon, *A History of Totalitarian Democracy* (London: Secker and Warburg, 1952), p. 270. Talmon summarizes the extreme Rousseauian position as the view that the citizenship of a state excludes membership of the Christian fraternity, or even human-kind. Also writing in the early years of the Cold War, Hannah Arendt noted 'the conformism inherent in society', which 'always demands that its members act as though they were one enormous family which has only one opinion and one interest'. Hannah Arendt, *The Human Condition* (Chicago: University of Chicago Press, 1958), pp. 41 and 39.

Integration refers, as Weil and Crowley point out, 'in a classic sociological Durkheimian sense' to shared practices, social interactions, and perhaps also to shared beliefs and goals.[4] In the context of this book, however, the issue of integration relates not to individuals, as over most of the history of democracy, but to groups.[5] This is a problem which has historically bedevilled states in such forms as religious wars, attempts at secession, claims of regional autonomy, and the persecution of minorities perceived as 'enemies within'. In the contemporary context it has arisen through the discourse of multiculturalism, which has permitted the very idea of separate groups or communities to be seen as compatible with the stability of the state, and in certain contexts has put a positive spin on it. Yet regardless of multiculturalism there can be no doubt that all states with democratic aspirations have to accept the emergence and flourishing of groups outside the control of government. Citizens have the right to associate for all kinds of private purposes. They also have the right, and the capacity, to join forces as pressure-groups, political parties, religions, localities, and economic associations. But these and other forms of activism all have the potential not only to resist an oppressive government, but to divide a society against itself beyond the limit which is compatible with the effective functioning of a democratic state. Their activities therefore always attract some form of regulation, the criteria for which relate to the extent to which groups' rights and privileges should be guaranteed, but also limited, by the state.[6]

The rapid increase in diversity which has occurred in many European states over the last 30 years has brought the issues of integrationism and multiculturalism, with their various perceived virtues and defects, very much to the fore. Indeed, a polarization has occurred which is reflected in the models under examination here. But what does 'integration' imply when applied to groups in a modern democracy? The literature does not provide us with clear guidance in relation to the fundamental constitutional issues. A recent project for the Migrants Information Territorial Index (MITI) saw the problem as requiring the team to focus on 'the number of immigrants, their integration in different fields such as housing and labor market and their access to rights such as health and marriage, in order to be able to compare foreigners' and migrants' level of integration within EU Member States'.[7] But this is to raise

[4] Patrick Weil and John Crowley, 'Integration in Theory and Practice: A Comparison of France and Britain', in Martin Baldwin-Edwards and Martin A. Schain (eds), *The Politics of Immigration in Western Europe* (London: Frank Cass, 1994), p. 111.

[5] John Dunn, *Setting the People Free: The Story of Democracy* (London: Atlantic Books, 2005).

[6] The idea of regulation from an integrationist perspective contrasts with that which became common in the EU after the wave of privatizations in the 1980s, namely the tendency of states and the EU to delegate much activity to particular economic and professional groups, relying on technical scrutiny and on the law to hold the ring. Indeed, this trend is more analogous with the multiculturalist project. See Giandomenico Majone, 'The Rise of the Regulatory State in Europe', *West European Politics*, 17/3 (1994), pp. 77–101.

[7] *Measuring Integration—The French Case: Regional Indices of Social and Labour Market Inclusion of Third Country Nationals. Final Report* (Paris: Sciences Po—CERI, 2008), p. 59. MITI was financed by the European Commission.

questions of fairness and equality which apply in all countries, regardless of their approach towards diversity. It does not tell us about what an integrationist state regards as acceptable in terms of groups' autonomy. The Migrant Integration Policy Index (MIPEX), which collates a substantial amount of data, itself does not pay much attention to the problem of criteria, while pointing out that '[f]ew countries base integration policy changes on hard facts. The focus on numbers of immigrants and test scores/levels says little about whether society is integrating over time. Some governments monitor statistics on integration trends, but fewer evaluate if policies had any impact on them'.[8]

If we extrapolate from both the actual behaviour of integrationist states, and the criticisms made of the multiculturalist project, we can get closer to the characteristics of integrationism as an ideal type, at least in the negative sense of the restrictions which a committed integrationist state would impose on group rights. These restrictions are set out in Table 3.1 for democracies only, as autocracies are likely to restrict group rights even more, and in an arbitrary fashion. Even France, the European country which asserts integrationism most self-consciously, does not in practice implement it so thoroughly as suggested by the examples in Table 3.1, which represent only a direction of travel. In light of the underdeveloped nature of theory about integrationism in relation to ethnocultural groups, we have no option but to extrapolate from particular historical experiences.

The history of the United States has been a major point of reference for Europeans on the issue of integrating new groups, as in many other respects. The welcoming of millions of immigrants into the New World required from the outset some notion of how this would affect the existing, barely established, social system, which had only recently come through a traumatic civil war. This arrived in the form of the '(s)melting-pot' metaphor, which had its origins in the earliest years of the American republic but took off only in the early twentieth century, following the play written by Israel Zangwill.[9] In principle this was the first representation of integrationism, with its egalitarian

[8] 'Key Findings', Migrant Integration Policy Index [online tool and reference guide], <http://www.mipex.eu/key-findings> accessed 28 July 2012. MIPEX traces behaviour in 31 countries and seven policy areas, using 148 policy indicators 'designed to benchmark current laws and policies against the highest standards through consultations with top scholars'. The seven policy areas are: labour market mobility, family reunion for third-party nationals, education, political participation, long-term residence, access to nationality, and anti-discrimination. Migrant Integration Policy Index, 'MIPEX Methodology', <http://www.mipex.eu/methodology> accessed 28 July 2012. An admirable level of detail is provided, with the focus on equality and anti-discrimination. But the ultimately philosophical issue of how these goals are best achieved in the context of the tension between individual and group rights is not addressed.

[9] Samuel P. Huntington, *Who are We? America's Great Debate* (London: Simon & Schuster, 2004), pp. 128–31. Also, 'Melting Pot' [Wikipedia entry], <http://www.en.wikipedia.org/wiki/Melting_pot> accessed 18 December 2012.

Table 3.1. The integrationist model and its implied restrictions[10]

Activity	Examples of integrationist policies
Religion	Limits on certain kinds of preaching; restrictions on minority cemeteries and funeral practices; ban on minarets; no recognition of minority religious holidays or prayer-times at work.
Language	Only one official language; no state subsidies for translations; language proficiency tests.
Education	No private schools on the basis of religion or ethnicity; no concessions to concerns about girls' participation in sports or about the form of dress required.
Civil rights	Restrictions on overt displays of religious symbolism, especially in public institutions; no forced marriages; no face-coverings; no para-state uniforms; no exemptions from health and safety rules, e.g. for Sikh motorcyclists; no circumcisions of minors.
Diet	Bans on ritualistic killings, e.g. for Halal or Kosher purposes. No exemptions from animal cruelty legislation.
Political rights	No formal recognition of, or support for, groups other than political parties; other groups stay in the private realm; creation of offences against the state, and/or enlargement of emergency powers through fear of subversion; no positive discrimination; a narrow definition of citizenship.
Military service	No exemptions from conscription (where it applies) on religious or ethnic grounds; no special provisions for religious practice, or exemptions from particular missions, in the professional armed services.

implication that the whole is only created by the fusion of many diverse parts—although from the outset there has been controversy as to whether in practice it meant rather that immigrants were to be assimilated into the existing WASP culture.[11] The idea of the melting-pot is thus usefully ambiguous: on the one hand it suggests a natural and voluntary process of melding over time; and on the other it implies the gradual loss of newcomers' original identities as they are subject to the processes of interaction with an existing, self-confident, host society.

But few observers still think that the 'melting-pot' notion, with its teleology of a homogeneous society, still applies, even in the US itself. Incomers, and the groups they have formed, have proved that their identities are too strong to be submerged. The dominant image has thus come to be that of 'hyphenated Americans', as in 'Greek-Americans, or 'Polish-Americans'. Michael Walzer has articulated the common view that 'an ethnic American is someone who "in

[10] The obverse of these characteristics is provided in a list of the features of multiculturalism, by Steven Vertovec and Susanne Wessendorf in the introduction to their edited book, *The Multiculturalism Backlash: European Discourses, Policies and Practices* (London: Routledge, 2010), pp. 1–31.

[11] This view had another metaphor—that of the Anglo-Protestant tomato soup, which absorbs new ingredients but stays tomato soup. Huntington says that 'the melting pot is working but at the individual, not the societal level'—by which he meant 'sustained intermarriage' across ethnicities by millions. Huntington, *Who are We?*, pp. 129 and 299.

principle", lives his spiritual life as he chooses, on either side of the hyphen'.[12] Some observers have even said that the United States has developed a form of multiculturalism.[13] But as the reference to 'spiritual life' indicates, the freedom to have an ethnic identity is regarded generally as relating to people's private life, and in particular to their religion. There can be no doubt that, just as the word common to all these constructs is 'American', there would be strong resistance (not least in official circles) to the idea that the public space of the country could be allowed to become a mere amalgam of different micro-cultures, held together more as *Gesellschaft* than true community. Walzer himself once claimed, indeed, that 'the American side of the hyphen' was actually strengthened by the process of empowering ethnic groups, which then had a sense of the US moving from host to mother-country, to which they accordingly felt indebted.[14] He saw the peculiar mix of assimilationism and multi-ethnicism which has characterized US history since 1865 as ultimately a source of civil peace—so long as managed by the 'friendly state'.

Thus even in its *locus classicus*, the melting-pot is not a realistic image for the development of modern multi-ethnic societies. The kindred idea of 'integration' has some of the same characteristics, and defects, but refers more to a continual process, with fewer idealizing overtones. For many, nonetheless, it represents a state of affairs which is at once undesirable and infeasible. For those who favour multiculturalism, and for broader reasons than the simple protection of minorities, integrationism is oppressive, inward-looking, and narrowly nationalist. It denies the creative conflict which derives from the encounter between varying traditions and attempts to privilege one, historically contingent, way of life. Furthermore, it represents a Canute-like attempt to prevent transnational forces from washing over an individual society, in a world where the mobility of people, goods, money, and ideas is increasingly irresistible.

This attitude reveals the inherent link between integrationism, as an approach to state–society relations, and international politics. The integrationist approach is closely related to the principle of sovereignty and to the concept of the Westphalian state. This is because the idea of a country which is homogeneous and with a strong sense of its own society *requires* a sovereign—that is, a legally independent—state to sustain and project externally its most distinctive

[12] Michael Walzer, *What it Means to be an American* (New York: Marsilo, 1992), cited in Tony Smith, *Foreign Attachments: The Power of Ethnic Groups in the Making of US Foreign Policy* (Cambridge, MA: Harvard University Press, 2000), p. 137. The word 'personal' could be usefully substituted for 'spiritual' here.

[13] Diane Ravitch, a New York educationalist, said that 'paradoxical as it may seem, the United States has a common culture that is multicultural'. Cited in Arthur M. Schlesinger, Jr, *The Disuniting of America* (New York: Norton, 1992), p. 135.

[14] Michael Walzer, *Politics and Passion: Toward a More Egalitarian Liberalism* (New Haven, CT: Yale University Press, 2004), pp. 42, 48, 82–4, and 87–9.

qualities, particularly with reference to citizenship, territory, and collective memory. Arguably, it also implies the need (or wish) for a strong state. Conversely, as the great variety among the United Nations' 193 Member States illustrates, a sovereign state does not require full-blooded integrationism in order to function properly—even if, as suggested earlier, all states by definition are integrated to some degree.

This association means that multiculturalists are not particularly attracted to the state. Indeed, they may think it inherently integrationist, and thus undesirable. Some may see it as an obstacle to their values and/or incompatible with the requirements of justice. This is understandable and logical if the premises of a cosmopolitan, globalized, perspective are accepted.[15] But if groups are to have rights, they can only be guaranteed by the state. By extension, integrationism can all too easily be tarred with the same brush as the state, without the balance-sheet of its advantages and disadvantages—or those of the alternatives—being fully considered. The problems of the state as a vehicle for social life and human achievement do not necessarily mean that it should, or can, be abandoned in favour of other forms of organization—let alone in some difficult-to-imagine international constitutional act.

Equally, while the case against directed social homogenization may be strong,[16] this does not mean either that the state is dispensable, or that integration is necessarily a misguided strategy. For just as each state/society has a different composition, history, and needs, so integrationism may turn out to be the most functional approach for some of them. It may have the deficiencies of any over-clear, procrustean remedy for a host of complex problems, but as one model of how to deal with the challenging task of managing inter-group relations amidst diversity, it has some coherence, and an historical track-record. Much depends on the normative assumptions of the observer about group rights and identities, on the one hand, and on his or her understanding of historical change on the other. In short, as with the multiculturalist model, integrationism is a tendency more than a full-blown social or political theory, requiring the combined perspectives of the political philosopher, the historian, and the analyst of world affairs to be fully understood.

[15] Linklater vigorously promotes the idea of 'cosmopolitan citizenship' on the grounds that 'with globalisation, it is absurd to assume that the most significant moral community comprises fellow-citizens or co-nationals'. That leaves as alternatives the local community, the region, and humanity as a whole—plus various societal groups. Linklater sees all as having valid claims. Andrew Linklater, *The Transformation of Political Community: Ethical Foundations of the Post-Westphalian Era* (Cambridge: Polity Press, 1998), pp. 31 and 198–212.

[16] Ilan Zvi Baron, 'The Problem of Dual Loyalty', *Canadian Journal of Political Science*, 42/4 (2009), pp. 1025–44.

INTEGRATIONISM IN PRACTICE

Some degree of nationalism is inevitable among integrationists, in the sense of a concern for national identity, more emphasis on the things which society holds in common than on pluralism, a conscious resistance to group rights and thus to the philosophy of multiculturalism. But an emphasis on the nation, the state, and thus the nation-state, is far from being the same as rampant nationalism, which in any case is not necessarily found in integrationist systems. Nor is it the same as political conservatism, or even republican secularism; values often associated with the idea of the nation. Within the category of those states which display integrationist tendencies, there is a significant variety of perspectives, and of mechanisms, because of the distinctiveness of each country's past. The same has been true of other broad categories of types of state, such as fascist, communist, and democratic. Such terms cover a multitude of sins—or virtues.

Variation within the category of integrationism may occur over time, as with the French backing away from pure assimilationism, or in terms of mechanisms, since republican secularism is only one possible means of implementation. It also occurs because some states are more self-conscious about the issues involved than others. Taking a global perspective, it is clear that many countries—perhaps the majority, given the largely theoretical status of the term 'nation-state'—face the problem of how to manage ethnocultural pluralism, a process usually subsumed under the concept of 'nation-building'. Some tend towards multiculturalism, and/or devolution, while others tend towards integrationism. Within the latter category some have pursued integration at the purely political level. Syria is a case in point, with a minority group (the Alawis) able to rule through a combination of a certain religious toleration and the dissemination of fear. The revolt which began in 2011 showed that this is an inherently vulnerable system, but it endured for 40 years on the basis of the Baath Party's police state, with the suppression of both individual and group rights. As his rule started to crumble, President Bashar al-Assad made a hollow appeal which could stand as the credo of integrationism: 'The strength of the state stems from the strength of the people . . . let the people and the state come together.'[17]

Other one-party states, such as China, have a dominant majority, with minorities (in this case notably the Uighurs and Tibetans) whose demands for autonomy are seen as threatening the very integrity of the system. Accordingly, they are subject to a punitive form of integration which has achieved control at the expense of sharpening the underlying antagonism—and

[17] Televised address to the Syrian people, 20 June 2011, reported on the BBC News website, 'Syria: President Bashar al-Assad Keeps to Hard Line', <http://www.bbc.co.uk/news/world-middle-east-13835393> accessed 18 December 2012.

internationalizing it. Russia, desperate to avoid further fragmentation after the collapse of the USSR, sent out an even harsher message through its 'mailed fist' policy in Chechnya, while having to balance top-down integration with federation in the country as a whole.

Many other states take a broadly integrationist approach to their perceived minority problems, but they generally stop short of such brutality. For example Indonesia and Israel both contain significant minorities which they regard as being essentially alien to their identity (in the first case Chinese, in the second Israeli Arabs) and which complicate international relations as much as domestic politics. Their responses are essentially integrationist, in the sense that group rights are restricted to the extent that their members feel themselves to be second-class citizens. A crucial qualification should also be entered in these cases: the Indonesian and Israeli governments do not expect their Chinese or Arab subjects to change identity—they simply want them to be quiescent, not to grow in numbers and not to expect to shape public life—in short, they do not want true integration.

A third form of integrationism which can be observed among the world's states is that which occurs after traumatic conflict, as a state attempts to build or rebuild a nation. This has been happening in Rwanda over the last fifteen years, where President Paul Kagame has answered criticisms of restrictions on personal liberty with statements such as 'we are all Rwandans now', understandably stressing the need to move beyond the identities of Hutu and Tutsi which precipitated the genocide of 1994.[18] An endorsement of multiculturalism can hardly be expected in certain circumstances, precisely because the reality beneath the surface is that of separate and divided communities—as is the case in Bosnia, where international forces have kept the peace between nationalities which they would like to integrate, but have no capacity to do so.

A more benign form of integrationism is that evident in countries with a long history of growing together and thus a strong sense of common identity which they naturally seek to protect when encountering the forces of globalization. A prime example of this is Japan, where geography, historical isolation, and social homogeneity have produced a strong sense of national identity. This makes it defensive towards externally derived change, including the immigrants increasingly required to service an ageing population. There is

[18] Most recently Kagame's Minister of Internal Security, Fazil Harerimana, said at a genocide commemoration event that 'we are all Rwandans, and we should stand strong by upholding the truth about what happened in our country', Grace Mugoya, 'Rwanda: Essi Secondary School winds up Commemoration Week', *The New Times*, 18 June 2011, <http://allafrica.com/stories/201106210571.html> accessed 17 December 2012. But this line cannot wish away opposition. The BBC's 'Profile: Rwanda's President Paul Kagame' cites much opposition, for example the question from one observer 'how can anyone say there is no tribe in Rwanda?', <http://www.bbc.co.uk/news/10479882?print=true> accessed 17 December 2012.

an element of xenophobia in this reaction, but it is also clear that the Japanese people are simply bewildered over how to treat those whom they see as profoundly different from themselves. The government in Tokyo thus sees it as its role to preserve the dominant culture, while largely ignoring minority groups, which have no rights as such. This is integration by default.[19]

Inside the European Union there are various states which could be said to pursue integrationist policies. Some are to be found among the new entrants to the EU of 2004—states which are still insecure about their sovereignty, given the limitations imposed on it for so long, and thus strive to reinforce their national identity through homogeneity. Poland, the Baltic states, and Cyprus all fall in their different ways into this category. Malta resists immigration from North Africa for the same reason, but also because it is simply too small to accommodate newcomers. Three of the more established EU Member States represent better case studies of integrationism as it has been practised over decades: France asserts the value of the approach unapologetically, given its long history of immigration and its proud republican tradition; Denmark is a small and rich state which, as one of the world's most generous donors of overseas aid, can hardly be accused of racism or parochialism. Yet internally it stands in strong contrast to its multiculturalist neighbour Sweden. Greece, while it has no long-standing tradition of immigration or of generosity to the Third World, has been a radical critic of Western imperialism as well as vigorously nationalist. Greece represents another variant of integrationism, more similar to that of Japan, with a long history defined by a heroic myth, and a determination not to be overwhelmed by a perceived Other, which in modern history has most often meant the Ottomans and Turks. It is pride rather than mere xenophobia which sustains the integrationist model in the Greek case.[20] I now take each of these cases in turn.

France

France is the first of our three European cases, and that which occupies the lion's share of the discussion, given that it is the most assertively integrationist democracy in existence, and that it plays a key role in international politics. The enormous global impact of the French Revolution produced an

[19] Only 1.6 per cent of the Japanese population is made up of ethnic minorities, and of these about 60 per cent come from China and South Korea. 'Japan' [online reference guide], *The World Fact Book*, CIA, <https://www.cia.gov/library/publications/the-world-factbook/geos/ja.html> accessed 18 December 2012.

[20] The serious financial crisis which began in 2008 has produced the rise of a radical, xenophobic right, in the form of the Golden Dawn party. But it has fed on a pre-existing integrationism, not produced it.

exceptionalist narrative of French history, rooted in the republican, egalitarian, and rights-based tradition often strangely labelled 'Jacobin'. This term really refers to the powerful centralizing and top-down nature of the Revolution, which insisted on France 'one and indivisible'.[21] In such a context it is inevitable that issues of immigration and diversity should represent serious dilemmas for governments in Paris, as they will stir up the most fundamental questions of national identity.

Until the last thirty years or so, France was a country which welcomed immigration, given its chronic problem of a low birth-rate. Newcomers were not seen as any threat to the 'certain idea' which the French had of their country, as they were assumed either to be guest-workers who would return to their country of origin, or to be willing to become fully assimilated—that is, to follow the way of life of the existing population. A significant potential tension did, however, emerge in the twentieth century, as a result of imperialism. France saw its colonies as extensions of the metropole—literally *territoires d'outre-mer*. But that was not to mean, ultimately, that the citizens of the colonies were automatically regarded as French men and women with rights of abode in the host country.[22] The massive increase in immigrants from the Maghreb from the 1960s led to the creation of an impoverished underclass which felt increasingly excluded from mainstream society—and in the end itself began to despair about integration.

After 1945 the indigenous French themselves moved through three sets of attitudes toward newcomers: from assimilation, through 'insertion', to integration; although these may be regarded as distinctions without much of a difference.[23] Insertion was the dominant idea from the mid-1970s on, partly because of reactions in the age of decolonization against the implicit notion of superiority in the concept of assimilation, and partly because of increasing doubts in some quarters about the realism of trying to assimilate North Africans.[24] But because it implied the recognition of separate communities 'inserted' into France, the spectre of multiculturalism *à l'anglaise* arose in the 1980s. Both left and right then started to prefer the term 'integration', which made a gesture towards the idea of change by all parties while retaining the value of a strongly unitary culture.[25] In the subsequent quarter-century there has been considerable upheaval, with the issues of immigration and national

21 Fernand Braudel, *The Identity of France* (London: Collins, 1988), p. 39.

22 Apart from Algerians, and their children, born before that country's independence in 1962. See Andrew Geddes, *The Politics of Migration and Immigration in Europe* (London: Sage, 2003), p. 61.

23 Weil and Crowley, 'Integration in Theory and Practice', pp. 113–16.

24 Weil and Crowley, 'Integration in Theory and Practice', p. 114.

25 Weil and Crowley, 'Integration in Theory and Practice', p. 115. See also Catherine Withol de Wenden, 'Immigrants as Political Actors in France', in Baldwin-Edwards and Schain (eds), *The Politics of Immigration in Western Europe*, pp. 91–109.

identity ever more linked and to the fore of national politics. But the French state, and most of its people, have not relinquished their attachment to integrationism, even if ethnicity as a concept cannot be excluded from public discussion, not least because of the stridency of the self-proclaimed standard-bearers for Frenchness, the *Front National*, in constantly drawing attention to it.[26]

Ethnicity could not be ignored in part because of white racism, in part because of the natural tendency of poor Maghrebian immigrants to cluster together in the same deprived urban estates, and in part through official fears for national security. The Fourth Republic had been brought down in 1958 by the 'savage war of peace' in Algeria, with its second front in France over the next four years, and the Fifth was indelibly marked by De Gaulle's decision to end the war by moving the country towards independence, thus leading the French settlers, or *colons*, to attempt to assassinate him on the grounds of betrayal.[27] The proximity of Algeria, in particular to the region of Marseille to which *maghrébins* flocked in the 1960s, with its strongly radical politics after independence, meant that Paris was always looking nervously southwards.[28] Yet even discrimination and insecurity were secondary factors in preventing the emergence of multiculturalist policies. More fundamental was the genuine conviction of the majority that the recognition of minorities as such would endanger the very way of life that attracted so much foreign admiration. This in turn rested on a unitary notion of the state which had also resisted strongly the claims of geographical communities such as the Bretons and Corsicans—despite, in the latter case, resistance which at times verged on insurrection.

This structural difficulty of homogenization became even more evident through the increased visibility of Islam as a source of identity for many immigrants—from Turkey as well as North Africa. Religion, through the wars of the sixteenth century, followed a century later by the expulsion of the Huguenots, had been powerful factors in shaping France's sense of its own history, and of the dangers of internal division. By comparison the English Civil War, where

[26] See Valérie Amiraux, 'Crisis and New Challenges? French Republicanism Featuring Multi-culturalism', in Alessandro Silj (ed.), *European Multiculturalism Revisited* (London: Zed Books, 2010), especially pp. 76–80.

[27] Alistair Horne, *A Savage War of Peace: Algeria 1954–1962* (3rd edn, New York: New York Review of Books, 2006), pp. 543–4. On the war of independence see also Martin Evans, *Algeria: France's Undeclared War* (Oxford: Oxford University Press, 2012).

[28] Neil MacMaster, 'Islamophobia in France and the "Algerian Problem"', in Emran Qureshi and Michael A. Sells (eds), *The New Crusades: Constructing the Muslim Enemy* (New York: Columbia University Press, 2003), pp. 294–5. MacMaster notes that many of the 2.3 million French soldiers who had seen service in Algeria, often with brutalizing effects, also settled in Provence-Alpes-Côtes d'Azur (PACA), together with many *pieds noirs*. This was where the key electoral successes of the *Front National* were to be achieved. See also Martin A. Schain, *The Politics of Immigration in France, Britain and the United States: A Comparative Study* (New York: Palgrave Macmillan, 2008), pp. 48 and 100.

religion was also important, has been primarily interpreted as a political struggle. The Revolution brought secularism and anti-clericalism to the fore, precipitating a century-long struggle over the limited place of the Catholic Church in France, which was ended by the 1905 Law on the Separation of the Churches and the State, which effectively established *laïcité* by forbidding the official recognition or subsidization of any religion.[29]

It was interesting that agreement on this law was reached in the wake of the Dreyfus affair which ran for a decade from 1894, revealing the depth of French anti-semitism.[30] Despite the insinuations by Dreyfus's enemies of a loyalty problem, the Jewish community in France had never asked for special treatment, and indeed had conformed to the ideal of assimilation, which made the behaviour of the Vichy regime in sending their fellow-citizens off to Nazi death-camps (including Dreyfus's grand-daughter) particularly shameful.[31] The enduring trauma and guilt which this history produced led to sensitivities over how to treat the newly arrived Muslim minority, but that was soon overlaid by resentment at its size (there are now perhaps as many as 6 million Muslims in France) and by the anti-semitism of some in the Maghrebian community itself, triggered by hostility towards Israel and solidarity with the Palestinians.[32] At one point the Israeli prime minister Ariel Sharon even suggested that French Jews should immediately emigrate to their ancestral land.[33] To officials in Paris

[29] Cécile Laborde, *Critical Republicanism: The Hijab Controversy and Political Philosophy* (Oxford: Oxford University Press, 2008), pp. 7–8. Also Jonathan Laurence and Justin Vaisse (eds), *Integrating Islam: Political and Religious Challenges in Contemporary France* (Washington, DC: The Brookings Institution, 2006), pp. 139–42.

[30] Dreyfus had been unjustly accused of spying for Germany, with the implication that a Jewish officer was inherently less attached to France. See Chapter 6, pp. (168–9).

[31] What had happened was hidden for more than two decades behind the myth of national resistance to the Nazis, until in 1969 the film *Le chagrin et la pitié* revealed the truth. Eventually, and belatedly, the 'Vichy syndrome' became a national obsession, fuelled by the revelations of President Mitterand's right-wing past. See Richard J. Golson, 'The Legacy of World War II in France: Mapping the Discourses of Memory', in Richard Ned Lebow, Wulf Kansteiner, and Claudio Fogu (eds), *The Politics of Memory in Postwar Europe* (Durham, NC: Duke University Press, 2006), pp. 73–8. Also Jan-Werner Müller, 'Introduction', in Jan-Werner Müller (ed.), *Memory and Power in Post-War Europe* (Cambridge: Cambridge University Press, 2002), pp. 23–4. On the treatment of Dreyfus's grand-daughter, see George R. Whyte, *The Dreyfus Affair: A Chronological History* (Houndmills: Palgrave, 2005), p. 459.

[32] The exact numbers are unclear, as the state has until recently refused to produce official statistics on ethnicity for fear of validating communalism. See 'French Plan to Break Taboo on Ethnic Data Causes Uproar', *The Guardian*, 23 March 2009. See also Patrick Simon and Valérie Sala Pala, '"We're Not Multiculturalists Yet": France Swings Between Hard Integration and Soft Anti-discrimination', in Vertovec and Wessendorf (eds), *The Multiculturalism Backlash*, pp. 92–110. On anti-semitism, President Mitterrand pointed out that 150 anti-semitic attacks had occurred in France between 1979–82, and that the government was determined to punish those responsible. 'Television Interview with M. François Mitterrand, President of the Republic', 17 August 1982 (London: Ambassade de France, Service de Presse et d'Information, 18 August 1982).

[33] 'Indignation en France après les propos de Sharon', and 'L' "alya" positive des juifs de l'Hexagone', both in *Le Figaro*, 20 July 2004. Sharon had talked of French Jews suffering 'Un

it was all too easy to fear that once again foreign conflicts were being played out on French soil.[34]

Such fears could not have gained ground, however, without the increasing numbers of Muslims living in France, and the increasingly important place which religion was playing in their lives—as a form of identity, over and above nationality, and as a source of self-esteem in the dire socio-economic circumstances in which they largely found themselves. The attempts of groups like SOS-Racisme and France-Plus to reduce racial discrimination (and thus foster integration) had only limited success, with the result that the increasing numbers of young, second-generation Maghrebians found themselves living in large, inhospitable, estates without hope of jobs or social success. They were less willing than their parents to accept the situation, and had no wish to return to North Africa. In this condition of *anomie* they were, much against the expectations of French officialdom at the time, all too ready to turn to Islam. The trend was fostered by the fact that in Algeria itself a growing tide of Islamist opposition to the military autocracy rule of Houari Boumedienne and his colleagues had been growing throughout the 1970s, centred around the notion that the country was not yet free from colonial influence: for the Islamists, too many Algerians had drunk the 'poisonous milk' of France.[35]

Such hostility to France, spreading to co-religionists inside the Hexagon, was the first indication of the way domestic and foreign policy were to become increasingly inter-penetrated through the controversies over Islam and over immigration. Young Muslims began to make demands of their government in Paris which not only echoed those made by those in Algeria, the Gulf, and elsewhere, but were actively supported by their external supporters. Difficult conflicts suddenly arose over mosques, education, and the *hijab*, as young Muslims reacted against secularism as a form of social control which denied them the ability to practise their religion fully, paradoxically finding in a more strict observation of their faith than their first-generation immigrant parents, an important source of individual identity.[36] Since it is probably true to say that in a secular society Islam makes more demands for special provisions

des anti-sémitismes les plus sauvages', although his spokesman subsequently tried to nuance the remarks.

[34] Mitterrand had said, self-servingly, in 1982 that 'extremists of all kinds want to attack France because she is the main factor of peace in the current Near-East conflict'. Mitterrand, 'Television Interview', 18 August 1982.

[35] Gilles Kepel, *Allah in the West: Islamic Movements in America and Europe* (Cambridge: Polity Press, 1997), pp. 157–62. George Joffé also makes the argument that the Islamist framing (on both sides) of the revolt in Algeria in the 1990s obscures the hostility to a repressive, and by implication neo-colonialist, state structure, George Joffé, *Islamist Radicalization in North Africa: Politics and Process* (Abingdon: Routledge, 2011), pp. 4–5.

[36] A point made in an important sociological study of the cultural dilemmas of African immigrants in France. Hugues Lagrange, *Le déni des cultures* (Paris: Seuil, 2010), pp. 84–91.

than other religions—especially as French Catholicism has already made its historic compromise with *laïcité*—this quickly posed serious dilemmas for the authorities at all levels.

External factors were an important catalyst of the growing domestic problems, and not just because the end of the Cold War meant other issues attracted more attention. The Rushdie affair in Britain polarized opinion in France as elsewhere, while the Gulf War of 1991 convinced a number of young Muslims that 'the West' was making war on their religion, and by extension on themselves, given the notion of the *umma*, the community of belief which transcends political boundaries. As their country was part of the UN-authorized coalition fighting in Iraq, France itself became an enemy, and Saddam Hussein a hero of the resistance.[37] Rather more significant was the quiet but determined French support for the military government in Algiers, which had taken power after the Islamic parties had won a wholly legitimate victory in the 1991 elections. The civil war which ensued lasted until 1998 and produced violence of a scale and ferocity seldom seen. By its support for the suspension of the election in Algeria, France was saying that it feared an Iranian-style regime just across the Mediterranean, and the spread of fundamentalism at home, and that this end justified support for a regime as ruthless as its opponents.

Such a policy was bound to bring forth a strong reaction. Some disaffected Muslim youths were recruited from the poor estates, to be trained in Pakistan and Afghanistan for terrorist purposes. They were subsequently involved in bombings in Spain. But French Muslims were seen by many as providing the sea in which bigger fish, from Algeria's own Armed Islamic Group (GIA), could swim unnoticed. The latter hi-jacked an Air France flight from Algiers to Paris which was apparently intended to crash into the Eiffel Tower over Christmas 1994, and carried out bombings on the Metro during 1995 which killed eight people and wounded more than 170. There were also serious attacks on the TGV network near Lyon. The security services managed to prevent further atrocities, but some of those wanted fled to the United Kingdom, where, to the great frustration of Paris, they found refuge before finally being extradited a decade later.[38]

Although only a small number of French Muslims had anything to do with these events, and the majority probably disapproved of them, it was not surprising that social tensions rose over the place of Islam in society. The sometimes hysterical media coverage, which tended to elide debates over the veil with the issue of international terrorism, did not help. But the growth of

[37] Wihtol de Wenden, 'Immigrants as Political Actors in France'. Yet, see also Laurence and Vaisse (eds), *Integrating Islam*, pp. 219–20. Laurence and Vaisse argue that the opposition to the war in 1991 came from the left, with Muslims not playing a distinctive part.

[38] 'Mastermind of Paris Metro bombings jailed', *The Times*, 29 March 2006.

anti-semitism in the form of attacks on Jewish graves and other symbols, associated with anger over Palestine, inevitably reinforced the views of those who already believed in a 'clash of civilizations'.[39]

In the years since 1995, France did not suffer a serious terrorist attack until the murders committed in Toulouse in 2012, while its foreign policy has not been seriously embarrassed by domestic opposition.[40] It would be easy to ascribe these two facts to the distance which Paris kept from Anglo-American interventionism after the events of 11 September 2001. But this would be too simple.[41] France has been part of the Coalition fighting in Afghanistan since October 2001, and its realpolitik in North Africa, which left it severely embarrassed when the Arab Spring broke out in 2011, was more than enough to attract the venom of the jihadists. Kepel's view leaves out foreign policy altogether, 'the combined results of secularism, conscious integration and a preventative security policy in France—the inverse terms of multiculturalism—has meant that the country has been spared terror attacks for a decade'.[42]

This has more plausibility, but the truth probably lies in a combination of factors, internal and external, with not much credit to be given to official strategy. On the one hand, the UK's willingness to side unequivocally with the United States in an illegal war, focused attention on Iraq for five years after 2003. France's overt opposition to the war, especially given the defeat of fundamentalism in Algeria, gave it some breathing-space from external subversion. On the other hand, the alienated youth of the *banlieues* show no sign of becoming more integrated into mainstream society—indeed there were serious riots in cities all over France during three weeks of October 2005.[43] The French football team has been regularly whistled at in the Stade de France in Paris when playing teams from North Africa—and this despite having won the World Cup in 1998 with a multi-ethnic team which seemed to presage a new form of French identity. One close observer has pointed out that 'Le stade,

[39] Laurence and Vaisse (eds), *Integrating Islam*, p. 218; MacMaster, 'Islamophobia in France', pp. 301–6.

[40] In March 2012 Mohamed Merah killed three Muslim French soldiers, and then attacked a Jewish school, killing three children and a teacher. He was reported as justifying his actions as a protest against the killing of Muslims by the French in Afghanistan and by Israel in Palestine. See the transcript of Merah's conversations with police before being shot dead himself, 'Conversation secrète entre Merah et la DCRI', *Liberation*, 16 July 2012.

[41] Briquetti concludes that a combination of effective counter-terrorist measures and the French model of integration best explains 'the French exception', not foreign policy. Sophie Briquetti, 'The "French Exception" in the Field of Islamist Terrorism Since the End of the Cold War', thesis submitted for the degree of MPhil in International Relations, University of Cambridge (2012).

[42] Gilles Kepel, 'Europe's Answer to Londonistan' [online article], *Opendemocracy*, 24 August 2005, <http://www.opendemocracy.net> accessed 18 December 2012, cited in Amiraux, 'Crisis and New Challenges', p. 71.

[43] Simon and Sala Pala, '"We're Not Multiculturalists Yet"', pp. 100–1.

c'est un des rares endroits où 'l'on peut encore manifester publiquement'—and there was no mistaking the deliberate anti-patriotism of the young people who were whistling.[44] One member of the French national team who plays in England put the problem sharply, observing with amazement that black players in the UK identify themselves as English, or British, whereas in France they identify with their country of origin, '... there isn't the sense of belonging... France has, at its heart, a problem where it has been unable or unwilling to accommodate the sons and daughters of its former colonies'.[45]

Yet the fact remains that alienated Muslim youth in France have not committed terrorist acts against their fellow-citizens, as in London or Madrid. They may still aspire to Frenchness, as indicated by their tendency to describe themselves with such phrases as '*français d'origine algériennne*'—a kind of *de facto* hyphenation.[46] Moreover, foreign policy as such does not appear to be a major source of anger. Olivier Roy argued that the riots of 2005 were 'no intifada of the *banlieues*'. There was 'a complete absence of Palestinian flags, references to the war in Iraq and elsewhere in the Muslim world, or even symbols of Islam'.[47] The riots were largely about socio-economic issues, and revealed a wish for more of the fruits of integration, such as jobs, better housing, facilities for young people—and sheer respect. There is no doubt also a preference for these things to be provided through Muslim organizations, which integrationist philosophy still mostly resists. But, remarkably, the French state has proved able to impose its restrictions on the *hijab* and on the *burka* without the degree of resistance that would have been inevitable in many other Western countries.[48] The sheer conviction behind French secularism has produced results. It may also be relevant that French foreign policy under the Fifth Republic has been made in such a determinedly elitist and bipartisan fashion that there is no expectation of popular participation of any kind, whether from the mass or a minority.[49] It should be noted, however, that in subsequently accepting investment initiatives in the *banlieues* from the rich

[44] Interview with William Nuytens, a sociologist at the University of Artois, *Le Monde*, 15 October 2008.

[45] 'In England minds are open—that's why French players here don't want to go back', *The Guardian*, 12 May 2011. The player was Benoit Assou-Ekoto, a Cameroonian brought up in France. His views were later echoed by another French player with experience of the UK, Louis Saha, in his book, *Du quartier aux étoiles. Le safari du footballeur* (Paris: Éditions Anne Carrière, with a foreword by Charles Biétry, the Director of Al Jazeera Sport, 2012), pp. 252–62. Translated as *Thinking Inside the Box: Reflections on Life as a Premier League Footballer* (Kingston upon Thames: Vision Sports, 2012).

[46] I owe this point to the observations of Dr Helen Drake.

[47] Olivier Roy, 'Foreword' in Laurence and Vaisse (eds), *Integrating Islam*, p. xi.

[48] On the long-running '*L'affaire du foulard*', on which the government moved towards a hard-line in 2004, see Simon and Sala Pala, '"We're Not Multiculturalists Yet", pp. 101–3, and Christian Joppke, *Veil: Mirror of Identity* (Cambridge: Polity, 2009) pp. 27–52. Also Laborde, *Critical Republicanism*, pp. 7–9 and 51–5.

[49] This is the view of Laurence and Vaisse, *Integrating Islam*, pp. 215–18.

Muslim statelet of Qatar, Sarkozy tacitly acknowledged the unavoidability of the transnational dimension.[50]

The relative absence of terrorism is a success for the authorities, but they recognize that in other respects the condition of inter-ethnic relations in France is potentially serious, as the gradual tendencies to accept the discourse of integration, and to set up various intermediary associations, indicate.[51] Furthermore, the interaction of internal and external factors remains important. From the early 1990s external funding has been forthcoming from the Gulf states for Muslim causes in France—precisely because the republican model forbids domestic subsidies. This in its turn heightened the sense of paranoia in some quarters about an international fundamentalist conspiracy to undermine the French way of life, made worse by the occasional taking of French hostages abroad in reaction to policy on the *hijab*. Furthermore, foreign policy has acted indirectly on the Muslim community by increasing the sense of polarization in society. Although France did not suffer its own 9/11 in the decade after the attacks on the US, the 'War on Terror' fuelled anxiety and antagonism wherever significant Muslim communities lived as minorities in Western states. The long-running wars in Afghanistan and Iraq led to a steady flow of distressing images in the media over the suffering of innocent civilians on all sides. Western governments, including that in Paris, were anxious to rally moderate Islam to their side, but these events were bound to impede integration.

For its part, French foreign policy has always been careful to lean in a *tiersmondiste* direction, although more for strategic than domestic reasons. Yet it is arguable that in 1991 and 2003 the caution of both Mitterrand and Chirac (the former joined in with Operation Desert Storm, but only after a long attempt at mediation) were cautious because of the sheer size of France's Islamic community. Moreover, the experts in the Elysée and the Quai d'Orsay found themselves taken aback on at least two major issues through the unexpected interaction between home and abroad.

Firstly, the referendum held in 2005 on the draft European Constitution led to a shock rejection by the electorate. The reasons were complex, but seem to have had little to do with the Constitution itself, and quite a lot with a growing concern over the type of European Union which was evolving, including concern over immigration, much of which was due to free movement within the EU, and over enlargement.[52] On the first occasion when the voters were

[50] 'Le Qatar lance un fonds pour financer des projets économiques dans les banlieues', *Le Monde*, 9 December 2011. At the launch of the scheme the Qatari ambassador in Paris hoped that 'Les Français d'origne arabe peuvent nous aider dans notre partenariat avec la France'.

[51] On this ambivalence, see Amiraux, 'Crisis and New Challenges?', pp. 82–6.

[52] Sarah Binzer Hobolt and Sylvain Brouard, 'Contesting the European Union? Why the Dutch and the French rejected the European Constitution', *Political Research Quarterly*, 64/2 (2011), pp. 309–22.

asked for their view on this elite-driven process, therefore, they delivered a rebuff, from which it was clear that the accession of Turkey would produce even more uproar. Since then French policy has been firmly against Turkish accession. Before the 2005 Referendum President Chirac had attempted to separate the issues of the Constitution from that of enlargement by inserting a provision in the Constitution for a separate referendum on any proposal to enlarge the EU further. His successor Nicolas Sarkozy then finessed the provision by providing for either a referendum, or a joint parliamentary vote with a three-fifths majority.[53] A further twist to the debate was added by the Armenian lobby in France, which persuaded the National Assembly to pass a motion making it an offence to deny the genocide of 1915 in Turkey—a move which led to outrage in Ankara.[54] French policy is not generally troubled by ethnic lobbies on the American model, but the Armenians do not conform to the low socio-economic status of most immigrant groups, and they skilfully played into anxieties over Turkey and thus Islamic influence inside the EU—especially in the run-up to presidential elections.

The second case of the domestic complication of foreign policy relates to the fact that over the years since the EU's 'global' Mediterranean policy was inaugurated at Barcelona in 1995, France has hovered uneasily between its traditional support for secular authoritarianism in Muslim countries, and a professed sympathy for the democratic expression of the Arab voice, notably in Palestine. Given that it is home to the largest Muslim community in Europe, France can hardly ignore the claims of the 'Arab street', but the fear of fundamentalism, and possibly the personal contacts of its elite, led it into sustained relationships with the increasingly unpopular regimes in Tunis, Cairo, Damascus, and elsewhere, as well as to involvement with the murky activities of the military government in Algiers. Paris effectively insulated Algiers from international attention throughout the 1990s, despite a death toll in its internal war which rivalled that of the Balkans at the same time.[55] Its double standards were thus badly exposed by the 'Arab Spring' in 2011, producing a policy first of support for Ben-Ali in Tunis, and then his rapid abandonment. This was followed by a further volte-face in favour of humanitarian intervention in Libya. France has not behaved so erratically in foreign policy since the Suez crisis and its aftermath. Ironically, humanitarian intervention which does not work can produce serious domestic

[53] As part of the Constitutional Amendments of 23 July 2008, see Article 88-5 of the Constitution: 'Constitution of 4 October 1958', Assemblée Nationale, <www.assemblee-nationale.fr/english/8ab.asp#Warning!> accessed 19 December 2012. Despite his manoeuvres Sarkozy felt strongly about Turkey—or was aware of the votes at stake. He cancelled at short notice a visit to Sweden in 2009 after Foreign Minister Carl Bildt had made clear Sweden's support for Turkish entry. 'Bildt s'oppose à Sarkozy sur la Turquie et le protectionnisme', *Le Figaro*, 28 May 2009.

[54] President Chirac visited Armenia in September 2006 and confirmed that Turkey should accept the genocide before it could enter the EU. He never visited Turkey.

[55] Horne, *A Savage War of Peace*, p. 16.

effects, as Tony Blair found out in the UK. France's new sympathy for the masses in the Maghreb makes it newly vulnerable to an interest in foreign policy being taken at home, especially as Muslims and secular intellectuals are likely to pull in different directions.

French integrationism is premised on a sharp distinction between home and abroad, but one that it cannot fully sustain. Indeed its apparent philosophical clarity is compromised by the fact that while France has refused to recognize minorities inside the state, it sees *la francophonie* as an embattled minority in a globalizing, Anglo-Saxon, world. On the home front the French state has had to give some ground on recognizing the importance of ethnic and religious identities, mainly through strong internal opposition to the *Front National*, but also through the indirect impact of major developments in international relations.[56] French Muslims have developed a sharper sense of their rights through the interplay between their own frustrations and external actors, initially in Algeria and the Gulf.

In terms of foreign policy, France has discovered that a rationalist elite operating on realist criteria no longer enjoys freedom from domestic complications. Few American-style lobbies exist to exert pressure, but the problems of social peace linked to the existence of the large Muslim community and the reactions of both left- and right-wing secularists cannot be kept in a domestic compartment. Issues such as EU enlargement, especially towards Turkey, and human rights in the Arab world, are now to some extent hostages to public opinion. Some subjects are particularly neuralgic. Even the pro-American Sarkozy felt the need to take a sharply different line from that of President Obama at the UN General Assembly discussion in September 2010 of the Palestinian drive for the recognition of its statehood. The domestic context was almost certainly a factor here.[57] Conversely, during the approach to the presidential election of 2012, Paris tried to downplay Algerian preparations for the celebration of fifty years of independence, which threatened to open up old wounds domestically and internationally. It was as well for Paris that the sixteen pages of advertising taken in *Le Monde* by President Bouteflika's government only appeared later, on 3 July.[58] If, as is possible, the arrival of

[56] In 2010, for example, President Sarkozy acknowledged that it had been a mistake three years previously to set up a Ministry of Immigration, Integration, National Identity, and Interdependent Development ('développement solidaire'), a linkage which had caused uproar. He brought Immigration back into the Ministry of the Interior, and disavowed talk of national identity. Yet during the election campaign of 2012 he returned to the identity discourse. See 'Nicolas Sarkozy Says Sorry for National Identity Ministry', *The Guardian*, 17 November 2010; also 'Le candidate Sarkozy réhabilite l'identité nationale', *Le Monde*, 5 March 2012.

[57] I am grateful for Anand Menon's advice on this and other aspects of recent French foreign policy.

[58] Natalya Vince, LSE Blog, 19 July 2012, <http://www.blogs.lse.ac.uk/europpblog/category/authors/natalya-vince/> accessed 29 July 2012. The paid supplement appeared in *Le Monde*, 3 July 2012, but also in *The Times* and other internationally known newspapers, while on 5 July

François Hollande in the Elysée leads to a formal apology to Algiers for the brutalities of the past, it is bound to produce more domestic divisions, along predictable lines.[59]

Denmark

The contrast between Danish and French integrationism is instructive. Whereas France is consistent in its antipathy to multiculturalism and its insistence on the separation between church and state, Denmark has allowed that diversity may have some value, albeit mainly within the community of those already defined as Danish. It gives a privileged place to the Evangelical–Lutheran Church in affairs of state, it is the 'People's Church', and other religious organizations do not enjoy the same legal status, needing to apply for various levels of approval.[60] At the same time, Denmark has a very strong sense of its identity, which has often been said to be based on a closer connection between state and nation than in almost any other country (outside Scandinavia). It seeks to protect this identity by a conscious commitment to integration—there is even a Ministry of Integration—which in practice is hardly distinguishable from top-down assimilationism.

The origin of the strong attachment which Danes feel to their nation-state lies in a sense of pride in their achievement in constructing a successful modern society, given their position of geopolitical vulnerability (Denmark is a small country and difficult to defend) and in their final emergence after 1918 from the difficulties caused by a multinational composition. The Schleswig–Holstein question, which Palmerston said was only understood by three people, was really about the clash between the Danish- and German-speaking peoples in the two regions of Schleswig and Holstein. Denmark lost both to war in 1864, regaining the Danish part of Schleswig (Southern Jutland) at the Treaty of Versailles, which consolidated Denmark as a place for Danes, while creating a reluctance to repeat the experience of multinationality.[61]

This falling back on nationality, however, did not produce xenophobia. The population of Denmark had little choice but to submit to occupation in 1940,

Le Monde published an article criticizing Bouteflika's use of the public purse, 'Après Le Monde Bouteflika se paie une grosse pub dans Le Times, USA Today, Al Hayat'.

[59] Jonathan Laurence, 'Why Is It So Hard to Say "Sorry" in French?', *Foreign Policy*, 5 July 2012, <http://www.foreignpolicy.com/articles/2012/07/05/why_is_it_so_hard_to_say_sorry_in_french> accessed 29 July 2012.

[60] Tina Gudrun Jensen, '"Making Room": Encompassing Diversity in Denmark', in Silj (ed.), *European Multiculturalism Revisited*, pp. 188–9.

[61] Lene Hansen, 'Sustaining Sovereignty: The Danish Approach to Europe', in Lene Hansen and Ole Wæver (eds), *European Integration and National Identity: The Challenge of the Nordic States* (London: Routledge, 2002), pp. 55–9.

but when three years later the Nazis tried to round up Danish Jews, their compatriots mobilized en masse to ensure that most were able to escape to Sweden. Of the 7,485 Danish Jews, almost all survived the war.[62] This notable reaction derived from the mix of egalitarianism and integration which characterizes Danish society—leading to a sense of responsibility for all fellow-citizens, whatever their religion. The Jews were seen as Danes like any other, unlike more heterogeneous and/or prejudiced societies. Danes are rightly proud of this episode in their history, which was echoed in the law enacting the Genocide Convention in 1951 in their country, a law considered by Raphael Lemkin, the driving force at the UN, to be an example for all other states.[63]

Since the end of the Cold War, the maintenance of Danish integrationism has run into certain problems. The wave of immigration arising from both asylum claims and economic migration has placed question-marks against both Danes' strong sense of egalitarianism, and their attitude towards diversity in principle. A central notion in Danish culture is the *folket*, into which strangers are expected to integrate, to become part of.[64] This inevitably takes time, a period in which newcomers may suffer suspicion and hostility—while some resist integration if the price is too high in terms of the loss of religious and cultural autonomy. Furthermore, the strong identification which exists between society and the welfare state has led to fears for the impact of immigration on Denmark's social achievements and way of life. It is no coincidence that the country was one of the last of the EU-15 to open its doors to non-European labour.[65] Unlike France, which is a shaper of EU policy, as a small state Denmark is hyper-sensitive about its national sovereignty within the Union, which it sees as a potential threat to its identity and to its ability to make choices on vital interests. Thus Denmark secured crucial opt-outs on defence, justice, and the common currency.

Like all countries, Denmark has its divisions, which have been evident in the various closely fought referenda on EU integration. The DPP has succeeded in becoming an important part of Danish politics, but it does not dominate. There continue to be strongly liberal instincts at work. Yet it remains true that Danes prefer to pursue the international and cosmopolitan aspects of their

[62] Richard J. Evans, *The Third Reich at War* (London: Allen Lane, 2008), pp. 390–1.

[63] Karen E. Smith, *Genocide and the Europeans* (Cambridge: Cambridge University Press, 2010), pp. 42–3.

[64] Meaning 'the people'. See Hansen, 'Sustaining Sovereignty', pp. 58–61.

[65] J. M. Schwartz, *Reluctant Hosts: Denmark's Reception of Guest Workers* (Copenhagen: Akademisk Forlag, 1985), cited in Tina Gudrun Jensen, '"Making Room"', p. 189. Furthermore, the rate of admission was initially slow, leading to delayed domestic reactions compared to other European states. The inflow into Denmark doubled between 1990 and 1995, during which time the flows were decreasing or stabilizing elsewhere. See Table 1.1 'Inflows of Foreign Populations into Selected European Countries, 1990–99', in Andrew Geddes, *The Politics of Migration and Immigration in Europe*, p. 9.

liberalism outside their own country. And this they do to great effect. Denmark is the world's fourth most generous giver of Overseas Development Aid, having reached the level of 1 per cent of GNI in 1992. Although by 2011 it had fallen to 0.88 per cent, that was still well above the UN's target of 0.7 per cent.[66] It has for several decades been an important player in southern Africa in particular, and a regular participant in UN peacekeeping. Denmark has also at times stood alone in criticizing China on human rights grounds, in full knowledge of the inevitable economic price to be paid.[67] Danes are thus more active than most in working for a better world—but that does not mean that they want to merge with it. Furthermore, their view of Europe tends to be cultural and identity-based, which means strong support for the accession of the Baltic states and opposition to the prospect of Turkish entry.[68]

The transnational dimension of modern politics produces significant problems even for states like Denmark which enjoy a high degree of internal confidence and the ability to exercise sovereignty. It is all too easy to become embroiled in an international dispute without having committed any foreign policy *faux pas*. This painful truth was brought home sharply in 2005–6 through the 'Cartoon Crisis', when the actions of two groups of Danish citizens led to the country being vilified, and boycotted by Muslims worldwide, with Danish missions being sacked in three countries. This was 'a paradigm example of how globalisation and transnational ties can create a grave foreign policy crisis'.[69] More than one hundred people were killed in violent demonstrations (none of them Danes, but the cartoonists did receive police protection in response to the many death threats they received). Neighbours Sweden and Norway were drawn into the controversy, with the Norwegian Embassy in Damascus being attacked, and the Swedish Foreign Minister being forced eventually to resign. The United States and the EU reluctantly took a public line in support of their small ally. As a result, the Danish Foreign Minister Per Stig Møller called the episode 'probably the most serious foreign policy crisis for Denmark since the Second World War'.[70] It also created deep domestic divisions which reverberated in the years that followed.

[66] Statistics from 'Millennium Development Goals Indicators' [online database], UN Stats, <http://www.unstats.un.org/unsd/mdg/SeriesDetail.aspx?srid=568> accessed on 26 June 2011.

[67] Henrik Larsen, 'Denmark: A Committed Member—With Opt-outs!', in Reuben Wong and Christopher Hill (eds), *National and European Foreign Policy: Towards Europeanization* (London: Routledge, 2011), pp. 93–110.

[68] See Marianne Riddervold and Helene Sjursen, 'The Importance of Solidarity: Denmark as a Promoter of Enlargement', in Helene Sjursen (ed.), *Questioning EU Enlargement: Europe in Search of Identity* (London: Routledge, 2006), pp. 81–103. See also Chapter 2, footnote 53.

[69] Hans Mouritzen, personal communication.

[70] Henrik Larsen, 'Danish Foreign Policy and the Balance between the EU and the US: The Choice between Brussels and Washington after 2001', *Cooperation and Conflict*, 44/2 (2009), p. 222. For the details of the crisis and for policy analysis, see also Henrik Larsen, 'The Cartoons Crisis in Danish Foreign Policy: A New Balance between the EU and the US?', in Nanna Hvidt

Of the two groups of Danish citizens responsible for the crisis, the first consisted of the staff of the newspaper *Jyllands-Posten*, who set out deliberately to assert the right to free speech in Denmark, and to criticize what they saw as self-censorship over Islam, by publishing twelve cartoons of the Prophet Mohammed, some of which provocatively associated the Prophet with terrorism and the suppression of women's rights. It is unlikely that the editors of the newspaper foresaw the extent of the international incident which followed, but they certainly willed a significant domestic controversy, while the era of Internet-based news coverage means that almost any issue has the capacity to evoke reactions in a wide range of different countries. There is a difference, however, between instant and evanescent comment, which is the fate of most news items, and the slow-burning accumulation of outrage over an issue which touches raw nerves. In this case the first foreign protests did not depend on the Internet, being made within a month through bilateral channels by the ambassadors of eleven Muslim countries, and via the Organisation of the Islamic Conference. In mid-November some of the critical governments went public, broadening the scope of the conflict. If the editors of *Jyllands-Posten* had wanted a test-case, they had clearly succeeded.

The second group of Danish citizens whose actions were critical was the Muslim community in Denmark, which immediately protested at the publication of the cartoons and moved to draw the attention of Muslim governments to the issue. Any competent Ambassador from Egypt or Iran (to name the two most active countries at the start) would have picked up on the dispute in Copenhagen, but the protests and requests for solidarity then made it even more difficult to contain matters, and to engineer a solution at the diplomatic level. In particular, a group of Danish Imams travelled to the Middle East to publicize their grievance and to seek powerful support.[71] Prime Minister Anders Fogh Rasmussen argued that the issue was hijacked by certain Middle Eastern countries for their own domestic reasons, but this is always a possibility in such cases. Rasmussen's own inept diplomacy, particularly his unwillingness to have a meeting with the eleven ambassadors, played right into the hands of the fundamentalists.[72] He seems not to have understood how easily a domestic dispute can turn into a foreign policy incident through the operation of transnational forces, although it is possible that he was not displeased to have this opportunity to remind voters of his national credentials. By January 2006 Saudi Arabia had recalled its ambassador and was encouraging a boycott

and Hans Mouritzen (eds), *Danish Foreign Policy Yearbook 2007* (Copenhagen: Danish Institute for International Studies, 2007), pp. 51–86. Helle Rytkønen, 'Drawing the Line: The Cartoons Controversy in Denmark and the US', pp. 86–109. For more normative discussions see Sune Lægaard, 'The Cartoon Controversy: Offence, Identity, Oppression?', *Political Studies*, 55/3 (2007), pp. 481–98, and Jensen, 'Making Room', pp. 201–8.

[71] Tina Gudrun Jensen, '"Making Room"', p. 203.

[72] Helle Rytkønen, 'Drawing the Line', p. 86–109, note 10.

of Danish products. Demonstrations and attacks on various Danish embassies followed in February, with around 100,000 people turning out in Sanàa, the Yemeni capital. Multilateralizing the crisis through the EU and US eventually helped to calm things down, but only after the cartoons had been republished in several other European countries, thus risking an even more widespread conflict with Islam, the avoidance of which had been a major strategic aim of the West since 2001. The Danish government subsequently tried to refurbish its reputation in the Middle East by relaunching its 2003 'Arab Initiative', which included public diplomacy and the opening of new embassies. But the endless ricochets between events outside and inside by now included a further strengthening of the Danish People's Party, which opposed increased funding for the venture.[73]

Thus despite the fact that Denmark has been a stalwart supporter of the United States and NATO, with forces sent to both Iraq and Afghanistan, it was not conventional foreign policy which got it into serious trouble. As a small state it actually benefited from multilateralism not only in terms of free-riding, but also through being able to shelter behind the main members of an alliance in a politically tempestuous environment. It was the US and Britain which attracted most jihadist odium for the interventions in Muslim states (notwithstanding the operation to liberate Kosovo), although it is possible to argue that had Denmark's position been different it might have received the benefit of the doubt from Muslim states over the Cartoon Crisis. Ultimately the country's progressive policies on aid and racism did not save it from attack.

What caused Denmark problems, more abroad than at home (where it had not suffered from serious unrest from its own Muslim community, let alone terrorism) was the interaction between a debate in civil society (on which, respecting the principles of free speech and an independent judiciary, the government stayed neutral) and the wider international environment, brokered by the unfettered transnational activities of some of its own citizens (including the free speech lobby, which looked for support in other liberal democracies). This was a shock for the Danish government as it looked back on a long tradition of foreign policy-making in which the *Folketing* (Parliament) has had considerable powers over war-making and over policy inside the EU, but where civil society was not generally active; outside the issues of European integration, development, and human rights, where interest-groups had become established actors.[74]

[73] Henrik Larsen, 'The Cartoons Crisis in Danish Foreign Policy', p. 81.

[74] For the Cold War position, see Ib Faurby, 'Foreign Policy-Making in Scandinavia', in W. Paterson and William Wallace (eds), *Foreign Policy-making in Western Europe: A Comparative Approach* (London: Saxon House, 1978), pp. 106–34. For the later period, see Ben Tonra, 'Denmark and Ireland', in Ian Manners and Richard Whitman (eds), *The Foreign Policies of European Union Member States* (Manchester: Manchester University Press, 2000), especially pp. 231–5.

Integrationism in Denmark has suffered some modifications, moving more towards the Swedish model, at the same time as Sweden has shown some signs of moving in the other direction. As Ulf Hedetoft has argued, some convergence can thus be observed.[75] But cultural variety is still only desirable if depoliticized, and there is much reluctance even to guarantee minority rights as explicitly as European Conventions require.[76] Since the shock of the Cartoon Crisis there has been more 'diversity talk' in official circles, but also a hardening of the conditions over immigration, citizenship, and access to welfare. Hedetoft, writing in 2008, presciently noted that the issue of tighter national rules and freedom of movement under the Schengen regime was 'looking to develop into a major crunch for Danish migration and integration policies'—and the crunch came with the unilateral reimposition of border controls in May 2011. Denmark is part of the Schengen zone of free movement, but shocked its partners with a unilateral reassertion of its border controls at the frontiers with Germany and Sweden, supposedly to counter transnational crime but also to appease the anti-immigration Danish People's Party (DPP). The ensuing row, in which the European Commission and Germany both criticized Copenhagen strongly, producing in turn a nationalist reaction from some members of the government, brought to the fore issues of identity, and anxiety about the impact of the outside world on Denmark.[77]

Relations with both the European Commission and Germany were damaged, with the German Foreign Minister Westerwelle issuing a strong and personal protest to his Danish opposite number.[78] Placed in a cleft stick, the

[75] Ulf Hedetoft, *Multiculturalism in Denmark and Sweden*, DIIS Brief (Copenhagen: Danish Institute for International Studies, December 2006); Hedetoft, 'Denmark versus Multiculturalism', in Vertovec and Wessendorf (eds), *The Multiculturalism Backlash*, pp. 111–29.

[76] Denmark, like France (but also Sweden and the UK) has not yet signed protocol 12 of the European Convention on Human Rights, which prohibits discrimination against minorities by public authorities. See Marc Weller, Denika Blacklock, and Katherine Nobbs (eds), *The Protection of Minorities in the Wider Europe* (Houndmills: Palgrave Macmillan, 2008), pp. 163–4, 68, and 169 note 43; also p. 279 on the patchy European ratification of the Framework Convention for the Protection of National Minorities.

[77] Hedetoft, 'Denmark versus Multiculturalism'. Fifty Customs Officers were deployed on the border on 5 July 2011, officially to stop drug smuggling. 'Danish Border Controls Break Schengen Law—Experts', *EUbusiness*, 13 July 2011, <http://www.eubusiness.com/news-eu/denmark-trade.b9f/> accessed 27 July 2012.

[78] Marlene Wind, 'The Blind, the Deaf, and the Dumb! How Domestic Politics Turned the Danish Schengen Controversy into a Foreign Policy Crisis', in Nanna Hvidt and Hans Mouritzen (eds), *Danish Foreign Policy Yearbook 2012* (Copenhagen: Danish Institute for International Studies, 2012), especially pp. 138 and 142. See also European Council Conclusions, Brussels ECO23/11, 23–24 June 2011, <http://www.register.consilium.europa.eu/pdf/en/11/st00/st00023.en11.pdf> accessed 20 December 2012. Here the Council attempted to gloss over the dispute, which played into the pre-existing clash between Italy and France over the former's granting of travel documents to illegal Tunisian migrants who were clearly in transit through Italy, heading for France. Much time was devoted to the migration issue, despite the pressing demands of the Greek economic crisis.

Danish government preferred to accept strong protests from its EU partners than to rebuff those at home who wished to assert the country's right to have border controls—with their barely concealed sub-text of stopping undesirables from entering. Denmark accepts migration, and the diversity that comes with it, up to a point, but stops well short of political multiculturalism, which has been rejected across the party spectrum. Politicians are, however, increasingly having to accept that this stance comes at the price of some new and potentially serious complications in external policy. Much depends on the movement of events and of public opinion—when the Liberal–Conservative government was defeated in the elections of September 2011, the border controls were dropped. Yet a year later, under the Danish presidency of 2012, Member States unanimously decided to exclude the European Parliament from decisions on Schengen borders, thus keeping the process wholly intergovernmental and in effect preserving the freedom to impose the unilateral suspensions of the kind which had been so controversial in 2011.[79]

Greece

Greece is an integrationist state both in its own current claims and in the sense used here of a state averse to recognizing group rights. But it is one which has little to do with the civic secularism or egalitarianism prominent in our other two cases. In 2010 its proposed legislation reforming the naturalization procedure stressed that citizenship on the French model of commitment to a territorial polity rather than to a blood community, was the basis of the state.[80] Yet in practice it is rooted in a nationalism which, while modernizing and subject to strong Europeanizing influences, is also the product of a deep historical and geopolitical insecurity. The importance of the Orthodox Church, which is recognized in the Constitution as 'the prevailing religion in Greece', together with the self-image of Greece as the hinge between east and west, has produced a powerful sense of exceptionalism.[81] Such tensions between theory and practice explain why the naturalization reform has still

[79] 'Danish Minister to face MEPs' anger over Schengen', *European Voice*, 8 June 2012.

[80] Law 3838/2010, *Provisions on the Greek Citizenship and the Political Participation of People of Greek Descent and Legally Residing Migrants and other Provisions* (Athens; Office of the President of the Hellenic Republic, English translation). The 'Statement of Reasons' accompanying the original draft legislation (Ministry of Foreign Affairs Translation Service, 16 April 2010) noted the detachment of Greek citizenship 'from its strong and exclusive link to the *jus sanguinis* principle'. It advocated trusting in 'the particular strength of the Greek citizen quality: the historical power to bring together different people in a creative common future'.

[81] Anna Triandafyllidou and Ruby Gropas, 'Constructing Difference: The Mosque Debates in Greece', *Journal of Ethnic and Migration Studies*, 35/6 (2009), p. 961. The Orthodox Church has a key place in Greek historical memory for its association with the independence struggle, and for consequently having suffered persecution under the Ottomans—as with the hanging of the

not passed into law and why there is so much resistance to the genuine integration of immigrants.[82]

The classical origins of Greece provide a unifying myth for the modern state, for which the rivalry of the ancient city states is less important than the sense of heroic resistance to the Persian invader. Since that zenith, more than two thousand years of occupation and subordination—to Romans, Ottomans, Venetians, and Germans—have left Greeks passionately determined to defend their sovereignty and Hellenic culture. Key events like the achievement of independence from the Ottomans in 1829, the war with Turkey in 1922 leading to a traumatic exchange of populations, the Axis occupation of 1940–4, resentment at foreign involvement in the civil war of 1944–9, and finally the strong identification with Greek Cypriots in their conflict with Turkey, have created the same thirst for autonomy which prevails in the ex-members of the Warsaw Pact. The notions of independence and cultural distinctiveness are mutually entangled in Greek political life. The relative newness of the modern Greek state, and the many threats it has suffered since 1829, have created a defensive nationalism in contrast to nineteenth-century liberalism, and indeed to the way in which Greeks had mingled with the other peoples of the eastern Mediterranean over the previous two millennia.[83]

This means that there is little sense of relaxed toleration about the existence of minorities in Greece, let alone a willingness to promote multiculturalism. Although, like Denmark, Greece had an honourable record of trying to protect its Jewish citizens from Nazi persecution, in the post-war period Greece often persecuted its sizeable Turkish Muslim minority in western Thrace, a remnant of the relatively relaxed multinationalism of the Ottoman empire, and nominally protected by the 1923 Treaty of Lausanne.[84] They were denied the same rights as ethnic Greeks, given poorer educational facilities, and even punished for attempting to appoint their own muftis.[85] This was in part the result of the

Patriarch and other key figures in 1821. See Richard Clogg, *Modern Greece: A Short History* (2nd edn, Oxford: Oxford University Press, 1992), pp. 11–13.

[82] As of August 2012 a decision was still awaited from the full Assembly of the Council of State and the Supreme Court, after a challenge from the right-wing party LAOS. I am grateful to Eda Gemi for information on this.

[83] John S. Koliopoulos and Thanos M. Veremis, *Modern Greece: A History since 1821* (Chichester: Wiley-Blackwell, 2010), especially pp. 1–23.

[84] On the brave but mostly unavailing attempts to save the Greek Jews, see Alexander Kitroeff, *War-time Jews: The Case of Athens* (Athens: Eliamep, 1995).

[85] On the Turks of western Thrace, see Nathalie Tocci, 'The Europeanization of Minority–Majority Relations in the Greece–Turkey–Cyprus Triangle', in Weller, Blacklock, and Nobbs (eds), *The Protection of Minorities in the Wider Europe*, pp. 259–61. Tocci points out that Athens has made efforts to improve the situation of the Turkish minority from the 1990s on (after sharp criticism from the State Department in 1991, see Clogg, *Modern Greece*, pp. 206–70). Yet in the same volume Will Kymlicka makes the point that in 1990 Greece raised its electoral threshold (for a party's presence in parliament under proportional representation 'precisely to prevent the

chronic fear of Turkish aggression, centred on the notion of a fifth column inside Greece, but also the product of the strong ethnocultural basis of Greek identity, citizenship, and statehood. In practice this means that the Greek language, the Orthodox Church, and the Hellenic heritage are key unifiers which any newcomer has to accept—even if Greeks themselves are not uniformly attached to the Church. Minorities have no formal recognition, which means that the Greek government has refused to sign the Framework Convention on National Minorities.[86] As Triandafyllidou and Gropas point out, 'There is as yet no debate on how to accommodate cultural and religious difference in inclusive and integrating ways, or how to make this diversity part of contemporary Greek society. In other words, dominant national self-understandings remain mono-cultural and mono-religious. The challenge of migration-related diversity is not yet fully addressed.'[87]

This approach might be thought to go beyond integrationism, amounting to assimilationism, but in practice even the latter is not an accurate description. Only a few immigrants, mostly those from neighbouring countries and/or of the Orthodox faith, are capable of full immersion, in terms of mastering the language and entering into the shared rituals of Greek life. Even those who meet these demanding criteria still face an uphill struggle if they seek naturalization. Muslims by definition are excluded from mainstream society given the Church's dominant role, while other groups are so small as to lack the capacity to mobilize in defence of their interests. This means that in general non-Greeks are neither integrated nor assimilated; in political and cultural terms they exist on the margins of society. This does not apply so much to prosperous Americans or Germans, say, who find their level among the *haute bourgeoisie*. But it makes a big difference to poorer immigrants, who form an under-class, especially in the Athens metropolitan area. The coming of the financial crisis in 2008, moreover, meant that they soon became scapegoats for some Greeks desperate for jobs and a share of the decreasing resources of the state. This led to the rise for the first time in Greece of a neo-fascist party, Golden Dawn, which succeeded in winning first 21 then 18 of the 300 parliamentary seats in the two general elections of Spring 2012. Social tensions were all too evident on the streets, associated with violence, fear, and discrimination, particularly in Athens where the proportion of immigrants has risen to more than 15 per cent.

possibility of Turkish MPs being elected'. Since then no Turkish Muslim party has been possible, with Turkish Muslims having to work through mainstream parties. Will Kymlicka, 'The Evolving Basis of European Norms of Minority Rights', p. 29.

[86] Martin Brusis, 'Enlargement and Inter-Ethnic Power-sharing Arrangements', in Weller, Blacklock, and Nobbs (eds), *The Protection of Minorities in the Wider Europe*, p. 234.

[87] Triandafyllidou and Gropas, 'Constructing Difference', p. 972.

For Greece has, over the last two decades, become a significant country of immigration for the first time, after a century of emigration. This is the result of growing wealth through EU membership, which has attracted economic migrants, fulfilling Greece's own needs for cheap labour. But it is also because of the country's position at the south-east extremity of the EU, with a land border with Turkey and many islands easy to reach from Anatolia. These have become major points of entry for illegal immigration, much of it nominally in transit, but in practice a major burden on Greece's limited administrative and welfare resources. How far, therefore, is Greece characterized by an empirical multiculturality at odds with its social philosophy?

At the start of the twenty-first century, Greece was experiencing high levels of illegal immigration, which it turned a blind eye to, given the 'draconian' laws on the statute-book in relation to rights of entry and access to public services.[88] But the element of sub-cultural diversity increased dramatically after the mid-1990s, with the stock of immigrants multiplying fivefold between 1988 and 2001. Statistics on migration are particularly difficult to find in Greece, given the 'chaos' of successive attempts at legislation, the reluctance of the Ministry of Public Order to release its data, and the particular problem of the *homogeneis*, or ethnic Greeks living abroad, who have been repatriated (especially from the ex-Soviet region) and awarded citizenship in large numbers without details being released.[89] Thus only a crude estimate of the immigrant total is possible. But it seems clear even on a conservative assumption that about 9 per cent of the Greek population of *c.*11.3 million is now made up of non-Greek citizens, while the proportions of the labour force and school-age children are higher at *c.*12–14 per cent and 15 per cent respectively.[90] The consequent mix has an unusual pattern, for Greece is the only European country to have more than 50 per cent of its immigrants from one source—in this case, Albania, which provides 56 per cent of incomers. The other groups—notably Romanians, Georgians, Americans, British, and Germans—do not amount to more than 3 per cent each, apart from the Bulgarians at 4.7 per cent. The illegal immigrants were initially predominantly from Albania, and other countries of the neighbourhood. But those coming via Turkey were mostly Afghans, Iraqis, and Asians from countries further afield.

88 Geddes, *The Politics of Migration and Immigration in Europe*, pp. 160–2, 166, and 169.

89 This, and what follows on Greek migration data, relies on Martin Baldwin-Edwards et al., *Statistical Data on Immigrants in Greece: An Analytic Study of Available Data and Recommendations for Conformity with European Union Standards* (Athens: Hellenic Migration Policy Institute, 2004), especially pp. 1–8.

90 Martin Baldwin-Edwards et al., *Statistical Data on Immigrants in Greece*, p. 4. Also Anna Triandafyllidou, 'Greek Immigration at the Turn of the Twenty-First Century: Lack of Political Will or Purposeful Mismanagement?', *European Journal of Migration and Law*, 11/3 (2009), p. 175. I am grateful to both Dr Triandafyllidou and to Dr Charalambos Tsardanidis for their guidance in this complex area.

Their removal 'is not an easy task, leading to the eventual illegal residence of most of these in Greece'.[91]

It is always important to make clear in the context of the discussion of multiculturality that the issue of immigrants is separate from that of the proportion of Muslims (or any other religious community) in a society, as many of the latter are citizens of long-standing (even if that is not the popular perception). Greece is particularly sensitive on this matter, as it refuses to recognize in ethnic terms its most long-standing Muslim community, that in western Thrace, fearing meddling by Turkey. On the most recent authoritative estimate (that of Triandafyllidou), if we add to the *c.*140,000 + Muslims from this region the *c.*350,000 immigrants from Albania (discounting the 'co-ethnic' Albanians of Greek extraction), together with those from other Muslim countries, we arrive at a figure of about 525,000, or at least 4.5 per cent of the population, which is a sizeable minority in a country obsessed with its large Muslim neighbour and basing its unity on the Greek Orthodox church.[92] It is not then surprising, especially in the context of the severe economic crisis since 2008, that the spectres of Turkish interference and even violent fundamentalism (although Greece has not experienced the latter) should be raised in political debate.

In recent years Greece has made significant moves to liberalize its approach to immigration and to citizenship, partly under the influence of pan-European norms.[93] In 2010 an element of *ius soli* was added to the (still dominant) *ius sanguinis* criteria for citizenship, so that second generation migrants would be able to naturalize more easily, and have full voting rights in local elections.[94] Most of the political spectrum seemed to be moving towards accepting that immigrants had legitimate concerns to be addressed, and that they should be regarded as more than a necessary evil.[95] For the Greek self-image is of a people which sides with the underdog. Yet, as with the granting of authority in 2000 to build a mosque in Athens, which has still to be built, there was a

[91] In 2004, 39,842 aliens were removed from Greek territory, the vast majority of them Albanians, which gives a sense of the pressure from illegal immigration. *Annual Report on Statistics on Migration, Asylum and Return in Greece (Reference Year 2004)* (Athens: Centre of Planning and Economic Research, KEPE, January 2008), pp. 7–8.

[92] Anna Triandafyllidou (ed.), *Irregular Migration in Europe: Myths and Realities* (Aldershot: Ashgate, 2010), Table 1.2. It should be noted, however, that Albanian immigrants are not always seen in the same light as others, through their tendency to return home in the summer, and the unobtrusive way in which they practise the Muslim faith.

[93] Georgia Mavrodi, 'Ulysses Turning European: The Different Faces of "Europeanization" of Greek Immigration Policy', in Thomas Faist and Andreas Ette (eds), *The Europeanization of National Policies and Politics of Immigration: Between Autonomy and the European Union* (Houndmills: Palgrave Macmillan, 2007), pp. 157–77.

[94] See footnote 80.

[95] Anna Triandafyllidou and Ruby Gropas, 'Migrants and Political Life in Greece: Between Political Patronage and the Search for Inclusion', *South European Society and Politics*, 17/1 (2012), pp. 45–63.

significant theory-implementation gap in the Greek approach.[96] Furthermore, with the coincidence of the unparalleled economic crisis and an increase in illegal immigration, there has been a resurgence of xenophobia, with significant outbursts of intolerance. Golden Dawn has both articulated the frustrations of some Greeks, and orchestrated them.[97]

Thus despite legislative changes, the debate between what Nikos Mouzelis has termed 'civic nationalism', based on residence and human rights, and 'ethnic nationalism', based on blood and descent, has moved back in favour of the latter. Quite apart from populist pressures there is a cross-party attachment to the central importance of 'Greekness' as the source of national identity, even if, as Mouzelis says, too fearful a reaction to change, 'leads to a conspiratorial view of the outside world, to a xenophobic retrenchment and a general tendency to view the native–foreign relationship in purity–pollution terms'.[98] Such a view means that the predictable expressions of concern from some Islamic states and INGOs over the welfare of Muslims in Greece, as over the need for a mosque in Athens, or criticisms from other EU societies of the treatment of immigrants more generally, have only led to further polarization.[99]

These representations indicate the links which exist between political culture on diversity matters and foreign policy. The latter has certainly come to incorporate immigration as a central diplomatic issue. As Charalambos Tsardanidis has noted, 'Greece has faced foreign policy choices about immigration that were complex, emotional and deeply intertwined with domestic concerns'.[100] Greece's borders are difficult to defend against immigration, yet the adherence to a mono-ethnic, monocultural society has made limiting the numbers on non-Greeks arriving a major priority. This has produced bilateral issues, notably with Albania and Turkey, which have then reverberated back into civil society. As the Kosovo crisis mounted, for example, the Simitis government refused to take any of the flood of refugees partly because of its ties with Serbia and partly due to its own anti-Albanian public opinion.[101] Gregoriadis has argued that the other side of this coin is the fact that 'Greece enjoys special historic and cultural links with Middle Eastern Christians', and

[96] Triandafyllidou and Gropas, 'Constructing Difference', pp. 963–5.

[97] In its wish to see strong government, Golden Dawn also displays signs of nostalgia for the military junta which ruled Greece from 1967–74.

[98] Nikos Mouzelis, 'Modes of National Identity in the Context of Globalisation', in Loukas Tsoukalis (ed.), *Globalisation and Regionalism: A Double Challenge for Greece* (London: London School of Economics and Political Science, The Hellenic Observatory/Athens: Hellenic Foundation for European and Foreign Policy, 2001), pp. 50–3.

[99] According to Tsardanidis, the following countries have made representations: Pakistan, Saudi Arabia, Morocco, Libya, Jordan, Kuwait, Indonesia. Charalambos Tsardanidis, 'Immigration and its Impact on Greek Foreign Policy', *Hellenic Studies* (Quebec), 15/1 p. 146.

[100] Tsardanidis, 'Immigration and its Impact on Greek Foreign Policy', p. 147.

[101] James Pettifer and Miranda Vickers, *The Albanian Question: Reshaping the Balkans* (London: I. B. Tauris, 2007), pp. 222–6.

thus has a special responsibility given the attacks on them in a number of Islamic states.[102] It seems unlikely that Greece has the power to do much, or even the will, given that few of the vulnerable communities are actually Greek Orthodox. But potential flashpoints do exist, as with the presence of a Greek Patriarch in Jerusalem. Greek–Israeli relations have improved in proportion to the decline in friendship between Israel and Turkey, but the wheel may yet turn again.

On the more classical issues of foreign policy Greece displays some interesting paradoxes: the fear of Islam, despite the pro-Arab and pro-Palestinian tradition on Middle Eastern politics; the fear of importing terrorism, in a country where home-grown political violence has been common; inward-lookingness to the point of having a minimal foreign aid programme, while also hoping for much from the EU; an ally of the USA, yet with a public that is often anti-American, to the extent that participation in the 2003 Iraq War, and more than a token role in Afghanistan, were unthinkable. Yet Greece does have genuine dilemmas to face through the interplay between its domestic character and its external relations. Despite the improvement since 1999 in relations with Turkey, as the result of a constructive and shrewd Greek initiative which also opened the way for its ally Cyprus to join the EU, the country remains over-shadowed by its large neighbour. The vulnerability of the Aegean islands to Turkish over-flying, maritime claims, or simply lax emigration controls, means that Greece will feel on the defensive towards Ankara for the foreseeable future, with its attitude towards its own growing Muslim community a not insignificant factor in the relationship.[103]

There is also a territorial dimension. The hyper-sensitivity shown about the new state of Macedonia, which Athens insists should be known as the Former Yugoslav Republic of Macedonia (FYROM)—possibly for fear of a greater Macedonia emerging which would attract its own province of that name, but more likely simply for reasons of national pride and identity—is another indication of how the internal structure of the Greek state inevitably affects foreign relations.[104]

To some extent Greece has used foreign policy to insulate itself, so as to create space for the preservation of its preferred way of life, although its margin of manoeuvre is not great. Until the unpredictable course of recent

[102] Ioannis N. Grigoriadis, 'Seeking Opportunities in Crisis Times: Greek Foreign Policy in the Middle East', *Eliamep Thesis* (Athens: Eliamep, March 2012), pp. 4–6.

[103] There is a tendency among ministers to blame Turkey for all illegal immigration, even if the statistics tend to show that only a minority arrive via the Aegean islands. Anna Triandafyllidou, 'Greek Immigration at the Turn of the Twenty-First Century', p. 169, note 16.

[104] Greece has, for example, strongly objected to the erection of a large statue of Alexander the Great in Skopje. It is unusual to have such a tug of war over national heroes. Simón Bolivar is another case in point, however, being claimed by Venezuela, Colombia, and other Latin American states.

economic events, it could look to the EU for financial support, and for help at the 'hard' external EU border with Turkey, via FRONTEX, the Union's operational agency charged with monitoring and deterring illegal entry. It also broadly went along with the Common Foreign and Security Policy, which provides helpful cover for small states in a dangerous world, while always retaining the right to keep a distance on vital national concerns such as Kosovo, or the name of Macedonia. Trying to frame something as 'a European problem', rather than a national one, enables Athens to contain pressures both at home and abroad. This is not always easy to do, however. In the case of the abduction of the Kurdish leader Abdullah Ocalan in 1999, which led to uproar among Kurds around Europe, it proved impossible to deflect the responsibility away from Athens, leading to the resignation of three ministers.[105]

If Greek foreign policy has thus become 'Europeanised' to a degree, the issue still remains as to how deep the process cuts. If it implies transforming the domestic base of foreign policy, then it has had little success in Greece.[106] Indeed, a deep ambivalence can be observed over both foreign policy orientation (i.e. between the EU and the Balkans) and national identity (between Orthodox and modernizing identities).[107] The two levels are connected, as part of the interplay between internal and external politics—at least in terms of political confidence. In 1998 Yiannis Kranidiotis, at the time Greece's Deputy Foreign Minister, observed, pointedly, 'If a country does not have the necessary social cohesion, if united national feeling is lacking, if economic vigour is missing, then that country cannot have a reliable policy in foreign affairs.'[108]

More than ten years later, Greece finds itself in a position where it still has a strong sense of national unity, but its traditional Hellenic basis is gradually being challenged by immigration and social change. What is more, it is going through an agonizing economic crisis whose domestic repercussions are unpredictable, but which certainly include resentment at the behaviour of exacting outside powers. In these circumstances a stable and effective foreign policy is truly difficult to achieve, though that is not to say that once the period

[105] Ocalan was abducted by Turkish agents in Kenya, where Greece had transferred him after the request for asylum in Athens. Mass Kurdish protests followed at Greek embassies around the world. See 'Kurdish Issue Explodes onto International Limelight Following Ocalan Arrest', *Hermes* (Athens News Agency, now ANA-MPA, March 1999), pp. 4–5.

[106] Spyros Economides, 'The Europeanisation of Greek Foreign Policy', *West European Politics*, 28/2 (2005), pp. 471–91. Charalambos Tsardanidis and Stelios Stavridis agree that some Europeanization has taken place, but are sceptical about its extent. See their chapter 'Greece: From Special Case to Limited Europeanisation', in Wong and Hill (eds), *National and European Foreign Policy*, pp. 111–30.

[107] Michelle Pace, 'Collective Identity: The Greek Case', in Walter Carlsnaes, Helene Sjursen, and Brian White (eds), *Contemporary European Foreign Policy* (London: Sage, 2004), pp. 227–38, especially 231–5.

[108] 'Yiannis Kranidiotis: Interview with Gerassimos Zarkadis, *Hermes* (Athens News Agency, now ANA-MPA, October 1998), pp. 7–8. Dr Kranidiotis, whose doctorate was in International Relations, was killed in an air crash the following year.

of turmoil has passed, the internal/external relationship cannot be reconfigured effectively. But much will depend on what kind of society Greeks—all Greeks—are able to forge together.

CONCLUSIONS

Integrationism as a model of society is under pressure. Immigration is difficult to manage, let alone stop, with the result that ethnocultural diversity increases beyond the rate at which assimilation (inevitably a slow historical process) can keep pace. External pressures to recognize groups arrive both from conventional intergovernmental sources—such as the EU's and Council of Europe's provisions on minority rights—and from transnational actors exploiting the space created by the mix of democratic states and global capitalism.

Yet such deeply embedded tendencies as that of integrationism cannot simply be discarded, even assuming the political will to do so. Social transformation is slow, and to some extent independent of formal decision-making. In any event, based on the cases we have examined in this chapter, it seems that integrationist states are bullish in their determination to tackle the challenges which the outside world brings in their own way. While all three have had to modify the tendency to pretend that diversity is not an issue, their determination not to privilege minorities, or the very idea of sub-national groups, has remained unaffected. Denmark, France, and Greece have all re-asserted the need for a strong state, a clear sense of national identity, and resistance to any attempts to interfere in their internal affairs—including those by the European institutions to which they subscribe. Their continued attachment to integrationism also implies, in conditions of increased *de facto* diversity, heightened suspicions of minorities and transnational diasporas, and the inevitability of conflict with other states or organizations which might object to their treatment of minorities. Opinion is no longer homogeneous on these points—indeed a more cosmopolitan view is gaining ground in all three states, while integration is actually a misnomer for the lived experience of their minorities, too often kept on the margins of society—but they still express the dominant political culture.

On the face of things the foreign policies we have examined seem largely unaffected by the issues of domestic diversity, which suggests that the integrationist model has succeeded in maintaining national unity and a clear distinction between the policies needed for home and abroad. It is true of any country, regardless of its domestic configuration, that much of its foreign policy will be shaped by international factors, while the impact of internal factors ranges beyond that of the issue of social diversity. But even if grand strategy has not been knocked off course, complications and signs of tension are all too evident in all three cases. For France, the vital issues of North Africa and EU enlargement are no longer the *domaine réservé* of an elite insulated from public opinion (although the special case of Algeria has long been interpenetrated with French life). For Denmark, asserting the value of free speech at home produced a major crisis with the Muslim world (just as earlier extending its values into criticism of China's approach to human rights led to ostracism by Beijing). Cultural relativism does not sit comfortably with Danes.

For Greece, immigration problems have increasingly become central to foreign policy, setting limits to the rapprochement with Turkey (from this viewpoint the Cyprus dispute may be seen as part of the same set of ethno-religious issues). At the same time Greece's weakness and vulnerability mean that it is caught between the need for support from its EU and NATO allies on the one hand, and its own nationalism on the other, producing awkward outbursts such as those over Macedonia and Kosovo. Diversity issues have also been complicated and over-shadowed by the massive linkage between foreign economic policy and domestic welfare. Denmark on the other hand, which is also small and vulnerable, is a far less erratic partner because it is richer, with a better functioning state, a more confident sense of its social cohesion, and is not an obvious gateway for poor migrants.

The argument emerging in this book is that foreign and domestic policies are increasingly caught in a perpetual loop of interaction. Even these integrationist states, which seek to preserve their essential character against the forces of globalization, have felt reverberations from outside, especially the events flowing from 9/11, which catapulted fundamentalism to the forefront of international relations. They also get backwash from their own external activities, as with the terrorist attacks in France of the 1990s, and the reduced cooperation between Turkey and Greece on illegal migrants at times of tension over Cyprus or the Aegean. Yet these things are not necessarily unmanageable. Indeed on a rare visit to western Thrace, Turkey's prime minister Erdogan explicitly told its Muslim population that their loyalty must be to the Greek state, while Denmark's fear that its opt-outs in the EU might cost it support during the cartoon affair, was not in the end realized.[109]

What is now true even for integrationist states is that geopolitics and domestic politics increasingly bleed into one another, with the result that the scope of 'foreign policy' has become enlarged to cover a range of societal issues. This in turn means that the definition of the national interest in

[109] In fact the visit in 2004 was the first by a Turkish leader to the region since 1952. Prime Minister Erdogan told his listeners: 'Nobody is Telling You to Lose or Give Up Your Turkish Identity, but Remember that You are Citizens of Greece', *Hurriyet Daily News*, 10 May 2004, <http://www.hurriyetdailynews.com/default.aspx?pageid=438&n=erdogan-visit-turns-new-page-in-ties-with-greece-2004-05-10> accessed 27 July 2012. Greece actually sees the minority as Muslim, not Turkish, but Erdogan was thinking of a Turkish audience.

external policy is more likely to be contested, and less likely to be left to a specialist cadre. Governments have a powerful role in this type of state in articulating the consensus on identity, but paradoxically this does not necessarily help them to maintain their traditional monopoly on dealings with the outside world. Nor are they able to take for granted their ability to manage their own multiculturality.

4

Parallel societies

Those European societies which follow neither an overtly multiculturalist path nor plough the opposite, integrationist, furrow could all be placed in a residual category. It would indeed be foolish to attempt generalizations which cover the experience in this area of Finland, Portugal, Ireland, and Poland. Apart from the fact that states are in very different stages of their encounter with ethno-cultural diversity, at times one simply has to surrender to the facts of particularity. Nonetheless, there are still some common reactions to diversity which can be observed among states which do not fit into one of the two main categories, yet which are also established and important players in the European Union.

In theoretical terms it might be expected that this set would consist of those making a compromise between multiculturalism and integration, as arguably can be seen in the United States with its famous concept of 'hyphenated Americans'. Indeed there is an element of compromise to be seen in the approaches of the three states discussed in this chapter: Germany, Italy, and Spain. But the matter is not so straightforward, since 'hyphenation' has yet to establish itself in Europe, except to a degree in Britain, where there has been some attempt to square the circle of competing identities, with such notions as the 'British-Jamaican' or 'Anglo-Irish' communities. But these concepts are so redolent of colonial days—an 'Anglo-Indian' really meaning someone of British descent who had worked for the Raj—that they do not provide a template for social development in the same way as the image of, say, a Polish-American. So far as compromise is concerned, the perpetual process of action–reaction which characterizes politics means that, as we saw in Chapters 2 and 3, both multiculturalists and integrationists have had to modify their positions, if still well short of convergence and consensus. In the states which cannot fit into either of these two categories, it is not so much a matter of splitting the difference between the two principal models as of societies finding their way towards an understanding of how to handle diversity, having had little previous experience of it, alongside managing other structural problems. Some would argue that these societies have in fact displayed a wilful refusal to confront the reality of their changed social compositions.

Such cases are best described in terms of 'parallel societies'.[1] That is, they are countries which have both a reasonably strong sense of their own identity, and an increasing element of social diversity. Yet they have not directly addressed the potential tension between these two phenomena, as Britain has by consciously promoting multiculturalism, or France has by asserting its sense of self unapologetically. They have either failed politically to recognize the issues at stake or have swept them under the carpet. As a result, significant minorities exist in such societies without any clear policy being adopted towards them. At the level of daily social interaction members of the ethnic communities are noticed—but often discriminated against. Their impact on the labour market, the extra burden they might place on welfare provisions, and the visibility of their social practices, are regularly commented upon. But the state, in the guise of the major parties which shape legislation, has not yet fully faced the question of how to relate minorities to its constitution and future development. There will be various reasons, and combinations of reasons, for this failure, depending on the state in question: becoming a society of immigration relatively late; preoccupation with building democracy after war or dictatorship; systems focused on geographical differentiation more than ethnicity or culture; uneasiness over the national capacity to cope with debates about social difference. It is possible that states with 'parallel societies', as they engage with the problem of diversity, will move decisively in the direction of multiculturalism or integrationism—or perhaps develop a settled form of hyphenated identity for its minorities. They use the language of each model promiscuously, without consistency or commitment. As a result, they remain in a kind of limbo.[2]

[1] The first reference to 'parallel societies' in this context seems to have been by Wilhelm Heitmeyer in the German language, i.e. 'parallelgesellschaften', in 1996: Wilhelm Heitmeyer, 'Für turkische Jurgendliche in Deutschland spielt der Islam eine wichtige Rolle', *Die Zeit*, Nr. 35, 23 August 1996. I owe this information to William Hiscott, '"Parallel Societies"—A Neologism Gone Bad' (Prague: Multicultural Center, July 2005), p. 3, <www.migration.cz> accessed 14 August. In English the term was given prominence by use of the phrase 'parallel lives' in the official report into the Lancashire riots of 2001: Ted Cantle (Chair) *Community Cohesion: A Report of the Independent Review Team* (London: Home Office, 2001). The report illustrated the idea of parallel lives by reference (para. 2.2) to a Muslim of Pakistani origin who said, 'When I leave this meeting with you I will go home and not see another white face until I come back here next week'. Report cited in Steven Vertovec and Susanne Wessendorf (eds), *The Multiculturalism Backlash: European Discourses, Policies and Practices* (London: Routledge, 2010), pp. 5, 8, and 30.

[2] As Carstensen-Egwuon and Holly point out, 'In recent years "integration" has become the key concept in the German immigration discourse'. But '[b]y using the concept of *integration*, people avoid debates about *Leitkultur* or "dominant culture" (considered too Right-leaning) or *multiculturalism* (the Leftist alternative) and promote a path beyond the risks of *parallel societies*'. Inken Carstensen-Egwuon and Werner Holly, 'Integration, Post-Holocaust Identities and No-go Areas: Public Discourse and the Everyday Experience of Exclusion in a German Region', in Heidi Armbruster and Ulrike Hanna Meinhof (eds), *Negotiating Multicultural Europe: Borders, Networks, Neighbourhoods* (Houndmills: Palgrave, 2011), p. 99.

STRUCTURAL COMPROMISES

Multiculturality is not so far removed from multinationalism in terms of the internal challenges posed to a state. Yet while the former describes a condition of intermingling between different groups and ethnocultural traditions, without clear-cut geographical zoning, the latter generally refers to a nation-state composed of various subaltern nations, each with its own regional identity and constitutional rights. As we shall see later in this chapter, where the two phenomena coincide, with multiculturality overlaying multinationalism, there can be confusion over where the potential threats to national cohesion lie and how best to sustain civil society. For the moment, however, it is worth pausing to reflect on the multinational question itself, given that it affects all three of the cases considered in this chapter. On the face of it, multinationality undermines the very idea of a 'nation-state', and by extension represents just as significant a challenge to a coherent foreign policy based on definable 'national interests' as does multiculturalism.[3]

The two most prominent examples of multinational states in Europe, after the demise of Yugoslavia and Czechoslovakia (which epitomized the issues at stake) are Belgium and Switzerland.[4] Both these states represent structural compromises, less between the majority and minorities, than between two halves of a divided society.[5] In Belgium's case the divide is between Walloons (French-speaking, 40 per cent) and Flemings (Dutch-speaking, 60 per cent), while in Switzerland the main divide is between French and German speakers, with the much smaller Italophone Ticino making up the numbers.[6] On the face of it such compositions should mean weakness, and a standing temptation to neighbours to intervene. Indeed, Belgium, an effective state only from 1839, represents an historic compromise between France and the Netherlands, with the issue of its territorial integrity a critical factor in the outbreak of two world wars. On the other hand, Switzerland, with a much longer history and a strong

[3] For a discussion of the various forms of cleavage that affect politics and society, and in particular of the roles of territory and religion at stake here, see Yves Mény, with Andrew Knapp, *Government and Politics in Western Europe: Britain, France, Italy, Germany* (2nd edn, Oxford: Oxford University Press, 1993), pp. 19–47.

[4] The United Kingdom is left on one side here given that it has already been considered under another category. But it is interesting to note that the multiculturalist overlay which has been so significant in the UK is far more characteristic of England than of Wales, Scotland, and Northern Ireland.

[5] For a brief historical comparison, see Kenneth Dyson, *The State Tradition in Western Europe* (Oxford: Martin Robertson, 1980) pp. 65–6.

[6] In Switzerland nineteen of the country's twenty-six cantons are predominantly German-speaking (63.7 per cent), with four French-speaking (20.4 per cent), including the key international city of Geneva. Italian is spoken by 6.5 per cent. It should be noted that around 22 per cent of the population is made up of foreigners. Source: 'Language Distribution', Federal Statistical Office of Switzerland, 2002, <http://www.swissworld.org/en/people/language/language_ distribution/> accessed 18 December 2012.

sense of its international distinctiveness, managed to stay out of the great conflicts of the twentieth century, despite its strategic vulnerability to the Third Reich.[7] Bearing in mind also the history of the United Kingdom, which like Switzerland (but in strong contrast to Belgium) has had assistance from geography, we may conclude that a multinational state is not automatically vulnerable to the depredations of international politics.

The interplay between internal and external politics is, however, central to the development of both countries. In the case of Belgium, the country is so deeply divided that it lacked a government for large parts of 2010–11, with many of its citizens expecting the eventual break-up of the state. Political parties, universities, and other key institutions are divided along linguistic lines, while the state has only survived this long through the adoption of a consociational system, by which the separate communities are guaranteed rights of political participation through a spoils, or quota, system. The country is divided geographically, broadly between north and south, but there are many cross-cutting cleavages. Arguably the state is only held together by its position between France, Germany, and the Netherlands, none of which wishes to be seen to be benefiting from Belgium's problems, and more particularly by membership of the European Union, with which it shares a capital city, and of which Belgium is the strongest possible supporter. A fully federal Europe is seen as likely to solve the problem of the country's internal divide, but that would still depend on what the units of the federation were deemed to be. In the meantime, the Belgian regions have acquired an unusual level of international treaty-making power, which naturally generates tensions with central government.[8]

The unresolved conflicts at the heart of Belgium have made it a weak state in terms of both its internal functioning and its external relations. Apart from the occasional spasm of independence over matters arising from its old empire, such as the Congo (where its moral and political credit is low), Belgium tends to follow the French lead in foreign policy on the occasions when it cannot find cover within the EU's Common Foreign and Security Policy. Thus it opposed the Iraq War, and in July 2011 became the second country (after France) to impose a ban on the wearing of the burka in public.

This brings us to the question of multiculturality in Belgium. Like France, the country has a sizeable foreign-born population, at around 14 per cent (up

[7] Switzerland survived between 1940 and 1945 partly through its willingness to blow up its Alpine tunnels, which were of strategic importance for the movement of German troops, and partly through the Nazis being perpetually distracted by other ambitions. But Hitler, who called Switzerland 'a pimple on the face of Europe', always had it in mind to invade the country and partition its territory with Italy. See Gerhard L. Weinberg, *A World At Arms: A Global History of World War II* (Cambridge: Cambridge University Press, 1994), pp. 173–4.

[8] M. Theo Jans and Patrick Stouthuysen, 'Federal Regions and External Relations: The Belgian Case', *International Spectator*, 42/2 (2007), pp. 209–20.

from 10.3 per cent in 2000).[9] The first wave of post-war immigration brought Italians and French, followed by Turks, Congolese, and Moroccans. An increasingly large proportion of these newcomers are Muslim by faith, between 4 and 6 per cent of the population. Most are concentrated in the two highly cosmopolitan cities of Antwerp (which has been so for centuries, with its Jewish and Armenian traders) and Brussels. The latter is now a largely international city, run by French and English-speakers despite being located in the Flemish part of the country. Unlike Jerusalem, a multicultural city which is the focus of discord, Brussels embodies Belgium in the eyes of the world, and works despite its uneasy relationship with the country's various communities.

Thus Belgium is a barely functioning multinational state, overlaid by the new phenomenon of multiculturality in some of its main urban areas. The latter has been the focus of new sharp disagreements, as the 9/11-effect led to anti-terrorism legislation and fear among both the Muslim and indigenous populations. But the country's fundamental and far more serious problem is untouched by this dimension.[10] Furthermore, as Bousetta and Jacobs have argued, 'the under [sic] development of an overarching vision of Belgian multiculturalism is largely prevented by the multinational character of the country and the complex decision-making procedures devised to pacify the tensions between the two dominant communities'.[11] Meanwhile on the external front, while Belgium's weakness as a small state is compounded by its inter-communal divide, the small-scale transnational activity generated by its ethnic minorities seems so far to have made little difference to the conduct of foreign policy. Even the continued concern with events in the Congo has more to do with tradition and colonial guilt than pressure from Congolese inside Belgium.[12]

Switzerland is a much more functional multinational state. Indeed, given its long history and strong sense of Swiss identity it can be argued that it is merely

[9] OECD International Migration Outlook 2012 'Stocks of Foreign-Born Population', <www.oecd.org/els/internationalmigrationpoliciesanddata/internationalmigrationoutlook2011.htm> accessed 18 December 2012.

[10] It is striking how an otherwise comprehensive and expert paper on Belgian counter-terrorism makes no reference whatsoever to the country's wider political and social structure. See Rik Coolsaet and Tanguy Struye de Swielande, *Belgium and Counterterrorism Policy in the Jihadi Era (1986–2007)*, Egmont Paper 15 (Brussels: Royal Institute for International Relations, 2007). See also Rik Coolsaet (ed.), *Jihadi Terrorism and the Radicalisation Challenge: European and American Experiences* (2nd edn, Aldershot: Ashgate, 2011), pp. 161–70.

[11] Hassan Bousetta and Dirk Jacobs, 'Multiculturalism, Citizenship and Islam in Problematic Encounters in Belgium', in Tariq Modood, Anna Triandafyllidou, and Ricard Zapata-Barrero (eds), *Multiculturalism, Muslims and Citizenship: A European Approach* (London: Routledge, 2006), p. 28. There is clearly an editing error here, in that 'underdevelopment' should read 'development'.

[12] Tanguy de Wilde D'Estmael, 'La politique étrangère de la Belgique 2004–2006. Un essai d'évaluation', *Studia Diplomatica. The Brussels Journal of International Relations*, 60 (2007), pp. 73–83.

multilingual and (highly) decentralized, rather than multicommunal in the way that Belgium or Canada are.[13] The divisions between Catholics and Protestants which caused bloodshed in the past no longer have significant political effects, while the devolution of so much power to the cantons, combined with the direct democracy use of referenda, has created common interests which override linguistic differences.[14] The external environment has also been a powerful unifying factor.[15] The long-held strategy of neutrality has proved effective both as a way of staying out of wider conflicts and as a set of values which binds the country together. By the same token it inoculates the German, French, and Italian cantons against the temptation to seek assistance, and thus interference, from neighbouring states. Such is its importance in this respect that the Swiss people have shown consistently that they do not wish to join the EU, where they would inevitably be drawn into closer relations with their big three neighbours, and for many years even preferred to stay out of the UN and the Bretton Woods institutions.[16] This powerful sense of both neutrality and independence combines naturally with the country's unique roles as the world's confidential banker and as a centre for such indispensable functional organizations as the Red Cross, the World Health Organization, and the World Trade Organization.

Switzerland has also acquired a multicultural overlay in recent decades, which paradoxically has had more impact than in Belgium, probably because of Switzerland's very stability and conservatism, which means both that it is not otherwise distracted, and that it is particularly sensitive to change. After the Second World War the country began to admit guest-workers from southern Europe, and indeed has a relatively high proportion of foreign-born

[13] For a reflection on the history of the Swiss federation, and its evolution from a confederation, see Murray Forsyth, *Unions of States: The Theory and Practice of Confederation* (New York: Holmes & Meier, 1981), pp. 18–30.

[14] For an excellent overview of Swiss federalism in relation to both traditional linguistic diversity and modern multiculturality, see Gianni D'Amato, 'Switzerland: A Multicultural Country Without Multicultural Policies', in Vertovec and Wessendorf, *The Multiculturalism Backlash*, pp. 130–51.

[15] Indeed, it can be argued that the Swiss state evolved from 1291 first through the need of small communities to band together against external threats, culminating in the trauma of French intervention between 1798 and 1813, and then through the interaction between external political ideas and internal religious disputes in the 1840s. This finally produced the move from confederation to federation in 1848. Forsyth, *Unions of States*, pp. 25–9.

[16] The key rejection was in the referendum of 1992 on the European Economic Area Treaty, which the Swiss government had seen as the precursor to EU membership. Although the popular vote was only narrowly against, eighteen out of the twenty-six cantons rejected the proposal. See Hanspeter Kreisi and Alexander H. Trechsel, *The Politics of Switzerland: Continuity and Change in a Consensus Democracy* (Cambridge: Cambridge University Press, 2008), pp. 172–89. After referenda rejecting UN participation in 1986 and 1994, membership was finally accepted by a vote in 2002. Hanspeter Kreisi and Alexander H. Trechsel, *The Politics of Switzerland*, pp. 31–3. Switzerland had joined the IMF and World Bank in 1992 after a referendum, and the WTO in 1995.

residents at 26.6 per cent (2010 figure, up from 21.9 in 2000).[17] But two-thirds come from the EU/EFTA states to which Switzerland formally opened its borders in the bilateral agreement of 2002, with a high proportion from Italy and Germany. They seem to have been assimilated without problems, even if a party resenting Italian day-workers crossing the border has grown up in recent years—ironically in the Italian-speaking cantons.[18] But the eventual influx of asylum-seekers from the Balkans, from Iraq, and from the Horn of Africa, produced a surge of anti-immigrant—and to some extent racist—feeling through the rise of the Swiss People's Party (SVP), which culminated in the 2007 electoral success, when it achieved the biggest vote share of any single-party (29 per cent) since 1919.[19]

Like many rich countries Switzerland has come to rely on immigrants to do menial jobs, without then being so willing to grant naturalization, even to their children, which leads to a form of parallel, even invisible, society. But since 9/11 the visibility of foreigners has increased, together with the pressures for regularization. This in turn has led to pressures for tighter immigration and asylum rules, with a focus by the SVP on the growing numbers of Muslims (probably between 4 and 5 per cent of the population) and their presumed impact on traditional Swiss culture.[20] One notable outcome of this campaign has been the ban on the construction of new minarets in the country, which was approved by 57 per cent of the population in a referendum in November 2009.[21] This despite the Federal government arguing that a ban would draw international condemnation from Muslims world-wide, and possibly expose the country to hostile measures.

This prediction turned out to be correct, but for reasons which were not just to do with minarets. The interplay between domestic and international factors took on an extra dimension through conflict with Libya, after the arrest of one of Colonel Gadaffi's sons in July 2008 for the apparent maltreatment of a hotel chambermaid. Multiculturalism would not have entered into the diplomatic row which followed, even allowing for the cynical behaviour of the Libyan leader in having two Swiss businessmen arraigned in Tripoli, and his call for the partition of Switzerland among its neighbours, had it not been for the ban on minarets. Gadaffi responded to this in February 2010 by referring to

[17] 'Stocks of Foreign-Born Population', OECD International Migration Outlook 2012, <www.oecd.org/els/internationalmigrationpoliciesanddata/internationalmigrationoutlook2011.htm> accessed 18 December 2012.

[18] *La Lega dei Ticinesi*, mirroring *La Lega Nord* across the border, <www.legaticinesi.ch/> accessed 20 December 2012.

[19] These data are taken from the very useful analysis in Julie Schindall's 'Switzerland's non-EU Immigrants: Their Integration and Swiss Attitudes', June 2009, <www.migrationinformation.org> accessed on 12 August 2011.

[20] 'The World Factbook: Switzerland', CIA, <https://www.cia.gov/library/publications/the-world-factbook/geos/sz.html#People> accessed 18 December 2012.

[21] Paul Scheffer, *Immigrant Nations* (Cambridge: Polity, 2011), p. 25.

Switzerland as the 'infidel harlot' and calling for a jihad against it 'by all means'.[22] The Swiss Embassy in Tripoli was besieged by police, and despite the presence of some EU ambassadors to demonstrate solidarity, the Swiss eventually surrendered the one businessman who had been given a prison sentence to the Libyan authorities.[23] The dispute spread, with Switzerland putting some Libyan nationals on the Schengen blacklist, and Gadaffi retaliating by refusing new entry visas to the citizens of all Schengen states, and imposing a full economic embargo on Switzerland. It was no surprise then that Berne was willing to compromise its neutrality by opening Swiss airspace to the coalition which intervened in Libya to protect Benghazi from Gadaffi's troops in March 2011.[24]

It is unlikely that Muammar Gadaffi's bizarre behaviour changed attitudes towards Islam in Switzerland or more widely—although it cannot have helped inter-faith relations. But what clearly did occur was a spiralling interaction between the internal Swiss arguments about minarets, immigration, and the unacceptable behaviour of an indulged foreigner, and foreign policy towards a Muslim country of some commercial significance. It also immediately drew in the EU, despite Switzerland's robust independence, given the sensitivities over relations with the Muslim world, and over the potential disruption to business—particularly oil.

The Swiss and Belgian cases show that states operating on the basis of consociationalism, that is, of a structural compromise between communities separated along broadly geographical lines, have their own inherent vulnerabilities to the external environment, and indeed that their very evolution has been governed by the need to cope with international politics. Moreover, on top of these accustomed dilemmas they now have the complications created by a less well-defined pattern of social diversity, created by a changing pattern of

[22] He is supposed to have said that 'Those who destroy God's mosques deserve to be attacked through jihad, and if Switzerland was on our borders, we would fight it', *Daily Telegraph*, 26 February 2010. See also Wikipedia on Libya–Switzerland relations, <http://en.wikipedia.org/wiki/Libya%E2%80%93Switzerland_relations> accessed 31 July 2012.

[23] Mr Göldi was released after four months and returned home immediately. It was subsequently confirmed, by the Swiss President Doris Leuthard no less, that the government had been considering a mission by special force commandoes to rescue him. *The Guardian*, 21 June 2010.

[24] Gadaffi's visa ban was rescinded after a month thanks to the good offices of Spain as EU President. But Mr Göldi had only been released after Switzerland had paid compensation of SFR 1.5million, ostensibly for the leaking of the police mugshots of Hannibal Gadaffi and his wife. See 'Looking Back at the Switzerland–Libya Dispute', *swissinfo.ch*, 3 December 2010, <http://www.swissinfo.ch/eng/politics/Looking_back_at_the_Switzerland-Libya_dispute.html?cid%20=%2028942506> accessed 31 July 2010. In mid-2010 the Swiss government had expected relations 'to normalise progressively', but had warned against all travel to Libya. 'Bilateral Relations between Switzerland and Libya', 12 July 2010 (the actual date given is 2011, but the content suggests this to be a typographical error), Federal Department of Foreign Affairs, Switzerland. The regular updating of the Foreign Ministry website means that this information is no longer accessible.

immigration. Newcomers are expected to fit in with civic nationalism—or not to expect rights. In these two cases—particularly Belgium, which has graver, constitutional, issues to face—the problems created so far have been relatively minor. But they provide significant pointers to the issues which can arise in states where multiculturality interacts with a pre-existing decentralized, even multinational, system. The EU contains three large states which fall into this category—Germany, Spain, and Italy—and it is to them we now turn.

Germany

As the biggest country and the most important economy in Europe, Germany is a critical site for the operation of multiculturalism, and for the future of international politics in the region. Yet Germany also occupies a unique position by virtue of its twentieth-century history, which makes it highly sensitive on issues relating to human rights and to minorities, while making others quick to comment at any sign—internal or external—of reviving German nationalism.

The reconstruction of German democracy in the form of the Federal Republic was designed to prevent a powerful central executive, and it thus privileged the role of the *Länder*. This produced, if not exactly a multinational state, then one in which the historically strong differences between the old German principalities re-emerged. The preeminent need to maintain national unity, and to create a new political culture, has meant that the differences, such as those between Bavarians and Rhinelanders, have been managed carefully, and with significant success. Even the process of unification, which began in 1990 and has entailed massive cross-subsidies and the absorption of nearly 17 million people, has not destabilized the German state. Although cultural differences clearly exist between the regions, and the 'Ossi/Wessi' fault-line remains, the impact of prosperity, a common language, and the evident success of 'modell Deutschland' has made federalism—as in the United States—a powerful force for unity, not division.[25] Nor do the *Länder* attempt to undercut federal foreign policy—although occasionally regional issues

[25] Via consensual and incremental change, as argued by Peter J. Katzenstein before unification, in his *Policy and Politics in Germany: The Growth of a Semisovereign State* (Philadelphia: Temple University Press, 1987). Since unification, Charlie Jeffrey has been said to argue that 'unification has made the German state more centralised and German society less homogeneous'. See Charlie Jeffrey, 'Federalism: The New Territorialism', and Peter J. Katzenstein, 'Conclusion: Semi-sovereignty in united German', both in Simon Green and William E. Paterson (eds), *Governance in Contemporary Germany: The Semisovereign State Revisited* (Cambridge: Cambridge University Press, 2005), pp. 7, 78–93, and 283–306. The particular quotation comes from p. 294.

cause difficulties with neighbouring states, as with the Bavarian Sudeten Deutsche and the Czech Republic in 1996–7.[26] Yet they are significantly involved by constitutional right in EU policy-making (short of the CFSP), and have certain rights of consultation with regard to federal treaty-making.[27] Moreover, as we shall see later, the domestic environment taken as a whole has a huge influence on how modern Germany behaves internationally, not least because, as Katzenstein has said, 'Since 1945, the interpenetration of domestic and foreign affairs has been constitutive of the Federal Republic: its state identity no less than the conduct of many of its policies.'[28] In principle, this means that the evolving nature of German civil society should have significant implications for the country's role in the world.

The most obvious changes in German society in recent decades have been wrought by immigration. As in Greece this has taken two forms: the influx of large numbers of people seen as sharing the same nationality, in this case ethnic Germans; and the entry of people coming from both outside the national community, and outside the European Union more widely. So far as the ethnic Germans, or *Aussiedler*, were concerned, they had a right of return and citizenship under the 1949 Basic Law. After 1990 (discounting the merger with East Germany), this produced large numbers of immigrants from eastern Europe and the ex-Soviet Union, to the extent that the FRG had to limit numbers according to birth-date and quotas, given the budgetary pressures on the *Länder*. Still, for every year from 1994–2003, the *Aussiedler* arrivals exceeded the applicants for asylum—despite the amount of public controversy attached to the latter.[29]

During the Cold War the foreign policy implications of the never-relinquished hope for unification ('two states, but one nation') and for repatriations were obvious: Bonn had to pursue a policy of never recognizing the

[26] Jürgen Hartmann, 'Organized Interests and Foreign Policy', in Wolf-Dieter Eberwein and Karl Kaiser (eds), *Germany's New Foreign Policy: Decision-making in an Interdependent World* (Houndmills: Palgrave, 2001), p. 275.

[27] See Uwe Leonardy, 'Federation and *Länder* in German Foreign Relations: Power-sharing in Treaty-making and European Affairs', in Brian Hocking (ed.), *Foreign Relations and Federal States* (London: Leicester University Press, 1993), pp. 236–51. Also Michèle Knodt, 'External Representation of German *Länder* Interests', in Eberwein and Kaiser (eds), *Germany's New Foreign Policy*, pp. 173–88.

[28] In Green and Paterson (eds), *Governance in Contemporary Germany*, p. 305.

[29] See Table 9.1 'Immigration and the non-national population in Germany, 1990–2003', in Simon Green, 'Immigration and Integration Policy: Between Incrementalism and Non-decisions', in Green and Paterson (eds), *Governance in Contemporary Germany*, p. 194. Compare Table 1 'Admission of Asylum Seekers and Ethnic Germans, 1980–1992', in Thomas Faist, 'How to Define a Foreigner? The Symbolic Politics of Immigration in German Partisan Discourse, 1978–1992', in Martin Baldwin-Edwards and Martin A. Schain (eds), *The Politics of Immigration in Western Europe* (Ilford: Frank Cass, 1994), p. 53, which shows both that the ethnic Germans arrived in steady numbers throughout the Cold War, and that their numbers shot up from 1987 on.

permanent exile of ethnic Germans, but also of promoting detente to the extent that family ties could be improved. From the mid-1990s, concern shifted towards managing the *Aussiedler* influx, which required agreements, and thus effective diplomatic relations, with Russia and the ex-Soviet republics. It also encouraged the view that the eastern enlargement of the EU should be pushed on as quickly as possible, even if there were other, more powerful motives for that policy.

The outcome of immigration from outside the EU has been similar to that in Belgium and Switzerland, in that it has produced a significant element of multiculturality, which now rests like a skein over the spatial structure of the federal state. From time to time this has led to fierce debates over multiculturalism, which have been fundamentally confused because the latter has never been launched as a 'state doctrine' (or what in this book is termed a 'project') in Germany.[30] Some have hoped that a rainbow society might emerge, as has been tried elsewhere, just as others have feared the very prospect. Chancellor Merkel, making common cause with Nicolas Sarkozy and David Cameron, went so far as to declare the (non-) experiment dead.[31] In practice the German state has not directly faced the issue of whether to pursue republican integration along French lines or explicit multiculturalism on, say, the Canadian model. Rather, it has taken refuge in the idea of a cultural unity derived from an historical sense of Germanness, yet without admitting until late in the proceedings that the population had come to contain at least seven million people who do not conform to this notion (through their citizenship, language, religion, or a combination of characteristics), or even that Germany had become a country of immigration.

The political elite continued to insist that Germany was *kein Einwanderungsland* (not an immigration country) up until 2001, when Interior Minister Otto Schily made a symbolically important declaration to the contrary. Yet by 1977, when the policy was first enunciated, four million foreign immigrants had already arrived![32] Provisional figures for December 2010 give a conservative figure of 81.8 million for the total German population, of which 7.2 million, or 8.8 per cent, are foreigners, mostly concentrated in the urban

[30] This highly appropriate term, perhaps more for Germany than for states without such a tradition of legal theories of the state, comes from Armin Nassehi (ed.), *Nation, Ethnie, Minderheit. Beiträge zur Aktualität ethnischer Konflikte* (Cologne: Bohlau, 1997), pp. 17–208, cited in Stephan Lanz, 'The German Sonderweg: Multiculturalism as "Racism with a Distance"', in Alessandro Silj (ed.), *European Multiculturalism Revisited* (London: Zed Books, 2010), p. 105.

[31] 'Merkel Says German Multicultural Society has Failed', BBC News online, 17 October 2010, <www.bbc.co.uk/news/world-europe-11559451> accessed 15 August 2011.

[32] For tables showing the growth of the numbers of foreigners in Germany from 1951–2006, and the size of the Turkish minority, Ayhan Kaya, *Islam, Migration and Integration: The Age of Securitization* (Houndmills: Palgrave Macmillan, 2009), pp. 41–2.

areas, and in the old West Germany.[33] The latter is a higher figure than it might be because of protracted naturalization procedures, despite reforms over the last decade. Thus members of second and even third generation immigrant families who in other countries would automatically have become national citizens are still classed as outsiders—a condition which they feel and resent. Furthermore, although the new Citizenship Law of 2000 did introduce a more humane approach, it was soon counter-acted by the effects of 9/11, so that naturalization applications now have to pass scrutiny by the Federal Office for the Protection of the Constitution (i.e. the security services), which since the Munich Olympics of 1972 has dealt as much with the threat posed by foreign nationals on German soil as with home-grown subversives.[34] Furthermore attitudes towards both general immigration and asylum seekers have become much more restrictive with the double effect of recession and social tensions.

As in many other countries, the German debate about immigration has partly been driven by concerns over jobs and partly by resentments, real and imagined, about changes to the 'German way of life'. In relation to the latter, the impact of Muslim incomers has taken centre stage, regardless of the powerful impact of other factors such as economic globalization (changes to trading hours) and secularization (the decline in church-going). Part of the problem lies in the distinction made throughout the Cold War between those immigrants who were returning Germans, and the 'guest-workers' who were imported to fuel the economic miracle, but on a rotating basis to ensure that individuals did not settle. Some have argued that this represents continuity with pre-1939 Germany in its inherent suspicion of the foreigner. The 1949 Basic Law does not allow for foreigners to be part of *das Volk*, or the sovereign people, while German citizenship was based until the 1990s on a mixture of descent (the *ius sanguinis*) and culture. Even after 2000, when a new citizenship law made provision for the place of birth as a criterion for naturalization (i.e. moving towards a *ius solis*), the notion of an organic, national German community which outsiders could only become part of over several generations, remained powerful, with the result that naturalization levels have remained relatively low.[35] Furthermore, social and labour mobility remains restricted, especially for those whose religion, skin colour, or customs make it particularly difficult to acquire Germanness.[36] A certain amount of progress

[33] Federal Statistical Office, and the Statistical Offices of the *Länder*, 31 December 2010, <https://www.destatis.de/EN/FactsFigures/SocietyState/Population/CurrentPopulation/Tables/PopulationBysexCitizenship.html> accessed 31 July 2012. It should be noted that the 'foreign-born' population is much higher, at 12.9 per cent, presumably through the return of ethnic Germans from the old communist bloc.

[34] Lanz, 'The German Sonderweg', p. 128.

[35] Green, 'Immigration and Integration Policy', p. 191.

[36] According to Karen Schönwalder, migrants are in 'a disastrous educational and labour market situation'. Karen Schönwalder, 'Germany: Integration Policy and Pluralism in a

has finally been made, as with the celebration of the impact of players of Turkish descent on the national football team's performances during the 2006 World Cup in Germany, but this is largely tokenism. Similarly, while the language of multiculturalism was common in Germany, its usual meaning was merely multiculturality and was in any case set back by the Sarrazin affair and the pronouncements of Chancellor Merkel (see pp. 111, 106). Germany tends to oscillate between an imagined multiculturalism and a *de facto* preference for integrationism.

The largest group of foreigners in Germany is composed of Turks, most of whom arrived as guest-workers but stayed on to make a family life. In 2009 there were 1,658,083 Turkish citizens present, compared to 517,474 Italians, the next biggest group. Since the next largest community of Muslim residents is from Bosnia, at 154,565, it is clear that in Germany, Turkish tends to mean Muslim, and vice versa.[37] Moreover, this figure understates the number of people of Turkish origin in Germany, which is around three million.[38] This matters because of majority perceptions of difference. Despite its economic indispensability, and the fact that it is not prone to fundamentalism, the Turkish community has been the focus of considerable criticism for a perceived unwillingness to integrate. At worst this has led to racist fire-bombings and the deaths of innocent people, especially in the eastern *Länder*, which have been less accustomed to cosmopolitanism.

Given Germany's continued prosperity, and the fact that it has not suffered terrorist attacks of the kind inflicted on Madrid and London, this degree of hostility can only be ascribed to resentment at the changing appearance of life in parts of some cities, and to a generalized anxiety about the future. It is not helped by the fact that *qua* state Germany has not prioritized the linked problems of immigration, citizenship, and social diversity. Accordingly this is the one area in which consensus has not easily emerged. The country has experienced one massive phase of change since 1945 and is perhaps not yet ready to face another. The famous incrementalism of Katzenstein's 'semi-sovereign state' has indeed been disjointed, a means of muddling through. Rather than insist on any one of integration, repatriation, or multiculturalism, it has produced—without really meaning to—'parallel societies'. This term—which originated in the Poland of *Solidarnosc* to describe the reality beneath

Self-Conscious Country of Immigration', in Vertovec and Wessendorf (eds), *The Multiculturalism Backlash*, pp. 152–69.

[37] *Statistisches Jahrbuch 2010* (Wiesbaden: Statistisches Bundesamt, September 2010), Table 2.20: 'Ausländische Bevölkerung in Deutschland', <https://www.destatis.de/DE/Publikationen/StatistischesJahrbuch/StatistischesJahrbuch2010.pdf?__blob%20=%20publicationFile> accessed 18 March 2013.

[38] Speech by Foreign Minister Guido Westerwelle, at the opening of the new Turkish Embassy in Berlin, 30 October 2012, <http://www.auswaertiges-amt.de/EN/Infoservice/Presse/Reden/2012/121030-BM_TUR_Botschaft.html> accessed 18 December 2012.

the surface of communism but became well known in Germany after Heitmeyer's article[39]—is not used here in the pejorative sense which became common in the German debate, and of which many complain. Rather, it is used as an analytical device to describe what seems to have occurred inside the country—and to a degree, the other states discussed in this chapter—whereby minorities have been neither integrated nor given special rights, but largely left to their own devices. In this sense 'parallelism' is not a matter of self-chosen or even imposed apartheid, but a mere consequence of the tunnel vision of successive governments which have found the matter too difficult to engage with.

Germany continues to be a social market economy with a strongly corporatist policy system in which economic interest-groups and the *Länder* play prominent parts. But since it is also predicated on the ethnocultural continuity of Germanness, minorities have remained very much on the margins. Their interest-groups find access to policy-making difficult, with even the large and long-established Turkish community lacking the kind of voice which it would have in the United States.[40] The barriers to citizenship also prevent them acquiring power as voters. Yet, paradoxically, this does not mean that they are irrelevant to Germany's external role, for some rather particular reasons.

Firstly, as signalled earlier, modern German foreign policy is profoundly affected by its domestic base in a normative sense. The education of the new generations after 1945 has almost worked too well in fostering a deep aversion to any kind of serious commitment overseas, and in particular to the use of force. Even the arrival of the 'responsibility to protect' arguments at the UN, which led Joschka Fischer to add 'never again Auschwitz' to the familiar mantra 'never again war', has only modified this pacifism, not changed it. On the other hand, human rights thinking, including support for national self-determination movements, is also part of the mentality created by the new model of German democracy. This, together with war-guilt, has produced persistent support for Israel, over and above that seen in most other EU states, and agonizing over the issues of recognition and human rights during the break-up of Yugoslavia in 1991—during which the sizeable Croat community, especially in Catholic southern Germany, was particularly vocal.[41] But it led to

[39] See footnote 1 in this chapter, and also Henryk M. Broder, 'What's So Bad About Parallel Societies?' *SpiegelOnline International*, 20 October 2010, accessed 14 August 2011.

[40] According to Hartmann, organized interests only influence the 'welfare and legitimacy function of foreign policy' in Germany. 'Their influence over security policy and "traditional" diplomacy is, by contrast, extremely minor'. Jürgen Hartmann, 'Organized Interests and Foreign Policy', p. 275. This is not quite the view of Eva Østergaard-Nielsen, who argues that Turks and Kurds inside Germany have constantly pressed on matters of high politics to do with events inside Turkey, albeit without much success because of their very status as 'outsiders'. Eva Østergaard-Nielsen, *Transnational Politics: Turks and Kurds in Germany* (London: Routledge, 2003), pp. 83–4.

[41] There is much controversy over both the German recognition of Croatia in December 1991 and the impact of Croats on German policy. What seems clear, however, is that domestic factors

hand-wringing in 2009 when the US asked Germany to accept nine Uighur Muslims released from Guantánamo, on the grounds that Munich has one of the biggest Uighur communities outside Asia. Although the Uighurs are ethnically Turkish, and thus close to Germany's main minority, Berlin was unwilling to further complicate already difficult relations with China on the Uighurs.[42]

Secondly, the large Turkish community has clearly influenced German policy towards Turkey. The difficult issue of Ankara's policy towards its own Kurdish minority, combined with the co-existence of Kurds and Turks within Germany, has gradually made Berlin exercise more caution, and avoid some of the stronger positions on Turkey's human rights which characterized policy in the 1980s and 1990s.[43] This is despite the relevance of the latter for the possible accession of Turkey itself to the EU, on which Germany has gradually taken a more negative stance. Although the SPD–Green coalition of 1998–2005 took a sympathetic view of Turkish entry, in line with its generally cosmopolitan outlook, it did not do anything to promote accession, being well aware of the mounting popular unease over immigration, and in particular of the potential impact on the single European market of being opened to a poor country of over seventy million people. The conservative government of Angela Merkel which followed has had no scruples in opposing Turkey's full membership, although it has been vague about the reasons.[44]

As a result of both this and the position of the *Gastarbeiter* (as they are often still called, revealingly), relations between the two countries have become strained. Recip Tayyip Erdoğan, Turkey's prime minister, went so far on a visit to Germany as to talk of his 'growing unease' about the treatment of his compatriots, and to advise them to learn Turkish before German, thus resisting the assimilationist interpretation of 'integration'.[45] This was in marked contrast to his emollient behaviour in Greece, referred to in Chapter 3.[46] Erdogan was partly playing to his own domestic audience, and

in Germany were thought at the time to be playing an important part. David Owen, *Balkan Odyssey* (London: Indigo/Gollancz 1996), pp. 201–2.

[42] The World Uighur Congress is based in Munich. 'German Foreign Minister Opposes Taking Uighur Guantánamo Inmates', *SpiegelOnline International*, 18 May 2009, <www.spiegel.de/international/germany/0,1518,625453,00.html> accessed 16 August 2010. On the other hand, Berlin had not been afraid to expel a Chinese diplomat in 2007, and later to expose four Chinese civilians, for suspected spying on the Uighurs. See 'Germany Suspects China of Spying on Uighur Expatriates', *SpiegelOnline International*, 24 November 2009, <www.spiegel.de/international/germany/police-raid-in-munich-germany-suspects-china-of-spying-on-uighur-expatriates-a-663090.html> accessed 1 August 2012.

[43] Eva Østergaard-Nielsen, *Transnational Politics*, pp. 131–2.

[44] However, Foreign Minister Westerwelle did sign the foreign ministers' letter of 28 June 2012 calling for a reinvigoration of the accession process. See Chapter 2, footnote 53.

[45] Helen Pidd, 'Erdogan Tells Turks to Resist Assimilation into German Society', *The Guardian*, 1 March 2011.

[46] See p. 94. It was not the first time that an Erdogan visit to Germany had constituted a blunt intervention in internal affairs. In February 2008 he had called assimilation a 'crime against

seeking votes from the diaspora, but he was also reacting to Merkel's statement in 2010 that 'multi-kulti' had failed, and to the storm whipped up by the provocative remarks of Thilo Sarrazin.[47] Sarrazin had to resign from the Executive Board of the Bundesbank after saying in public that 'no immigrant group other than Muslims [i.e. Turks] is so strongly connected with claims on the welfare state and crime', before going on to publish what became the best-selling politics book in Germany of the new century.[48] His argument that only those willing to make an effort to integrate should be allowed into Germany clearly struck a chord with many. Erdogan's own statement produced an immediate counter from the German foreign minister Guido Westerwelle on the importance of children learning German as their first language.[49] What was perhaps most interesting about the exchanges, however, was their belatedness. In comparison to other countries Germany is only just beginning to have an open debate about diversity.[50]

Once provocations issue from any quarter about minorities in the post 9/11 environment, concerns about terrorism are never far behind. In the German case the Palestinian attacks on Israelis at the 1972 Olympics left a deep scar, not least as the subsequent domestic terrorism of the Red Army Faction (RAF) was explicitly linked to the Palestinian cause. Moreover, in 1986 the bomb attack on US servicemen at the La Belle discotheque in Berlin was judged by the US to have been ordered in Libya. The subsequent US raid on Tripoli was followed by the sabotage in December 1988 of Pan Am flight 103, which crashed at Lockerbie but originated in Frankfurt, where Libyan agents or sympathizers seem to have planted the bomb. In the early 1990s there were violent demonstrations by Kurds (who constitute almost one-third of the 'Turkish' guest-worker population) in Germany against the Turkish government.[51] Thus the discovery that many of the 9/11 hijackers, led by Mohammed Atta, had lived and planned their attacks in Hamburg, fitted into a set of perceptions about the immigrant community acting as the sea in which

humanity'. 'Erdogan's Visit Leaves German Conservatives Fuming', *SpeigelOnline International*, 12 February 2008, <www.spiegel.de/international/germany/the-world-from-berlin-erdogan-s-visit-leaves-german-conservatives-fuming-a-534724.html> accessed 20 December 2011.

[47] 'Merkel Says German Multicultural Society has Failed', BBC News online, 17 October 2010, <www.bbc.co.uk/news/world-europe-11559451> accessed 20 December 2012.

[48] Thilo Sarrazin, *Deutschland schafft sich ab: Wie wir unser Land aufs Spiel setzen* (Munich: Deutsche Verlags-Anstalt, 2010). The title translates as, 'Germany is Doing Away with Itself: How Our Country is at Risk'). The book has sold well over one million copies, and the first edition sold out immediately. On the furore it provoked see Patrik Schwarz (ed.), *Die Sarrazin Debatte. Eine Provokation—alle Antworten* (Hamburg: Die Zeit, 2010).

[49] *The Guardian*, 1 March 2011.

[50] 'Compared with France's two decades of openly conducted political debate surrounding Islam, there has been much less of it in Germany', Christian Joppke, *Veil: Mirror of Identity* (Cambridge: Polity, 2009), p. 54.

[51] Green, 'Immigration and Integration Policy', p. 202.

dangerous fish were swimming. Despite the fact that the victims of racial violence in Germany have almost exclusively been Turks, events elsewhere, such as the murder of Theo van Gogh in Holland, also had a big impact.[52] Security measures, immigration controls, and measures against 'hate preachers' in Mosques have increased steadily over the last decade.[53]

The lack, so far, of any attempt at official levels to think seriously about what kind of society Germany should become once the reality of immigration has been recognized, has created, *de facto*, two parallel societies. The evasion of the problem has obvious disadvantages, but—together with the eschewing of foreign wars—it has enabled Germany to stay beneath the radar internationally. Non-decisions, or at least varied practices, as with the *Länder* and the issue of the veil, have meant avoiding too much acrimony and foreign interference. On the other hand, such quietism, combined with large Muslim zones in the bigger cities, has attracted a minority of (non-Turkish) jihadists in need of the anonymity in which to pursue their plans for attacks elsewhere.[54] The authorities have now caught up with this trend, just as the Turkish government has woken up to what it sees as structural discrimination against the *Gastarbeiter*.

Thus the period in which the connections between the issue of diversity at home and Germany's increasingly important foreign policy have been mostly indirect and undramatic, may be coming to an end. Even so, the unusually dominant place of the Turks among Germany's minorities, and their lack up to now of much interest in international affairs (beyond the issue of relations with Turkey), may continue to protect the Federal Republic from the difficult linkages experienced by other Member States.[55] It also makes it easier for the state to continue its belated groping towards a conception of the national interest, just when Britain and France, for example, are having to rethink their traditional reliance on the concept.

Spain

Like Germany, Spain has spent much of its recent history in the process of democracy-building. It also shares a decentralized state structure. Yet there are certain important differences. Unlike Germany, Spain has a long history of unity, and (between 1492 and 1898) of global and colonial power. It is also a

[52] Scheffer, *Immigrant Nations*, p. 161.

[53] Lanz, 'The German Sonderweg', pp. 128 and 132–3.

[54] According to one report of 'security service estimates' there were 36,270 German Muslims who supported 'Islamist aims' in 2009, with 200 'hard-core "jihadists"'. Ian Traynor, 'Hamburg Mosque which Links 9/11 to the Badlands of Pakistan', *The Guardian*, 8 October 2010. But such figures are suspiciously precise and notoriously unreliable.

[55] Joppke, *Veil*, pp. 59–60.

plurinational state, allowing regions and 'historical nationalities' which retain the right to use their own languages (Catalonia, Galicia, and the Basque country) to co-exist in a quasi-federal, asymmetrical structure based on 'autonomous communities'.[56] Spain also came much later to democracy than Germany, having been ostracized by most of Europe during the rule of General Franco, up until his death in 1975. Taking a comparative perspective, the history of Spain over the last thirty-five years amounts to little short of a miracle, given the challenge of creating and consolidating a democratic system for the first time in an environment of tension between central government and the regions, as well as massive social change, much of it unwelcome to the powerful Catholic church.

Separatist tendencies have been a perpetual concern. They have been expressed peaceably through enthusiasm in many quarters for the idea of a 'Europe of the regions', with states losing their rationale and the European Union providing a framework in which sub-national units can flourish. But at times they have also resorted to violence, most notably through the terrorist activities of ETA. The outcome has been a surprisingly stable nation-state, despite the contestation of Spanish nationhood. Nonetheless, separatism is a perpetual problem for governments in Madrid and links all too readily with foreign policy, as with the reluctance to recognize the independence of the Baltic states in 1991, and the continued refusal to recognize Kosovo. Both cases have awakened fears of fragmentation within Spain, and indeed have sharpened the sense of entitlement on the part of Catalan and Basque nationalists.[57] Spain's steady move towards a more cautious, even-handed approach towards the Israel–Palestinian dispute is probably also conditioned by its own sensitivity over issues of self-determination.

On top of these issues, like the other states discussed in this chapter Spain has experienced the arrival of a new kind of diversity over the last two decades, cutting across its regional structure. Until the last years of the twentieth century Spain did not see itself as a country of immigration, given the centuries of movement towards the New World, and the outflow of political refugees under Franco. Even after outsiders began to see the newly vibrant country—and member of the EU from 1986—as an attractive destination, the reaction inside Spain was largely positive. Hard-working and inexpensive migrant labour was sought to fuel economic growth, particularly in the agricultural and tourist sectors. Furthermore, many new arrivals came from Latin America, being therefore perceived as already part of *Hispanidad* (the

[56] See Michael Keating, *Federalism and the Balance of Power in European States* (Paris: OECD SIGMA Programme, 2006), pp. 22–5.

[57] Victor de la Serna, 'Baltic Factor Teases Spain', *The European*, 13–15 September 1991; Esther Barbé, 'Spain and Europe: Mutual Reinforcement in Foreign Policy', in Reuben Wong and Christopher Hill (eds), *National and European Foreign Policies: Towards Europeanization* (London: Routledge, 2011), pp. 133, 137–9, and 148.

world Hispanic community) and halfway to integration already. It was only the combination of economic difficulties, a more diverse intake, especially from Muslim countries, and the impact of 9/11 which eventually produced a wave of concern about immigration and some foreign policy ramifications.

On the other side of the coin the continuing reaction to the authoritarianism and isolation from the world of the period 1939–75 meant that many in Spanish society were sympathetic to asylum-seekers and to poor economic migrants, so that the emergence of an anti-foreigners movement on Swedish or Swiss lines was forestalled—not least because Spain's mainstream conservatives had already taken the name of the People's Party (PP).[58] The PP government itself did not play the anti-immigration card as conservatives have done elsewhere. In 2001 its Foreign Minister was still talking of 'the shortage of labour and the need to assure a certain influx of immigration'—although he added some cautious caveats about the need to discuss the cultural implications of immigration and the fact that 'we do not wish to have separate communities'.[59] Five years later, in the United States, José Maria Aznar declared that multiculturalism was Europe's most complicated problem, and that it favoured neither tolerance nor integration, but by then he was in opposition and immersed in the arguments about terrorism and the war in Iraq.[60]

In fact, although Spanish governments faced up to the reality of being an immigration country in 1991 as soon as the change became apparent—while official German heads were still stuck in the sand—it must be emphasized that the country never adopted multiculturalism as state policy. This is in part because of the very rapid and recent change in the number of foreigners living in Spain and in part because the range of their diversity has not been so great as in other states, and thus not yet sufficient to distract from the challenge of establishing Spanishness against regional nationalisms.

In terms of numbers, foreigners amounted to 0.7 per cent of the population of Spain in 1990, as opposed to 6.3 per cent in France, 4.6 per cent in the Netherlands, and 8.8 per cent in Germany. This figure had risen to 2 per cent by the year 2000—an increase from 278,700 to 801,300 in absolute

[58] Geddes, *The Politics of Migration and Immigration in Europe*, p. 164. The *Partido Popular*, under José Maria Aznar, governed Spain from 1996–2004. Spanish flexibility may have its limits, however. According to one study, 'ethnic tolerance' in the country ranked well below the EU15 average in 2002, although measurement in such matters is notoriously difficult. Jan Zielonka, *Europe as Empire: The Nature of the Enlarged European Union* (Oxford: Oxford University Press, 2006), pp. 79–82.

[59] Josep Piqué i Camps, 'Spanish Foreign Policy at the Turn of the Century' (lecture at the London School of Economics and Political Science, 24 January 2001), text released by Spanish Embassy, London.

[60] *The Tocqueville Connection*, 'Multiculturalism "a Big Failure": Spain's Ex-prime Minister Aznar', 27 October 2006, 'Aznar: "El Multiculturalismo divide e debilita los sociedades"', <http://www.20minutos.es/noticia/166754/0/Aznar/declaraciones/multiculturalismo/> accessed 18 March 2013 (my translation).

numbers—in a population of just over forty million.[61] The rate of increase then accelerated dramatically. By 2005 the number of foreign residents had reached 3.5 million and by 2007 was over 4.5 million, or almost exactly 10 per cent of the then population of 44.5 million.[62] This represents both a higher proportion than in France, Germany, and the UK, and an extraordinary rate of increase.

That there has been relatively little social unrest associated with this momentous change has, as indicated, partly been because it has not introduced a proportionate degree of ethnocultural diversity, with its potentially loosening effect on community cohesion. In 1998 about half of all immigrants came from developed countries, such as Spain's partners in the EU and EFTA, whose citizens may be assumed to share some values with their host country, and not to make dramatic demands on social services.[63] A significant number of Moroccans and other Africans made up the majority of the remainder. In the first seven years of the new century, however, the relative importance of these two groups diminished, with a rise in the number coming first from the Andean countries of Colombia, Ecuador, Peru, and Bolivia, and later from eastern Europe, particularly Romania.[64] The detailed survey conducted by ENI (Encuesta Nacional de Inmigrantes—the National Survey of Immigrants) for Spain's National Statistical Office (which has been particularly active in monitoring the profile and experiences of immigrants) shows that 80 per cent of incomers had already had some kind of 'contact' with Spain before their arrival.[65] 'Contact' means primarily links with family or friends in Spain, but could also refer to requests from employers.[66] Furthermore, 22 per cent of immigrants already held a Spanish passport, with around 40 per cent of the total coming from Latin America. Almost another 40 per cent arrived from the EU and other developed countries, with the remaining 20 per cent coming from the rest of the world, and in particular from the Maghreb and sub-Saharan African.[67]

[61] Table 1.3: 'Stocks of Foreign Population in Selected European Countries', in Geddes, *The Politics of Migration and Immigration in Europe*, pp. 12–13.

[62] See the detailed data and indispensable analysis in David-Sven Reher et al., *Informe Encuesta Nacional de Inmigrantes (ENI-2007)* Documentos de Trabajo 2/2008 (Madrid, April 2008), especially pp. 7–13, <www.ine.es/daco/daco42/inmigrantes/informe/eni07_informe.pdf> accessed 20 January 2013. Also the brief survey available for 2009, *Encuesta Nacional de Inmigrantes* (Boletin Informativo del Instituto nacional de Estadistica, Madrid, 1/2009), <www.ine.es/revistas/cifraine/0109.pdf> accessed 19 August 2011.

[63] Reher et al., *Informe Encuesta Nacional de Inmigrantes*, pp. 8 and 20. This is not to say that prejudices and suspicions do not exist about fellow EU citizens, as the treatment of the Roma, and the controversy about the 'Polish plumber' indicate.

[64] Reher et al., *Informe Encuesta Nacional de Inmigrantes*, pp. 8 and 20.

[65] *Encuesta Nacional de Inmigrantes*. 45 per cent of immigrants spoke Spanish as their mother-tongue.

[66] Reher et al., *Informe Encuesta Nacional de Inmigrantes*, p. 140.

[67] Reher et al., *Informe Encuesta Nacional de Inmigrantes*. Figure 1.2 'Extranjeros por nacionalidad en España', p. 9. See also p. 138, and Table A.2 'Nacidos en le extranjero según el país de nacimiento, la tipologia migratoria, el sexo, la edad media y el año de llegada', pp. 143–4.

Thus the ENI report concludes that 'it is evident that Spain has *foreigners* and it has *immigrants*. The differences observed are so strong as to make us wary of using the same term for both groups'.[68] The overall pattern shows entry from,

> a relatively limited number of countries, above all if we compare Spain with other European nations . . . This reduced variety of origins can be an advantage in some contexts (for example, in the presence of many people with a culture not so far distant from that of the Spanish) but also a disadvantage in others (in making more difficult the process of assimilation of numerous groups with a high level of internal cohesion).[69]

It is too early to tell whether the advantages of these limits on diversity will outweigh the disadvantages, but clearly Spain faces choices, over whether: (1) to accept 'the tendency of all immigrants to organise themselves in networks';[70] (2) to pursue an active policy of integration for all ethnic groups; (3) primarily to encourage Hispanic arrivals, who would merge into existing society without great difficulties.[71] Behind these choices lurk the general issues of multiculturalism and Otherness, and in particular the historic preoccupation in Spain with relations between Catholics and Muslims.

Spain's encounter with Islam has been the most profound of any major European state. After the successful invasion of 711 the Iberian peninsula was occupied by the Moors at least in part until 1492, with a legacy which can still be seen in the magnificent architecture of Córdoba and Granada. The creation of a modern unified Spain under the 'Catholic monarchs' of the sixteenth century was associated with the expulsion of Muslims (and, indeed, of the Jews), and finally in the first part of the seventeenth century of the Moriscos. These were Muslims who had been forced to convert in order to avoid expulsion, but whose presence had come to be seen as a possible fifth column which could be exploited by the neighbouring Ottoman empire.[72]

Proximity to the Muslim world continued to be of critical importance to Spain, not least through the possession of the North African enclaves of Ceuta and Melilla, which remain in Spanish hands today. In 1912 Madrid occupied the northern coastal parts of what is now Morocco, which remained a colony

[68] Reher et al., *Informe Encuesta Nacional de Inmigrantes*, p. 137. (My translation, but emphasis in the original.)

[69] Reher et al., *Informe Encuesta Nacional de Inmigrantes*, p. 136. (My translation.)

[70] Reher et al., *Informe Encuesta Nacional de Inmigrantes*, p. 11.

[71] Zapata-Barrero argues that it has been explicit policy to prefer immigrants from Eastern Europe and Latin America over Moroccans since the race riots of 2000. Ricard Zapata-Barrero, 'The Muslim Community and Spanish Tradition: Maurophobia as a Fact, and Impartiality as a Desideratum', in Modood, Triandafyllidou, and Zapata-Barrero (eds), *Multiculturalism, Muslims and Citizenship*, p. 147.

[72] David Abulafia, *The Great Sea: A Human History of the Mediterranean* (London: Allen Lane, 2011), pp. 470–6; J. H. Elliott, *Europe Divided 1559–1598* (London: Collins Fontana, 1968), pp. 186–9. The Ottomans in fact abandoned the Moriscos to their fate in an episode of what we now call ethnic cleansing.

until 1956. It was from there that General Franco launched his revolt against the Republic in 1936 which began the Civil War and ushered in forty years of authoritarian rule.

Thus modern Spain has an intimate and deeply ambivalent relationship with the Muslim world and particularly with the neighbouring territories of the Maghreb. It is revealing that the first visit to a foreign country of all four of Felipe González, José Maria Aznar, José Luis Rodriguez Zapatero, and Mariano Rajoy as newly elected prime ministers was to Rabat.[73] Spain is sensitive about the issue of illegal immigration across the straits of Gibraltar, knowing that it cannot be controlled without the cooperation of Morocco.[74] Indeed there are wider issues of security on the southern flank, as shown by the armed dispute with Morocco over the island of Perejil in 2002, the long-running conflict in its ex-colony of Western Sahara, and the fears of the Islamic fundamentalism spreading through North Africa.[75]

The bombing of the Atocha station on 11 March 2004, which killed 192 commuters and wounded nearly 2,000, was Europe's 9/11, and indeed it is known in Spain as '11-M'. Occurring only three days before a general election in which one key issue was the presence of Spanish troops in Iraq, it created controversy over foreign policy, party differences, and vulnerability to terrorism. Huge demonstrations immediately followed the bombs. The subsequent investigations by police and judicial authorities led to the deaths of four suspects in a siege, and the convictions of twenty-one more. These were almost all Muslims, and mostly from Moroccan backgrounds. It is still not clear who ultimately inspired and resourced the attacks, but al-Qaeda seems to have been their inspiration if not their author. In the immediate aftermath of the bombings the PP government blamed ETA, and instructed its diplomats to hold to this line. This proved impossible to sustain, so that the subsequent victory of the Socialists under Zapatero (the PSOE) owed a good deal to the general perception of the Aznar government's dishonesty and incompetence on the matter. The Socialists had promised to withdraw Spanish troops from Iraq in the event of their victory, a promise which they kept. It seems unlikely, however, that the bombings frightened the Spanish people into voting for the PSOE, given the pre-existing hostility of public opinion to the war in Iraq, and the relatively narrow margin of Zapatero's win.

[73] Paul Kennedy, 'Spain', in Ian Manners and Richard Whitman (eds), *The Foreign Policies of European Union Member States* (Manchester: Manchester University Press, 2000), p. 120. In the case of Zapatero the visit took place less than two weeks after the Madrid bombings. 'Spain Visit Boosts Moroccan Ties', BBC News website, 24 April 2004, <http://news.bbc.co.uk/1/hi/world/europe/3654943.stm> accessed 2 August 2012. Also 'Mariano Rajoy en Marruecos: un beso a la llegada, dos al marcharse', *El País*, 21 January 2012.

[74] Charles Powell, 'Dalla A(znar) alla Z(apatero)', *Aspenia*, 34 (Rome: Rivista of the Aspen Institute, Italy, 2006), pp. 200–8.

[75] Esther Barbé, 'Spain and Europe', pp. 142–4.

Spain had been used to terrorism through the activities of ETA, but not anything on the Atocha scale. It had also been used to the impact of transnational criminality, through the vulnerability of the southern coasts to intruders and the existence of the 'Costa del crime', home to hardened gangsters of many nationalities. This may explain the surprising lack of uproar over the presence of jihadist 'sleepers' in Spanish society. Nonetheless, the Zapatero government showed itself extremely concerned about the possibility of a recurrence, and pursued a policy of attempting to build bridges with the Muslim world—although it kept troops in Afghanistan, albeit in a low-key role, as a symbol of its commitment to the struggle against terrorism, in which Spanish democracy had been engaged since its creation.[76] Later in 2004, at the UN General Assembly, Zapatero called for 'an Alliance of Civilisations between the Western and the Arab and Muslim worlds', explicitly designed to avoid the 'clash of civilisations' predicted by Samuel Huntington.[77] This entailed commissioning a report from a 'High-Level Group' of eminent persons, in conjunction with the UN Secretary-General and Prime Minister Erdogan of Turkey, on what practical ways might be found to combat extremism.[78] What was particularly notable about this reaction was that while Spain was naturally increasing its cooperation on anti-terrorist measures with sympathetic states, it was also explicitly reaching out to the largest Muslim country in the Mediterranean region, and one aiming to join the EU, rather than—as it might have done—withdrawing into a stance of suspicion towards Islam and Muslim immigration. Spain's consistent support for Turkish accession thus derives *from* its relationship with Islam, rather than being pursued despite it.[79]

A constructive attitude towards the Muslim world did not mean, however, that Spain was unconcerned about immigration. As numbers began to rise in the first few years of the new century, and especially after the attacks in the

[76] Edward Burke, 'Spain's War in Afghanistan', FRIDE Policy Brief 23 (Madrid, Fundación para las Relaciones Internacionales y el Diálogo Exterior [FRIDE], January 2010). Spain kept no more than 1,500 troops in Afghanistan, with a mostly logistical role, and resisted US pressure for combat involvement. In June 2011 it announced a phased withdrawal, to be completed by 2014.

[77] 'Speech by the President of the Government of Spain, 59th Period of Sessions of the United Nations General Assembly', and 'Initiative by the Spanish Government for an Alliance of Civilizations, Memorandum 2004', both contained in the collection of documents entitled *Alliance of Civilisations* (Dirección General de Comunicación Exterior, Ministerio de Asuntos exteriores y de Cooperación, Madrid, November 2005). The Opposition People's Party continually ridiculed this initiative. See Albert Aixalà, 'The Parliamentary Session of Dissent', in Esther Barbé (ed.), *Spain in Europe 2004–2008*, Monograph of the Observatory of European Foreign Policy, 4 (Bellaterra, Barcelona: Institut d'Estudis Europeus, February 2008), Section 6, p. 3.

[78] The Alliance was launched by Secretary-General Kofi Annan on 14 July 2005. It became institutionalized, generating projects on youth, the media, education, and migration, offering Fellowships, and convening large international meetings. See <http://www.unaoc.org> accessed 20 December 2012.

[79] Economics was also important, as trade between the two countries tripled in eight years. Prime Minister Zapatero visited Turkey three times in his term of office. 'Zapatero reitera a Erdogan su deseo de ver a Turquía en la UE', *El País*, 7 September 2011.

United States, the inherently external dimension of migration policy was acknowledged increasingly, together with its security implications. This was most obvious at the Seville EU summit of 2002 chaired by Spain, but it also became a more significant concern for public opinion.[80] The Zapatero government initially hoped to substitute European cooperation for the bilateral agreements with sending countries preferred by its predecessor, but in the event needed both strategies after dramatic increases in irregular flows during 2005–6 into the Moroccan enclaves and the Canary Islands. Agreements were signed with West African as well as Maghrebian countries, linking development aid to emigration.[81] The external dimension of migration policy, and arguably the migration aspects of foreign policy, had become major priorities.

In contrast to Italy, and even to a cautious Germany, Spanish governments of both political complexions were explicit about foreign policy being central to the process of building Spain's prosperity, reputation, and influence—but also as inherently linked to the domestic environment. In 2001 Foreign Minister Piqué i Camps had talked of Spain being 'a radically different country from what it was only 20 years ago. This fact ought to be and is in fact reflected in our foreign policy', and of 'the strong sense of solidarity in Spanish society, reflecting the new responsibilities and the new commitments that Spain is now willing to shoulder on the international scene'.[82] Seven years later, Prime Minister Zapatero advocated, from the opposing camp,

> . . . the foreign policy of a progressive government, but one conceived as a policy of State, that is, as a policy that serves Spanish society as a whole. And by this I mean a policy not just *for* Spanish society but designed and carried out *with* it; in other words working with as many public and private sector forces as possible.[83]

Zapatero's rhetoric reflected Socialist philosophy and also the need for national unity in the aftermath of the Atocha bombings, but otherwise there was considerable continuity with the views of his conservative predecessor. The Barcelona Process for Mediterranean cooperation remained vital for Spain, even if it was embarrassingly reinvigorated by the French proposal for a Mediterranean Union in 2008.[84] Policy on the Israel–Palestine conflict

[80] Ricard Zapata-Barrero, 'Dynamics of Diversity in Spain: Old Questions, New Challenges', in Vertovec and Wessendorf (eds), *The Multiculturalism Backlash*, pp. 170–89.

[81] Gemma Pinyol, 'Spain's Immigration Policy as a New Instrument of External Action', in Barbé (ed.), *Spain in Europe 2004–2008*, Section 9, pp. 1–4. Zapatero preferred 'positive conditionality', i.e. more aid for more willingness to cooperate, compared to Aznar's preference for withdrawing aid from those who fail to comply with agreements. In practical terms this is a distinction without a difference.

[82] Josep Piqué i Camps, 'Spanish Foreign Policy at the Turn of the Century'.

[83] José Luis Rodríguez Zapatero, 'In Spain's interest: A Committed Foreign Policy', speech given at the Prado Museum on 16 June 2008 for the Elcano Royal Institute and other foundations.

[84] On Spain's important role in the origins of Barcelona, see Federica Bicchi, *European Foreign Policy Making Toward the Mediterranean* (Houndmills: Palgrave Macmillan, 2007), pp. 151–80.

had to remain even-handed, given both the abhorrence towards any form of terrorism and the need to cultivate the Arab world. Africa and Asia were talked up as 'the new pillars of Spanish foreign policy', given the concerns over migration on the one hand, and trade on the other.

In conclusion, therefore, we can see that foreign policy became an increasing priority for Spain, at the same time that it was transformed by a huge increase in immigration, and hit by a traumatic terrorist attack. This has led to pro-active steps in external policy, into which immigration policy is now virtually subsumed, but not to any new doctrine on the management of civil society, whether through multiculturalism or integration. The multiculturality evident on the streets is new in scale and extent, but does not seem so discontinuous given the historical and geographical proximity of Islam on the one hand, and the solidarity with *Hispanidad* on the other. Nonetheless, given the inevitable time lags which occur in relation to the impact of immigration, there may yet turn out to be significant consequences—at home and abroad—of the upheavals of the last decade.[85] Furthermore, the interplay between the multinational structure of the Spanish state, and the growing overlay of ethnic diversity, has the potential to cause problems, especially if some regions feel the financial and cultural impact of immigration more than others.

Italy

Mi scusi Presidente
Non è per colpa mia
Ma questa nostra Patria
Non so che cosa sia[86]

('Io non mi sento italiano', sung by Giorgio Gaber, 2003)

The last of our three cases of 'parallel societies' is Italy. Another latecomer to the status of an immigration country, for more than a century Italy had been

[85] An OECD report on immigration, with figures for 2009 which were given prominence in the Spanish press, showed that the economic crisis had only slowed the influx of immigrants, not halted it, while the unemployment rate among foreigners at 30 per cent was even higher than that in the population as a whole (21 per cent). Nonetheless, as the OECD explained, the unprecedented 'explosion' of Spanish immigration was not necessarily a burden, as most of it was legal and thus produced tax revenue. 'International Migration Outlook 2011, OECD, <www.oecd.org/els/internationalmigrationpoliciesanddata/internationalmigrationoutlook2011.htm> accessed 18 December 2012, cited in 'País de parados busca inmigrantes', *El País*, 13 July 2011, pp. 30–1. The economic crisis also led Zapatero to announce in May 2010 a reduction in his cherished ODA budget by 20 per cent, despite its preventive philosophy with regard to conflict and migration. Manuel Manrique Gil, 'Spain's Foreign Policy in Africa: Time to Reassess the Vision', FRIDE Policy Brief, 59 (Madrid, November 2010).

[86] A loose translation is: 'Excuse me Mr Prime Minister/it is no fault of mine/but this our dear country/I don't know what it is . . .'

accustomed to its own citizens searching in northern Europe and the New World for the jobs they could not find at home.[87] But from the 1960s onwards, the combination of a falling birth-rate and economic expansion led to an accelerated rate of immigration. The number of foreign residents rose from little more than 120,000 in 1971 and 320,000 in 1981 to 1,334,889 in 2001, by which time the proportion of the population had risen from 0.22 per cent to 2.34 per cent.[88] There followed a particularly rapid increase, so that by 2005 this had reached about 2.7 million, or about 4.5 per cent of the population—a wave second only to that of Spain in its size.[89] The rise continued, so that by 1 January 2010 the total was 4,235,059, or 7.0 per cent.[90] As these figures only describe legal residents the actual totals are probably up to 10 per cent higher, as can be judged by the large numbers who have responded to the regular amnesties offered to 'clandestine' immigrants.[91] Nor are the trends likely to be reversed, given the 'push' factor of poverty in the developing countries to Italy's south and east, and the 'pull' factor of one of the lowest birth-rates in the EU.[92]

The speed of these changes, combined with other factors, has meant that the immigrant community in Italy has not been able to integrate well with civil society. As Paul Ginsborg has pointed out, it is revealing that the Italian word for most of the newcomers is '"extracommunitarii", a peculiarly Italian label which in technical terms described immigrants from countries not belonging to the European Community, but which also had strong overtones of exclusion'.[93] Most newcomers live semi-visible lives, usually in segregated areas, whether Moroccans harvesting fruit and vegetables in the countryside, Chinese leather workers in the Tuscan city of Prato, or Romanians in the building trade. They are associated in the public mind with criminality, which has produced racist outbursts from a minority and simple distancing on the part of the majority.[94] Given the Italian paradox of a weak state but a

[87] Donna R. Gabaccia, *Italy's Many Diasporas* (London: UCL Press, 2000).

[88] Luca Einaudi, *Le politiche dell'immigrazione in Italia dall'Unità a oggi* (Roma-Bari, Editori Laterza, 2007), p. 405, Table A1, 'Gli stranieri nei censimenti dell'Italia unita (1861–2001)'. As Einaudi's balanced and scholarly analysis is the most authoritative source on immigration into Italy, I have relied on it heavily.

[89] Luca Einaudi, *Le politiche dell'immigrazione in Italia dall'Unità a oggi*, p. 407, Table A4, 'Evoluzione della presenza legale straniera in Italia (1970–2003)'. Also pp. 397–403.

[90] ISAT (Istituto nazionale di statistica), Table on 'The Foreign Population Resident in Italy, on 1 January 2010' (Rome, 12 October 2010), <http://demo.istat.it/> accessed 23 August 2011.

[91] ISAT (Istituto nazionale di statistica), p. x.

[92] Among the EU-15 only Austria, Germany, and Portugal had (marginally) lower fertility rates in 2009. The figures are low in most EU states, and would be lower without the higher birth-rates among immigrant communities, 'Fertility Statistics', Eurostat, <http://epp.eurostat.ec.europa.eu/statistics_explained/index.php/Fertility_statistics> accessed 1 August 2012. As against this, the economic recession from 2008 reduced job opportunities and the attraction to immigrants, especially in the south of the EU.

[93] Paul Ginsborg, *Italy and its Discontents, 1980–2001* (London: Allen Lane, 2001), pp. 62–3.

[94] See Einaudi, *Le politiche dell'immigrazione in Italia dall'Unità a oggi*, pp. 234–40, for a discussion of the difficult arguments over immigration and crime. In 2008 37.4 per cent of the

homogeneous society it has been difficult for any stranger to break into a settled, family-centred, way of life.[95]

On the other hand, there are some signs of change; for example, recent statistics show that 22.6 per cent of foreigners' households include one or more Italians.[96] Yet this is less likely to signify intermarriage than the presence of naturalized citizens, including children. Italians have come to accept that their society contains ever greater diversity in practice, but have yet to embrace it, or to accept it in principle. There has not even been a clear policy debate over multiculturalism versus integration, let alone the formulation of a political consensus on the best way forward.[97]

Apart from holding the problem of increasing ethnic diversity at arm's length, the three countries under discussion here also have in common a decentralized political structure and a difficult recent past from which they are still trying to emerge. In the case of Italy it has often been said that the civil war of 1943–5 has not yet been resolved, with powerful antagonisms between left and right still colouring every area of policy. The partisan heritage is a powerful factor on the left, while the dominant figure of the last two decades, Silvio Berlusconi, still referred to his opponents as 'communists' twenty years after the collapse of that ideology in Europe. Domestic terrorism, instigated by elements from the extremes on both wings, continues to cast a shadow even into the twenty-first century, with regular commemorations of the most shocking events.[98] Yet although the right–left antagonism does still dominate,

prison population were immigrants. On the other hand, immigrants tend to be poor, and criminality correlates with poverty. Maurizio Carbone (ed.), *Italy in the Post-Cold War Order: Adaptation, Bipartisanship, Visibility* (Lanham, MD: Lexington, 2011), pp. 96–7.

[95] Between the state and individuals lies what Robert Putnam called 'civic community', or the collective capacity to make modern states work. Putnam and his colleagues argued that this civic community was underdeveloped in southern Italy by comparison to the north, for historical reasons. Robert D. Putnam, Robert Leonardi, and Raffaella Y. Nanetti, *Making Democracy Work: Civic Traditions in Modern Italy* (Princeton, NJ: Princeton University Press, 1993). While most immigrants live in northern Italy, and have found the strong local communities difficult to break into, those in the south have found the absence of effective local government, and the subsequent reliance on family networks an even higher wall to surmount.

[96] ISTAT, 'Households with Foreigners: Indicators of Economic Distress 2009' (Rome, 28 February 2011), <http://www.demo.istat.it> accessed 23 August 2011.

[97] Also the view of Anna Triandafyllidou, 'Religious Diversity and Mutliculturalism in Southern Europe: The Italian Mosque Debate', in Modood, Triandafyllidou, and Zapata-Barrero (eds), *Multiculturalism, Muslims and Citizenship*, p. 135. There has, however, been much angry debate about Islam, as a possible threat to the Italian way of life, focused mainly on the writings of Oriana Fallaci, one of Italy's best-known foreign correspondents. See her *La rabbia e L'orgoglio* (Milan: Rizzoli, 2001), written in the aftermath of the attack on the Twin Towers. This and two other books in the same vein sold millions of copies in Italy and polarized opinion. 'Obituary: Oriana Fallaci', *The Guardian* (26 September 2006).

[98] For example the bombing of the Uffizi Gallery in 1993, killing a whole family, and the murder in Bologna of Professor Marco Biagi, an economist advising Prime Minister Berlusconi, in 2002.

the issue of multiculturalism has attracted much political disagreement over the last decade, cutting across the conventional polarity.

Italy's regionalism is not of the federal variety, although there is strong pressure from the Lega Nord for it to become so. The country does have distinctive regional cultures, but its primary split is along north–south lines; the product of both material circumstances and the construction by political forces in Lombardy, Piedmont, and the Veneto of a distinction between what they choose to see as a near Third World existence in the south, and an efficient, economically productive society north of Rome.[99] This has entailed the invention of a region called Padania, and various myths to sustain claims for its autonomy.[100]

Whatever the reasons for the undoubted contrasts in wealth and administrative culture between north and south, the reality is nothing like as simple as the Lega likes to paint it. For one thing the corruption scandals first exploded in Milan—*tangentopoli*, or bribesville—in the early 1990s, while the northern economy has survived for decades on attracting southerners to do the poorly paid jobs on which it depends. Many public sector employees, including in the police and *carabinieri*, are either from the south or descendants of families who moved north after 1945. Thus the issue of immigration in Italy involves far more than the most obvious issue of the newcomers from Africa and the Balkans. The south of the country in particular has been shaped over many centuries by diverse cultures and ethnicities, from Greece and the Normans to Spain and the Arab world. On top of this historical mix, long term and short term, has been placed the stratum of new immigrants, who had no choice but to live their lives in parallel, outside the relatively closed society they were trying to settle in.

But who are the new immigrants, and where are they clustered? Nearly half of foreign residents have their origins in eastern Europe, with 888,000 of those (21 per cent of the total) coming from Romania alone. Another 25 per cent come from eastern European countries outside the EU, particularly Albania (11 per cent) and the Ukraine (4.1 per cent). Of non-Europeans, the largest groups come from Morocco (10.2 per cent), China (4.5 per cent), Peru (2.9 per cent), and the Philippines (2.1 per cent)—with the latter two providing most foreign domestic carers. There have also been sharp rises recently in the numbers from India, Pakistan, and Moldova. Thus most immigrants, not surprisingly, come from poorer countries in search of work, with three

[99] One consequence is that identification with Italy has been low even amongst the indigenous population. In 1994 only 44.9 per cent said that they felt 'most of all' Italian, as opposed to 33.5 per cent European, and 21 per cent a citizen of their region or municipality. Table 4, Census Survey 1994, in Giuseppe Roma, *Italy: The Opportunities Represented by Confusion* (Washington, DC: Centre for Strategic and International Studies, 26 September 1996).

[100] Anna Cento Bull and Mark Gilbert, *The Lega Nord and the Politics of Secession* (Houndmills: Palgrave, 2001), especially pp. 106–12.

(Romanians, Albanians, and Moroccans) accounting for 42.2 per cent of the total.[101] In terms of religion, 1.3 million foreign residents, or 31 per cent of the total, come from predominantly Muslim countries, which is not as high a proportion as is popularly supposed.[102] On the other hand, the top ten sources of immigrants represent a wide mix of cultures and parts of the world, creating a definite impression of multiculturality. As a result, the last decade has seen much angry debate about Islam as a possible threat to the Italian way of life.[103]

In terms of the distribution of this mix across Italy, the overwhelming majority have settled in the more prosperous regions of the country—60 per cent in the north and 25.3 per cent in the centre. The remaining 13 per cent or so live in the south, which is, however, where the sharpest rate of increase is currently being seen—presumably because of a degree of saturation elsewhere.[104] It is therefore piquant that the voters for the Lega Nord, who are antagonistic towards their compatriots from the Mezzogiorno, let alone those from more far-flung cultures, are also those most in need of immigrant labour.[105] A further twist is that the lower fertility of indigenous Italians requires more immigrants, and the higher number of children per family they tend to produce, to achieve the kind of replacement rate which can sustain the economy and look after the ageing population. This is in turn creates more racial prejudice and inter-communal tensions—a vicious circle seen in most wealthy European states.

[101] Trends and data from the table 'The Foreign Population Resident in Italy on 1 January 2010', ISTAT (Rome, 12 October 2010; available at <http://www.demo.istat.it> accessed 23 August 2011). Data also from the tables (i) 'Cittadini Stranieri. Popolazione residente per sesso e cittadinanza al 31 Dicembre 2009. Italia—Tutti I Paesi'; (ii) 'Cittadini Stranieri. Bilancio demografico anno 2009 e popolazione residente al 31 Dicembre—Tutti I paesi di cittadinanza. Italia'. See also 'Immigrazione e presenza straniera in Italia 2009–10', Rapporto Sopemi Italia 2010 (Roma: Censis, November 2010), <http://www.censis.it> accessed 30 August 2011.

[102] The calculation is mine, from the ISTAT tables, but omitting all countries with less than 1,000 expatriates living in Italy. The figure also excludes those states with large Muslim minorities, such as India, which would probably increase the figure further. Another estimate, however, for January 2007, or three years earlier than the 2010 figures used here, is lower, at 850,000, although the percentage of the total immigrant population at 32.6 per cent is comparable to mine (31 per cent). Antonella Guarneri, 'Muslim diversity in Italy: An unacknowledged reality', *The International Spectator*, 43/3 (2008), pp. 117–35.

[103] See footnote 97. The reception of Oriana Fallaci's work foreshadowed what happened in Germany following the publication of Thilo Sarrazin's book. The high sales for both books revealed the existence of much popular anxiety. Another prominent voice was the one-time Muslim defender of multiculturalism in Italy, Magdi Allam, who converted to Catholicism in 2008 after making a 180-degree turn into apocalyptic warnings about Islam. See his 'Se i musulmani democratici sono estremisti', *Corriere della Sera*, 20 January 2007.

[104] 'The Foreign Population Resident in Italy on 1 January 2010', ISTAT, Rome.

[105] Einaudi, *Le politiche dell'immigrazione in Italia dall'Unità a oggi*, p. 398, and table A8 'La distribuzione regionale degli stranieri in Italia', p. 411. On the attitudes of the Lega voters see Robert Borcio, *La rivincita del Nord. La Lega dalla contestazione al governo* (Rome-Bari: Editori Laterza, 2010).

The foreign policy dimension of Italian multiculturality is not immediately obvious, if only because Italian foreign policy in general has been generally reactive, even since the end of the Cold War, during which it was almost invisible.[106] But just as the foreign and the domestic are structurally linked, so Italy has seen a regular two-way flow between issues of social diversity and foreign policy. For example, the onset of chaos in the Balkans following the collapse of Yugoslavia presented Rome not only with a serious geopolitical challenge, but also with an outflow of refugees. Most dramatic was the arrival in 1991 of large numbers of Albanians, finally benefiting from the opening of frontiers to escape not only from a broken state, but also from a serious agricultural crisis. Italy and Greece represented natural refuges, given their proximity and historical roles in the region. In three days during March 1991, 25,700 Albanians crossed the Strait of Otranto to find refuge in Italy. They were welcomed on humanitarian grounds, although only 11,000 obtained official permission to stay. When the next wave arrived in August of that year the reaction was that of fear at an uncontrollable invasion (10,000–12,000 people arrived at Bari on a single ship). After chaotic scenes which damaged Italy's international reputation, almost all were sent back to Albania. Thus migration had produced a serious foreign policy dilemma, which necessitated an immediate agreement with the government in Tirana over various forms of criminality as well as immigration. This led in due course to Italian vessels patrolling the Italian coast, to some effect.[107]

In 1997, however, another Albanian crisis, this time created by a popular uprising against financial duplicity which had wiped out the savings of thousands, produced an even more dramatic Italian intervention. After Britain and France refused to act, Rome initiated and led 'Operation Alba', a multinational expeditionary force of 6,000 men which succeeded gradually in restoring order in Albania. Once again there was fear of a mass population movement, which the intervention largely forestalled.[108] This was a major change in Italian foreign policy, proving (not least to decision-makers themselves) that the country could act independently, even lead, and that it had the technical competence to manage reconstruction in a crucial part of its near abroad (and ex-colony to boot).[109] Problems remained, however, especially

[106] For good overviews of Italian foreign policy, see Antonio Missiroli, 'Italy', in Manners and Whitman (eds), *The Foreign Policies of European Union Member States*, pp. 87–104; Elisabetta Brighi, 'Resisting Europe? The Case of Italy's Foreign Policy', in Wong and Hill (eds), *National and European Foreign Policies: Towards Europeanization*, pp. 57–71; Carbone (ed.), *Italy in the Post-Cold War Order*.

[107] The data in this paragraph is drawn from Einaudi, *Le politiche dell'immigrazione in Italia dall'Unità a oggi*, pp. 177–80.

[108] On Operation Alba and the Italian fear of more refugees, see James Pettifer and Miranda Vickers, *The Albanian Question: Reshaping the Balkans* (London: I. B. Tauris, 2007), pp. 30, 55, 60, and 65–77.

[109] For a wider perspective on Operation Alba, see Paolo Tripodi, 'Operation Alba: A Necessary and Successful Preventive Deployment', *International Peacekeeping*, 9/4 (2002),

that of intercepting the speedboats which trafficked illegal migrants across the Adriatic, provoking strong public reactions back in Italy. This in turn compelled further bilateral cooperation with Albania, leading extraordinarily to the setting up of a sizeable Italian base on the small Albanian island of Sasano. Gradually the flow of illegals was reduced, but the Kosovo crisis of 1999 produced another wave of 30,000—this time genuine refugees.[110] By 2000 more than 20 per cent of the Albanian population had moved overseas, mostly to Italy and Greece.[111] For the former, the perception was being created internationally of a state that was either willing to take in newcomers (as it was to some degree, for labour market reasons) or simply unable to prevent their arrival. This led to new pressures coming from Tunisia and Libya.

Because of the difficulties of controlling the movement of people, Italy, like other European states, has been drawn into a network of bilateral agreements on the 'readmission of persons', like that with Albania in 1998. By 2009 it had a total of fifty-one such agreements, including all states on the Mediterranean littoral except Israel.[112] The fact that they were needed with partners in the EU as well as non-EU states reveals the weaknesses of the Schengen system, at their most apparent in 2011 during the uprisings in North Africa, when the sudden influx of Tunisian migrants led the Italian government to deal with the problem by issuing them with temporary entry permits, in the knowledge that most would be heading for France. This led the French government temporarily to re-impose border controls at the Italian frontier, and to a sharp diplomatic exchange.[113]

It is hardly an exaggeration to say that over the last ten years migration concerns—which in turn are deeply connected to domestic society—have become central to Italy's foreign policy. Apart from Albania, the other country which has caused Rome headaches has been Libya, and in particular its former leader Muammar Gadaffi who played skilfully on the domestic/foreign policy connection. Over a decade he turned on and off the tap of desperate people without documents (usually from other African countries) who risked the sea

pp. 89–104. On Italian Balkan policy more generally, see Roberto Belloni, 'Italy in the Balkans: An Emerging Actor in its Neighbourhood', in Carbone (ed.), *Italy in the Post-Cold War Order*, pp. 215–37.

[110] Einaudi, *Le politiche dell'immigrazione in Italia dall'Unità a oggi*, pp. 228–34.

[111] Einaudi, *Le politiche dell'immigrazione in Italia dall'Unità a oggi*, p. 178.

[112] See the Return Migration and Development Platform (RDP) of the Robert Schumann Centre for Advanced Studies at the European University Institute in Fiesole: <http://rsc.eui.eu/RDP/registration> (registration required), accessed 30 March 2013. Also Jean-Pierre Cassarino, 'Informalising Readmission Agreements in the EU Neighbourhood', *The International Spectator*, 42/2, June 2007, pp. 179–96.

[113] 'Immigrati, la stretta della Francia: "Ecco come bloccare i tunisini"', *La Repubblica*, 7 April 2011. Such spats are all too predictable given the diverging national interests. Malta is another example. See 'Ferma in mare nave con immigrati. Scambio di accuse tra Maroni e Malta', *La Repubblica*, 18 April 2009.

journey to the Italian islet of Lampedusa, causing over-crowding there and uproar in Italian politics. Well understanding the weakness of a powerful country with its hands tied by maritime law on the use of force, and desperate to maintain access to Libyan oil, gas, and commercial contracts, Gadaffi also played on the nervousness of a civil society shocked by the sudden influx of *extracommunitarii*. He did this with a flair for media spectacles, and no little *Schadenfreude* given the history of Italian atrocities. It was also clear that he was paying no price for having expelled Italian residents without compensation in the 1970s.[114] It was the classic example of a small state's ability to tie down Gulliver. Despite various protests at home over the issue of dealing with a serious human rights violator, and likely sponsor of terrorism, successive governments pushed on with a policy of rapprochement on grounds of realpolitik (Prime Minister Massimo D'Alema was the first Western leader to visit Tripoli, in December 1999, after Gadaffi had finally surrendered the Lockerbie suspects to the Scottish courts).[115] The first readmission agreement was in 2000, but it became wearyingly apparent after each round of diplomacy that the Libyan leader would always come back for more concessions.

Italian diplomacy towards Gadaffi between 2000 and 2011 amounted to no less than appeasement, predictably accompanied by similar humiliations to those endured by Neville Chamberlain in 1938. In 2008 Italy agreed to pay 5 billion dollars in compensation for the era of colonialism, accompanied by Berlusconi's visit to Tripoli to 'offer in the name of the Italian people our apologies and to express our grief for what happened many years ago'.[116] Driven by commercial imperatives but also the knowledge that his voters wanted action on immigration, Berlusconi then allowed himself to be sucked into yearly commemorations of the agreement, notable for their cloying expressions of personal friendship, but also homilies from Gadaffi. The first in 2009 was held again in Tripoli, but it was Rome in 2010 which exposed the hold which Libya had gained over the Italian government. Gadaffi had recruited 200 Italian young women to hear about the virtues of conversion to Islam, while he sported a large photograph attached to his jacket of a Libyan hero executed by the Italians under colonialism. He also cajoled a grim-faced Berlusconi to view an exhibition of colonialism at the Libyan Academy of Rome.[117] By this time protests were being voiced even by Berlusconi's allies and officials. On the other hand, a *quid pro quo* was forthcoming; the landings of illegal immigrants

[114] Ghaddafi posed dilemmas for Italian foreign policy right from the outset. See Luigi Ferraris (ed.), *Manuale della politica estera italiana, 1947–1993* (Roma-Bari: Editori Laterza, 1996), pp. 279–80.

[115] In August 1999 Foreign Minister Lamberto Dini had been the first Foreign Minister to visit Tripoli in this new phase. Carbone (ed.), *Italy in the Post-Cold War Order*, p. 203.

[116] 'Italia–Libia, accordo da 5 miliardi', *La Repubblica*, 31August 2008. My translation. 'Gheddafi a Roma provoca l'Europa', *Corriere della Sera*, 31 August 2010.

[117] *Corriere della Sera*, 31 August 2010.

from the south coast dropped dramatically from 2009 on, until the revolutions of 2011 changed the whole scenario.[118]

The courtship of Libya was not just due to concerns about immigration and domestic politics. Italy's historic interests in the country, economic and political, were a powerful motive. But even on this last visit, Gadaffi knew that immigration was the easiest way to up the ante, threatening Europe as a whole with an invasion, to the extent that it would 'become Africa', unless he were given another € 5 billion per year.[119] Italy was nominally exempted from this threat, but it was clear where the main point of entry for such migrants would be, given that Malta could not physically absorb more than a few thousand.

In some European states the increase in ethnic diversity has been associated with terrorism, but not in Italy. As we have seen there have been terror attacks from internal groups of both the right and the left, as well as some associated with the Mafia and rogue elements of the secret services. So Italians are used to serious threats against the state emanating from their own population. Nonetheless, the fear of Islamic jihadism emerging from an ever more diverse society has been increasing since 2001. One of the perpetrators of the London bombings of 2005 found refuge among sympathizers in Italy before eventually being extradited. Even more dramatically, in 2003 the CIA abducted one of the targets of its 'extraordinary rendition' programme, Abu Omar, on the streets of Milan. This was probably with the connivance of sympathizers in Italian military intelligence—and indeed an Italian police operation was already tracking Omar—but in defiance of the law, and public opinion which was hostile to US foreign policy at the time. The long-term effects on community relations can hardly have been positive, but it must be said that Italy has not itself suffered an act of jihadist terrorism, with most controversy on multiculturality focusing on honour killings, religious symbols, and what Italians call 'microcriminalità' (presumably in contrast to what the mafia gets up to).

Italy has moved from a condition in which an unfettered executive pursued a quietist foreign policy for most of the Cold War, to the present uneasy oscillation between a desire to be a respected contributor to international order and interruptions from an increasingly turbulent domestic environment. Some of the latter is due to the inherent instability of governing coalitions, as in 2007 when internal disputes over the mission in Afghanistan forced Prime Minister Prodi to resign, or when the Lega Nord broke ranks to express its opposition to Italy's participation in the operation to support the

[118] Rapporto Sopemi Italia 2010, Chapter 4, 'L'immigrazione irregolare', pp. 17–19.

[119] Rapporto Sopemi Italia 2010, Chapter 4, 'L'immigrazione irregolare', pp. 17–19. Gadaffi bombastically repeated the threat at the EU-Africa summit three months later. But of the leaders of the big four EU states, only Berlusconi turned up to hear him. 'Immigrazione, Gheddafi insiste', *La Repubblica*, 29 November 2010.

Libyan rebels in 2011.[120] But it is also the result of a spreading recognition of the connections between internal and external politics. The Lega, which for much of its early existence took little interest in foreign policy, was gradually drawn into behaving like a para-diplomatic actor (largely ignoring the Farnesina) through concerns about immigration, Islam, and the fiscal impact of defence spending. Its international policies have been markedly erratic and lacking in credibility even when serving in a governing coalition, but it has consistently shown hostility to both globalization and multiculturalism. It also strongly articulates the hostility towards war common across the political spectrum in Italy, principally on the grounds that foreign interventions do not serve the interests of its voters.[121]

The only other regional entity to have had a significant external profile (since the decline of concerns in Friulia-Giulia-Venezia over property rights in ex-Yugoslavia) is the German-speaking minority in Alto-Adige South Tirol, which gained much autonomy in the 1972 settlement of the long-running communal dispute.[122] The region now enjoys wealth and stability, but remains a foreign policy question of much sensitivity in both Rome and Vienna, given the transnational dimension of the region and its implications for the two nation-states. Acts of terrorism committed by those opposed to Italian rule were committed as late as the decade running up to Austria's accession to the EU in 1995. The visit of President Scalfaro to Vienna in 1993 to improve relations was the first by an Italian head of state since the Second World War. Even then the signing of a Friendship Treaty had to be postponed because of difficulties over an amnesty for those guilty of terrorism.[123]

Ethnic and religious lobbies on the US model barely yet exist in Italy, apart from the special case of the Vatican. The Catholic Church is a powerful force

[120] For analysts this was all too predictable. In the first year of Prodi's coalition Elisabetta Brighi wrote that the government 'seems to come close to the abyss every time a major foreign policy decision needs to be taken'. Elisabetta Brighi, 'How to Change Your Foreign Policy in 100 Days: A New Course with the Prodi Government?', *The International Spectator*, 42/1, March 2007, p. 138. On the Lega's problem with the Libyan intervention of 2010, see 'Maroni: basta raid su Tripoli', *La Repubblica*, 16 June 2011. This led temporarily to Foreign Minister Frattini calling for a halt to the bombing, even though international and domestic protests soon produced a swing back in policy: 'Frattini: "Stop umanitario ai raid in Libia". No della Nato: "Gheddafi si riarmerebbe"', *La Repubblica*, 23 June 2011. 'Missioni all estero: il loro future non è merce di scambio', *L'Unità* 4 July 2011. On the general problem of foreign policy for Italian coalitions see Vittorio Emanuele Parsi, 'Conclusion', in Carbone (ed.), *Italy in the Post-Cold War Order*, pp. 262–6.

[121] Marco Tarchi, 'Recalcitrant Allies: The Conflicting Foreign Policy Agenda of the *Alleanza Nazionale* and the *Lega Nord*', in Christina Schori Liang (ed.), *Europe for the Europeans: The Foreign and Security Policy of the Populist Radical Right* (Aldershot: Ashgate, 2007), pp. 187–207.

[122] See Anthony Adcock, 'The South Tyrol Autonomy: A Short Introduction' (Londonderry; University of Ulster, 2001). Palermo's argument that regional foreign policy is on the rise in Italy has little evidence to back up its claims. See Francesco Palermo, 'The Foreign Policy of Italian Regions', *The International Spectator*, 42/2 (2007), pp. 197–208.

[123] Ferraris (ed.), *Manuale della politica estera italiana 1947–1993*, pp. 462–3.

inside and outside the country, including arm's-length diplomatic actors like the San Egidio Community, but it, even more than others, is torn between a humanitarian concern for the welfare of immigrants and its desire to sustain the Catholic traditions of Italy. The Vatican cannot be discounted by the secular powers in Italy, as during the Balkan wars with its pressure to recognise Croatia.

The only other major ethnocultural group is the Jewish community, whose suffering during the Second World War has brought it respect, and influence on relations with Israel.[124] For their part, the sizeable Muslim population (now the second biggest religion in Italy) has, as the commentator Gad Lerner has pointed out, virtually no political representation, which is likely to be a serious problem given the growing numbers of second generation young people, who seem far more engaged on foreign and domestic issues than their parents.[125] The initiative of the Ministry of the Interior in 2005 to set up the Council of Italian Islam (*Consulta Islamica*) has not inspired much trust among Muslims themselves, partly because of their own diversity, and partly because of its top-down quality, along the French model.[126]

CONCLUSIONS

The three countries at the centre of this chapter have not displayed any clear direction of travel, let alone made a conscious choice, about how to deal with the issue of ethnic diversity. In this they probably represent the majority of European states, which are neither clearly multiculturalist nor committed to a policy of top-down assimilation. The matter is confused by the promiscuity of political rhetoric which leads to policies of almost all hues being labelled 'integrationist'. This matters little where a country's minorities are small in number or where the rate of change is slow. But in cases like those of Germany, Italy, and Spain the absolute numbers are now large, and the rate of change over the last decade dramatic. At the same time, governments have tended to act as if nothing has happened, leading to a potentially serious gap growing up between official discourse and views on the streets, and in

124 For example, its view was important in leading Israel to decide after eight years of caution that the ex-leader of the Italian neo-fascists, Gianfranco Fini, should be invited to Jerusalem, after his disavowal of anti-semitism, 'Fini condemns his country's "disgraceful past"', *Haaretz* (Tel Aviv), 24 November 2003.

125 Gad Lerner, 'Quei giovani arrabbiati destinati alla ribellone', *La Repubblica*, 26 September 2008.

126 Andrea Coppi and Andrea Spreafico, 'The Long Path from Recognition to Representation of Muslims in Italy', *The International Spectator*, 43/3 (2008), pp. 101–15.

structural terms to the existence of 'parallel societies', where minorities are neither discouraged nor given privileges, but mostly ignored.

This, then, is the condition of multiculturality with no imminent prospect of integration. In all three countries the social life of the majority continues unaffected by much contact with ethnocultural minorities, which have succeeded even less in penetrating the political establishments. Such myopia on the part of the state and its representatives could simply be condemned out of hand, but it is not surprising when one takes into account the competing preoccupations. Given that all three states (like Belgium and Switzerland) have strong elements of devolution, the problems of coherence and community relations take primarily a regional form. Ethnic diversity is not trivialized, but the question of how to handle it is complicated by supervening identities and by uncertainties over legal competence. Its growing networks lie asymmetrically over the decentralized structure of government, obscuring the relationship between state and civil society. The result, thus far, has been a preference for non-decisions.

A second characteristic linking Germany, Italy, and Spain is their increasing tendency to pursue a more confident national foreign policy. Spain has been the most pro-active, determined to escape from the isolation of the Franco years, but also to build a stronger position in the European Union. Germany is the strongest of the three, but also the most cautious given the antagonisms it can still awake. Nonetheless, Germany has moved steadily towards the status of 'an ordinary country' and to the verge of serious involvement in crises beyond its borders. Italy has been the most hesitant, but it too is far more active, especially in the Mediterranean region, than it ever was during the Cold War. Thus the three states share both a rapidly changing domestic environment, albeit one whose changes they have barely acknowledged, and more exposed foreign policy profiles—a combination which has already started to cause problems on both sides of the equation. Immigration has become central to public policy, and fully implicates foreign policy. Bilateral relations with neighbours have often been tense as a result. The fear of terrorism dominates security strategies, and has led to enhanced surveillance of ethnic minorities and the consequent ratcheting up of social tensions. EU enlargement has both led to domestic problems and become hostage to them. Domestic energy needs also condition the trade-offs which have to be made with neighbouring states.

Despite this plethora of difficulties, and isolated outbreaks of racism, it is notable that increasing ethnic diversity has not produced serious instability in any of the three countries concerned—which in Spain is remarkable, given that the death toll at Madrid station in 2004 was inflicted by Islamist migrants. The impact of social changes, however, always involves time lags. Foreign policy, on the other hand, has already been disturbed in all three cases by the changing domestic environment. Thus there are clear similarities to be observed. Each state is naturally unique, and the interactions between society and external relations are too complex to allow any pre-determined paths. Spain's historical encounter with Islam, Germany's special relationship with Turkey, but also deep vulnerability on the treatment of minorities, and Italy's lack of a strong state, all shape their respective reactions to multiculturality and the implications for foreign policy. Yet the onset of rapid social change with both external origins and a cosmopolitan dimension has presented all three states with challenges which they have not yet met head-on.

5

Identity—friends, enemies, and roles in the world

In this second part of the book I turn to the major dilemmas which confront European states—that is, both policy-makers and citizens—as a result of the interplay between changes in both their patterns of social diversity and their international relations. The analysis will range over the three different paths of development identified earlier, while identifying where possible how practical dilemmas differ according to the path followed. The states figuring in Chapters 2–4 provide most of the illustrative material, but the main focus in the second half of the book is analytical, conceptual, and at times theoretical. The current chapter opens the discussion by focusing on the issue of the identity, or rather *identities*, which underlie a state's external behaviour. In what sense does a society feel itself to be distinctive, and have concerns to promote beyond the basics of survival, territorial integrity, and prosperity? To the extent that there has been consensus on such matters in the past, perhaps articulated and even partially constituted by a well-defined foreign policy, how far has this been called into question through the changing ethnocultural profile of society? Conversely, how have changing foreign policy orientations impinged upon community relations and ideas about national cohesion? To address these questions the chapter begins by considering the relationship between the ideas of national identity and national interest, and moves on to discuss the impact on them of changes in society, in conceptions of international relations, and in actual foreign policy. The thread which runs through the discussion is the issue, in Huntington's words, of 'who are we?', or more precisely, 'who do we think we are?', and how far the sense of ourselves is affected by relations with the outside world. Because of the attempt to take into account what Chapter 1 termed 'the social basis of foreign policy' the analysis goes beyond the usual FPA focus on elite discourses, although without trying to do more than sketch the parameters of self-understanding at the popular level.

NATIONAL IDENTITY AND NATIONAL INTEREST

We saw in Chapter 1 that the idea of national interests is deeply flawed as a guide to both action and the relationship between civil society and foreign policy-makers. Yet because it is ubiquitous, in fact unavoidable in a world of sovereign states, the idea is constantly being reworked, according to context and political need. Over the last two decades of International Relations theory, constructivists have used this observation as a jumping-off point for arguing that foreign policy is powerfully shaped by ideas, and that a certain plasticity is therefore built into national behaviour—in contrast to the various rationalist, materialist, or structuralist accounts which assume in their various ways narrow limits to state choice.[1] I go some of the way down this road, but also wish to ask the next question—about where key ideas come from, and what shapes the interpretations which decision-makers make of the constraints and opportunities which lie before them. To say, paraphrasing Alexander Wendt, that interests are what you make of them, opens the question up usefully but does not answer it.[2] My own response follows Wendt in broad terms, assuming that both external and internal factors affect the formulation/understanding of the national interest, through a process of continual interplay and feedback which involves not only dominant ideas (and discourse), but also new material factors which have to be taken into account if the goals fundamental to all political systems—of survival, integrity, security, and prosperity—are not to be compromised.[3] By 'material', far more is meant than just economics. As used here the adjective includes geography—both human and physical—ecology, political forces, and social trends. Their meaning, in turn, has to be interpreted by human beings, that is, filtered through the 'psychological environment' of decision-makers.[4]

This set of assumptions opens up the frame to allow for the fact that changes in a state's domestic society affect its foreign policy, firstly through creating a new calculus of interests for those responsible for taking decisions

[1] A key early work in this context was Martha Finnemore's *National Interests in International Society* (Ithaca, NY: Cornell University Press, 1996). Just as influential was Peter Katzenstein (ed.), *The Culture of National Security: Norms and Identity in World Politics* (New York: Columbia University Press, 1996).

[2] Alexander Wendt, *Social Theory of International Politics* (Cambridge: Cambridge University Press, 1999), especially pp. 92–138.

[3] For the problem of the goals of foreign policy, see Christopher Hill, *The Changing Politics of Foreign Policy* (Houndmills: Palgrave Macmillan, 2003), ch 5, especially pp. 118–26.

[4] I have used this now rather passé term to indicate the continuity—not always recognized—between modern constructivism and the work of the pioneering students of foreign policy-making. See, for example: Kenneth Boulding, *The Image: Knowledge in Life and Society* (Ann Arbor: University of Michigan Press, 1956); Harold and Margaret Sprout, *Foundations of International Politics* (Princeton, NJ: Van Nostrand Co., 1962), pp. 122–35; Robert Jervis, *Perception and Misperception in International Politics* (Princeton, NJ: Princeton University Press, 1976).

and secondly through changing a society's idea of itself, and of its relationship with the outside world. This can happen in both directions: inside-out, for instance where political reform or economic regeneration lead a state to present a new face to the rest of the outside world—as Vietnam has begun to do in the twenty-first century; and outside-in, whereby changes in the wider environment compel new thinking about past, present, and future—if this is usually a process of evolution it can, however, also be dramatic, as in January 2011 when the revolution in Tunisia suddenly confronted Egyptians with a new sense of possibilities about their own polity. The focus of this book is on the domestic environment, but this does not mean that external factors—local or systemic—are discounted. Far from it, for most domestic change is connected in some way or other to broader developments, while many states are intensely vulnerable to the forces of world politics. Indeed the general argument here is that societies and their governments are enmeshed in a constant process of transnational and transgovernmental interaction which shapes their choices whatever they try to do. It is thus critical to understand the relationship between the two levels and how change operates. One way of doing this is through the concept of identity.

Identity has been central to political analysis throughout the modern era, even if the terminology has varied. Just after the Second World War thinking focused on the idea of 'national character', subsequently abandoned for its personifying quality.[5] During the Cold War the dominant mix of realism and hard-edged social science meant that any such notions were seen as vague, anthropomorphic, and barely relevant to actual behaviour, which was largely attributed to the workings of power and interest. But since 1990, the fluidity of the international system has created space for thinking about the influence of cultural and ideational factors on politics, with identity emerging as a key point of reference. Despite its popularity, however, when applied to nation-states identity is an inherently problematic concept, promising as it does to communicate the core features of the self-understandings supposedly held in common by a large and diverse group of people. Unlike attitudes on particular issues it is unmeasurable, and highly susceptible to subjective interpretation. On the other hand, any functioning society undoubtedly shares certain distinctive characteristics, including a few dominant self-images. This is what social scientists try to access by a range of techniques, whether operational codes, cognitive maps, discourse analysis, opinion polls, or historical generalization.

[5] The best-known study, described by the author as 'cultural anthropology', is Ruth Benedict's on Japan: *The Chrysanthemum and the Sword* (London: Secker & Warburg, 1947). More recently a survey has appeared of two centuries of thinking about the English. See Peter Mandler, *The English National Character: The History of an Idea from Edmund Burke to Tony Blair* (New Haven: Yale University Press, 2006).

These methods are normally used in conjunction with detailed empirical research. Here the approach is rather to trace the *possible* links on the one hand between increased diversity and national identity, and on the other between identity and foreign policy. Identity applied to states is a macro-level concept which subsumes material and ideational factors. That is, while identity is subjectively held, it emerges out of the physical and historical situation of a people—as with 'the island race' for Britain, or 'the polder model' for the Netherlands. Although in a state of continual evolution, a country's identity changes slowly because perceptions of such fundamentals as the state, the nation, and civil society are at its heart.[6] To the extent that identity is strongly defined it will act as a significant (if general) driver and/or constraint of public policy.

It should be noted that identity is not to be equated with public opinion, for the latter relates to particular issues, whereas if national identity exists it does so in and of itself, as the 'real or imagined collective memory of a polity'.[7] It is probably the main means by which an individual identifies with society, creating a sense of 'we' at the mass level without necessarily lapsing into the agonistic mentality of nationalism. It may be defined briefly as who we think we are, at the level of society combined with polity.[8] For, as Anthony Smith has argued, 'whatever else it may be, what we mean by "national identity" involves some sense of political community, however tenuous'.[9] Yet as our own sense of national identity is bound to be imprecise and even contested, we cannot expect it to translate easily outside the country, which means that there is scope for misunderstandings, both popular and diplomatic. This is the case even if we accept Bhikhu Parekh's more objectivist definition of national identity, as 'the way a polity is constituted . . . what makes it the kind of community it is', for he goes on to specify such things as ideals, values, fears, collective memories, and dominant myths as constituting a polity, as well as its 'central organising principles and structural tendencies'.[10] If Parekh is on the right lines, as I think he is, then national identity is an aggregate of

[6] Ole Wæver is convincing on the centrality for identity of the state–nation relationship, but omits reference to civil society, for which 'nation' is too narrow a straitjacket. Ole Wæver, 'Identity, Communities and Foreign Policy', in Lene Hansen and Ole Wæver (eds), *European Integration and National Identity: The Challenge of the Nordic States* (London: Routledge, 2002), pp. 20–49.

[7] Ilya Prizel, *National Identity and Foreign Policy: Nationalism and Leadership in Poland, Russia, and Ukraine* (Cambridge: Cambridge University Press, 1998), p. 35.

[8] This definition owes something to Samuel Huntington's crisp survey of the issues at stake, but ultimately Huntington does not provide a clear definition of the term, tending to blur national identity with nationalism. Samuel P. Huntington, *Who Are We? America's Great Debate* (London: Simon & Schuster, 2004), pp. 3–33.

[9] Anthony D. Smith, *National Identity* (London: Penguin Books, 1991), p. 9.

[10] Bhikhu Parekh, 'The Concept of National Identity', *Journal of Ethnic and Migration Studies*, 21/2 (1995), p. 257.

intersubjective understandings which evolve on the basis of experiences—political, social, and international. Because 'by its very nature a community's identity needs to be constantly reconstituted in the light of its inherited resources, present needs and future aspirations', issues of both social diversity and foreign policy are bound to have an impact.[11]

The particular relevance of foreign policy to identity-formation was argued originally by David Campbell, who said that the former was critical in determining the ontological boundaries between one group and another. It is on this view a discursive practice with self-reproducing qualities, many of which may be undesirable in terms of setting human beings against each other.[12] This approach tends to underplay the materialist constraints on states, but it has the strength of making it normal to think about the relationship between what goes on inside a society and how it behaves collectively in international politics. As Sonia Lucarelli has said, 'foreign policy is relevant to the process of the political self-identification of the individual in a group, not only because it is one of the important frameworks within which core values and principles of a political group are interpreted . . . but also because it is the main context in which the group interacts with external Others'.[13]

The capitalization of 'Others' suggests the view that identity and foreign policy entail 'Othering', or the necessary establishment of self through differentiation from others. But while that can produce stereotypes of another state or community, the polarization of foreign relations, and rigidities in one's sense of self from which it may be difficult to escape, identity is not wholly interdependent with Others. The United States does not necessarily change identity because China is now more of a rival to it than Russia. On the other hand, as this book wants to suggest, changes in both society and external relations, and the two interacting, may over time produce changes in how we see ourselves, in the way we organize ourselves (our 'way of life'), and possibly in our degree of distinctiveness.

[11] Bhikhu Parekh, 'The Concept of National Identity', p. 268.

[12] David Campbell, *Writing Security: United States Foreign Policy and the Politics of Identity* (rev. edn, Manchester: Manchester University Press, 1998). Campbell did, however, distinguish between 'Foreign Policy' as a relatively narrow state practice and 'foreign policy' as 'all practices of differentiation or modes of exclusion (possibly figured as relationships of Otherness) that constitute their objects as "foreign"' (see pp. 68–9). This has obvious relevance for the issue of multiculturalism, which I will return to in Chapter 9. For a European country-study influenced by this approach see Ben Tonra, *Global Citizen and European Republic: Irish Foreign Policy in Transition* (Manchester: Manchester University Press, 2006), especially pp. 4–15.

[13] Sonia Lucarelli, 'European Political Identity, Foreign Policy and the Others' Image: An Underexplored Relationship', in Furio Cerutti and Sonia Lucarelli (eds), *The Search for a European Identity: Values, Policies and Legitimacy of the European Union* (London: Routledge, 2008), p. 35.

The idea of national interest is sometimes seen as inextricably yoked to that of national identity, as by Tony Smith when he talks of 'the problem' of defining them both.[14] But while a clear sense of identity makes the definition of collective interests easier, it is not indispensable—for the latter is about *Staatsräson*, and relates to the outer, not inner, world. Conversely, the sources of a nation's identity cut deeper than calculations of interest, for an identity is not the kind of thing that can easily be preserved or promoted by strategic action, at home or abroad—notwithstanding the resources poured into public or cultural diplomacy, through entities like China's Confucius Institutes, or such tropes as 'Cool Britannia'. Those activities are essentially epiphenomenal.

Still, debates about national interests are bound to provide a link, or two-way transmission belt, between national identity and the practice of foreign policy. What is more, the definition of interest is more open to change and subjectivity than is slow-moving identity—for all that realists like Palmerston claim that interests are 'eternal'. If the sense of collective self is in flux, through social change, this might lead to the recalibration of particular interests, for example in relation to EU enlargement, or to new thinking about those international groupings with which the state identifies. On the other side of the coin, major shifts in the external environment and the challenges it presents can lead a given community to begin to question the sense of 'who we are', or might become. Clearly the Russian Revolution, for example, had that effect on many societies around the world.

In 1991 William Wallace could observe that 'successive governments have adjusted to increased interdependence and decreased British standing in the world without thinking it necessary to redefine national goals or launch an agonised debate about history and identity'.[15] Yet the twenty years which followed have witnessed just such a debate—over Britain's feelings about empire, Europe, Ireland, devolution, and multiculturalism. All of these straddled the domestic/foreign divide and have generated particular dilemmas about the interests which the country should pursue. Other European states have had their own, equivalent, debates about both identity and national interests. The first part of this book has provided examples of how the domestic and the international interact to create dilemmas for different models of society, and foreign policies, in a range of European states with varying historical experiences. What follows is an examination of how identity politics plays out in the context of this nexus.

[14] Tony Smith, *Foreign Attachments: The Power of Ethnic Groups in the Making of US Foreign Policy* (Cambridge, MA: Harvard University Press, 2000), p. 140.

[15] William Wallace, 'Foreign Policy and National Identity in the United Kingdom', *International Affairs*, 67/1 (1991), p. 67.

NATIONAL IDENTITY AND SOCIAL CHANGE

Over the last two hundred years society has been in perpetual motion, despite descriptive categories like 'democracy' or 'capitalism' tending to freeze it in time. The remorseless succession of overlapping generations, each bringing new attitudes and achievements, combines with powerful forces—social, economic, political, and cultural—to drive change, always on the presumption that things can be better, and that nothing is permanent. Yet beyond this basic condition of modernity, a society can be subject to quite rapid change through exogenous factors such as war and immigration. As so many European countries have experienced significant inflows of newcomers over recent decades, and from a wide range of sources, so their societies have experienced an extra impulse of change in the direction of social diversity. This in turn has had some distinctive effects, with the potential for more. Some are regressive, as with the strong conservative instinct for retrenchment and tradition seen in most countries confronted with mass immigration. Others can accelerate existing processes of change and finally consign certain ways of being to the past—as has occurred with much thoughtless racial prejudice on the part of otherwise decent people.

Yet in between these two extremes lie more complex processes. In the first instance a sudden increase in diversity must weaken some of the bonds of a given society, even if it may ultimately replace them with something richer or stronger. In particular when it leads to an explicitly multicultural project, as in the UK, Sweden, and the Netherlands, it will allow strong bonds within particular groups even at the expense of national cohesion. This is what Amitai Etzioni has called a 'community of communities'.[16] Yet even when the consequence is not to acknowledge group rights, as in France, social life on the ground will still entail the diversification of myths, memories, religious practices, and other cultural reference points. This may produce in a given minority a feeling of separation from the majority in the host community, and in some an indifference, even hostility, towards the state which ostensibly protects them—an issue discussed in the chapter which follows. The outcomes will vary according to which model a country employs for handling diversity, but also on how well chosen it is, and on how well it is made to work.

The consequence of weakening social bonds, even on a temporary basis, is that the political consensus on which the major planks of public policy rest, foreign policy included, may start to erode, leading to more contestation (which can be a positive virtue if democratic debate has stagnated) and to erratic swings of the pendulum.

[16] Amitai Etzioni, *The New Golden Rule* (New York: Basic Books, 1996), ch 7, cited in Smith, *Foreign Attachments*, p. 162.

What is the evidence for changes at the level of identity within these European states? Any attempt to answer raises a massive epistemological problem, in that there is no scholarly agreement on how or where to find evidence of identity. Opinion surveys on what the majority feel themselves to be can be of some assistance, such as that conducted for the Pontignano seminar in 2008 on British and Italian youth, which found that 65 per cent of young Britons thought that the sense of national identity over the previous five to six years had weakened (only 13 per cent thought that it had strengthened) as opposed to 50 per cent of young Italians (another 24 per cent of them thought it had actually strengthened). The main factors deemed responsible for this dilution were the quality of national politicians (55 per cent Italy; 23 per cent UK), and immigration (34 per cent Italy; 60 per cent UK). Among various other factors it was notable that 23 per cent of young Italians also blamed the emergence of separatist movements (of which the *Lega Nord* is the prime candidate; the figure was 9 per cent for the Britons, presumably with Scotland in mind).[17]

This kind of quantitative evidence is useful at the mass level, although one has to be cautious given variations in the political climate, and in the kinds of questions asked. But in terms of the state taken as a whole it is at least as useful to read back changes from the evolution of public policy and of political argument more broadly. In most of the states of western Europe, changes in social composition over the last two decades have led to much discussion of multiculturalism and of integration with, as we have seen in Chapters 2–4, a range of different responses. Debate has raged among engaged publics as to how far multiple identities are inevitable, desirable, and/or compatible with existing national formations. Many have feared for their long-held traditions, others for their still fragile nation-building efforts, and yet others for the dangers of nationalist reactions and racism. In some respects the battle between two different versions of democratic thought—a globalization plus universal human rights perspective on the one hand, and a statist, communitarian perspective on the other—is being fought out in the polities of western Europe. Furthermore, regional integration gives the debate an extra twist, with some seeing the EU as a bastion of Judaeo-Christian civilization now under threat, and others looking to it to set an example of rights-based internationalism, even cosmopolitanism.[18]

[17] Web-based survey of 1,000 British and 1,000 Italian young people between the ages of 18 and 35 by Publica ReS for the Anglo-Italian Pontignano Conference, 26–28 September 2008. Serena Saltarelli, Riccardo Cova, and Enzo Risso, *Identities in Transition: Who Do We Want to Be? The Opinions of Italian and British Youth* (Trieste and Bologna: Publica ReS, 2008), pp. 16–17, author's copy.

[18] Timothy Garton Ash identifies what he calls the inevitable 'historical inconsistency' of such cultural approaches. See 'Chapter 6: What Europe Can Be' in Timothy Garton Ash, *Free World: Why a Crisis of the West Reveals the Opportunity of Our Time* (London: Penguin, 2004), pp. 209–23.

The very existence of these disagreements indicates that identity is in question within individual countries and across the region. In certain cases there is an evident gap between the existence of a vigorous, even growing, sense of national identity (sometimes the more powerful for having been only recently unleashed, as in Spain and Germany) and the growing reality of cosmopolitanism, especially in the big cities. In others, such as Belgium, Britain, and Italy, the arguments over cohesion have played into existing tensions on a regional, sub-national basis. Either way, immigrants and their descendants often feel excluded from the country in which they live, while members of the majority are not infrequently heard voicing the view that they no longer feel at home in their own country.[19] In these circumstances it is clear that national identities across Europe are not settled or at ease with themselves. In practice they have never been fully settled, but for most of the 1945–90 period, because of both the Cold War and the need for economic and political reconstruction, most societies operated on the basis of a fairly clear ethnocultural identity, albeit with some flux in Britain and the Netherlands, among the first countries to encourage migration from the ex-colonies. Now the situation is one of uncertainty, leading to legal and social heterogeneity across Europe. It may be that solid new senses of identity will emerge from this, either national or European, based on what Tarak Barkawi has called (in relation to Britain) 'a fully inclusive ideal of citizenship', rather than 'a governmental multiculturalism that lets the natives keep their traditions', but this is not currently on the horizon anywhere.[20]

A PLACE IN THE WORLD

What might this uncertainty over national identity mean for a country's view of its place in the world, and thus for its foreign policy? Conversely, how might events at the international level impact on identity? The two are entangled because issues like migration represent a permanent two-way bridge between the internal and external, but also because powerful historical memories, and the myths associated with them, do not distinguish clearly between the experiences of citizens as individual human beings, and the fate of their country as a

[19] Adrian Favell points out that even in liberal Amsterdam it is very difficult for foreigners—even those from other EU Member States—to penetrate the secrets of Dutch society. Adrian Favell, 'Immigration, Migration, and Free Movement', in Jeffrey T. Checkel and Peter J. Katzenstein (eds), *European Identity* (Cambridge: Cambridge University Press, 2009), pp. 180–1.

[20] Tarak Barkawi, 'How Multiculturalism Can Save UK Grand Strategy', 28 July 2011 (London: Royal United Services Institute), available online <http://www.rusi.org/analysis/commentary/ref:C4E316C8388D65/> accessed 19 December 2012.

whole. This is not just true of peoples who have suffered the traumas of defeat, occupation, or genocide.[21] The very fact of having successfully resisted a continental hegemon on three occasions since 1792 is central to the values which direct British democracy and attitudes towards the rest of Europe. It has been argued, indeed, that eighteenth-century foreign policy, with its 'three victories and a defeat', determined how Britons were to define themselves, as Europeans of a very particular character.[22] Thus identity, which equates to the collective sense of self, is intimately tied up with the interplay between a state's particular history and its experience of international relations, even if much of this is orchestrated by elite myth-making and then becomes absorbed into the reservoir of communal experience.[23]

In the context of western Europe this process varies according to three broad categories of national experience. The first contains the states for which the loss of empire has been relatively recent, and also traumatic. Britain, France, Belgium, and the Netherlands fit this description. Despite the rapid process of decolonization, mostly complete by the mid-1960s, the effects are still working themselves out today. Part of this is manifest in what Miles Kahler called 'the domestic consequences of decolonization', in particular the natural attraction of the metropole to migrants from the ex-colonies.[24] But it also involves the orientation of foreign policy along path-dependent lines, so that in the developing world Belgium remains focused on the Congo, while the Netherlands is still oriented towards Indonesia and what is now Suriname—although these ties diminish with time, unless reinforced by diaspora groups. Finally, it can be argued that both the positive and negative aspects of a country's self-image, as expressed by its political class, show that for the bigger states, at least, the age of empire is not easily shuffled off. Britain and France both still assume responsibilities as leaders in the international system, with Britain seeing itself as one of the principal agents of the 'international community', and France convinced of its greatness, 'cultural as much as military'.[25] In macro terms this is a matter of identity, and of the roles which

[21] The impact of trauma on Japan, Turkey, and Russia is examined in Ayse Zarakol, *After Defeat: How the East Learned to Live with the West* (Cambridge: Cambridge University Press, 2011).

[22] Brendan Simms, *Three Victories and a Defeat: The Rise and Fall of the First British Empire, 1714–1783* (London: Allen Lane, 2007), especially pp. 674–84; also Linda Colley, *Britons: Forging the Nation, 1707–1837* (London: BCA by arrangement with Yale University Press, 1992).

[23] As reflected, for example, in Danny Boyle's 'Isles of Wonder' creation for the London Olympics Opening Ceremony, 2012, which gave the world a view of the historical origins of Britishness—albeit omitting war and empire!

[24] Miles Kahler, *Decolonization in Britain and France: The Domestic Consequences of International Relations* (Princeton, NJ: Princeton University Press, 1984). Kahler points to the greater difficulties experienced by France in decolonization, but the indirect effects which he also noted, in terms of migration, race relations, and political instability, were also significant.

[25] David McCourt shows how, even before the interventionism of New Labour, Britain connected its own honour to the defence of 'right international conduct'—not a universal trait

internal politics and the international system have bestowed on states.[26] But since the empire lives on in a more practical sense in terms of changed societies, the actual policy choices of these states are regularly affected by a distinctive set of concerns and transnational linkages.

The second group in terms of identity consists of those states recovering from authoritarianism at home and/or pariah status abroad—that is, Germany, Greece, Italy, Spain, and Portugal. These states, although varying in size, share a need to re-establish their international reputation while also nurturing the still tender plant of democracy.[27] This has led them into some distinctive postures, combining hyper-sensitivity over certain issues (for example eastern Europe and Israel for Germany, and Turkey for Greece), with a low profile in general, being cautious over undertaking major commitments even in multilateral frameworks. Some movement has been observable in both aspects in recent years, but not enough to change the pattern. The sense of vulnerability both to external criticism and internal upheaval remains, together with the awareness that any new departure in foreign policy could all too easily be derailed by domestic politics. This is one reason why membership of the EU has provided such crucial shelter internationally for all these states; other partners can be allowed to take the lead, while domestic criticisms can often be deflected by reference to the need for European solidarity.

The last group, in terms of the dominant characteristic of their identity, is that of small states. Those given attention in this book are Denmark, Sweden, and Switzerland, but Austria, Finland, Ireland, Luxembourg, and Norway also fall into the category. For the most part these are countries which are wealthy but lack the capacity to exert significant influence in international affairs. At the same time they are vigilant about their independence—with four ex-neutrals among them, and an ex-colony (Ireland). This means that the protection provided by international institutions, that is, the EU and/or NATO, has been indispensable for all except Switzerland, which is a free rider. Their pasts and domestic characteristics vary, but they, like those in

among states. David M. McCourt, 'Role-playing and Identity Affirmation in International Politics: Britain's Reinvasion of the Falklands, 1982', *Review of International Studies*, 37/4 (2011), pp. 1599–621. On France, see Robert Gildea, 'Myth, Memory and Policy in France Since 1945', in Jan-Werner Müller (ed.), *Memory and Power in Post-War Europe: Studies in the Presence of the Past* (Cambridge: Cambridge University Press, 2002), p. 75.

[26] McCourt, 'Role-playing and Identity Affirmation'. McCourt argues convincingly that identity alone does not provide much guidance about agency, and that we need therefore to distinguish identity from the 'roles', partly chosen, partly ascribed, which states perform on the international stage. In my view, however, the idea of 'role' itself suffers from significant problems. Christopher Hill, 'Britain's Elusive role in World Politics', *British Journal of International Studies*, 5/3 (October 1979), pp. 248–59.

[27] In economic terms, Greece, Portugal, and Spain, at least, have also been playing a game of catch-up on development. See M. Fatih Tayfur, *Semiperipheral Development and Foreign Policy: The Cases of Greece and Spain* (Aldershot: Ashgate, 2003).

the first two groups, have all experienced changes in civil society as the result of increased immigration. Even rich, tranquil, and thinly populated Norway suffered the trauma of a massacre in 2011 committed by a deluded opponent of what he saw as a new wave of Islamic conquests. Such changes have led some of these states to consider whether their identity might be mutating, and whether they might need to relate to the outside world in different ways. At times they have had no choice in the matter, as in the cases of the Danish cartoons discussed in Chapter 3 or the rise of Jörg Haider's nationalist and anti-immigration Austrian Freedom Party, which generated strong opposition even within the EU. Because of their size, relatively small changes in social composition, or isolated incidents involving minorities, can have a disproportionate impact on community relations, and dominate the country's image abroad.[28]

Thus identities matter for foreign policy because they shape the self-understanding of international roles. And identities emerge in turn from the historical interplay of domestic and international experiences and social change, with circumstances and the ascription of roles by outsiders as powerful factors in the mix. As Prizel has said, 'national identity serves not only as the primary link between the individual and society, but between a society and the world'.[29] This evolutionary process, however, is not necessarily clear or linear. Roles which appear to be losing relevance can appear to be brought back to life by structural upheavals outside the control of individual actors. The end of the Cold War, for example, with its apparent ratification of the 'triumph of the west', suddenly made the role of medium European powers like Britain and France, which had been struggling with relative decline since the mid-1950s, seem significant again, especially in contrast to the collapse of the Soviet Union and the weakness of its successor.[30] The subsequent emergence of the doctrines of 'humanitarian intervention', and the 'responsibility to protect' reinforced this new European version of a manifest destiny on the basis of an artificially revived self-confidence, obscuring the changes which had been gathering pace in both civil society and international position. This led them, unhappily, into new conflicts with the very post-colonial world with which they had been trying to build a new relationship since the 1960s.

[28] Small countries are particularly sensitive to their image abroad, and try to improve it—often in vain. Image is not the same as identity, but the two phenomena overlap and may cause confusions. See Alan Chong and Jana Valenčič (eds), 'The Image, the State and International Relations: Conference Proceedings', EFPU Working Paper No. 2001/2 (London: London School of Economics and Political Science, 2001). Also Simon Anholt, *Places: Identity, Image and Reputation* (Houndmills: Palgrave Macmillan, 2010).

[29] Prizel, *National Identity and Foreign Policy*, p. 19.

[30] This phrase seems to have been first coined by J. M. Roberts in his book (and television series), *The Triumph of the West* (London: BBC, 1985).

The governments of those countries which explicitly embraced multiculturalism as a project, and particularly the New Labour ministers who took office in Britain in 1997, did attempt to face the parallel changes they observed in society and the wider world, concluding that identity and its external face required a radical rethink. For the most part this was driven by the ideology of 'globalisation', or the view that the world was rapidly becoming homogenized by economic and technological forces, with the divide between national and a presumed global civil society fast eroding.[31] The more open the economy to trade, finance, and migration the more likely this issue was to be confronted. In Britain Tony Blair pressed forward on all fronts to reinvent the nation's identity, courting the Asian middle-class to help present an image of a multi-ethnic country *ouvert aux talents* which would appeal to coming generations at home and abroad, all this as part of the Third Way's focus on breaking with the old tribal politics. However, there is an inevitable superficiality about any attempt to rebrand a society, and this approach brought about its own reactions.[32] Over a longer time-frame the Dutch celebration of liberal cosmopolitanism, which had seemed so progressive, also turned sour.[33]

The polarization which developed at home was mirrored, and ultimately compounded, by a foreign policy increasingly directed towards the 'War on Terror', fought on every front. The globalization perspective had paradoxically, and tragically, produced not a 'global civil society' but a deep series of antagonisms which knew no frontiers, and thus disturbed in many countries community relations which had long been fostered, and whose delicate balance was all too vulnerable to the crashing rhetoric and often brutal actions of post-9/11 *realpolitik*. Societies were rapidly resecuritized after years of painstaking emergence from wartime mobilization, Cold War suspicions, and (in some cases) dictatorship. The price paid in Britain and Spain, which sacrificed their images of openness and hybridity in favour of solidarity with US neo-conservatism, was to be a heavy one.

Yet if the hope for new identities had thus proved naïve and to some degree hypocritical, there had at least been some recognition that life had changed, inside and outside Europe, over the previous twenty years. This sense has not been wholly abandoned. In Spain the push to build a new kind of society in reaction to Francoism continued, expressed through the victory of Zapatero over Aznar immediately after the Madrid bombs, and through the gradual

[31] For an account and balanced assessment of the globalization paradigm, see Ian Clark, *Globalization and International Relations Theory* (Oxford: Oxford University Press, 1999).

[32] See Andrew Gamble, 'The Meaning of the Third Way', in Anthony Seldon (ed.), *The Blair Effect 2001–5* (Cambridge: Cambridge University Press, 2005), pp. 430–8.

[33] As argued as early as 2000 by Paul Scheffer in an article which caused uproar in the Netherlands by warning of threats to the country's social peace: 'Het multiculturele drama' (the multicultural drama), *NRC Handelsblad*, 11 May 2000, cited in Paul Scheffer, *Immigrant Nations* (Cambridge: Polity, 2011), p. 325. See also Chapter 2, this volume.

achievement of peace in the Basque country. Even in Britain, the reaction has not been overwhelming, and the Conservative David Cameron, as prime minister in the Coalition government from May 2010, has attempted to graft some cosmopolitan thinking onto the traditional values of his party in both foreign and domestic policies.[34] He has also continued his predecessor's commitment to power-sharing between the two communities in Northern Ireland, and indeed a role for the Republic of Ireland in the peace process, despite what this implies for the limits of British state power.

Compared to the countries pursuing a multiculturalist project, and the special case of renascent Spain, most European states have fared better in terms of keeping their foreign and domestic policies in separate compartments, with little consequent change in their sense of identity. Germany and Italy, it is true, have gradually become more self-assertive, tied in the former case to an internal debate about emerging from historical guilt.[35] But this has led only to occasional spasms of activism in foreign policy, and limited moves towards cosmopolitanism in either country. Switzerland finally accepted that a limited degree of internationalism might be acceptable, in the form of becoming a member of the UN in 2002, but even then only 55 per cent of voters were in favour.[36] Greek policy underwent a radical shift towards rapprochement with Turkey, but this took place in 1999, before the flood of illegal migration from the east which has subsequently complicated Greek–Turkish relations.[37] For the most part, therefore, any change in identity or foreign policy associated with the evolution of civil society in these countries has been indirect, not least because of competing versions of identity yet to be reconciled.

In France, however, the strong attachment to 'a certain idea' of the country produced a degree of cognitive dissonance. By this I mean not only that the elite is strongly attached to civic nationalism and its assumption that

[34] 'The guiding doctrine has been one of "liberal conservatism"'. Michael Harvey, 'Forged in the Crucible of Austerity', *The World Today*, 67/4 (2011), p. 16.

[35] The *Historikerstreit*, or 'historians debate' took place in the 1980s. The fall of the Berlin Wall soon afterwards further liberated Germany to think of itself as 'an ordinary country'. Jeffrey Herf, 'The Emergence and Legacies of Divided Memory: Germany and the Holocaust since 1945', in Müller (ed.), *Memory and Power in Post-war Europe*, pp. 184–205. Germany is the country which has engaged in most debate over the relationship between foreign policy and its identity. Most useful here are Peter J. Katzenstein (ed.), *Tamed Power: Germany in Europe* (Ithaca, NY: Cornell University Press, 1997), and J. P. G. Bach, *Between Sovereignty and Integration: German Foreign Policy and National Identity after 1989* (New York: St. Martin's Press, 1999).

[36] In 1986 a referendum had seen 75 per cent reject membership of the UN. There is thus a correlation between the arrival of non-European migrants and the changing of attitudes, but it remains only a correlation. 'Moving towards the UN in Slow Motion', *Swissinfo.ch*, <http:// www.swissinfo.ch/eng/politics/foreign_affairs/Moving_towards_the_UN_in_slow_motion.html?cid=291972> accessed 6 August 2012.

[37] John S. Koliopoulos and Thanos M. Veremis, *Modern Greece: A History since 1821* (Chichester: Wiley-Blackwell, 2010), pp. 193–4. On the subsequent migrant issue see Anna Triandafyllidou and Thanos Maroukis, *Migrant Smuggling: Irregular Migration from Asia and Africa to Europe* (Basingstoke: Palgrave Macmillan, 2012), pp. 200–3.

Frenchness is accessible to all, despite the evident alienation on the part of many *beurs* (the children, born in France, of Arab immigrants), but also that its foreign policy has avoided any serious debate about a 'descent from power', of the kind which took place in Britain in the 1960s and 1970s. Thus there is a tension between the attachment to the traditional French identity and place in the world on the one hand, and a growing awareness of their shifting domestic foundations on the other. It was in response to this tension that President Sarkozy took his short-lived initiatives to set up a Ministry of Immigration, Integration, National Identity, and Interdependent Development ('développement solidaire'), and to launch a national debate on identity.[38] One might suppose that something will have to give eventually, but the capacity of human beings (and political systems) to endure contradictions is surprisingly great. The long time-lags involved in coming to terms with change and reworking identities are a factor here, and affect all states whatever their internal conformation.

Whether Europeans as a whole are suffering from cognitive dissonance is a matter for debate, but it is plausible to believe that the region is going through what Tony Judt has called an 'interregnum' in terms of identity.[39] From being central to modernization and the creation of a global international system, as well as to the horrors of ideological conflict and world war, the continent has suffered a form of relegation first through the rise to primacy of the United States and the Soviet Union, and then through the emergence of the new powers of China, India, and Brazil. Its very success in the triumph over Soviet communism, and as a zone of relative peace, has meant that it now represents the status quo and is no longer a cockpit of international politics. Defensiveness about the morality and consequences of the colonial era has created uncertainty over whether it should still seek a global role or retreat into neighbourhood politics. Europeans are not quite sure whether to see themselves as standard-bearers for democracy, human rights, and a post-modern move away from power politics, or to apologize for their wealth, privilege, and need to do deals with unsavoury regimes to promote exports or gain access to raw materials. The arrival of a serious crisis in the European economy, and by extension in the EU itself, has produced further introspection, with various pockets of social turbulence.

Such dilemmas inhibit the ability of the European states to act decisively in international politics, not least because it makes consensus among twenty-seven Member States even more difficult to achieve. Confusion and internal

[38] See Chapter 3, footnote 56. Also 'L'identité nationale, thème récurrent de Nicolas Sarkozy', *Le Monde* (26 October 2009).

[39] '. . . a sort of interregnum, a moment between myths when the old versions of the past are either redundant or unacceptable, and new ones have yet to surface'. Tony Judt, 'The Past is Another Country: Myth and Memory in Post-war Europe', in Müller (ed.), *Memory and Power in Post-War Europe*, p. 180.

divergences make for uncertainty, as over the future of enlargement, now that the early post-Cold War confidence has dissolved. Resistance to immigration and multiculturalism, combined with the onset of economic crisis, has put paid to the possibility of states with large populations such as Turkey and Ukraine joining the EU in the foreseeable future. Some of the resistance is due to concern about jobs, and some to the conservative wish to hold on to the uneasy mix of Christianity and Enlightenment secularism which constituted European culture until the last quarter of the twentieth century. Thus although only 14 kilometres of water separate Morocco from Spain (far less than Malta's distance from Italy), while Rabat and Athens are at an equal distance from Brussels, it is generally accepted within the EU that Morocco is inconceivable as a candidate for entry.[40] In the case of Turkey, over which there is ambivalence and disagreement among Member States, Ankara has only been a plausible candidate for so long because the country seemed to aspire to share Europe's model of secular democracy—and because it was a key member of NATO whose suit was pressed by Washington. But Turkey's gradual move over the last decade away from secularism has played into anti-Islamic feeling inside the EU, which compounds the fears of large numbers of migrants seeking ever scarcer jobs, to swing the balance against its accession.

The erratic behaviour over enlargement is one product of the fact that Europeans have started to demand that their politicians step back from the 'milieu' goals of promoting democracy and stability beyond their borders, to concentrate on more instrumental, or 'possessional', concerns.[41] This pressure operates both at the collective level in terms of the EU being expected to look after Europeans more than outsiders, and at the national level, where each state has experienced to some degree a revival in national feeling. Domestic difficulties have undermined the integration project and turned Europeans inward. The spirit of generosity, even cosmopolitanism, which characterized attitudes towards development assistance and peacekeeping, as well as asylum and race relations, has been compromised—although by no means destroyed. But the balance between a cosmopolitan approach to world politics, whereby most thoughtful Europeans saw their institutions as making a key contribution to building a more peaceful and civilized world order, and a more communitarian emphasis on the needs of their own region, especially their own nation-states, has moved in favour of the latter.[42] Given the fluid

[40] Indeed, its application was brusquely rejected within months of being made in 1987.

[41] The distinction between milieu and possessional goals corresponds to that between the long-term and the systemic, versus the more immediate and self-regarding. Arnold Wolfers, *Discord and Collaboration: Essays on International Politics* (Baltimore: Johns Hopkins University Press, 1962), pp. 67–80.

[42] Chris Brown, *International Relations Theory: New Normative Approaches* (Hemel Hempstead: Harvester Wheatsheaf, 1992). Brown subsequently came to regard the cosmopolitan/communitarian dichotomy as too crude to do justice to international thought. See Chris Brown,

relationship between factors inside and outside, however, the pendulum may well swing again, as it did during the Arab spring of 2011. The combination of geo-politics and energy concerns, with human rights pressures from both public opinion and Maghrebian exiles, made it difficult to adopt a strictly isolationist position.

FRIENDS, ENEMIES, PARTNERS, RIVALS

If national identity is a meaningful concept it must arise from the interaction of a society with its activity in international affairs. In this context, identity-formation has two faces. In part, identity is a matter of defining oneself in relation, and contra-distinction, to others. Thus there has been much academic writing about 'Othering', or the need to create an image of an unwanted Other in order to shore up a sense of self. Iver Neumann has done most to relate this Lacanian idea to the empirical study of Europe.[43] The other part of identity-formation occurs through the opposite process, of *identification* with like, and like-minded, states. By examining each aspect we discover things both about how a state sees itself, and how its self-image has come to be formed.

The history of international relations has been cast in terms of friends versus enemies, but in the post-Cold War period this has become too sharp a dichotomy for most states.[44] For Europeans in particular there has been an attempt to construct a foreign policy paradigm which does not rely on enmities, or for that matter on any kind of binary description of world politics.

Sovereignty, Rights and Justice: International Political Theory Today (Cambridge: Polity, 2002), p. vii. Yet as a guide to public debates it still has some traction.

[43] Europe for Russia, Russia for Europe, Turkey for Europe, Terrorists for the West, have all been variously seen in these terms. See for example Iver B. Neumann and Jennifer Welsh, 'The Other in European Self-definition: A Critical Addendum to the Literature on International Society', *Review of International* Studies, 17/4 (1991), pp. 327–48; Iver B. Neumann, *Russia and the Idea of Europe: A Study in Identity and International Relations* (London: Routledge, 1996); Iver B. Neumann, *Uses of the Other: The 'East' in European Identity Formation* (Manchester University Press, 1999); Richard Jackson, *Writing the War on Terrorism: Language, Politics and Counter-Terrorism* (Manchester: Manchester University Press, 2005). And this has passed into practical politics (and turned on its head), as illustrated by the attempt by some of President Obama's opponents to represent him as foreign. 'Othering: The GOP's 2012 Strategy', *International Policy Digest*, 7 March 2011.

[44] Wendt saw the three main logics, the Hobbesian, Lockean, and Kantian, producing three kinds of role—enemies, friends, and rivals. I have added 'partners' here as a further option. Wendt, *Social Theory of International Politics*. All such terms are anthropomorphizing, as Wendt acknowledged (p. 298), and as McCourt has pointed out, they need not exhaust the way decision-makers, or analysts, might think about roles. McCourt, 'Role-playing and Identity Affirmation in International Politics', p. 8.

Rather, they have moved towards the language of interdependence, multilateralism, and soft power—which in this context means persuading as many others as possible to share the same goals.[45] There is a degree of idealism in this on which individual EU Member States are not confident enough to rely. In consequence, the United States remains a key ally, and a close partner for most European states, with France rejoining NATO and reconstructing its relationship with Washington after the low point of conflict over the Iraq War.

While there are variations between individual countries, and also over time, the nature of European political culture, expressed variously through EU foreign policy, the welfare state model, and Europe's increasingly cosmopolitan post-imperial societies, has led to transatlantic divergences on some basic attitudes. American commentators have noticed this change, notably Robert Kagan in his (overplayed) metaphor of Mars versus Venus.[46] The Bush administration was deeply unpopular across the political spectrum in western Europe, while Barack Obama was welcomed as 'one of us' on his pre-election trip to Germany, and continues to be more popular in Europe than at home.[47] While mixed race origins and a multilateralist, cosmopolitan outlook antagonize many US conservatives, they are precisely what appeal to most Europeans. Yet even under a Democratic President there is still an element of explicit differentiation in the relationship with the United States, sharpened by disagreements over social issues like capital punishment, abortion, and religion, where Europe's mix of secularism and a growing Islamic population contrasts with the strength of Christian evangelism on the other side of the Atlantic.[48]

There are also the more straightforward elements of economic rivalry and unease about the global exercise of power, particularly in support of Israel, and in the pursuit of jihadists through rendition or the use of drones. Thus to the extent that Europeans have a growing sense of their collective identity, it has been formed less through the contrast with enemies than through a sense of not being the United States. If Europe is not yet a pole in a multipolar world it is becoming now its own cultural reference point, and no longer merely a

[45] Joseph S. Nye, Jr, *Soft Power: The Means to Success in World Politics* (New York: Public Affairs, 2004); Christopher Hill, 'The European Union and Soft Power', in Inderjeet Parmar and Michael Cox (eds), *Soft Power and Hegemony in US Foreign Affairs: Theoretical, Historical and Contemporary Perspectives* (Abingdon: Routledge, 2010).

[46] Robert Kagan, *Of Paradise and Power: America and Europe in the New World Order* (London: Atlantic, 2003).

[47] In 2012 over 80 per cent in Germany, France, and Britain had confidence in Obama, as opposed to 61 per cent of US respondents. Pew Global Attitudes Project, 'Confidence in the U.S. President', Key Indicators Database [webpage], <http://www.pewglobal.org/database/?indicator=6> accessed 7 August 2012.

[48] Pew Global Attitudes Project, 'Confidence in the U.S. President'. In the 'American ideas and Customs' section of the survey, to the question' 'Is it good or bad that American ideas and customs are spreading here?' the responses for eight EU Member States varied between 40 per cent of Italians and 23 per cent of Germans replying 'good', p. 91.

subordinate part of the West. This is, however, a long historical process in which the changing nature of European societies is only one, reinforcing, factor.[49]

If the United States represents a different way of being Western, but is still an ally, there are those which constitute actual rivals, if not obvious threats, to Europeans. The situation is complicated by the EU's aspiration, articulated in its Security Strategy of 2003, to make almost all potential rivals 'strategic partners'.[50] Thus China, India, and Russia fit in with European conceptions of a world in which power has to be shared, and solutions to major problems like climate change and nuclear proliferation sought through cooperation with states of very different political complexions. Wariness and realism will still be necessary, but not at the expense of trade and diplomatic coordination.

But where does civil society fit in to this pragmatic approach? Indians have been present in the UK for many years, and have become the nearest thing to an effective ethnic lobby that country possesses. More recently increasing numbers of Russian and Chinese immigrants have come to live in European societies but have tended to maintain a low profile, not least due to the fact that many attain economic self-sufficiency. This is not quite true of Britain, where the combination of disaffected Russians, some of them rich oligarchs, with hostile reactions from the Russian government, seriously damaged relations between London and Moscow, especially after the murder of Alexander Litvinenko in 2006. In Germany the mix of many *Aussiedler*, or ethnic German refugees, with the 18 million inhabitants of the old DDR who have become nostalgic for the old order complicated attitudes in a different way. Russia is a key country for Germany and for German public opinion, for reasons of history, geopolitics, and energy supply.[51]

Less dramatically, exiled Chinese and Tibetan protests against the Chinese government in a number of countries have from time to time complicated relations with Beijing. The small numbers of active dissidents who campaign to expose human rights abuses in either China or Russia get a sympathetic but not very responsive hearing from public opinion in the EU. Apart from occasional expressions of concern, as over Chechnya, Tibet, and abuses such

[49] Robert Cooper, *The Breaking of Nations: Order and Chaos in the Twenty-First Century* (London: Atlantic Books, 2003) pp. 155–72; Michael Smith and Rebecca Steffenson, 'The EU and the United States', in Christopher Hill and Michael Smith (eds), *International Relations and the European Union* (2nd edn, Oxford: Oxford University Press, 2011), pp. 404–31.

[50] The Strategy listed the USA, Russia, Japan, China, Canada, and India as the targets for strategic partnerships. Javier Solana, *A Secure Europe in a Better World: European Security Strategy* (Paris: European Union Institute for Security Studies, 2003), pp. 20–1.

[51] In the 1990s there were battles between the Foreign Ministry and the Ministries of Finance and the Interior over the balance between the various interests at stake in the handling of the many issues generated by the changes in regime and by migration. Wolf-Dieter Eberwein and Karl Kaiser (eds), *Germany's New Foreign Policy: Decision-Making in an Interdependent World* (Houndmills: Palgrave, 2001), pp. 45–6 and 231–2.

as the persecutions of the Falun Gong in China, or the pressure on critical journalists in Russia, they have had little influence on official policy.

There is one dimension, however, which does provide a notable, if indirect, link between civil society in Europe and Russia, China, and India—three of the so-called BRIC rising powers. This is the perceived threat coming not from any nation-state, but from the transnational force of Islamic fundamentalism. India has a large Muslim minority of around 140 million, and is nervous of religion fanning the flames of social and economic unrest, abetted by outside states—in particular by Pakistan. China and Russia by contrast are more concerned about the secessionist impact Islam could have, among the Turkic Uighur people of the Xinjiang region in the first case, and in the Muslim periphery of the Russian Federal Republic in the second.[52] Some of the concern is over terrorism, which I return to later, but too often that is a cover for concern about the distinctive political and cultural identity which Islam represents, in states nervous about disunity.

To some degree the same syndrome is evident in Europe, leading some political tendencies to be sympathetic to calls for international solidarity among those threatened by fundamentalism. There is a certain piquancy in the fact that this appeal to defend 'Western civilisation' makes allies of ex-communists like Vladimir Putin, conservative supporters of the Christian traditions of Europe—including populists like Silvio Berlusconi—and secularist children of the Enlightenment.[53] They are opposed by those who are angry about human rights abuses in Russia and China, and/or concerned for minority rights inside the EU, or believers in the multicultural ideal. Thus the divisions within European states on the changing nature of civil society are mirrored in diverging positions on how to handle fundamentalism at the international level, and whom to engage with.

Terror, with al-Qaeda as its main exponent, is almost universally acknowledged by Europeans as the main contemporary threat to their security. But opinion polls equally suggest that most people agree that Islam per se is not a violent religion. However misguided the 'War on Terror', even that strategy attempted to make a clear distinction between Islam as a faith and the fundamentalists who had taken to terror. Yet extremists always breed their counterparts, so that the far right in Europe predictably reworked its racism into an anti-Muslim crusade. But Islam is now embedded inside most European societies; the last time it clashed with Christianity on a civilizational level was at the siege of Vienna in 1683, and that was the last major episode of a conflict which had been at its height a century earlier. Those who oppose it

[52] On the Uighurs in German–Chinese relations, see Chapter 4, footnote 42.

[53] According to Tony Blair, who spoke to the Russian leader on 11 September 2001, Putin spoke spontaneously and was 'outraged'—also then hoping for support in his war in Chechnya. Anthony Seldon, *Blair* (London: The Free Press, 2005), p. 488.

now are mostly concerned on cultural grounds, not liking the manifestations of diversity which it brings to everyday life but also concerned about the exemptions some adherents claim from human rights regimes.[54]

Yet this picture of broad tolerance challenged by tiny minorities on both extremes is not the full picture. The organized cells of actual jihadists who operate in Europe find shelter where they can according to tactical needs, and strike where they think the strategic gain will be greatest. They are able to do this because of the anonymity they find when living among the larger Muslim populations, which is why the security services give so much attention to the latter, often with heavy-handed and counter-productive investigations. This is not just a matter of extremists seeking an environment in which they do not stand out, although this is even more relevant for the 'lone wolves' who seek to emulate al-Qaeda without being under its command. It is clear that a significant minority of Muslims, especially young people from the second and third immigrant generations, oppose some of the tenets of Western democracy, and have a degree of sympathy for jihadism, even for some acts of terrorism. This is particularly true in Britain, where the Rushdie affair of 1989 inaugurated a long period of tension over issues of blasphemy and freedom of speech. The foreign policy of the Blair government then compounded these difficulties, with the result that a 2007 poll showed that 37 per cent of Muslims aged between 17 and 24 would prefer to live under Sharia than British law, as opposed to 17 per cent of those over 55. It was notable that as many as 86 per cent of respondents said that religion was the most important thing in their lives—faith being the source of identity for those with mixed roots and cultures.[55] This makes for a dramatic contrast with non-Muslim Britons.[56] Furthermore, right across Europe many young Muslims alienated by discrimination and lack of job opportunities have found their identity through religion rather than nationality or political ideology.[57]

[54] Gideon Calder and Emanuela Ceva (eds), *Diversity in Europe: Dilemmas of Differential Treatment in Theory and in Practice* (London: Routledge, 2011).

[55] Poll conducted by Populus for the conservative think-tank Policy Exchange. See Munira Mirza, Abi Senthilkumaran, and Zein Ja'far, *Living Apart Together: British Muslims and the Paradox of Multiculturalism* (London: Policy Exchange, 2007), available online <http://www.policyexchange.org.uk/publications/category/item/living-apart-together-british-muslims-and-the-paradox-of-multiculturalism>.

[56] A 2011 European survey asked respondents whether they thought of themselves primarily as Christians or as nationals of their home countries: 21 per cent in Britain thought of themselves first as Christian, compared to 8 per cent in France, 23 per cent in Germany, and 22 per cent in Spain. Pew Global Attitudes Project, 2011 Spring Survey Topline Results (21 July 2011), p. 49, <http://www.pewglobal.org/files/2011/07/Pew-Global-Attitudes-Muslim-Western-Relations-Topline.pdf> accessed 7 August 2012.

[57] Olivier Roy, *Secularism Confronts Islam* (New York: Columbia University Press, 2007), pp. 65–90.

Generalizations mask the diversity which characterizes Muslims as much as any religious group.[58] Nonetheless, there are certain attitudinal tendencies which inhibit social integration just as much as do physical ghettoes. Table 5.1 shows that at the high-point of the search for Osama Bin Laden, in 2006, a significant minority of Muslims in the bigger EU states identified with the al-Qaeda leader. The figures were clearly highest in the two countries which had actually suffered terrorist attacks from within—Spain and the UK.

The numbers in Tables 5.1 and 5.3 showing sympathy for Islamism or considering that suicide bombers might have some justification, are not so small as to be insignificant. They might conceivably have been inflated by a degree of bravado, particularly on the part of the younger respondents, but we

Table 5.1. Muslim degrees of confidence in Osama Bin Laden (as %; 'don't knows' have been excluded)

	A lot/some	Not much/none
British Muslims	14	68
French Muslims	5	93
German Muslims	7	83
Spanish Muslims	16	75

Question asked: 'How much confidence do you have in Osama Bin Laden to do the right thing regarding world affairs?'
Source: 'The Great Divide: How Westerners and Muslims View Each Other', thirteen-nation Pew Global Attitudes Survey, surveys of between 400 and 413 Muslim respondents in each country conducted April–May 2006 (Washington DC: Pew, June 2006), pp. 25 and 60–1. Available online <http://www.pewglobal.org/files/pdf/253.pdf>.

Table 5.2. Islamic faith in relation to life in modern society (%)

	% Yes conflict	% No conflict	% Don't know/refused answer
France	26	74	0
French Muslims	28	72	0
GB	54	35	11
GB Muslims	47	49	4
Germany	70	26	4
German Muslims	36	57	7
Spain	58	36	6
Spanish Muslims	25	71	4

Question asked: 'Do you think there is a natural conflict between being a devout Muslim and living in a modern society, or don't you think so?'
Source: 'The Great Divide: How Westerners and Muslims View Each Other', 13-nation Pew Global Attitudes Survey, p. 49.

58 A point stressed by the authoritative *Muslim Networks and Movements in Western Europe*, a report published by the Pew Forum on Religion and Public Life (Washington, DC: Pew Research Center, September 2010), available online <http://www.pewforum.org/Muslim/Muslim-Networks-and-Movements-in-Western-Europe.aspx>.

Table 5.3. Attitudes to suicide bombing (%)

	Often justified	Sometimes	Rarely	Never	Don't Know/Refused
French Muslims	6	10	19	64	1
GB Muslims	3	12	9	70	6
German Muslims	1	6	6	83	3
Spanish Muslims	6	10	9	69	7

Question asked: 'Some people think that suicide bombing and other forms of violence against civilian targets are justified in order to defend Islam from its enemies. Other people believe that, no matter what the reason, this kind of violence is never justified. Do you personally feel that this kind of violence is often justified to defend Islam, sometimes justified, rarely justified, or never justified?'
Source: 'The Great Divide: How Westerners and Muslims View Each Other', 13-nation Pew Global Attitudes Survey, p. 57.

Table 5.4. Attitudes to Muslims (%)

States	(1) Total % with a very favourable or somewhat favourable view of Muslims	(2) Total % thinking Islam the most violent religion
Britain	64	75
France	64	90
Germany	45	79
Spain	37	87

Questions asked: (1) Please tell me if you have a very favourable, somewhat favourable, somewhat unfavourable or very unfavourable opinion of Muslims; (2) Which one of the religions that I name do you think of as the most violent—Christianity, Islam, Judaism, or Hinduism?
Source: Pew Global Attitudes Project, 2011 Spring Survey Topline Results, pp. 46 and 49.

might also speculate that many Muslims would be cautious about revealing sympathy for the declared enemies of the country in which they live. So far as the perception of a clash between religious devotion and life in a modern society is concerned (which was also asked about Christianity but produced percentages at about half the level of the replies about Islam), the data in Table 5.2 indicate that at least a quarter of Muslims in these major EU states (nearly a half in the UK) feel conflicted over following their faith in what is a largely secular, and increasingly suspicious, society. Except in France, where faith is a strictly private matter, the general population is even clearer about this conflict, with over half seeing Islamic devotion and modernity as incompatible. The perception of difficult relations between Muslims and other citizens has been confirmed by subsequent polls: for example, despite generally favourable views of Muslims as such, a majority of people in four large European states named Islam as the most violent religion (Table 5.4), which denotes a continuing distance between large numbers of people on a matter central to their lives and to social cohesion.

Thus there exists objective evidence for a small number of activists who reject any identification with the majority culture of the countries in which they (or more likely their parents or grandparents) have settled. This minority

Table 5.5. Immigrant populations: Popular estimates versus official statistics[a]

	Perception	Reality
UK	27	10
France	26	9
Netherlands	25	11
Spain	24	13
Germany	23	13
Italy	23	6
AVERAGE	24.7	10.3

[a] Foreign-born, as % of population (data a combination of OECD statistics and national statistical offices, 2008).
Question asked: 'In your opinion, what percentage of the total (COUNTRY) population are immigrants?'
Source: *Transatlantic Trends: Immigration 2009* (German Marshall Fund and Partners, 2009), p. 7. Available online <http://trends.gmfus.org/files/archived/immigration/doc/TTI_2009_Key.pdf> accessed 30 March 2013.

creates problems for the Muslim communities in which they live, both of a practical nature through security monitoring and psychologically because of uncertainties over identity—do they reject their own militants entirely? Can they feel fully accepted by wider society given such opinion amidst their ranks? For its part the majority cannot help but be concerned about possible fifth columns, particularly when attacks have already taken place. And it is all too easy to slide from fear of a small number of hostile jihadists into antagonism towards the Muslim community as a whole, and thence to minorities or immigrants in general. This is particularly so given that all populations seem to have a tendency to exaggerate wildly the actual numbers of immigrants amongst them. In a 2009 poll (Table 5.5) respondents in six European countries thought on average that a quarter of their national populations consisted of immigrants, whereas official statistics show the average number to be close to 10 per cent. Such estimates are no doubt affected by the assumption that differences of colour and dress must denote immigrant status, when the individuals observed may well have been born in the country concerned.

It is clear, therefore, that notions about 'friends' and 'enemies' in the international arena overlap with domestic society and politics through various transnational mechanisms, some tangible through the movement of people and resources, but some simply at the level of ideas, perceptions—and fears. Conceptions of difference and solidarity within society have always been determined in part by international conflict, as with attitudes towards communists in Cold War America. For when the most serious choices of life seem at stake, over security, principle, and in this case faith, fracture lines open up in attitudes towards a polity. People are expected, by government and by the majority, to identify with the country they are living in. Those who either have doubts, or are thought to have them, will come under suspicion, however unreasonably. The more pronounced the social and religious mix in a given society, the more this polarization is likely to happen under conditions of strain. Moreover, the idealism of the European Union and its foreign policy is not enough to make either citizens or individual governments feel secure. They have retained the right to act at the national level, not least because that is where feelings of identity still predominantly reside.

CONCLUSIONS

This chapter has surveyed the issues of national identity and interest in the context of the increasing social diversity being experienced by European states. It has attempted to show that official foreign policy, being one of the major means by which the internal and external are brought into contact, helps to shape national identity as well as being the frame within which debate about national interests takes place. This point has been made elsewhere, albeit largely at the theoretical level. What the analysis here adds, apart from the comparative European perspective, is a focus on the nature of civil society, and how that has become embroiled in a two-way interaction with foreign policy issues. As a result, aspects of national identity have been called into question, and depending on the state in question may even be said to be in flux. This is evident in how decision-makers, and publics, conceive of themselves in relation to Europe, to the rest of the world, and to transnational factors, whether actors or ideas. Critical in this process have been notions of friends and enemies, 'us and them', communities and threats, which are no longer easy to cast just in terms of relations between states. Identity involves defining the self both against presumed difference and through identifying with presumed similarity, processes which are now complicated by social mobility and diversity.

On one view, state identities are largely a fiction, convenient for politicians but without significance for actual behaviour. Yet we saw in Chapter 4 how those states which have a sense of themselves which is conflicted because of difficult recent histories, or because of centrifugal forces, find it particularly difficult to deal with the new challenge represented by large-scale immigration. They tend to avoid choices on the matter, leading to 'parallel societies'. Conversely, states which are confident in their own identity, such as France and Denmark, tend (for good or ill) to take a straightforward, mono-cultural, approach to minorities. But neither group is free of foreign policy complications, any more than are those states which espouse multiculturalism and who seem more obviously vulnerable. This is partly because dedicated adversaries of the West like al-Qaeda do not distinguish between variations of Western society, for all of Bin Laden's propaganda, and because in principle all Muslims look beyond the state to the *umma* as their primary reference group. More profoundly, it is because external events reverberate often and unpredictably in an environment of diversity, where diasporas proliferate and the relationship between state and society is in flux.[59]

If the passing of time were to mean that minorities lost their distinctiveness, enabling them to take part in the political process on equal terms with the majority, then national identities would be reinforced through the process of integration. Alternatively both nations and minorities would be subsumed under some emerging version of a common European identity—a notion which seems more realistic to outsiders than to Europeans themselves.[60] As Wæver has pointed out, while Member States of the EU may cooperate on a given common policy, 'the story sustaining this policy is very different from one country to another'.[61] By extension, there are also always different stories being told within each country; if they turn out not to impede consensus on certain key values and institutions, then social cohesion and a broad sense of shared identity become possible. If, on the other hand, diversity extends to the deepest layers of customs, beliefs, and principles, this can present a state with major challenges. In particular, it can mean that the domestic sources of foreign policy become more complex and less predictable, just as foreign policy itself now stirs up divisions in civil society, calling national identity into question far more than in the days when decision-makers enjoyed a free hand.

One of the key issues arising from these complications is that of how far the increasingly transnational dimension of society affects loyalty—to the state and to the nation. A perceived exclusion from shared identity opens up space for allegiances to go elsewhere. This has become a serious anxiety in the age of terrorism, and is felt keenly in the realm of foreign and security policies. On the other hand, while loyalty may be central to bureaucrats and to military discipline, it may not be an appropriate quality to expect in civil society. It is to this discussion which we now turn.

[59] On Bin Laden see Chapter 2, footnote 72. Certain *foreign policies*, however, do draw more fire, as argued in various parts of this book.

[60] With the exception of theorists like Jürgen Habermas, whom Castiglione rightly criticizes for underestimating the diversity of Europe, and constructing a single ethnicity for it. Dario Castiglione, 'Political Identity in a Community of Strangers', in Checkel and Katzenstein (eds), *European Identity*, p. 46.

[61] Ole Wæver, 'Identity, Communities and Foreign Policy', p. 40.

6

Loyalty, security, and democracy

Uncertainty over a common identity can be perfectly compatible with a functioning and peaceful democracy, as Canada continues to demonstrate. Furthermore, identity is not necessarily the cause of the difficult internal conflicts it may be associated with—the two phenomena may share deeper roots. But a failure to accept *any* shared understanding of national identity—whether on the part of minorities or of the majority—is certainly an indicator of problems in store. In the eyes of the majority, and even more importantly of those acting on behalf of the state, the perception that a given group has a strong sense of separate identity all too easily shades into accusations of disloyalty. This is especially the case if that identity is seen as taking priority over nationality in the state in question, and/or if there are significant transnational ties to an original homeland or faith community. In democratic states like those of the European Union tensions soon arise over the competing values—all to be honoured in their own way—of patriotism, liberty, security, diversity, consensus, and human rights. When passionate differences over foreign policy are added to the mix, the potential arises for serious internal cleavages, and even violence. This chapter seeks to explore the tensions over the issue of loyalty which arise through the transnational dimension of ethnocultural diversity, in the context of: firstly, the practice and potential for subversion; second, the problems which arise over recruiting minorities into government service; third, the dilemmas over making foreign policy in a democratic system where minorities may feel at the same time excluded and highly motivated to participate. All of these issues relate to the problem of security, but also to the question: security for whom?

SUBVERSION

Prejudice against minorities has historically often taken the form of fear that they might constitute 'Trojan horses' or fifth columns working in the interests of a hostile foreign power. In early modern Europe religion was usually the marker for such groups, with the Jesuits in Elizabeth's England being seen as the agents of Spain or France, while in his turn Philip II of Spain was fearful of French Huguenots fomenting rebellion in Catalonia.[1] Much of this was exaggerated and a cover for the real preference, which was religious orthodoxy and the avoidance of domestic factionalism. But in each case there were enough individuals actively working against the state and with encouragement from outside to provide the motive—or excuse—for moves against a whole community. By the twentieth century the principle of national self-determination had largely replaced religion as the source of suspicion over ethnic minorities, with notable cases being the Armenians in Turkey and the Germans in Alsace-Lorraine after 1918. The Jews were a convenient scapegoat in all periods, despite their lack of any homeland to show preference to, culminating in the genocidal persecution by the Nazis.[2] War-time inevitably heightens the desire to hammer down any nail sticking up from the surface, as the Japanese say about non-conformists. The slow spread of democracy after 1945, and of values which gave some respect to minority rights, lessened the tendency to see dangers in difference, while the Cold War decoupled foreign policy from domestic issues of multinationality. Fears about subversion then focused more on the ideological enemies within, as with the hysteria of McCarthyism. It was only when the Cold War ended that the pressures for national self-determination were explosively released, leading immediately to the break-up of Yugoslavia, the Soviet Union, and Czechoslovakia and to the emergence of fracture-lines in such multinational states as Italy, Spain, and the United Kingdom.

On top of such geopolitical developments, the challenges to national unity represented by globalization, in particular increased migration and the revolution in personal communications, meant that concerns over subversion could easily arise given the right conditions. These are: the facilitation of transnational politics by the free movement of people, goods, money, and ideas in the EU's single market, combined with foreign policy activism, and sources of internal disaffection. Two of these conditions were enough in the UK in the 1980s, when clandestine help from Libya, fuelled by Gadaffi's ideological hostility to Western colonialism, sustained the Provisional IRA's bombing campaign. They have applied more widely since 9/11 and the onset of the War on Terror.

Of the three conditions, that of vulnerability to transnational political operations applies to all the European Union states, by virtue of the Single Market, although the opt-outs of Britain and Ireland from the Schengen regime give them a degree of special insulation. But it applies most to the states

[1] J. H. Elliott, *Europe Divided, 1559–1598* (London: Collins, The Fontana History of Europe, 1968), pp. 302–4; J. H. Elliott, *Imperial Spain, 1469–1716* (London: Edward Arnold, 1963), pp. 226–7.

[2] At first the Nazis encouraged Jewish emigration in the hope of actually creating a new homeland in Palestine, but soon came to see this as a potential threat to Germany. Richard Evans, *The Third Reich in Power* (London: Allen Lane, 2005), p. 557.

which have particularly large ethnic minority populations, and thus people who feel connected to one or more of: their original homeland, their global diaspora, and their fellow-religionists. The second condition, foreign policy activism, is more difficult to identify, not least because activism per se does not necessarily cause domestic opposition—it is what is done with foreign policy that counts. But the more active a foreign policy (especially if it intervenes in the affairs of other states), the greater the chances of a collision between the national interest as interpreted by decision-makers and the particular concerns of a minority. People may complain about passivity in foreign policy, but few are likely to conspire against the authorities because of it. On this basis the European states most active beyond the borders of the EU over the last two decades have been, in roughly descending order, the UK, France, Italy, Spain, Denmark, the Netherlands, and Germany. In consequence all have at times adopted stances with the potential to stir up unrest at home as much as abroad.

Domestic opposition to foreign policy is only likely to shade over into actual subversion if the third condition is also met, namely the pre-existence of a disaffected minority. In the case of the IRA the 'enemy within' was all too obvious, but governments are sometimes not aware of the existence of serious alienation until it literally blows up in front of them. This was the case for the Spanish government in March 2004 when a group made up mostly of Moroccans resident in the country planted the bombs on the Madrid commuter trains which claimed nearly one thousand casualties. The Aznar government immediately blamed ETA, perhaps in a cynical attempt to deflect blame from its own commitment to the war in Afghanistan, but it was not so illogical at the time to assume that the main threat to civil peace would come from Basque terrorists. The disproportionate effect of actions such as these means that the existence of general disaffection in a society is not the main consideration where subversion is concerned. A mere handful of dedicated individuals working beneath the radar of official awareness can wreak havoc in the lives of their co-citizens, with social and political effects which ripple out far beyond even that.

The other European state which has suffered significantly from subversion connected to the existence of ethnocultural minorities is the United Kingdom.[3] A year after the Madrid bombings fifty-two commuters died as the result of four carefully coordinated suicide bombs on London transport (this

[3] The transnational factor should not blind us to the continued presence of subversion from completely external sources, which is inherently a matter of foreign policy. A notorious example is the murder of Alexander Litvinenko in November 2006 by polonium-210 poisoning, an act the British authorities consider to have been carried out with the connivance of elements from the Russian intelligence services. This was the kind of event familiar from the Cold War, and did not depend on the existence of a fifth column in British society. The severe damage it caused to UK–Russian relations, however, is an indication of how seriously states take any suggestion of subversion.

was the first time suicide bombing had occurred in Europe).[4] Two weeks later a similarly deadly attack was attempted, only to end in failure and the arrests of the perpetrators. In 2006 a plot to blow up seven transatlantic flights out of Heathrow using explosives concealed in liquids was foiled, with three men eventually sentenced to exceptionally long prison terms, at the price of lengthening the queues to pass through airport security for years to come.[5] On 30 June 2007 another plot narrowly failed to kill large numbers of young people at a central London nightclub, whereupon the perpetrators fled to Glasgow, driving a car loaded with explosives into the main door of the airport terminal, but fortunately causing harm only to themselves.

Various other plots seem to have been foiled in the succeeding years.[6] In the two years from January 2007 to January 2009 eighty-six people were convicted of Islamic terrorist offences in Britain.[7] Almost all these attacks on British society and institutions were carried out by British citizens, who had often had help from their transnational contacts, but were hardly the brain-washed victims of a foreign puppet-master. They had taken a calculated decision, persisted with over time, to kill members of their own society in the hope of disrupting the policies of the British state, and in particular its foreign policy. Some, like Richard Reid, the 'shoe-bomber' who failed to blow up the flight he took from Paris to Miami in December 2001, or Germaine Lindsay, who killed nineteen people on the Piccadilly Line on 7 July 2005, were of Afro-Caribbean origin, but the majority came from Anglo-Pakistani backgrounds, usually second or third generation immigrants, while all espoused radical Islamic creeds.[8] The consequence was that the British state was forced to invest heavily in security measures against domestic subversion over the next decade, some of which entailed the sacrifice of long-cherished individual liberties, while France, the United States, and other allies began to talk of 'Londistan' and to demand action against the potential threat it represented to their own security.[9]

[4] As Gandhi had foreseen, 'Western humanism's ever more strident insistence on the supreme value of human life' had distanced itself from other traditions, making such kamikaze attacks profoundly shocking. Charles Townshend, *Terrorism: A Very Short Introduction* (Oxford: Oxford University Press, 2011) pp. 107–8.

[5] Christopher Andrew, *The Defence of the Realm: The Authorized History of MI5* (London: Penguin Books, 2010), pp. 828–33.

[6] Andrew, *The Defence of the Realm: The Authorized History of MI5*, p. 828. Andrew says that in the two and a half years after 7/7, MI5 disrupted six other plots.

[7] Andrew, *The Defence of the Realm: The Authorized History of MI5*. p. 836.

[8] Reid had been a petty criminal in south London who found a purpose in life first through Islam and then jihadism. He travelled to Belgium and then France to launch the attack, but was assisted in the plot by a British Muslim, Saajid Badat.

[9] For a detailed if occasionally lurid account of the impact of charismatic foreign preachers on second generation (or 'post-migrant') British Muslims, see 'Chapter 10: The Lords of Londistan' of Robert S. Leiken, *Europe's Angry Muslims: The Revolt of the Second Generation* (Oxford: Oxford University Press, 2012) pp. 151–88. France had protested well before 9/11 at the British toleration of mosques which preached jihad, and in particular at the harbouring in London of Maghrebian radicals whom they considered responsible for the bombs on the Paris Metro in 1995.

Despite the continued denials of Tony Blair, prime minister between 1997 and 2007, there seems little doubt that the direction of British foreign policy in this period was a key factor in catalysing the hostility which led to such acts of terrorism.[10] The head of MI5 at the time of the Iraq War, Eliza Manningham-Buller, has said that she was not surprised that UK nationals were involved in the 7/7 bombings, as the war had raised the terrorist threat to the country by radicalizing some young Muslims. In evidence to the Chilcot Inquiry on the Iraq War she said that 'the real change came 2003/2004, when there was a sharp increase of threat intelligence relating to British citizens', because there was 'an increasing number of British-born individuals living and brought up in this country, some of them third generation, who were attracted to the ideology of Osama bin Laden and saw the west's activities in Iraq and Afghanistan as threatening their fellow religionists and the Muslim world'.[11] Indeed, as early as 2004 the Permanent Under-Secretary at the Foreign and Commonwealth Office, Sir Michael Jay, had noted, in an internal document: 'Experience of both Ministers and officials working in this area suggests that the scope of British foreign policy and the perception of its negative effect on Muslims globally plays a significant role in creating a feeling of anger and impotence amongst especially the younger generation of British Muslims'.[12]

Unsurprisingly, British Muslims themselves took the same view. In a survey of more than four hundred and fifty Muslim students in further and higher education after the July 2005 bombings, 62 per cent said that British foreign policy had played a 'major' or 'complete' part in leading to the attacks, and more than a quarter said they felt a conflict between their loyalty to the UK and their loyalty to the *umma*.[13] The exhaustive Chilcot Report on the Iraq War is likely to remove any further doubt on the matter.[14]

[10] It was clear before 2001 that British Muslims were becoming increasingly agitated by international issues such as Bosnia, sanctions against Iraq, Palestine, Chechnya, and Kashmir, although before the invasion of Afghanistan it had little specific focus on British foreign policy.

[11] Transcript of Evidence given by Baroness Manningham-Buller, 20 July 2010, pp. 16 and 19, <http://www.iraqinquiry.org.uk/media/48331/20100720am-manningham-buller.pdf> accessed 9 December 2012. Lady Manningham-Buller noted that the Security Services were therefore not surprised by the attacks of 2005; they had been fearing some kind of atrocity. She had already made such observations in a speech at Queen Mary College, London in 2006, explicitly agreed and cleared with the then Home Secretary, John Reid (p. 20).

[12] Foreign and Commonwealth Office internal communication, Sir Michael Jay to Sir Andrew Turnbull (18 May 2004), available online at *The Guardian* website, <http://politics.guardian.co.uk/foi/images/0,9069,1558170,00.html> accessed 14 January 2013. For a development of this argument see Christopher Hill, 'Bringing War Home: Making Foreign Policy in Multicultural Societies', *International Relations*, 21/3 (2007), pp. 269 and 273–6.

[13] The survey was by the Federation of Student Islamic Societies, 'Muslims Admit Loyalty Conflict', *Times Educational Supplement*, 30 September 2005. A Sky Television opinion poll came up with very similar findings. Sky News poll of UK Muslims, fieldwork on 20–21 July 2005, conducted by Communicate Research, <http://www.comres.co.uk/polls/Sky_News_Poll.pdf> accessed 14 January 2013.

[14] At the time of writing, the publication of the Report has been delayed by disputes with the Cabinet Office over what confidential documentation should be put into the public realm.

It is unlikely that even strenuous opposition to what was perceived as an 'unethical foreign policy'[15] would have led to such dire domestic consequences had a significant degree of alienation not already existed among young British Muslims. Paradoxically the development of multiculturalism in the UK had only sharpened the contrast between the serious and in some cases puritanical lives which some Muslims were turning to for identity reasons, and the free and easy lifestyles of secular youth.[16] The substitution of anti-Islamic prejudice for racism based on the mere colour of a person's skin probably also sharpened the sense of hostility. It was the combination of these domestic traits with international relations which helps to explain why the UK has suffered more than any other European country from attempts at subversion.

Only Britain has seen a persistent series of attacks, which can be ascribed to the combination of its strong association over a long period with American power, its forward foreign policy in Iraq and Afghanistan, and the existence of a large number of alienated second and third generation Muslims living in the kind of separate ethnic communities (encouraged by multiculturalism) which make the gathering of good intelligence a major challenge. Among EU states Britain is associated most with the Western policies which have led to so many Muslim deaths in the Middle East, and has thus been seen as a high-value target by al-Qaeda. It is also important that many of its Muslim families came from, and retained their contacts with, the remote Pakistani villages along the Afghan border, where a martial spirit and memories of British imperialism remain part of the local culture.[17] They saw UK foreign policy as being anti-Muslim, regardless of the country's (admittedly tardy) underwriting of Bosnian independence, and role in the war which freed Muslim Kosovo from Serbia. The confluence of these factors made British society particularly vulnerable to terrorism from within.

Other countries also possess significant populations of disaffected Muslim youth, notably France. But here, as in other matters, we come up against 'the

[15] In 2006, thirty-six Muslim associations and leading figures sent a letter to Downing Street calling for Britain to adopt 'a principled foreign policy', and saying that UK foreign policy had made the country a target for terrorism. The reference to the New Labour claim to have introduced ethics into external policy did not go unnoticed. 'Muslim Leaders Want UK to Adopt "Principled" Foreign Policy', <http://www.arabicnews.com> accessed 15 August 2006. 'Muslim leaders say foreign policy makes UK a target', *The Guardian*, 12 August 2006.

[16] Leiken, *Europe's Angry Muslims*, pp. 117–216. There were clearly tensions between the pressures to live like the majority of young Britons, and a certain disgust (and self-disgust) at the contrast with the traditional values of family and religion—the rediscovery of which then produced in some a fanatical fervour. Osama bin Laden himself had made such a 180-degree turn from youthful indulgence to adult asceticism. Leiken, *Europe's Angry Muslims*, p. 88.

[17] There are many cases of British Muslims having gone to Pakistan for training. For example, in November 2011 two men from Ilford in east London were reported as having been killed in US drone strikes in South Waziristan. They had apparently fled from the UK while under control orders, while the brother of one of the men received a life sentence in the UK for having conspired to cause explosions. *The Guardian*, 19 November 2011.

French exception'. Just as the French seem to be able to imbibe cheese and cream without suffering the rising cholesterol levels seen elsewhere, so the French state has managed to avoid domestic terrorism (since 1995 at least) despite the presence of large numbers of disaffected youths from ethnic minorities. A simple explanation of this paradox is that French foreign policy was opposed to the invasion of Iraq and has, since 1956, been seen as generally pro-Arab. Indeed, American neo-conservatives accused President Chirac of having stayed out of the 2003 War precisely through fear of domestic insurgency.

This last motive seems much less plausible than the traditional wish of French leaders to maintain a distance from Britain and the United States, and to maintain good relations with Arab states; a tendency which in its turn may have had a more significant influence on perceptions in the Muslim world than differences over a specific policy. After all, France has taken part in the mission in Afghanistan from the onset, while jihadists have had no illusions about its part in the Western-dominated international order. Fifty-eight French troops were killed in the Lebanon bombs of 1982, and a French airliner was brought down over Niger in 1989 by Libyan-sponsored terrorists. In 2011 France, by this time feeling the wind from a different direction in North Africa, was to be a leading player in the coalition which helped to bring down Colonel Ghaddafi in Libya.

At least as important as an explanation of the relative absence of terrorism inside France in recent years is the fact that however angry and neglected Muslims in the country may feel, their discontent focuses mostly on internal problems, over such matters as poor housing, unemployment, and a lack of respect. Paradoxically, the relative benefits which British multiculturalism has bestowed on minorities has freed up their angry minorities to focus on international issues, whereas in France they are still preoccupied with trying to gain acceptance as citizens and workers. Young Maghrebians in Paris whistle the French football team at the national stadium, but when they riot—as Olivier Roy has pointed out—they tend not to display the support for jihad, or even the symbols of Islam, seen regularly in British demonstrations.[18]

In practice, those willing to engage in actual subversion are a very small minority of the minorities, and they may be found—as individuals or small cells—in any country. Their attacks are intermittent and ephemeral in the sense that they rarely produce sustained campaigns. In Spain there has been no major incident of Islamic terrorism since 2004, which again suggests the relevance of the foreign policy connection, since the new Zapatero

[18] Olivier Roy, 'Foreword', in Jonathan Laurence and Justin Vaisse (eds), *Integrating Islam: Political and Religious Challenges in Contemporary France* (Washington, DC: The Brookings Institution, 2006), p. xi.

government fulfilled its promise to withdraw troops from Iraq, while the mandate of the Spanish forces in Afghanistan is effectively limited to non-combat activity. Equally, Spanish immigration has only reached high levels in recent years, while its Muslims come mostly from the closely neighbouring state of Morocco, without close links to the conflicts of the Middle East. Since Morocco also fears Islamic fundamentalism, security cooperation between the two countries on counter-terrorism has increased significantly since the Madrid bombings.[19]

Thus subversion associated with ethnocultural diversity has been a relatively rare and patchy occurrence in Europe, despite the dramatic effects it has had when visible. As is always the case with terrorism, a very small number of determined people, causing a limited number of deaths, has had a huge impact in terms of creating fear, antagonism, and social tension. They can also tie up huge state resources in the attempts to prevent recurrence and catch perpetrators. One 'spectacle' created by a few individuals all too easily creates an 'evoked set' of negative and fear-strewn perceptions towards a whole community.[20] But events such as those in Madrid and London in 2004–5 would have not happened at all had it not been for the coincidence of migration, heightened social diversity, and major foreign policy events which have raised issues about loyalty and security for both the state and some of the minorities within it. Civil societies which had become stable, if only over the last thirty years in the case of the post-dictatorships of Spain and Greece, were thus suddenly plunged into spirals of fear, uncertainty, and antagonism, with panic-stricken authorities taking measures which then further heightened tensions. Security measures were understandable in that citizens have the right to expect their governments to protect them from terrorism, regardless of the relatively small numbers of victims by comparison, say, with war-time bombing. If contentious foreign policy issues were gradually to disappear, that might help to refurbish civil peace, but the truly dedicated enemies of Western society will strike where and when they can, without regard to political niceties. Moreover, even moving out of the grim shadow of terrorism does not mean that civil society is free of all divisive issues.

[19] Sarah Wolff, *The Mediterranean Dimension of the European Union's Internal Security* (Houndmills: Palgrave, 2012) pp. 173–4.

[20] The 'spectacle' refers to the idea of Guy Debord about the commodification of modern society, and how we are merely the audience of a show, not in control of our own lives. Guy Debord, *La société du spectacle* (Paris: Buchet-Chastel, 1967). On the impact of these ideas on attempts at terrorism see Gordon Carr, *The Angry Brigade: A History of Britain's First Urban Guerrilla Group* (London: Gollancz, 1975), pp. 17–24. The 'evoked set' is a term used in psychology to refer to the human tendency for a whole group of associations to be triggered by a given stimulus. See Robert Jervis, *Perception and Misperception in International Politics* (Princeton, NJ: Princeton University Press, 1976), pp. 203–16.

PUBLIC SERVICE AND RECRUITMENT

In the normal course of things, issues of loyalty arise on both sides between the state and its citizens. On the one hand, those holding state offices can be too quick to see internal protest or non-conformity as evidence of subversion. On the other, citizens often regard even the standard demands made of them as excessive given their conception of the modern state as a vehicle for providing their security and welfare, but at the lowest tax level possible. Democracies try to avoid making extra demands on their citizens except in emergencies, when civil liberties may be suspended, new taxes raised, or conscription into the armed services introduced. All tend to strain consensus and loyalty to the limit, particularly military service, which entails the risking of life for the collective good. Nonetheless, most people are loyal most of the time, even under extreme conditions, as witnessed by the extraordinary acceptance of duty by millions during the carnage of world war.

These structural tensions may be exacerbated by an increase in social diversity, especially when ethnic or cultural groups are inward-looking. Matters come to a head when citizens are pressed into extra duties in the service of the state, or when some wish to enter public service but find their way barred by suspicions over the reliability or patriotism of the particular group to which they belong—or by simple prejudice. Conscription in most Western countries has been abolished over the last few decades, so issues like that which arose over the boxer Cassius Clay's refusal to serve in the Vietnam War, changing his name to Muhammad Ali, are unlikely to arise. Israel, as so often, is a special case, refusing to call up its Arab citizens, whether Muslim or Christian, on the face of it protecting them from a potentially agonizing choice between their state and their identity, but also entrenching the elements of division in Israeli society through the questioning of loyalty which such a policy implies.[21] As the military profession is built upon the principle of unquestioning obedience to orders, there has been a general trend towards professional soldiering which will suffer less from having to reflect the full spectrum of society—including the principle of conscientious objection so important to religious and ideological minorities.[22]

[21] Alon Peled, *A Question of Loyalty: Military Manpower Policy in Multi-Ethnic States* (Ithaca: Cornell University Press, 1998), pp. 14–15 and 127–68. Even the Druze, whose battle performance was exemplary, were kept in a segregated unit for many years (until 1991). Israeli governments took the view that it would be both cruel and dangerous (for the state) to conscript Israeli Arabs. See also Hillel Frisch, *Israel's Security and its Arab Citizens* (Cambridge: Cambridge University Press, 2011), which argues that Israel's security concerns over its Arab population are not unreasonable, and derive from the inherent link between internal and external threats.

[22] See Bruno Coppetiers, 'Political Loyalty and Military Disobedience: Militarism, Pacifism, Realism and Just-war Theory Compared', in Michael Waller and Andrew Linklater (eds), *Political Loyalty and the Nation-State* (London: Routledge, 2003), pp. 74–88. Interestingly, France, with

Among the fifteen states which were members of the EU in 2000, only Austria, Denmark, and Greece still retain conscription, and they each require less than a year's service.[23] But the move to a professional military can still produce identity problems. Germany delayed its change as long as possible (until July 2011) because, paradoxically, it saw military service as a way of inculcating democratic and pacific values. By the same token that aim might now be more difficult to achieve, not least because recruitment to the professional forces reveals a disproportionate intake of those from the ex-Communist eastern *Länder*, where unemployment is at its highest.[24] If Germany is to take part in more foreign missions in future that would mean the death toll being higher in the poor east than elsewhere—although this is a familiar phenomenon for countries like Britain and Italy, with their clear regional differences of both wealth and recruitment.[25] The issue of ethnic diversity remains in the background for the moment, but could complicate matters even further.

The Dreyfus case stands as a permanent reminder to all European states of both the shame of discrimination on ethnic or religious grounds (in this case through anti-semitism) and the turmoil which can be caused by the presumed disloyalty of minority groups. Alfred Dreyfus, who was not only a Jew but an Alsatian and thus doubly suspect given France's open sore after the loss of Alsace-Lorraine in 1871, was wrongly accused in 1894 of having spied for Germany.[26] He was incarcerated on Devil's Island, only emerging after four years thanks to the powerful campaign led by Emile Zola. Even then Dreyfus was not fully exonerated, and the arguments over his guilt or innocence continued to represent a marker between right and left in French society for the remainder of the Third Republic—some would say even to this day.[27]

its strong civic nationalism, was particularly slow to recognize conscientious objection. See Margaret Levi, *Consent, Dissent and Patriotism* (Cambridge: Cambridge University Press, 1997), pp. 185–90.

[23] Austria requires seven months' service, Denmark four, and Greece nine, though conscripts usually have to be reservists afterwards for a period. Switzerland also retains conscription. See also p. 191, this volume.

[24] 'The Draft ends in Germany, but Questions of Identity Endure', *New York Times*, 30 June 2011. The report cited an unnamed 'expert' study which said that 30 per cent of military personnel came from the east as opposed to 16 per cent of the population.

[25] UK armed services have traditionally drawn on the poorer (ex-)industrial areas, such as Scotland, Lancashire, and South Wales. The Italian armed services, including the *Carabinieri*, have been one of the few routes to employment for young men from the *Mezzogiorno*.

[26] The loyalties of French Jews in relation to foreign policy had been questioned after their opposition to the French government's support for the persecution of an innocent Jew in Syria in 1840. See Ilan Zvi Baron, 'The Problem of Dual Loyalty', *Canadian Journal of Political Science*, 42/4 (2009), pp. 1031–2.

[27] Fernand Braudel once cited approvingly Julien Benda's remark of the 1930s that the history of France has in many ways been 'a permanent Dreyfus affair'. Fernand Braudel, *The Identity of France*. Volume I: *History and Environment* (London: Collins, 1988), p. 120. For a blow-by-blow account of the Dreyfus affair and its vicious prejudices, see Frederick Brown, *For the Soul of France: Culture Wars in the Age of Dreyfus* (New York: Knopf, 2010), pp. 175–230, and for one

The suspicions and maltreatment (through renditions and imprisonment in the Guantánamo Bay camp) inflicted on some Muslim suspects in the aftermath of 9/11 have uncomfortable echoes of the Dreyfus scandal. The United States has been the major player, but various European governments—notably the British—have cooperated with Washington while struggling to convince domestic critics that human rights and respect for minorities have not been sacrificed. The latter position became much less credible when it emerged that as part of its policy of engagement with Colonel Ghaddafi after 2003 Britain had extradited some opponents of the regime to a dubious fate back in Tripoli—only then to see them emerge as victors in the revolution of 2011.[28] Most of the victims of rendition seem to have been in transit through the EU, but some, like Moazzam Begg and Babar Ahmad, are themselves citizens of a Member State (in their cases Britain), which inevitably increases the degree of fear and alienation felt by those in their particular minority community.[29] Thus the moderate website *Sala@m* maintains a 'Database of arrests and outcomes', as well as an 'Islamophobia dossier', to monitor the high level of suspicion towards UK Muslims.[30]

This reduction of trust on both sides must make Muslims less likely to apply to serve in the police or armed services. Indeed those who consider the

which places it in the context of the Third Republic's politics, see Alfred Cobban, *A History of Modern France*. Volume III: *1871–1962* (Harmondsworth: Penguin, 1965), pp. 48–57.

[28] The Council of Europe's 'Marty Report' showed that at the very least some EU states, including Germany, Italy, Sweden, and the UK, had turned a blind eye to dubious CIA activities on their territory in relation to prisoner transfers. 'Europeans "assisted CIA renditions"', *Financial Times*, 7 June 2006. This was denied by the Member States concerned, but their denials have rung increasingly hollow. The European Parliament subsequently endorsed the Marty Report: 'Extraordinary Rendition: Text Adopted 6 July 2006, P6_TA(2006)0316', available online <http://www.europarl.europa.eu/sides/getDoc.do?pubRef=-//EP//TEXT+TA+P6-TA-2006-0316+0+DOC+XML+V0//EN&language=EN> accessed 27 December 2011. For the Marty Report itself see Council of Europe Parliamentary Assembly, Committee on Legal Affairs and Human Rights, 'Alleged Secret Detentions and Unlawful Inter-state Transfers Involving Council of Europe Member States', Draft report—Part II (Explanatory memorandum) (7 June 2006), available online <http://assembly.coe.int/committeedocs/2006/20060606_ejdoc162006partii-final.pdf> accessed 14 January 2013.

[29] Moazzam Begg, and three other British citizens, were released from Guantánamo in January 2005 after several years of detention and growing public outcry. Begg admitted that he had flirted with the jihadist movement, but denied any military activity. In November 2010 the British Government reached a financial settlement with Begg and the other detainees over their claims of UK complicity in their illegal detention and possible abuse. Babar Ahmed is a British citizen who has been detained in custody since 2004, fighting extradition to the USA on charges of promoting terrorism. In December 2011 a debate took place on extradition in the House of Commons triggered by 140,000 signatures demanding a debate on the Ahmed case. *Hansard*, House of Commons Debates, 5 December 2011, Columns 82–130, available online <http://www.publications.parliament.uk>. This occasion was notable for the fact that so many Conservative MPs expressed concern over the holding of a man in prison for seven years without trial, and for the cross-party concern over current extradition arrangements. None of this prevented Ahmed's eventual extradition in October 2012.

[30] Sala@m, <http://www.salaam.co.uk/index.php> accessed 27 December 2011.

possibility will have to take into account the possible threats to their person made by jihadists who see them as traitors, as with the four sent to prison in 2008 for plotting to behead a British Muslim soldier. The judge said of them: 'This was not only a plot to kill a soldier but a plot to undermine the morale of the British army and inhibit recruitment'.[31] The rise in tension also places barriers to the acceptance of those Muslims who do apply to the armed forces or civil service. For one thing it creates unjustifiable suspicions over 'dual loyalties' where there were none before, as research on attitudes in the Austrian, Dutch, and German armed services has shown.[32] For another, there are some legitimate security issues over the employment of people (even more in specialist areas like airport security or nuclear reprocessing) who might be concealing a serious hostility to the state. Despite the justifiable concerns over the wholesale discrimination it implies this means that 'profiling', or the paying of special attention to those from certain backgrounds, is bound to be used in recruitment to sensitive jobs, when the security services will also take a close interest. Less significant than the fear of rogue insiders, such as US Major Nidal Hasan who killed thirteen of his colleagues at Fort Hood in 2009, is concern over the security threat posed by the passing on of useful information about in-house procedures which even people in menial catering jobs can be privy to.[33]

The combination of minority alienation and official risk aversion results in the low representation of minorities in public service, which in turn reduces the pool of talent available to the state and further heightens mutual incomprehension. Before 2001 the major obstacles were lack of familiarity with the military and the common perception by minorities of institutionalized racism.[34] There can indeed be formal entry barriers, as with the requirement in the Netherlands that recruits to the professional armed services possess a Dutch passport, which those from the main entry countries of Morocco and

[31] 'Ringleader of Beheading Plot Jailed for Life', *The Guardian*, 18 February 2008.

[32] Iris Menke and Phil C. Langer (eds), *Muslim Service Members in Non-Muslim Countries: Experiences of Difference in the Armed Forces in Austria, Germany and The Netherlands*, vol. 29, *FORUM International* 29 (Strausberg, Germany: Sozialwissenschaftliches Institut der Bundeswehr, 2011) e.g. pp. 29, 47.

[33] On Major Hasan, see the summary in the *New York Times* online version, <http://topics.nytimes.com/top/reference/timestopics/people/h/nidal_malik_hasan/index.html> accessed 10 January 2012.

[34] As found by the first extensive survey of ethnic community attitudes towards the armed services in the UK, conducted just before 9/11 (although exact dates are not provided). See Mohammed Ishaq and Asifa Hussain, 'British Ethnic Minority Communities and the Armed Forces', *Personnel Review*, 31, 5/6 (2002), pp. 722–39. Also Asifa Hussain and Mohammed Ishaq, 'British Pakistani Muslims' Perceptions of the Armed Forces', *Armed Forces and Society*, 28/4 (2002), pp. 601–18. Both surveys also suggest a greater willingness to consider a British military career among those with family who had served either in their homeland military or in the colonial forces.

Turkey can only acquire as second or third generation immigrants.[35] But the resurgence of terrorism gave a new impetus to the recruitment efforts of the diplomatic, intelligence, and military professions, which suddenly found themselves in desperate need of cooperation from minority communities. As Maria Böhmer, the German Minister for Integration, has said, 'In the light of the [sic] increasing globalization, the integration of Germany in international missions all over the world, intercultural competence is getting more and more important for the Bundeswehr'.[36] By 2006 MI5, the British internal security service, had increased its staff by 50 per cent over 2001 levels, with 6 per cent being from ethnic minorities, and fifty-two languages covered. The aim was for a further expansion by the same degree by 2008.[37] Other states, notably Denmark and the Netherlands, also upgraded their capacity significantly.[38]

The United Kingdom is again a special case in that it has both active pockets of hostility to the state within its ethnic minorities, and a high-profile military presence in the Muslim world. The kind of open clashes on the streets between supporters of the armed services and members of the 'Muslims against Crusaders' group which have occurred in Luton, or over the burning of Remembrance poppies, have not been seen in other European countries.[39]

[35] Conscripts, as in Austria, tend to be more representative of the general population, but the practice is dying out. Hussain and Ishaq, 'British Pakistani Muslims' Perceptions of the Armed Forces', *Armed Forces and Society*, pp. 16–17, 49, and 105–6. Where an effort is made to increase numbers, change can occur, as in the UK, where the percentage of minority ethnic personnel rose from 1.0 per cent in 1998 to 1.7 per cent in 2001 and 6.6 per cent in 2010 (although the rise for the officer class is far less, from 1.2 per cent in 2001 to 2.4 per cent in 2010). For the data on the earlier years, see Christopher Dandeker and David Mason, 'Diversifying the Uniform? The Participation of Minority Ethnic Personnel in the British Armed Services', *Armed Forces and Society*, 29/4 (2003), Table 1, p. 485. For 2010, see UK Defence Statistics 2010, Chapter 2—Personnel, 'Table 2.10 Strength of UK Regular Forces by Service, Ethnic Origin and Rank, at 1 April 2010' [webpage], <http://www.dasa.mod.uk/modintranet/UKDS/UKDS2010/c2/table210.php> accessed 28 December 2011.

[36] Menke and Langer (eds), *Muslim Service Members in Non-Muslim Countries*, pp. 33–4. This passage, together with p. 138, contains a useful comparative discussion of the role of ethnic minority soldiers as 'culture-brokers', and the difficulties that they nonetheless suffer when on missions abroad through lack of the special religious facilities which the European military have got used to providing on home soil. For examples of both the vocal, if highly untypical, individual Muslims who have virulently opposed serving the British state, and the efforts of the authorities to counter their message, see Shiraz Maher, *Ties that Bind: How the Story of British Muslim Soldiers Can Forge a National Identity* (London: Policy Exchange, 2011), pp. 71–6, available online, <http://www.policyexchange.org.uk/images/publications/ties%20that%20bind%20-%20sep%2011.pdf>.

[37] See 'The International Terrorist Threat to the UK', speech by Dame Eliza Manningham-Buller at Queen Mary's College, London, 9 November 2006, available online, <https://www.mi5.gov.uk/home/about-us/who-we-are/staff-and-management/director-general/speeches-by-the-director-general/the-international-terrorist-threat-to-the-uk.html> accessed 9 December 2012.

[38] David Spence (ed.), *The European Union and Terrorism* (London: John Harper Publishing, 2007), p. 7.

[39] 'Soldiers Targeted by Muslim Extremists in Luton Will March Again in Watford', *Daily Telegraph*, 11 March 2009. See also 'Armistice Day Poppy-burning Demo "Sickened" Observer', <http://www.bbc.co.uk/news/uk-england-london-12551338> accessed 27 December 2011,

The latter not only tend to deploy fewer troops on the front lines than does Britain, but also contain relatively small populations from the 'arc of crisis' where the conflicts of the last decade have occurred, namely Pakistan, Afghanistan, Iraq, and the Gulf. Moreover, such communities as do exist on the continent are formed primarily by refugees who see their new abodes as safe harbours, rather than the image of imperial arrogance which is evoked in a significant minority in Britain.[40] With over 1 million citizens of Pakistani and Bangladeshi origin, and around 1.4 million journeys taken between Pakistan and the UK every year, it takes only a small amount of disaffection to create significant problems for both the state and the Muslim community.[41]

In principle, any state needs to ensure recruitment from its ethnic minorities for four reasons: social, so as to ensure equity and foster cohesion; political, so as to prevent alienation; strategic, so as to help penetrate the communities from which enemies might come; and international, so as to have a more diverse profile in its dealings with the outside world. But this very effort risks putting some citizens, many with only shallow roots in society, in the position of having to choose between their loyalty to the state and/or national community, and their loyalty to their faith and deepest personal principles. Being conflicted in this way is likely to push a small but potentially dangerous group into subterfuge. Over time these dilemmas get overcome, as the common cause in battle so often made by English, Scottish, Welsh, and Irish regiments demonstrates—to say nothing of the huge sacrifices made in both world wars by soldiers from the British and French colonies, who would have had every justification for an unenthusiastic, even subversive attitude.[42] But the time to adjust is not necessarily available. States need to make their

referring to an incident on 11 November 2010. As Lord Leveson, the senior judge responsible for sentencing, later explained, the small fines handed out to the poppy-burners reflected the need to balance the offence given to many with the right to free speech and protest, <http://www.bbc.co.uk/news/uk-12675911> accessed 27 December 2011.

[40] The Director of MI5 said publicly in 2006, 'If the opinion polls conducted in the UK since July 2005 are only broadly accurate, over 100,000 of our citizens consider that the July 2005 attacks in London were justified'. Manningham-Buller, 'The International Terrorist Threat to the UK'.

[41] I am grateful to Fouzia Suleman for guidance on the Pakistani diaspora. The figure of 1.4 million can be found at the India Pakistan Trade Unit [website], 'Pakistani Relations with the UK', <http://www.iptu.co.uk/content/pakistan_economy.asp#7> accessed 27 December 2011.

[42] For example the *tirailleurs indigènes* from North and West Africa in the French Army, or the Indians and black South Africans who fought for the British. Such service did not necessarily help them or their descendants in getting proper treatment over immigration or pensions, as the Gurkhas found out (until a campaign led by the actress Joanna Lumley shamed the British government into a change of course in 2009). France also backed down (after forty years) under pressure from the entertainment world, but those Moroccans unfortunate enough to have served in Franco's army in Spain have languished in increasing poverty. John Lichfield, 'Film Moves Chirac to Back Down Over War Pensions', *The Independent*, 26 September 2006; Boughaleb el Attar, 'Los marroquíes en la Guerra Civil', *El País*, 10 April 2009. On the historical multinationality of the British forces, see Dandeker and Mason, 'Diversifying the Uniform', pp. 493–4.

minorities feel valued, respected, and—most of all—equal under the law. Then there is a chance that they will seek to enter public service and be trustworthy when they do—as Frederick William III of Prussia discovered when, after making Jews full citizens, they then enlisted in disproportionate numbers for his war against France.[43] War and foreign policy, however, can also open up potential fracture-lines. The decline in Irish enlistment to the British Army in the nineteenth century coincided with the rise of Irish Catholic nationalism. By the time of the First World War the British Government had concluded that any attempt to impose conscription on the Irish would be simply too risky.[44]

THE FUNCTIONING OF DEMOCRACY

Transnationalism may inherently provoke some concerns over identity and loyalty, but in a democracy these must always be balanced by an acknowledgement of the right of individuals to their freedom—of expression, conscience, worship, association, and movement. These rights would normally trump any vague complaints about identification with outsiders, or a lack of patriotism, except in the specific case of spying. But in an environment coloured by both rapid change towards multiculturality, and the polarizing discourse of the War on Terror they have been regularly called into question. This halfway house between normal democracy and a full war footing has been characterized as the 'politics of exception' by Huysman and Buonfino.[45] We thus need to consider how the functioning of democracy has changed, and perhaps become compromised, under these new conditions, specifically with reference to the debate about foreign policy and the national interest, but also more generally.

One way of approaching the problem is to set the negative factors against the positive. The most obvious candidate in the first group is the taking of emergency powers to deal with the apparent threats to European societies after September 2001. All states naturally went on alert, increased their state of readiness, and over time showed more willingness to engage in cooperation on

[43] Yossi Shain, *Kinship and Diaspora in International Affairs* (Ann Arbor: University of Michigan Press, 2007), pp. 3–4.

[44] Levi, *Consent, Dissent and Patriotism*, pp. 54–8.

[45] Jef Huysmans and Alessandra Buonfino, 'Politics of Exception and Unease: Immigration, Asylum and Terrorism in the Parliamentary Debates in the UK', *Political Studies*, 56/4 (2008), pp. 766–88. See also Toby Archer, 'Welcome to the *Umma*: The British State and its Muslim Citizens since 9/11', *Cooperation and Conflict*, 44/3 (2009), p. 331. 'Unease' was first conceptualized by Didier Bigo in his article 'Security and Immigration: Towards a Critique of the Governmentality of Unease', *Alternatives: Global, Local, Political*, 27/1, Supplement (2002), pp. 63–92.

Table 6.1. Individuals tried in EU Member States on terrorism charges (2006–10)

Country	No. of individuals
Austria	2
Belgium	58
Denmark	38
France	266
Germany	52
Greece	17
Ireland	48
Italy	118
Netherlands	50
Spain	916
Sweden	9
UK	151
TOTAL	1725

Source: Adapted and updated from Table 10.1 in Rees, 'The External Face of Internal Security', in Hill and Smith, *International Relations and the European Union*, p. 232. Original source (used for updating): *EU Terrorism Situation and Trend Report*, Europol TE-SAT 2011, Annex 4: Data Convictions and Penalties (EUROJUST), p. 38.

counter-terrorism, especially at the EU level.[46] States inevitably varied in the speed and intensity of their reaction, with the UK in the vanguard. The British government rushed the 'Anti-Terrorism, Crime and Security' Act through Parliament in 2001 and was unique in derogating from Article 5 of the European Convention on Human Rights, so as to be able to intern suspects without trial, although states like Italy and Germany already had measures in place given their past experiences with domestic terrorism.[47]

Table 6.1 shows that states have subsequently followed proper judicial procedures to indict suspects on terrorism charges, although there are interesting variations between them. The relatively low total for the UK, for example, may be explained by the use of Control Orders under the 2005 Anti-Terrorism Act, which replaced internment with house arrest, still avoiding the need to bring a formal charge. Italy, by contrast, has not been so preoccupied with terrorism. The 2010 Report from the Italian Ministry of the Interior on Criminality and Security makes it clear that the concern with immigration, dating in fact from before 9/11, from the late 1990s, has been driven by concerns over criminality and social cohesion,

[46] Wyn Rees, 'The External Face of Internal Security', in Christopher Hill and Michael Smith (eds), *International Relations and the European Union* (2nd edn, Oxford: Oxford University Press, 2011), especially pp. 231–7.

[47] Subsequently quashed by the House of Lords in 2004, leading to Control Orders being substituted for detention without trial. 'Article 5: The Right to Liberty and Security', *Human Rights Review 2012*, p.177–9 (UK's Equality and Human Rights Commission, 2012), available online <http://www.equalityhumanrights.com/uploaded_files/humanrights/hrr_article_5.pdf> accessed 9 December 2012.

rather than terror.[48] Probably Rome had become so accustomed to the kind of Mafia atrocity represented by the murder of its investigating magistrates that the prospect of an occasional al-Qaeda bomb changed little. In Britain and Spain, however, especially after 2004–5, and to a lesser extent in France and Germany, the fear of a European equivalent of the Twin Towers attack, possibly worsened by the use of WMD, represented a nightmarish vision that could not be risked, notwithstanding the libertarian cost. It should also be noted that of the 332 convictions or acquittals on terrorism charges in 2010 in the various Member States, 25.3 per cent related to Islamist terrorism and 60.5 per cent to long-established separatist causes (in Spain, France, Ireland, and the UK), where violence was diminishing but not eradicated.

Thus the arrival of 'the surveillance society' was not brought about by 9/11 alone.[49] Increasing use of sophisticated technology by police-forces, and below-the-horizon international cooperation on criminal and security matters, had been happening in Europe since the creation of the Trevi network in the mid-1970s.[50] The EU encouraged more extensive coordination on 'Justice and Home Affairs' from 1993 onwards via the Treaty of European Union, which heightened awareness amongst its Member States of the growing problems caused by the trafficking of drugs and people, and the laundering of funds from the black economy.[51] Yet *pace* the analysis of Huysman and Buonfino, which shows that in Britain the immediate strong reactions to atrocity (in both 2001 and 2005) were soon replaced by a more measured approach (the 'politics of unease'), there can be no doubt that at the level of public opinion, both majority and minority, the debates over terrorism have created a sense of apprehension and social polarization.[52] The general public wanted to know why they were suddenly at risk of death in going about their

[48] Marzio Barbagli and Asher Colombo (eds), *Rapporto sulla criminalità e la sicurezza in Italia 2010* (Milan: Gruppo 24 Ore and the Fondazione Intelligence, Culture and Strategic Analysis, for the Ministero dell'Interno, 2011), especially pp. 62–72.

[49] *A Surveillance Society?* UK House of Commons, Home Affairs Committee, HC 58 (London: House of Commons, 2008), cited in David Omand, *Securing the State* (London: Hurst & Co., 2010), p. 110. Omand himself talks of the 'nightmare... of the Panoptic State'.

[50] On Trevi, see Christopher Hill, 'European Preoccupations with Terrorism', in Alfred Pijpers, Elfriede Regelsberger, and Wolfgang Wessels (eds), *European Political Cooperation in the 1980s: A Common Foreign Policy for Western Europe?* (Dordrecht: Martinus Nijhoff, 1988); also Christopher Hill, 'The Political Dilemmas for Western Governments', in Lawrence Freedman et al., *Terrorism and International Order* (London: Routledge and Kegan Paul for the Royal Institute of International Affairs, 1986).

[51] Valsamis Mitsilegas, Jörg Monar, and Wyn Rees, *The European Union and Internal Security: Guardian of the People?* (Houndmills: Palgrave Macmillan, 2003).

[52] Huysmans and Buonfino, 'Politics of Exception and Unease'. See also Lauren McLaren, 'Immigration and Trust in Politics in Britain', *British Journal of Political Science*, 42/1 (2012), pp. 163–86, who argues that concern about immigration can seep through into the wider polity, with 'a weakening of ties between the governed and the governors' (p. 184). Also survey in *The Observer*, 8 January 2012.

daily business, and Muslims resented the assumption that their community now represented an enemy within.

In parallel, various 'new crimes' have found their way onto the statute books in many European countries, ranging from the planning and preparation of a terrorist plot, through taking photographs of public buildings, to (even) the possession of large amounts of unexplained cash.[53] In principle these new restrictions are non-discriminatory, but it seems clear that they have bitten hardest on those who are profiled as possible adherents to jihadism. At various levels of society and public life a degree of stereotyping has occurred which too often has led to someone obviously Muslim, or indeed just foreign, being ostracized or even suspected of terrorist activity (as in the tragic case of Jean Charles de Menezes, mistakenly taken to be carrying explosives and shot dead by London police officers). This kind of 'securitizing' of everyday life has become intertwined with, and compounded by, popular resentments about increased immigration, competition for jobs and welfare, and the visibly changing character of the cities. The resulting problems pose a big challenge to the democratic process, given the fact that most national parliaments struggle to hold executives to account in such semi-emergency and fast-changing conditions, while there is always a significant lag effect in their ability to mirror society and its changing composition.

There is another, more positive, side to this coin. In the first place, despite the predictable mileage which the radical right has made out of Islamist terrorism, and the fear of electoral losses which have pushed governments into tougher positions on security and immigration, the latter have generally been hyper-alert to the need to distinguish between the law-abiding Muslim majority and the very small numbers of subversives. If real problems have arisen from the undeniable fact that would-be terrorists conceal themselves by immersion in their own ethnocultural communities, then mainstream politicians have mostly reacted by asking minority leaders for help while issuing reassurance about religious freedom and the need for mutual respect. Thus two weeks after 9/11 Tony Blair met representatives of British Muslims at Downing Street to condemn attacks on Muslims in the street and to stress that the atrocities in the US were 'not the work of Muslim terrorists . . . [but] terrorists, pure and simple'.[54] Two months later it was notable that the Conservative Shadow Home Secretary, Oliver Letwin, stressed in the House of Commons:

[53] Kim Lane Scheppele, 'Bringing Security Services under the Rule of Law in the Global Anti-Terror Campaign', in Martin Scheinin, organizer, 'European and United States Counter-terrorism Policies, the Rule of Law and Human Rights', RSCAS Policy Paper 2011/3 (Fiesole, European University Institute: Robert Schumann Centre for Advanced Studies, 2011), pp. 43–8.

[54] 'Blair Meets British Muslims', *The Guardian*, 27 September 2001. See also Christopher Hill, 'Putting the World to Rights: The Foreign Policy Mission of Tony Blair', in Anthony Seldon and Dennis Kavanagh (eds), *The Blair Effect, 2001–5* (Cambridge: Cambridge University Press, 2005), p. 389.

> These are dangerous times—I think that is agreed across the House—and there are loopholes in our national security . . . However the purpose of the House and of Parliament as a whole at a time such as this is not merely to enact into law the first set of propositions that occur to Her Majesty's Government, but to achieve an appropriate balance between public safety, which it is the Home Secretary's responsibility to protect, and individual liberty, which this House and Parliament as a whole were established to protect.[55]

Over the last decade all British governments have made persistent if sometimes ham-fisted efforts to engage constructively with the Muslim community, partly for the tactical imperative of maximizing cooperation and intelligence, but also because it was all too evident that unless multiculturalism could be nudged along a more integrationist path, without threatening existing freedoms, there was a risk that inter-communal tensions could degenerate into serious violence.[56]

Other European governments have also broadly preferred the responsible line of not seeking to persecute their Muslim communities, even if in France and Germany that is associated more with maintaining a low profile on the issue of religion in politics than of active reassurance. In the Netherlands the challenge has come from below in the form of intercommunal tensions even without dramatic terrorist acts, but the state has still found it a struggle to preserve Dutch traditions of tolerance, with the challenge of trying to incorporate Islam as one of the 'pillars' of its system.[57] In Italy, similarly, social prejudice against Islam, so evident in the popularity of the writings of Oriana Fallaci, has not produced any significant official move away from respect for Islam as a faith or towards seeing Italian Muslims as an inherent danger. That kind of unease has probably been more marked in the Scandinavian countries, whose progressive traditions have come under great strain as they try to work out how to tolerate those with illiberal views and practices, rooted in faith rather than democratic theory.

The most striking case is that of Spain, where the carnage at the Atocha station in March 2004 has led to regular arrests of Islamist suspects ever since (see Table 6.1), but not to significant anti-Islamic prejudice, despite the fact that the attacks were launched from within the rapidly growing Maghrebian community in the country. This is probably because Spain was already accustomed to the extensive counter-terror measures in place against ETA, but also because Zapatero's PSOE government committed itself from the

[55] Oliver Letwin, speech of 19 November 2001, Hansard, col. 39, cited in Huysman and Buonfino, 'Politics of Exception and Unease', p. 771. 'Notable' because the Conservative Party has usually favoured greater police powers.

[56] Toby Archer, 'Welcome to the *Umma*'.

[57] Paul Scheffer, *Immigrant Nations* (Cambridge: Polity, 2011), pp. 118–30. Dutch multiculturalism has its origin in the late nineteenth-century idea of separate but equal 'pillars': Protestants, Catholics, and Socialists. See also Chapter 2.

outset not to fall into the trap of racism and xenophobia.[58] It may also be, bearing in mind the Italian case, that Islam finds a readier acceptance in countries which have learned to coexist with the Arab world through centuries of proximity, and where religion has a more significant place in daily life than in northern Europe—so long as it does not challenge the dominant orthodoxy.

More broadly, there is a dialectic to be observed in the way that the real tensions over terrorism, religion, and immigration have brought international politics sharply into focus in citizens' daily lives, as only war tended to do previously. Indeed, terrorism and the measures taken to counter it have literally 'brought war home'.[59] At least for a period this has probably led to a more vigorous debate about foreign policy; it has certainly connected it up, for better or worse, to the domestic issues of inter-community relations, immigration, and religion. The proliferation of internationally oriented pressure-groups in Europe, developing in parallel through concerns about human rights and development, has accentuated the process. Insofar as ethnocultural minorities are also beginning to organize themselves better, partly because of their strong motivation on particular external issues, we should increasingly expect to see interest-group pluralism extend into the more politically sensitive aspects of foreign policy—as with the Armenian-Turkish argument in France, the Serb protests in various EU states over Kosovo, and the Tamil campaign over their rights in Sri Lanka.

At the level of the formal institutions of the state there is, as usual, a lag between the emergence of a pressure or need, and the ability of the system to meet it. Parliaments and their national foreign affairs committees have rarely proved capable of acting as focal points for effective debate, which has predictably been forced into the media or onto the streets. The former have responded—terrorism and war make international politics front page news more often than in the past—but the mass market titles in particular all too easily fall back on a populism and xenophobia which governments and interest-groups struggle to contain. The new social media have moved into the gap which remains, with Facebook and Twitter providing a semi-underground, transnational facility for young people to discuss international politics. The consequences have not been so evident in Europe as in North Africa and the Middle East during the Arab Spring, but Internet phenomena like Wikileaks have provided a huge stimulus to discussion—and to scepticism over official sources. In the long run this may well feed through into party and electoral politics.

So far as minorities are concerned, the aspersions cast on their loyalty to a particular society can rebound disastrously, especially when exploited by the

[58] Zapatero inauguration speech, 15 April 2004, cited in 'Setting an Example? Counter-terrorism Measures in Spain', *Human Rights Watch*, 17/1, D (January 2005), especially pp. 8–14.

[59] Hill, 'Bringing War Home'.

media or by opportunist political parties. A religious or ethnic community can become alienated from their fellow-citizens as easily in this way as by the racism and intolerance which so often accompanies it. Alienation from the *state itself*, however, is unlikely to take place unless there is a feeling that its laws and institutions cannot be relied upon for protection. One other critical factor might be the sense that there is no way through normal democratic processes of having very strong objections to a foreign policy stance taken into account—that is, if foreign policy is treated by decision-makers as something to be ring-fenced, in the 'national interest', as it so often has been.[60] Yet if controversy, prejudice, and injustice can ultimately produce a greater engagement on the part of minorities with the political system from which they have largely been marginalized, that would represent a significant advance. If it could be paralleled by a growing sense of involvement in the discussion of foreign policy and its relation to domestic issues on the part of society as a whole, that would be an even more significant step forward. If ghettoes are bad for society, then the same goes for foreign and security policy—it needs to be made part of normal politics.

CONCLUSION: LOYALTY, DEMOCRACY, AND THE NATIONAL INTEREST

This chapter has analysed, in the particular context of foreign policy-making, the tensions which arise over the issue of loyalty—that is, culturally diverse European democracies open to a range of transnational influences. Lying behind the analysis have been some difficult normative questions: firstly of how to balance effectiveness and democracy in conditions of diversity, transnationality, and at times also crisis; and secondly of how much loyalty should be expected of citizens who may fiercely disagree with official foreign policy. The particular issues of subversion and recruitment were examined as a way of approaching the problem.

It is clear that even taking into account the special circumstances of the decade after 9/11, actual subversion is a relatively rare occurrence and a less serious threat to the common weal (with the important exception of a possible dirty bomb) than is generally supposed. But the effects of a single terrorist act ripple out far beyond its immediate context. The sight of the Twin Towers collapsing in New York was sufficient to put all European societies on high alert before any sign had been detected of a threat to them. The elements of

[60] For example, documents released in Britain in 2012 under the '30 year rule' show that Mrs Thatcher decided to purchase the Trident nuclear deterrent system without Cabinet authorization, and in consultation with officials more than ministers. *The Guardian*, 30 December 2012.

fear and suspicion which then entered community relations, enhanced by the preventive measures governments took, and multiplied when Islamist terror arrived in Europe, had damaging effects on social cohesion. Muslims fell under suspicion, especially those who dressed distinctively, with the result that they tended to fall back on their own communities, with a small number sufficiently fuelled by resentment to react violently. In the explicitly multiculturalist societies years of work on building up intercommunal understanding were set back, for the genie of distrust cannot easily be put back into the bottle. In the societies which were only just beginning to come to terms with *multiculturality*, hopes for integration now faced new obstacles. Although most governments have made active efforts to insist that the great majority of ethnic minority citizens are no less loyal and law-abiding than anyone else, the very nature of the counter-terrorism measures they passed has made it difficult to get that message across. This despite the fact that in Britain, Germany, Italy, and Spain at least, terrorism was already a familiar phenomenon, having been experienced frequently over the last decades of the twentieth century. But then those attacks had not usually been associated with a movement like al-Qaeda—at once foreign and linked to insiders who seem indifferent to the country itself, not just antagonistic to the government and its foreign policy.[61]

Some of this increased social tension would have happened as a result of the changes in international politics following on from the attacks of 11 September 2001. But it would probably not have caused such difficulties without the war in Afghanistan, and in particular the determination of some EU states, notably Britain, Spain, Italy, and Denmark, to support the US invasion of Iraq. Western Europe is vulnerable to terrorism through the spreading net of transnational links, of which increased migration and diversity are both causes and symptoms. Whatever emergency restrictions governments may introduce, these are basically open societies committed through the EU's Single Market to the free movement of goods, services, capital, and people, which makes it difficult—even for Britain, opted out of the Schengen system of open frontiers—to monitor the trafficking of migrants or drugs, the laundering of money, and the clandestine activities of international terror rings. In prolonged periods of tension this means that levels of distrust, between the authorities and minorities, but also intercommunally, remain high.

A practical manifestation of distrust is the difficulties which arise over the recruitment of people from minority backgrounds into state employ. The existing barriers of discrimination, unfamiliarity, and established networks are compounded by official concerns over loyalty or hidden motives, and the

[61] In Germany during the 1970s the internal Red Army Faction did have close contacts with Palestinian terrorists, dramatically demonstrated by the murders of Israeli athletes at the 1972 Olympics. But their numbers were limited by the ideological nature of their solidarity, as compared to those of blood and faith evident in recent jihadism.

fears of potential applicants that they might be ostracized (by their own community as well as by the workplace majority) and/or face agonizing conflicts between their faith and the requirements of their job. Both terrorism and controversial foreign policy positions (whether or not causally connected) create serious extra complications for Muslims, in particular those wishing to pursue a diplomatic or military career, or even in such civilian occupations as aviation. They may feel, in the words of Waller and Linklater, that the state 'speaks for the dominant nation or culture and not for the citizenry as a whole'.[62]

By the same token, in the post-9/11 climate of fear, the authorities have become much more motivated to recruit from the minority communities so as to reduce polarization, legitimize policy, and (in the case of the police and security services) make possible the penetration of suspect cells at home and abroad. In this as in other aspects of the problem the UK is an outlier, with perceived threats at a higher level than elsewhere in the EU, but also relatively greater success in providing opportunities to ethnic minorities. The multicultural model of society in general encourages such an approach, but states falling into the other two categories, of integrationism or 'parallel societies', feel less urgency, whether because they perceive less threat or simply through an unwillingness to acknowledge the need for action on equal opportunities. But minorities continue to feel excluded in all states, with international politics now worsening the problem of the snail-like passage of change in social attitudes and patterns of recruitment to elite institutions.

The evidence surveyed suggests that the complex interplay of socio-cultural diversity, foreign policy debate, and transnational politics has sharpened the problems faced by modern European states in the provision of both security and social peace for their citizens. Yet here too there is a dialectical element to the process of change. Governments are increasingly forced to acknowledge the impacts of the digital revolution, greater social diversity, and transnationalism, on their policy environment. Foreign policy, in the sense of the need to deal with the world outside a given polity, has not gone away, but it has itself taken on a transnational character through the broadening of its subject-matter and the need often to address a domestic audience.

Not only do decision-makers have to cope with this social and diplomatic revolution, but they have to accept that their basic assumptions about the nature of representative democracy, and even of loyalty to the state, may need to be re-examined. Governments are having to consider how best to reach out to minorities—or to the majorities within the minorities—without appearing to allow their foreign policies to be held hostage by special interests. They also have to engage in more directly normative justifications of their foreign policies

[62] Waller and Linklater (eds), *Political Loyalty and the Nation-State*, p. 4.

than they have been used to. On the face of it this splinters the sense of a straightforward national interest underpinning policy without providing an alternative; but in the long term it might create a clearer understanding on all sides of the critical distinctions between genuinely shared interests, legitimate differences of view, and challenges to the very rationale of the state.

7

Interventions, blowbacks, and the law of unforeseen consequences

In any democracy the issue of whether—and when—to intervene forcibly in the internal affairs of another state is not only a primordial question of international politics, but also a potential source of controversy at home. That said, major Western interventions such as those in the civil war which followed the Russian Revolution, or during the Cold War in Cuba, the Dominican Republic, and Grenada, barely excited public opinion. The grip of an ideological antagonism towards communism made it easy to present intervention as self-evidently in the national security interest. (The Vietnam War, which went on for a decade and cost 58,000 American lives, was a huge exception.) In the European states of Britain and France, where domestic unrest over 'small wars' did occur, it was largely in the context of the end of empire, as during the Suez crisis of 1956. In the UK the conflicts in Cyprus, Kenya, Rhodesia, and Aden led to increasing unease at home, which reinforced the loss of official confidence in empire marked by Harold Macmillan's 'wind of change' speech in 1960. France had persistent, serious, and complex internal divisions over Algeria before and after formal independence in 1962.[1] Yet, despite the end of its formal empire Paris showed more confidence than London in post-colonial interventions, as in Cameroon in 1961 and Gabon in 1964, partly because, in Stephen Smith's view, French public opinion 'with rare exceptions did not object to the neo-colonialism of the *trente glorieuses*'.[2]

The same period showed that a failure to intervene can sometimes cause uproar, as with the humanitarian disaster in Biafra in the late 1960s, and the

[1] See the illuminating discussion of the left in Britain and France during the 1950s and 1960s in Miles Kahler, *Decolonization in Britain and France* (Princeton: Princeton University Press, 1984), pp. 161–264 and 369–71. Both were more concerned with intra-party matters than with rousing public opinion on such issues.

[2] Stephen W. Smith, 'Nodding and Winking: The French Retreat from Africa', *London Review of Books*, 32/3 (11 February 2010). The '*trente glorieuses*' were the recovery years for France of 1945–75, notwithstanding the damaging colonial wars in Indo-China and Algeria. For a survey of the 1960s as a whole, see Frederic S. Pearson, 'Foreign Military Interventions and Domestic Disputes', *International Studies Quarterly*, 18/3 (1974), pp. 259–90. The domestic disputes discussed by Pearson, however, relate to the states which were the targets of interventions.

expectation of Britain's Greek Cypriot community that London would live up to its treaty obligations to act against the Turkish invasion of 1974. These were the first hints of a growing demand for foreign policy to reflect humanitarian concerns.[3] Yet until the end of the Cold War these occasional bursts of indignation were largely conceptualized in traditional terms, as criticisms of sheer incompetence, immorality, or political cowardice—arguments which would have been familiar to Gladstone and Disraeli. Insofar as expatriate groups were vocal, as they were in different ways over Algeria, the Congo, Cyprus, Rhodesia, South Africa, and the South Moluccas, they were generally seen as politically motivated groups on either side of the struggle over decolonization. They were not to be taken as indicating a basic change in the social or political base of the ex-imperial states of western Europe. Thus the developments of the two decades after 1991, with significant changes in the ethnocultural composition of most European societies, and the parallel emergence of a new wave of interventionism, shook up the working assumptions in government circles about the relationship between foreign policy and domestic society. This chapter examines the way in which intervention became a major dilemma for Europeans after the Cold War, and how this implicated domestic society, itself evolving towards a condition of greater diversity. To what extent has the new phase of foreign involvements had destabilizing effects on the delicate balance of intercommunal relations inside the different social models discussed in Chapters 2–4? Conversely, how far has the direction of foreign policy been shaped, or hamstrung, by new domestic pressures? In particular, what unforeseen consequences—or 'blowbacks'—have flowed from interventionism? To tackle these issues the chapter begins by examining first the nature of the new interventionism and second the particular challenges it has posed for Europeans, before analysing the record of European interventions with a view to seeing where the biggest impacts, in society and foreign policy, have occurred, and why.

THE NEW INTERVENTIONISM

The post-Cold War period has witnessed a mix of different types of intervention, as well as the inevitable mix of motives.[4] The extent of intervention has

[3] 'Human rights are now part of the calculation of what is legitimate internationally'. John Vincent, *Human Rights and International Relations* (Cambridge: Cambridge University Press, 1986), p. 132. For the earliest signs of humanitarianism in foreign policy, see Gary Bass, *Freedom's Battle* (New York: Vintage Books, 2008), and Brendan Simms and D. J. B. Trim (eds), *Humanitarian Intervention: A History* (Cambridge: Cambridge University Press, 2011).

[4] See James Mayall and Spyros Economides (eds), *The New Interventionism: United Nations Experience in Cambodia, former Yugoslavia and Somalia* (Cambridge: Cambridge University Press, 1996), especially pp. 1–10 and 22; also David Chandler, *From Kosovo to Kabul and*

ranged from the full-scale invasion of Iraq in 2003, through the reliance on air power alone (Iraq, 1998; Serbia, 1999; Libya, 2011) to the 'laser sanctions' against Robert Mugabe and his clan. What is 'new' about the new interventionism is firstly that European states have been ever more involved, thus emerging from the association with colonialism which had hung heavily over them since the end of empire in the 1960s. Post-colonial diffidence had produced inhibitions about intervening in the Third World, accentuated by the relative decline in Europe's international power position—apart from France in West and Central Africa, where it continues to assume a privileged role despite the huge damage to its reputation of the Rwandan genocide of 1994.[5] The second new face of interventions in the 1990s was the preoccupation with humanitarian issues, in part driven by public opinion. In time this evolved into the view that interventions were justifiable where they could be shown not only to have a moral purpose, but also to be legitimized by being pursued multilaterally—at a minimum through a coalition of the willing, but preferably via both the EU and the UN.

The realist motives for intervention—security, wealth, prestige, and relative power—have still been significant, not least in the first decade of the twenty-first century, when the wish for 'pre-emptive defence' against terrorists and the state sources of terrorism became prominent even among the more 'civilian' powers. The conservative wish for a restoration of international order was once again to the fore in European foreign policies, as it was in the years following 1815, 1848, and 1945.[6] This produced an amended version of the democratic peace hypothesis, whereby states that are either failing or seriously threatening their own people (or both) have come to be seen as constituting an inherent threat to the peace, making them a legitimate target for interference from outside.[7] The emerging and related idea of a 'responsibility to protect' thus took strength from a new form of insecurity, created by the virulent form of fideism which is Islamic jihad.[8] Reactions to this new thinking about the

Beyond: Human Rights and International Intervention (London: Pluto, 2005); and Jennifer M. Welsh (ed.), *Humanitarian Intervention and International Relations* (Oxford: Oxford University Press, 2004).

[5] Catherine Gegout, *Why Europe Intervenes in Africa* (2013, forthcoming), Chapter 5.

[6] Paul W. Schroeder, *Systems, Stability, and Statecraft: Essays on the International History of Modern Europe* (New York: Palgrave Macmillan, 2004), pp. 37–57, though Schroeder prefers 'hegemony' to 'order'.

[7] Gegout, *Why Europe Intervenes in Africa*, pp. 31–4.

[8] The doctrine of 'the Responsibility to Protect' was articulated in 2001 by the report of the International Commission on Intervention and State Sovereignty'. It followed Tony Blair's attempt to articulate a 'doctrine of the international community' in a speech in Chicago in 1999. Jennifer M. Welsh, 'A Normative Case for Pluralism: Reassessing Vincent's Views on Humanitarian Intervention', *International Affairs*, 87/5 (September 2011), pp. 1196–9. 'Fideism' denotes the reliance on faith for political judgment, often producing a crusading instinct. See Michael Donelan, *Elements of International Political Theory* (Oxford: The Clarendon Press, 1990).

responsibility of 'the international community' inevitably arose, especially from sovereignty-obsessed powers like China and Russia. Yet in Western states the conservative and liberal agendas have tended to converge; interventions have occurred, as over Kosovo in 1999, when humanitarian and balance of power considerations have come together, in the minds of decision-makers if not in international law.[9]

In modern democratic states of the kind prevalent in Europe today any significant adventure abroad is bound to provoke considerable debate. It is highly desirable from both the democratic and quality control points of view that this should happen. Conversely domestic pressures can firm up the resolve of an uncertain government, as over Libya in 2011 when President Sarkozy—smarting over the criticisms of French policy before the Arab Spring—saw electoral advantage in leading the campaign to save the population of Benghazi from Ghaddafi's onslaught. In the context of this book this means that the concerns of minorities, particularly those with diasporic or religious links to a particular site of conflict, may come strongly into play, even if this is not necessarily evident until a later stage, as with the British Muslims motivated to join jihadist training camps in Pakistan by what they saw as the abandonment of their Bosnian co-religionists. For while public opinion is often reified through reliance on mass polling ('the public favours X or Y') on foreign policy issues it is usually differentiated, with a majority holding views of low intensity and various small clusters feeling very strongly about a given problem.[10] Such minorities may be politically or ideologically based, but they are also now likely to be ethnocultural, with concerns about particular parts of the world, but also such themes as ethnocentrism, neo-colonialism, and the place of religion. They represent a distinctive contribution to debates on foreign policy.

In principle this could lead to deeper and more effective debates about 'duties beyond borders', and the definition of national interests, than has hitherto been the case. On the other hand, the disparity between majority indifference and minority anger can deepen existing divisions and at the extreme produce violence. The situation is complicated by the fact that very few interventions are clean and short. Once a military involvement in the

[9] Christopher Hill, 'Foreign Policy', in Anthony Seldon (ed.), *The Blair Effect: The Blair Government 1997–2001* (London: Little Brown, 2001) pp. 340–3. Even China and Russia have not been unaffected by the normative drift in relation to intervention, as can be seen by their willingness to allow the UNSC Resolution on Libya.

[10] Public opinion is certainly changing as the result of international and social factors, and in certain ways becoming more important to foreign policy—this is in part the argument of the current book. But even the 'revisionists' who argue that it is becoming more informed and outward-looking do not suppose that mass opinion is strongly held outside major crises. See Brigitte L. Nacos, Robert Y. Shapiro, and Pierangelo Isernia (eds), *Decision-making in a Glass House: Mass Media, Public Opinion and American and European Foreign Policy in the 21st Century* (Lanham: Rowman & Littlefield, 2000), especially pp. 240–3, and 247–64.

affairs of another state has begun it is difficult to bring to an end—indeed, interventions all too often move from a specific goal into *processes* represented by abstract nouns such as nation-building, stabilization, security, or democracy. Britain, for example, stayed in Iraq from 2003–11, and its presence in Afghanistan is scheduled to be from 2001–14. France has had an ambiguous military presence in the Ivory Coast from the start of its crisis in 2002 to the present day. Despite the political talk about combating terrorism over 'the long haul', few politicians (let alone citizens) can have expected at the beginning of these wars that they would entail combat over a period twice as long as the Second World War. Such prolonged ventures have significant unanticipated consequences, including on the home front. Even French society, which as we saw in Chapter 3 has been largely free from foreign policy-induced terrorism, in March 2012 suffered the shocking murders of three soldiers with Arab names and four Jewish civilians (of whom three were children). This was at the hands of an alienated French Muslim of Algerian extraction who claimed he was avenging Palestinian and Afghan deaths—for which French policy in the Middle East was apparently responsible.[11] This event reverberated in the presidential election campaign over the following month, bringing both social and foreign policy divisions to the fore. It showed how the parameters of domestic politics can be overturned by a small-scale but dramatic reaction to foreign policy on the part of a marginalized individual.

Even limited foreign adventures can have a notable domestic backwash. In Italy the ultimately successful dispatch of troops to restore order in Albania in 1997 led to unease in parliament on both the right and the left, weakening the centrist government of Romano Prodi and leading to his resignation the following year.[12] Prodi was also forced to offer his resignation during his second term of office in 2007 after losing the support of his left-wing coalition allies in a vote of confidence on the issues of Italian troops in Afghanistan and the expansion of a US Air Force base in northern Italy. As Foreign Minister D'Alema said in the debate, 'A country like Italy, which is not a great power, cannot face such delicate and complex challenges without strong and clear political consensus'.[13] In such cases it is both the initial decision to commit,

[11] 'Did France Ignore the Islamic Radical Threat?', BBC News, 22 March 2012, <http://www.bbc.co.uk/news/world-europe-17476996> accessed 14 December 2012; 'Avant Merah, peu d'Islamistes avaient grandi et frappé en France', *Le Monde*, 29 March 2012. At the time of writing it seems that the killer, Mohamed Merah, was not simply a demented individual, but part of a small jihadist cell: 'Mohamed Merah sur le point d'être inhumé à Toulouse', *Le Monde*, 29 March 2012. See also Chapter 3, note 40.

[12] Christopher Hill and Filippo Andreatta, 'Struggling to change: The Italian state and the new order', in Robin Niblett and William Wallace (eds), *Rethinking European Order: West European Responses, 1989–1997* (Houndmills: Palgrave, 2001), pp. 248 and 257; also Elisabetta Brighi, 'How to Change Your Foreign Policy in 100 Days: A New Course with the Prodi Government?', *The International Spectator*, 42/1 (2007) pp. 129–40 (Houndmills: Palgrave: 2001), pp. 248 and 257.

[13] 'Prodi Resigns as Italian Premier', *The Guardian*, 21 February 2007. Prodi did, however, recover from this crisis and the government lasted another year.

and the unforeseeable movement of events, which risk stirring up the discontent which can shake a government's purpose.[14]

Thus activism abroad can be vulnerable to domestic circumstances without even considering the complications of ethnocultural diversity. But the latter has the potential to affect foreign policy in certain contexts and circumstances, as an increasingly significant part of a state's domestic environment. This was indeed the case for Italy in 1997 over Operation Alba, in that one motivation for taking the lead was to prevent a further wave of chaotic Albanian emigration, with the inevitably hostile reaction inside Italy which it would produce. Furthermore, where either (*1*) a national position matters greatly to a particular minority; or (*2*) intercommunal tensions map onto conflicts elsewhere in the world, both social cohesion and the effectiveness of foreign policy may get called into question. The interplay between cohesion and effectiveness bears out the application of the 'strategic-relational' approach to foreign policy, which stresses how goals and contexts affect each other through endless feedback loops.[15] These loops are explored in more detail in the second half of this chapter, which deals with the complexities arising from intervention on the part of the five Member States most implicated in interventions.

THE CHALLENGES FOR EUROPEAN SOCIETIES

All states face dilemmas when facing up to a potential military intervention overseas, but for European societies the issues have very particular resonances. These are in part the consequence of history, in particular two world wars and the rapid rise and fall of colonial empires. But the arrival of increased heterogeneity at home has presented familiar issues in a new light while putting new ones onto the table.

The first challenge relates to the use of force. No European society is pacifist, but several tend in that direction, taking what has been termed a 'pacific-ist'

[14] A recent assessment of Italian military operations overseas argues that their proliferation after 1990 could not have happened at all without both bipartisan consensus and an increasingly majoritarian political system. See Fabrizio Coticchia and Giampiero Giacomello, 'All Together Now! Military Operations Abroad as "Bipartisan" Instrument of Italian Foreign Policy', in Giampiero Giacomello and Bertjan Verbeek (eds), *Italy's Foreign Policy in the Twenty-First Century: The New Assertiveness of an Aspiring Middle Power* (Plymouth: Lexington, 2011), pp. 135–54. The authors also note (p. 136) that 'a cultural analysis of the evolution of the Italian defense policy is still missing'.

[15] On the approach itself, see Bob Jessop, *State Power* (Cambridge: Polity, 2007); for an application, see Elisabetta Brighi, *Foreign Policy, Domestic Politics and International Relations: The Case of Italy* (London: Routledge, 2013).

approach to international relations.[16] By this is meant a distinct aversion to the use of force in all circumstances short of dire national necessity. It is a good description of the attitudes during much of the post-1945 period of Italy, the Federal Republic of Germany, and the European 'neutrals' of Austria, Finland, Ireland, and Sweden. Even after the end of the Cold War, with the fading relevance of neutrality and the move of Germany towards 'normal country' status, these countries still display, particularly at the level of public opinion, what one might think is a wholly proper caution and distaste towards the prospect of the state going to war. On the other side of the coin, those European states not scarred by their own past aggression and subsequent defeat in the Second World War, and those without a tradition of neutralism, still tend to see the use of force as inherent to international politics. Britain and France in particular, anxious to retain their status as permanent members of the UN Security Council, maintain significant armed services and have been willing to deploy them out of the European area. Denmark, Greece, and the Netherlands have also had particular reasons for scepticism towards the pacific-ist model. Even this group of countries, however, has been far less willing to envisage force projection than in the colonial era—the end of which left its mark on them. The memories of the losses of two world wars combined with the failures to resist anti-colonial insurgencies to create war-fatigue in most European states. This was reinforced by an embedded caution about military action and the fear of quagmires, as the 'lessons of Vietnam' had not been imprinted on American minds alone.[17]

Diffidence towards the use of force is therefore a structural feature of European states, deriving from historical trauma and their relative decline from power. Even the new wave of interventionism, with its humanitarian gloss followed by concerns about terrorism, has not fully overcome these inhibitions. Yet such pacificism is not a function of the changing social composition of European states. Indeed, it is arguable that some minority communities would enthusiastically support force if the circumstances were to their liking—as with those Muslims who called for Bosnia to be armed in the early 1990s, or the Kurds eager to see Saddam Hussein overthrown.

More significant as a reinforcement of the drift away from war is the sheer cost which military capabilities impose upon a state—financial, economic, social, and human. This second challenge for contemporary Europe is not a straightforward matter. States such as Britain and France, with established military traditions and industrial sectors tied in to defence through arms production and

[16] The term was coined by A. J. P. Taylor. It was given prominence and a full conceptual analysis by Martin Ceadel in *Thinking about Peace and War* (Oxford: Oxford University Press, 1987).

[17] See Ernest R. May, *'Lessons' of the Past: The Use and Misuse of History in American Foreign Policy* (Oxford: Oxford University Press, 1973), and Robert S. McNamara, *In Retrospect: The Tragedy and Lessons of Vietnam* (New York: Random House, 1996).

Table 7.1. Size of armed forces, and defence expenditure as percentage of GDP, of three EU states

	Armed services			Defence expenditure		
	1985	1999	2010	1985	1999	2010
Britain	327,100	212,400	192,300	5.2	2.6	2.56
France	464,300	317,300	233,600	4.0	2.7	2.01
Netherlands	105,500	56,400	47,660	3.1	1.8	1.43

Sources: For 1985 and 1999: *The Military Balance, 2000, 2001* (London: Oxford University Press for the International Institute of Strategic Studies, 2000), Table 38, p. 297.

For 2010: European Defence Agency database, <http://www.eda.europa.eu/DefenceData/> accessed 14 December 2012.

the increasingly sophisticated technologies associated with it—to say nothing of nuclear weapons—exhibit a distinct path dependency and unwillingness to envisage radical change. This is one reason why it has been so difficult to establish common European procurement programmes—individual states are not ready to give up their independent capabilities, or indeed the foreign policy postures which are associated with them. The ability to find resources for the Libyan operations of 2011 in the midst of a financial crisis is a striking case in point.

Even so, and well before that crisis, which from 2008 led to major cuts in public expenditure, even the larger European states had been forced to accept the limitations on their ability to sustain both extensive welfare provision and a forward international policy. Table 7.1 shows the changes in the size of armed forces, and defence expenditure, of Britain, France, and the Netherlands, three countries with traditionally global roles, between 1980 and 2010. (The Federal Republic of Germany has been excluded given the special constraints on its use of force.)

The data show a fall of between one-third and a half in both manpower and share of GDP devoted to defence over the quarter-century after 1985. The figures are deceptive to the extent that growing wealth meant that there were still large amounts of public money devoted to defence, while more sophisticated technology ensured that the smaller numbers in uniform did not necessarily reduce the projectable power of the main European states. Nonetheless, the end of the Cold War, with its 'peace dividend', still marked a major downgrading of the military as a priority of public policy, as it did the fall-off of intellectual interest in 'strategic studies'.[18] But the collapse of the superpower rivalry was not the whole story. Changing attitudes towards foreign and defence policy which predated 1989 also played a part. The expectation that Europeans would need or wish to send expeditionary forces beyond their own region was significantly in decline from the mid-1960s (the major period of decolonization) onwards.

[18] Richard K. Betts, 'Should Strategic Studies Survive?', *World Politics*, 50/1 (1997), pp. 7–33.

Two significant exceptions in the last decades of the twentieth century involved Britain: the retaking of the Falklands Islands in 1982, and the expulsion of Iraq from Kuwait in 1991, where the UK made the second biggest contribution to the US-led coalition. France was also a major player in Operation Desert Storm, sending 18,000 ground troops.[19] Yet both these cases involved UN-legitimized reactions to flagrant, border-crossing, violations of national sovereignty, actions which were increasingly perceived as anachronistic and likely to occur only rarely. More probable, it seemed, was involvement in the 'new wars' epitomized by the implosion of Yugoslavia.[20] Even here, in Europe's 'backyard', Britain and France dispatched troops with great reluctance, while the Netherlands was shamed by the impotence of its UN peacekeeping brigade in the face of the Srebrenica massacre. These experiences led even Britain, so anxious to retain its credibility as an effective ally of the United States, to conclude that it would need to seek economies of scale in defence, finally embarking on the path of European defence cooperation at the Anglo-French St Malo summit of 1998. The costs—in terms of losing men and *matériel*, but also political through public scepticism about adventurism—were seen as too high for individual states to bear.

This was particularly true in relation to the idea of military service. It seemed that the nation no longer wanted to be 'in arms'. Britain had abolished conscription by 1962, concentrating its resources on professional and increasingly high-tech forces, although the rest of Europe did not follow suit until after the turn of the twentieth century, realizing that the costs of putting reluctant young people into uniform and finding things for them to do were not justified by any military benefits. The media spectacles of family grief over the bodies of young conscripts killed in action, as with the Italians killed in Somalia in 1993, were now politically intolerable, despite the rarity of the occurrence.[21] The Netherlands abolished the draft in 1997, France in 2001, and Italy in 2005.[22] The unpopularity of conscription was general, but as we saw in Chapter 6 the growing proportion of young people coming from minority backgrounds has further complicated the issue of attachment to 'my country right or wrong', and the idea—already weakened—that the government of the day is by definition pursuing a consensual national interest

[19] Other EU states were only involved in support (Belgium, the Netherlands, and Italy) or through cheque-book diplomacy (Germany).

[20] Mary Kaldor, *New and Old Wars: Organized Violence in a Globalized Era* (Cambridge: Polity Press, 1999).

[21] The images of the Argentinian conscripts killed in their unequal battles with British regular soldiers over the Falklands in 1982 had set in train this growing disquiet. Sixty years on from the mass slaughter of the Great War, war had once again come to be seen as a matter for the professionals.

[22] In legal terms the Netherlands and Italy have only 'suspended' conscription, so that it may easily be reintroduced. But given political will, the same is true for any state. See also Chapter 6, pp. 167–8.

abroad. Their ties to third countries, and their tendency to take an interest in foreign affairs, further undermine the wisdom and practicability—especially in the eyes of professional soldiers—of sending conscripts to fight in foreign wars. The draft had become reduced to the status of concealed unemployment, subsidized by the state. With the public purse coming under ever greater strain, this was an institution ripe for abolition.

The third challenge which the new interventionism poses is the extent to which it entails the export of a particular set of values. Intervention for security reasons, such as Israel's into Lebanon, derives straightforwardly from realist thinking. The domestic values of the intervening society are not relevant—even if outsiders and dissenting citizens may claim that the action is inconsistent with the internal morality of the society in question. But when intervention occurs on the basis of human rights derogations it entails, *ipso facto*, the claim that the intervener's ethical standards are higher than those of the target state. That the right to act might then be based on some notion of the common standards of mankind, enshrined in UN declarations, does not change the perceptions of many outsiders that the intervention is either hypocritical, being essentially driven by self-interest, or ethnocentric, being the attempt to impose a particular set of values on societies which hold to different traditions.

Many Europeans themselves are concerned about the question of whether it is right to impose their own way of life on other cultures, agonizing over dilemmas of gender politics and the place of religion. Certain EU members are particularly conflicted in this regard. Germany is hesitant over its right to lecture others and/or to return to sites where the memories of Nazi occupation are just beneath the surface. For their part the old imperial powers are always vulnerable to accusations of neo-colonialism, or of attempting to maintain traditional spheres of influence. It was no accident that on one of his trips to Rome, Colonel Ghaddafi treated his Italian hosts to an exhibition of images of colonial atrocities, while many Afghans see the British presence in ISAF as merely the latest of an historical series of attempts at subjugation, starting in 1839.

Such views are echoed inside European states, and not only by left-wing parties.[23] Attentive opinion is deeply divided between those who believe that societies which claim to be civilized cannot stand aside without acting to stop atrocities like those in Bosnia or Rwanda, and those who see intervention as cynical power politics.[24] In this context the views of minority communities will themselves vary. Depending on the issue, there is always likely to be a vociferous group of exiles calling for the overthrow of the regime they

[23] The columnist Simon Jenkins in *The Guardian* is a most articulate non-intervener. In Italy the *Lega Nord* has been almost wholly inward-looking. See Anna Cento Bull and Mark Gilbert, *The Lega Nord and the Politics of Secession* (Houndmills: Palgrave, 2001), e.g. p. 182.

[24] John Pilger is the best-known critic of this kind. See also Tarak Barkawi, 'On the Pedagogy of "Small Wars"', *International Affairs*, 80/1 (January 2004), pp. 19–37. Barkawi's critique attributes interventions as much to Western illusions of superiority as to mere realpolitik.

abhor, as with Hussein's Iraq or Mugabe's Zimbabwe. On the other hand, the generalized hostility to Western imperialism among minorities, given their Third World origins, means that many will oppose Western interference, taking their stand on sovereignty and anti-hegemonic grounds. It is also the case, however, that minorities are no different from any political community in that many people, perhaps a majority, are indifferent or ill-informed about external affairs, being preoccupied with their own lives and locality.[25]

The confluence of the trend towards humanitarian intervention with the emergence of jihadist attacks on the West has come to present European societies with a fourth, and very particular, challenge. Sending troops into a Muslim country is perceived by many around the world as an attack on Islam itself, regardless of the motive. The large number of civilians killed during the occupations of Iraq and Afghanistan compared to the losses of US or European troops, combined with the all too frequent episodes of disrespect for the Qur'an, or for prisoners, compounds the anger felt in the Muslim world over the plight of the Palestinians in Gaza and the West Bank. Even if Europeans try to dissociate themselves from hard-line Israeli policies (as opposed to Israel's right to exist), they are still tarred with the brush of the West's apparent indifference to Muslim suffering.[26]

This fact represents a foreign policy problem which the EU states manage in different ways, assisted by the cover which their self-consciously even-handed Common Positions on the Middle East provide.[27] But for those which are prominent interventionists as well as containing large numbers of Muslims in their domestic populations, it also represents the potential for blowback at home. There is no simple correspondence between these two factors on the

[25] One survey of British Muslims found that while foreign policy was the main issue of concern, fewer than 20 per cent could actually name the President of the Palestinian Authority or the Prime Minister of Israel, which does not suggest such a deep level of engagement. Munira Mirza, Abi Senthilkumaran, and Zein Ja'far, *Living Apart Together: British Muslims and the Paradox of Multiculturalism* (London: Policy Exchange, 2007). Gilles Kepel had similar findings in an in-depth study of the Parisian *banlieues* of Clichy-sous-Bois and Montfermeil. Between the two poles of a strong Islamic community on the one hand, and those drawn to French secular values on the other, he found 'une vaste gamme d'attitudes de personnes qui cherchent à négocier au mieux leur situation, en fonction des ressources culturelles et matérielles dont elles disposent'. Gilles Kepel, with the collaboration of Leyla Arslan and Sarah Zouheir, *Banlieue de la République: Résumé* (Paris: Institut Montaigne, October 2011), p. 2, <http://www.institutmontaigne.org/medias/documents/banlieue_republique_resume_institut_montaigne.pdf> accessed 6 April 2012.

[26] And as Musu points out, the Israeli attack on Gaza in 2008 led to attacks on Jewish property in various European countries which polarized matters further. Costanza Musu, *European Union Policy Towards the Arab–Israeli Peace Process: The Quicksands of Politics* (Houndmills: Palgrave, 2010), p. 148 and 192. Israel, nonetheless, sees the Europeans as biased towards the Palestinians, Musu, *European Union Policy Towards the Arab–Israeli Peace Process*. p. 88.

[27] Roy H. Ginsberg, *The European Union in International Politics: Baptism by Fire* (Lanham, MD: Rowman & Littlefield, 2001), pp. 105–79.

one hand and internal upheaval on the other. But it is evidently true (*1*) that the larger the Muslim community, the more likely it is that an external force like al-Qaeda will be able to recruit the small number of sympathizers whose help it needs to plan attacks on its enemies—internally or internationally; (*2*) the more visible a European state is in military operations within a Muslim state, the more its own Muslim citizens will feel an obligation to oppose the action on behalf of their co-religionists—even if most will remain passive, and the vast majority of protests are within the law.

This is still a new and significant complication for governments. When even one individual reacts violently, the consequences are unforeseeable. The killings in Toulouse in March 2012 transformed a presidential election campaign which up to that point had not involved the question of Islam in France, leading to widespread security measures which in turn threatened to polarize attitudes about religion even further.[28] A foreign policy cannot be conducted on the basis of avoiding all such incidents at home—seen as examples of terrorist blackmail to which one gives in at even greater cost—but European governments have slowly had to become aware that when they intervene in a country which professes the Muslim faith, even with the best of intentions, they risk inflaming tensions over the very 'clash of civilisations' which they are at pains to deny exists, and at home as well as abroad.[29]

The last challenge which interventions pose to European states in the context of their increasing ethnocultural diversity relates to the choice of their allies and partners. Those dictated by the logic of security, by treaty obligation, or by tradition may be less acceptable to a society whose composition is changing—a point often made with respect to the United States, whose growing Hispanic population is said by some to be loosening its traditional ties with Europe, and in particular the United Kingdom.[30] We have already surveyed the issue of partners in Chapter 5, in the context of identity. Here the point is simply that—given European states are now unlikely to launch an intervention alone (with the exception of France in parts of Africa[31])—the choice of partners becomes a highly sensitive issue, and opens a new front for public opinion. Internal

[28] Steven Erlanger, 'A Presidential Race Leaves French Muslims Feeling Like Outsiders', *International Herald Tribune*, 4 April 2012.

[29] States vary as to how they respond to this dilemma. After the 2004 bombs in Madrid, Spain pursued an 'Alliance of Civilizations' in harness with Turkey, and kept a low profile over military intervention. France and Britain, however, were swift to support the Libyan rebellion against Ghaddafi of 2011, although they were ultra-cautious about admitting the presence of troops on the ground, and made sure the Arab League was on board.

[30] Samuel P. Huntington, *Who Are We? America's Great Debate* (London: Simon & Schuster, 2004), pp. 171–7. See also Chapter 5, this volume.

[31] As this book went to press in January 2013 France sent troops into Mali to help the government against Islamist rebels. It was, however, receiving discreet support from various NATO allies.

debates about the merits of the intervention—purpose, place, means—easily blur with those about the desirability of the allies in question.

Many partners have the potential to cause unease on the home front, particularly when support is evinced for Israel (often wrongly referred to as an 'ally' of Britain by the BBC, for example), for the monarchies in the Gulf, or for African governments fighting al-Qaeda-inspired insurgencies. But the most obvious case in point is the United States, as the leader of NATO and the key ally of most EU members. There were powerful reactions within Europe against Washington during the Cold War arising from tactical differences over policy towards the Soviet Union.[32] But now that NATO's main activity is in the Middle East or Africa, in areas which many of the minority communities call home, the potential for anti-American feeling to arise over joint military operations is higher. The matter is complex, in that not all diasporas may be presumed to take a negative view of the superpower's world role. Still, the more heterogeneous nature of European societies adds an extra reason for caution into the calculations of those considering military action alongside the United States. It suited both the Europeans and the US that France and Britain were willing to take the public lead over Libya in 2011, as it did in 2006 when France and Italy provided peacekeeping forces for the Lebanon after the war with Israel. Internationally, and at home, the American alliance is now even more of a two-edged sword.

One further point of relevance is that sometimes an intervention can be spurred by pressure from a minority group which is desperate to assist its co-nationals back home. In this event military intervention is unlikely; national foreign policy is not put at such risk for a special interest.[33] But, as with the German recognition of Croatia in December 1991, it is not impossible for a powerful campaign to raise the profile of an issue to the point where wider support is attracted, and a government feels it must act.[34] Something similar had happened in 1982, when the UK lobby for the Falkland Islanders helped to tip the balance in favour of sending a task force to expel Argentinian troops.[35] In France the Armenian lobby has achieved an official recognition of the 1915

[32] E.g. over the Euromissiles crisis; see Diana Johnstone, *Politics of Euromissiles: Europe's Role in America's World* (London: Verso, 1984).

[33] Preventive action, and/or special forces operations, however, might be possible, as in the Indian Ocean over piracy and the taking of hostages.

[34] Josip Glaurdić, *The Hour of Europe: Western Powers and the Breakup of Yugoslavia* (New Haven: Yale University Press, 2011), pp. 188–90. Glaurdić argues, however, that similar campaigns in other EU states were resisted by governments. Caplan's view is that Germany put its foreign policy 'at risk' by this move, driven by both 'domestic pressures and strategic considerations'. But the vocal Croatian community of *Gastarbeiter* did not count electorally, and without wider political and media support could not have been decisive. Richard Caplan, *Europe and the Recognition of New States in Yugoslavia* (Cambridge: Cambridge University Press, 2005) pp. 42–8.

[35] Lawrence Freedman, *The Official History of the Falklands Campaign:* Volume I. *The Origins of the Falklands War* (London: Routledge, 2005) pp. 85–131.

genocide, thus pressurizing Turkey and compromising relations between Ankara and Paris.

EUROPEAN INTERVENTIONS—THE RECORD

The military interventions by Europeans in the wider world which have gained most attention in recent years are those under the auspices of the EU's Common Security and Defence Policy (CSDP).[36] As of March 2012 there had been twenty-four CSDP missions. But the majority of these were civilian. Of the eight military actions, only three have lasted for more than two years—those ongoing in Bosnia Herzegovina, Somalia, and the Indian Ocean. As Somalia is mostly a military training operation (and is in any case linked to the EUNAVFOR against off-shore piracy), this means that the EU has only mounted serious collective interventions in two theatres. This is not to underestimate their intrinsic importance, but they need placing in the context of the non-EU operations conducted by various European states, sometimes under the auspices of the UN and sometimes not, variously in Somalia (1992), Rwanda (at the end of the 1994 genocide), Comoros (2005), Central African Republic (1996–7, and 2006), Congo-Brazzaville (1997), Albania (1997), Democratic Republic of the Congo (1998), Kosovo (1999), Sierra Leone (2000–2), Afghanistan (2001–present), Iraq (2003–9), Lebanon (2006–present), Chad (2006), Ivory Coast (2002–present), Mauretania and Niger (2010), and Libya (2011).[37]

European interventions of both kinds have been motivated by a range of considerations, in varied combinations according to circumstances: security, human rights, pressures from the United States and the United Nations, conflict-resolution, and concerns for the long-term stability of the international system. Table 7.2 lists the wide range of deployments of the EU-15 Member States. But these have been more than chess-board calculations by rational actors; domestic factors have often shaped the decisions of individual states, and certainly their evaluations over the passage of time. From a reluctance to get involved at all to a sense of firm obligation, from a distinctive regional or cultural connection with a given problem to priorities elsewhere, EU Member States

[36] See Roy H. Ginsberg and Susan E. Penska, *The European Union in Global Security: The Politics of Impact* (Houndmills: Palgrave Macmillan, 2012). Also Mette Eilstrup-Sangiovanni, 'The Future of the CSDP' (forthcoming); and Jolyon Howorth, 'The EU's Security and Defence Policy: Towards a Strategic Approach', in Christopher Hill and Michael Smith (eds), *International Relations and the European Union* (2nd edn, Oxford: Oxford University Press, 2011), pp. 197–225.

[37] Britain, France, and Italy have been the main states involved in these operations, many of which have been short-term stabilization or citizen-rescue missions.

Table 7.2. Sites of EU-15 troop deployments, in order of number of Member States sending contingents of more than fifty at any given time between 1995 and 2007

Site of deployments	Number of Member States deploying
Bosnia, Serbia	14
Afghanistan	13
Lebanon	11
Croatia	8
Albania	7
FYROM, Iraq	6
DRC	5
Chad/Central Africa Empire, Ethiopia/Eritrea	4
Cyprus	3
Haiti, Iraq/Kuwait, Kuwait, Liberia, Med. Sea, Saudi Arabia, Turkey	2
Bahrain, Côte d'Ivoire, Djibouti, Kenya, Kyrgyzstan, Sierra Leone, Syria/Israel, Tajikistan, Timor Este, Uzbekistan	1

Source: Adapted from Bastian Giegerich and Alexander Nicoll (eds), *European Military Capabilities: Building Armed Forces for Modern Operations* (London: International Institute for Strategic Studies, 2008), Appendix, pp. 157–70.

have varied in the ways in which their internal environments have affected their views of interventions, both in prospect and in implementation.

The other dimension is the impact of a foreign involvement on domestic society—which also varies between cases. This is the 'blowback' already referred to, a term suggestive for its connotation of the unforeseen (and potentially dramatic) consequences which flow from any action as serious as interference in the affairs of another country.[38] Even being associated with an intervention can lead to controversy at home, while the actual dispatch of troops and commitment of major resources can spin out of control into a prolonged presence which then becomes a major issue of domestic politics. Conversely, a single trauma like that of the Dutch at Srebrenica may even have effects at the level of national identity. At the most extreme, interventions can produce revenge terrorist attacks on the home front, usually generated by a combination of internal and external enemies. The bigger European states, as the most visible and capable of contributing to military interventions, are also the most vulnerable to blowbacks. What follows therefore focuses on the experience of the 'big five': Britain, France, Germany, Italy, and Spain. Table 7.3 identifies the interventions which had significant domestic reverberations, for some if not all of the five. Table 7.4 shows how these states committed the most troops to such missions, although it should be noted

[38] The 'law of unintended consequences' was first outlined in Robert Merton's 1936 essay: 'The Unanticipated Consequences of Purposive Social Action', in Robert K. Merton, *Sociological Ambivalence and Other Essays* (New York: Free Press, 1976). See also Karl Popper, *The Open Society and its Enemies* Vol. 2 (London: Routledge, 1966).

Table 7.3. European 'big five' interventions 1991–2012 with a significant domestic dimension

Case	Dates	States Intervening
Bosnia Herzegovina	1992–5	Britain, France
Albania	1997	Italy, France, Spain
Kosovo	1999	Britain, France, Italy, Germany
Sierra Leone[a]	2000	Britain
Afghanistan	2001	All five with varying time-spans
Ivory Coast	2002	France
Iraq	2003–11	Britain, Italy, Spain – varying time-spans
Lebanon	2006–present	France, Italy, Spain

[a] It can be argued that Britain had already intervened in Sierra Leone in 1997, through using the mercenary outfit SandLine International to break the UN arms embargo. Andrew M. Dorman, *Blair's Successful War: British Military Intervention in Sierra Leone* (Aldershot: Ashgate, 2009), pp. 40–2; Tanja Schümer, *New Humanitarianism: Britain and Sierra Leone, 1997–2003* (Houndmills: Palgrave, 2008), pp. 69–70.
Note: To qualify as an intervention here a state has to have >50 troops on the ground.

Table 7.4. EU-15 Member States' troop deployments, 1995–2007

Member State	Total no. of troops deployed 1995–2007[a]	Number of sites on which troops deployed[b]	Number of deployment years[c]
United Kingdom	150,068	14	82
France	125,070	15	94
Italy	78,794	10	68
Germany	76,658	13	47
Spain	30,778	8	33
Netherlands	27,779	10	35
Greece	16,241	5	27
Denmark	15,017	6	36
Belgium	14,207	4	28
Finland	13,493	4	23
Austria	12,965	6	38
Portugal	12,329	8	36
Sweden	10,424	6	22
Ireland	8,512	5	29
Luxembourg	386	0	0

[a] The figures in the first column were obtained by adding the totals given by IISS for each year, excluding observers. Evidently there were overlaps of personnel over succeeding years, so the numbers do not indicate the total number of individual soldiers involved.
[b] This column indicates the number of geographically separate places where a given Member State deployed troops. For example, Finland sent contingents (that is, more than fifty in a year) to four sites over the period in question: Afghanistan, Bosnia, Croatia, and Serbia.
[c] This column is calculated by adding up the number of years a state had troops in the various sites to which it sent contingents. For example, Finland sent troops to Afghanistan for five years in total, to Bosnia for eight, to Croatia for two, and Serbia for eight—a total of twenty-three 'deployment years'.
Source: Adapted from Giegerich and Nicoll (eds), *European Military Capabilities: Building Armed Forces for Modern Operations*, Appendix, pp. 157–70.

that Greece and the Netherlands, in a different category by virtue of their smaller populations, made proportionately bigger contributions than Spain.

For much of the period and for all of the five states the usual condition applied—whereby the attention of domestic publics turned much more to issues such as the economy than to foreign policy, with the result that decision-makers were largely able to operate without the nervousness over repercussions at home. But the emergence of the new interventionism combined with increased levels of social diversity, has introduced a higher level of uncertainty and complexity into the conduct of foreign policy and its domestic context. External policies are now more likely to rebound at home, and unpredictably given that shared understandings of the national interest can no longer be taken for granted.

On this basis only a schematic analysis can be offered of the pattern of impacts at the national level. At one extreme British politics and society have been much affected by the country's foreign policy, and at the other France has been relatively immune. As the two states possess the most active foreign policies among EU Member States their contrasting experience in this respect is interesting. It suggests that an active international role in itself is not critical in determining whether or not a foreign policy is disruptive at home. That may relate more to the kind of activity pursued, and to the nature of the particular domestic environment. We return to this issue in Chapter 9, but for the moment it is worth noting that the United Kingdom has been heavily involved in wars in Muslim countries while being relaxed about fostering minority groups at home. France has, broadly speaking, done the opposite. Italy, Spain, and Germany fall somewhere in between their two poles, with feedback loops between foreign policy and society which are perhaps more obvious than in executive-dominated France, but still more intermittent and indirect than has recently been the case in the UK. Their experience of ethnocultural diversity is also relatively recent.

In order to understand the patchiness of the interplay, it is useful to turn to the different sites in which it is manifest. There are seven counts on which the various interventions of the big five European states have produced blowbacks, often in surprising ways and occasionally in deeply shocking ones. Of these seven, three relate primarily to the *values* present in an intervening state (meaning here the sets of attitudinal preferences about desirable conduct in world politics), three primarily to *interests* (meaning the various stakes inside a state on which an intervention impacts), and one—the issue of Islam—to a significant *combination* of the previous two themes.

At the level of *values*, foreign interventions have raised various levels of concern according to country, over human rights, imperialism, and pacificism (hostility to the use of force). Bearing in mind that here we focus not on the motives for intervention but on the internal reverberations that followed (except in the sense that governments could be sensitive to the possibility of domestic criticism if they did not act[39]), human rights was a significant factor in three of the cases listed in Table 7.3—Bosnia, Sierra Leone, and Kosovo. The Sierra Leonean minority in Britain, let alone elsewhere, was not big enough to stir up difficulties over any intervention, but the ham-fisted Sand-Line operation of 1997, breaking a UN arms embargo, and in which the British government seemed implicated, caused an embarrassing parliamentary row for the new Foreign Secretary, Robin Cook.[40] In Bosnia once the British government finally decided to intervene, in 1992, the presence of its troops only drew more criticism for its limited scope and inability to stop Serbian and Croatian aggression. But even three years later, as Brendan Simms has commented, in Britain 'the Srebrenica massacre [of 1995] provoked public horror, political mortification, and important operational changes, but no fundamental change in government policy'.[41]

There was to be a fundamental change in policy, but it came four years later over Kosovo, when the New Labour government showed itself affected by the sense of guilt which had spread through the political class over Bosnia, playing a major part in the air war which defeated Slobodan Milosevic. The same process was at work within other European societies, particularly Germany, for whom intervention in Kosovo broke post-war taboos about the Balkans, the UN, and the role of force. Guilt over the Bosnian inaction changed the climate of opinion within the Federal Republic.[42] It reinforced the humanitarian

[39] David Owen, *Balkan Odyssey* (London: Indigo/Gollancz, 1996), p. 19. The British Prime Minister John Major said in the summer of 1992 that he did 'not detect any support in Parliament or in public opinion for operations which would tie down large numbers of British forces in difficult and dangerous terrain for a long period . . . [but] I do not rest on that. We have to look all the time at fresh possibilities' (letter from John Major to David Owen, 3 August 1992). Lord Owen notes (*Balkan Odyssey*, p. 20) that John Major 'had left the door slightly ajar in case public opinion demanded more action'.

[40] Also Sir Thomas Legg and Sir Robin Ibbs, *Report of the Sierra Leone Arms Investigation*, ordered to be printed by the House of Commons, 27 July 1998 (London: The Stationery Office); Commons Foreign Affairs Committee, 2nd Report, 3 February 1999 on Sierra Leone, and response by the Secretary of State for Foreign Affairs, April 1999, Cmd 4325; and Hill, 'Foreign Policy', in Seldon (ed.), *The Blair Effect*, pp. 331–53.

[41] Brendan Simms, *Unfinest Hour: Britain and the Destruction of Bosnia* (London: Penguin Books, 2001), p. 317.

[42] An important motive for Germany in 1999 was to demonstrate solidarity with its allies, and thus its own 'normalization', as stressed by Martin Wagener's 'Normalization in security policy? Deployments of Bundeswehr forces abroad in the era Schröder, 1998–2004', in Hanns W. Maull, (ed.), *Germany's Uncertain Power: Foreign Policy of the Berlin Republic* (Houndmills: Palgrave Macmillan, 2006), especially pp. 79 and 86. But this had not been a decisive factor on previous occasions. In 1999 the impact of Bosnia, together with a Red–Green government in Berlin, finally unshackled Germany from its past, creating the conditions for 'German armoured columns . . . [to be] shown on German television rolling across the green fields of Macedonia', and for 'German flight commanders, cool and self-confident . . . [to be] interviewed in the media'. Thomas Berger, 'The power of memory and memories of power: The cultural parameters of German foreign policy-making since 1945', in Jan-Werner Müller (ed.), *Memory and Power in Post-war Europe: Studies in the Presence of the Past* (Cambridge: Cambridge University Press, 2002), p. 78.

instincts which had produced an early recognition of the independence of some of the republics of Yugoslavia back in 1991–2, while those Croat guest-workers left in Germany must have indulged in a touch of *Schadenfreude* watching Serb discomfiture.[43]

The more significant consequences of Bosnia for British society, and perhaps elsewhere in Europe, were barely visible until the start of the next century. Beneath the surface of politics some British Muslims, deeply disturbed by the suffering in Bosnia, had come to the conclusion not only that their own government was not on the side of right, but that it should be classed as the enemy. This image was not reversed by the willingness in 1999, even without a UN Resolution, to protect Muslim Kosovars from the possibility of genocidal violence. Relatively small numbers had become alienated, but some of their activities would eventually prove devastating. Omar Saeed Sheikh was a middle-class boy who left his course at the London School of Economics to join the fighters in Bosnia, going on to be responsible for the kidnap and sadistic murder in Pakistan of the American journalist Daniel Pearl.[44] For others the impact of Bosnia was more slow-burning, but there seems little doubt that it laid the seeds for the hostility to the British government, and to some extent to civil society, which emerged more strongly among young Muslims after the invasions of Afghanistan and Iraq. As Bronitsky's detailed study concludes, 'Throughout the Bosnia War of the early 1990s, British Islamists rallied support for the Khilafah (Caliphate) by hailing its re-establishment as the only true guarantor of Muslim security. Their campaign centred upon a parallel drawn between the societal issues faced by Muslims in Britain and the unspeakable conditions endured by their co-religionists in Bosnia'.[45] Events in Bosnia further radicalized those concerned, who had been alerted in the first place by events at the British universities which young Muslims had begun to attend in increasing numbers, encouraged by the multicultural ethos of the 1980s.[46]

The other two value-related issues which arose from interventions are anti-imperialism and pacifism. The first concern was evoked on the left in all the big five countries by Kosovo, Afghanistan, and Iraq—to some extent as a reflex action, on the assumption that joint action with the United States necessarily represented NATO expansion and an instinct for the domination of countries

[43] Glaurdić, *The Hour of Europe*, pp. 262–85; Paul Hockenos, *Homeland Calling: Exile Patriotism and the Balkan Wars* (Ithaca, NY: Cornell University Press, 2003), pp. 61–73.

[44] 'Model Pupil to Militant', *The Guardian*, 9 February 2002. It is impossible to know how many British Muslims went to Bosnia, but it seems likely that there were several hundred, at least, mostly engaged in relief work. Jonathan Bronitsky, *British Foreign Policy and Bosnia: The rise of Islamism in Britain, 1992–1995* (London: King's College, International Centre for the Study of Radicalization and Political Violence, 2010), p. 18.

[45] Bronitsky, *British Foreign Policy and Bosnia*, p. 1.

[46] Bronitsky, *British Foreign Policy and Bosnia*, pp. 1–14. It should be said that Bronitsky paints an apocalyptic picture of Muslim activity on university campuses in the 1990s.

which might possibly challenge Western interests. This response polarized debate over foreign policy and thus raised its political profile, but failed to overcome the countervailing stimuli of the idea of the 'responsibility to protect' (Kosovo) and the desire to resist Islamist terrorism (Afghanistan). There was some variation between countries, with the left-wing critique of intervention as a tool of the United States being stronger in Italian society than in more self-confident France, but it was everywhere difficult to distinguish from the sheer aversion to war.[47] And of course the anti-colonialist critique was only rarely voiced by immigrants from poor countries themselves, facing so many obstacles in their access to politics and the media. It was rather the indigenous left which asserted its right to speak for them and for those living in the sites of interventions.

So far as pacifism is concerned, only Germany and Italy have political cultures in which this reaction is likely to be evoked. As we have seen, in Germany the dominant anti-militarist tendency was trumped over Kosovo by the human rights argument, and by loyalty to the alliance.[48] This was less true in Italy, but the latter's own (domestically popular) intervention in Albania in 1997 meant that it was difficult for a movement in public opinion to arise on pacifist grounds two years later. Still, Italians were unusual in wanting a quick return to diplomacy after the first phase of bombing, which can be explained by the fact that in Italy pacifism has a hold on the Catholic right as well as on the left, where it combines with anti-imperialism.[49] Here as in Germany a possible use of force brings to the fore several value sets entrenched in political culture which are not insuperable, but together can provide major obstacles to participation. Thus although the attacks of 9/11 pushed pacifists on both states onto the defensive, freeing the way for support for the Afghanistan invasion of October 2001 (if not the subsequent prolongation of the war), in the case of

[47] The analysis here refers to the big five—in Greece the majority of the public looked on NATO's actions with hostility. P. Everts, 'Chapter 8: "War Without Bloodshed": The Conflict Over Kosovo', in the same author's *Democracy and Military Force* (Houndmills: Palgrave Macmillan, 2002), pp. 134–57, especially the data in the Annex which shows support for NATO's air strikes running at between 35 and 55 per cent in Italy from March to June 1999, as compared to a range of 40–72 per cent in France, with averages of 44 per cent over eighteen polls in Italy as compared to 57 per cent over eleven polls in France (pp. 154–5). It is, however, difficult to disaggregate the various reasons for supporting/opposing the strikes.

[48] Everts, '"War Without Bloodshed"', p. 151, shows that German opinion continued to support NATO's actions despite its scepticism that Milosevic would be forced to comply.

[49] Everts, 'Chapter 8: "War Without Bloodshed"', p. 146, Table 8.3 shows that an average of 65 per cent over ten polls between 26 March and 17 May 1999 wanted a return to diplomacy. See also Pierangelo Isernia, 'Italian Public Opinion and the International Use of Force', in Philip Everts and Pierangelo Isernia (eds), *Public Opinion and the International Use of Force* (London: Routledge, 2001), pp. 100–4. Italy's Prime Minister Massimo D'Alema hesitated perhaps less than his predecessors would have done over such an intervention, but even he was all too aware of the 'nervosismo' in the domestic environment. See Marta Dassù, *Mondo privato e altre storie* (Torino: Bollati Boringhieri, 2009), pp. 88–91.

Iraq the mix of pacifism and anti-imperialism in Italy, together with sheer scepticism over Anglo-American motives in both countries, combined to create a wave of popular opposition to the war. At the public level, indeed, this extended right across Europe. In such cases Muslims, and other minorities, were part of a general social movement, and did not therefore feel particularly alienated or exposed. This fact may go some way to explain why neither Germany nor Italy suffered from major jihadist plots at the time.

It is always difficult to keep values and interests in wholly separate compartments, and this is especially evident in Europe with respect to Islam. Since the publication of Samuel Huntington's 'clash of civilisations' thesis in 1993 (if not before), a global debate has provoked conflicting views on Islam's role in the world, and indeed over the revival of religion more generally as a factor in international politics.[50] Many societies have seen sharp clashes of interest over the rights claimed by or denied to Muslims, often in local and practical contexts but also raising broad constitutional issues.

So far as the consequences of interventions are concerned the two key cases are again Afghanistan and Iraq. The attacks on the USA of September 2011 raised the twin spectres of al-Qaeda and their protectors in Afghanistan, leading to an ultimatum to the Taleban that—once predictably ignored—led to invasion and regime change. In Europe almost as much as in the US, Islamic fanaticism was framed as the systemic enemy, to be ground down in a 'War on Terror'. Tony Blair and others insisted that Islam, as 'a peaceful, tolerant religion', should not be associated with terrorist violence, but the political forces released by 9/11 made it difficult to sustain the distinction at the level of public discourse once the initial victory in Afghanistan had turned into long-term occupation and low-intensity warfare.[51] This increasingly polarized opinion in the contributing European states, notably in the UK, with its large Muslim population and foreign policy closely aligned with that of Washington. On the one hand, suspicions grew among the majority population about the loyalties of Muslim citizens, and the very nature of Islam as a religion. On the other, the Muslim community felt more embattled, especially once police surveillance and profiling at the UK border increased, with some becoming seriously alienated. These trends may well have been evident without any complications from foreign policy, but there can be little doubt that the invasion of Iraq in particular accelerated and exacerbated them. The subsequent parallelism between two long-drawn-out wars in Muslim lands, with much civilian suffering, continued the process, although the anger felt by

[50] Samuel P. Huntington, 'The Clash of Civilisations?', *Foreign Affairs*, 72/3 (Summer 1993), pp. 22–49. See also Samuel P. Huntington, *The Clash of Civilizations and the Remaking of World Order* (New York: Simon & Schuster, 1996).

[51] Blair's remark was made in an article published in October 2001, cited in Anthony Seldon, *Blair* (London: The Free Press, 2005), p. 526.

British Muslims was shared by many Christian and secular citizens. Equally, the regular uncovering of bomb plots, and the legal but provocative demonstrations of disrespect towards the armed services, fostered the growth of such groups as the English Defence League and, more significantly, eroded consensus over the benefits of multiculturalism as a model.

Other countries did not have this kind of blowback from Afghanistan and Iraq to anything like the same degree. France was only vulnerable in relation to the former, and even there seems to have been insulated by the combination of its reputation for opposing the Iraq War, and the focus of French Muslims more on their own problems than on foreign policy. They were also, by their history, oriented to the Maghreb rather than to the mountains of Pakistan and the Afghan border, where most jihadist training was taking place. In its turn the lack of terrorism, plus the opposition of the French state to multiculturalism, also limited the excesses of Islamophobia—until the Toulouse killings of 2012, and the presidential election campaign on which they impacted.

Spain, as we saw in Chapter 4, did suffer the devastating attacks of March 2004, probably deriving from its presence in Iraq, but since its withdrawal from that country (strongly supported across society) its continued presence in Afghanistan has produced few internal tremors—perhaps because there have been regular 'preventive' arrests for fear of further terrorism, in part by jihadists trained in Afghanistan.[52] Over ninety Spanish troops have died in Afghanistan, but mostly as the result of accidents. Public opposition has grown to the mission, but given the economic crisis which supervened from 2008 onwards, it has not been a determining factor in Spanish politics.[53]

In relation to the *interests* inside society affected by foreign adventures, the most tangible is that of the soldiers killed or maimed on active service. There is a considerable literature, going back to the aftermath of the Vietnam War, on

[52] Rafael L. Badarjí and Ignacio Cosidó, 'Spain: From 9/11 to 3/11 and Beyond', in Gary J. Schmitt (ed.), *Safety, Liberty and Islamist Terrorism: American and European Approaches to Domestic Counter-Terrorism* (Washington, DC: American Enterprise Institute, 2010), pp. 48–61. The authors argue that the high number of Islamist detainees in Spain is 'not only a sign of the success of Spanish police in pre-empting acts of terrorism, but equally important, a reflection of the presence and activity of Islamic terrorist groups in Spain', p. 55. See also Rogelio Alonso, 'Jihadist Terrorism and the Radicalization Process of Muslim Immigrants in Spain', in Michal Finkelstein and Kim Dent-Brown (eds), *Psychosocial Stress in Immigrants and in Members of Minority Groups as a Factor of Terrorist Behavior* (Kiryat Shimona, Israel: IOS Press, NATO Science for Peace and Security Series, 2008), pp. 109–21.

[53] 'Prime Minister Jose Luis Rodriguez Zapatero Defends Spanish Presence in Afghanistan', *Barcelona Reporter*, 16 September 2010, available online <http://www.barcelonareporter.com/index.php?/pg_print_article/prime_minister_jose_luis_rodriguez_zapatero_defends_spanish_presence_in_afg/> accessed 25 April 2012. Public opinion in Spain had been almost equally divided on the value of the presence in Afghanistan, but by 2009 59 per cent wanted it to be reduced or brought to an end, while 35 per cent wanted it maintained or increased. See the polls in the 'Twentieth Edition of the Barometer of the Elcano Royal Institute', March–April 2009, available online <http://www.realinstitutoelcano.org/wps/portal/rielcano_eng/Content?WCM_GLOBAL_CONTEXT=/elcano/elcano_in/barometer/barometer20> accessed 25 April 2012.

the 'casualties hypothesis', or the view that there is a correlation between the number of troops brought home in coffins and opposition to the mission they were engaged in.[54] This is a complex and controversial issue. What can be said in the current context is that the fact or possibility of losses did not prevent the big five from committing to Afghanistan over a long period, Britain and France from putting troops on the ground in Bosnia, or Britain, Italy, and Spain from deploying in Iraq—although it did induce all of them to err on the side of caution and restraint. On the other hand, as time went on the regular spectacle of grieving relatives in the mass media helped to stir up debate on the purpose and morality of conflicts which were already under question for other reasons.

This was particularly evident for Italy after the loss of twelve Carabinieri at Nasiriyah in southern Iraq, which evoked memories of the traumatic withdrawal from Somalia in 1993 after the killing of Italian conscripts; and increasingly for Britain, France, and Spain in Afghanistan. President Sarkozy, sensitive to French opinion before the elections of 2012, and to his rival François Hollande's promise to end the Afghan mission, announced that he would speed up France's pull-out after four French soldiers were killed by an Afghan colleague.[55] Back in the 1990s the fear of losses had shaped British, French, and Dutch reluctance to engage with aggression in Bosnia, and the consequent reliance on airpower to subdue Serbia over Kosovo. We can safely conclude therefore that in modern, mediatized, conditions a military intervention represents a significant risk for European governments in terms of the domestic anguish and conflict which can result from both the actions of troops abroad (since the killing of foreigners can no longer be closed down by reference to a self-evident national interest) and from their own losses, no longer certain to be grieved by all sections of society. Support for the armed services is traditionally taken for granted by those working within a nation-state frame of reference; even opponents of particular wars would have shared a concern for 'our boys'. But some members of minority communities seeing the impact of European military action on their country of origin may find this a distasteful notion.

The second set of domestic interests which is engaged by intervention relates to immigration. Wars always produce refugees, while modern Europe

[54] For a useful (and skeptical) analysis, see Everts, *Democracy and Military Force*, pp. 158–81. Among the many discussions of the American evidence, see S. S. Gartner and G. M. Segura, 'War, Casualties and Public Opinion', *Journal of Conflict Resolution*, 42/3 (1998), pp. 278–300, and for some recent reflections from a leading exponent of the view that casualties affect public support, John Mueller, *War and Ideas: Selected Essays* (Abingdon: Routledge, 2011), pp. 172–8, 199–204, and 214–15.

[55] *The Guardian*, 21 January 2012. Edward Burke also sees the killings as a catalyst for many discontents. 'Why France is Leaving Afghanistan', blog entry (London: Centre for European Reform, 2 February 2012), <http://centreforeuropeanreform.blogspot.co.uk/2012/02/why-france-is-leaving-afghanistan.html> accessed 14 December 2012.

is a particular magnet for its prosperity, geographical accessibility, and post-colonial diversity. When European states are themselves the intervenors they become susceptible to the arguments of obligation from those who may have shared their cause in a given conflict (for example, Iraq) which they have fled to avoid reprisals, or from those who think themselves let down by the failings of European foreign policies (such as Bosnia). On occasions, policy is explicitly directed towards containing the sudden floods of immigrants, as with Operation Alba in 1997 or the Arab Spring in 2011. In both cases Italy was particularly exposed, but was also just a conduit to areas further north, leading to the spat with France in 2011 over the closing of the land border at Ventimiglia.[56] The EU's internally open frontiers mean that all the Member States are potentially affected by the fall-out from a particular crisis, even if few may be immediately involved. It means that attempts to limit immigration at the EU's common 'hard' external frontier become particularly important, as do relations with neighbouring states.[57]

Yet apart from the dramas caused by the occasional influx, long-drawn-out conflicts produce a steady stream of displaced persons, sharpening already difficult debates over the right of asylum and over the capacity of European states to absorb newcomers. The disintegration of Yugoslavia, for example, led to an increase in the number of foreign nationals in Germany deriving from that region, from 610,499 in 1989 (12.6 per cent of all foreigners) to 1,054,705 (14.3 per cent) in 2003.[58] Afghanistan and Iraq became new sources of migrant pressure on European societies, creating choke-points at places like the Sangatte camp in Calais or on the Greek–Turkish frontier.[59] Although some of these people were in fact keen to return home as soon as conditions allowed, this was rarely taken into account in the simplistic public debate on immigration, with the result that the diverse circumstances of economic migrants, refugees from war and/or persecution, and those seeking family reunions, were blurred together in generalizations about jobs and ways of life under threat. This was not so surprising given that many refugees did decide that they wished to stay permanently—only to find that their arrival was not welcome among those whose economic and social interests they allegedly

[56] See Chapter 4, p. 126.

[57] For a good survey of the internal and external significance of Schengen, see Ruben Zaotti, *Cultures of Border Control: Schengen and the Evolution of European Frontiers* (London: University of Chicago Press, 2011), especially pp. 159–91. See also Chapter 8, in this volume.

[58] Rafaela M. Dancygier, *Immigration and Conflict in Europe* (Cambridge: Cambridge University Press, 2010), Table 7.1, p. 225. It should be noted, however, that by the time Germany itself intervened militarily in Kosovo, the numbers of asylum-seekers had dropped back to pre-1990 levels (Dancygier, *Immigration and Conflict in Europe*, Figure 7.4, p. 254).

[59] The Sangatte camp became a focus for Iraqi Kurds and Afghans wanting to find a way of entering the UK illegally between 1999 and 2002, when it was closed. Asylum seekers still remain in Calais in smaller numbers.

threatened.[60] In this respect the human fall-out from interventions affected Spain and France rather less than the other three of the big five, as their immigration pressures come from Latin America in the first case and Africa—where the long tradition of French interference in the north and west is itself a factor—in the second.

The last set of domestic interests at stake is electoral. Politicians coming up to democratic elections will be aware that their fortunes may turn on the outcome of any foreign intervention which they or their opponents have undertaken. This may lead to calculations about the further prosecution of the war in question, and/or about similar future actions. The burden of scholarly opinion is that historically election campaigns have rarely been affected significantly by foreign policy debate.[61] Voters mainly decide on such bread and butter issues as taxes, jobs, education, and health. Even so, war—even far from the home theatre—is always potentially the gravest activity a government can undertake, which means that when it goes wrong the potential for political embarrassment is huge. In contemporary conditions, furthermore, the emerging humanitarian and diasporic dimensions bring foreign policy issues more to the fore even when disaster has been avoided.[62] If foreign policy is important for even 10 per cent of voters, decision-makers will know that they are vulnerable to a decisive adverse swing.[63] A prolonged involvement in a foreign conflict, with the losses in lives and resources discussed earlier, will increase the chances of an electoral reaction, as Lyndon Johnson concluded in 1968 when deciding not to run again for President because of Vietnam.

We have already noted President Sarkozy's nervousness over the impact of the Toulouse terrorist attacks on the 2012 presidential election, attacks which were themselves apparently in response to French foreign policy. Others have ascribed his eagerness to intervene in Libya in 2011 to the hope for a boost in declining opinion poll figures, along the lines of Mrs Thatcher's profiting at

[60] Dancygier's systematic study (footnote 58) argues strongly that competition over scarce resources is more important than ethnic and cultural issues in causing social conflicts (see especially pp. 292–8). She barely takes into account, however, the impact of international politics or the religious issues associated with it.

[61] A point developed in Christopher Hill, *The Changing Politics of Foreign Policy* (Houndmills: Palgrave Macmillan, 2003) pp. 258–61. The classic statement is in Bernard C. Cohen, *The Public's Impact on Foreign Policy* (Boston: Little Brown, 1973).

[62] Steven Kull and I. M. Destler argue forcefully that the American public, while ignorant of detail, is not uninterested or uncaring about foreign policy. They 'have a sense of history, a recognition of global interdependence, and a desire to see their nation make a meaningful contribution for both selfish and altruistic reasons'. *Misreading the Public: The Myth of a New Isolationism* (Washington, DC: Brookings Institution, 1999), p. 264.

[63] A point made on the basis of a 1988 poll about US voters' concerns by Miroslav Nincic, 'Elections and U.S. Foreign Policy', in Eugene R. Wittkopf and James M. McCormick (eds), *The Domestic Sources of American Foreign Policy: Insights and Evidence* (4th edn, Oxford: Rowman & Littlefield, 2004), pp. 117–27.

the 1983 general election from the Falklands War a year earlier.[64] Foreign policy successes can certainly burnish the image of leadership, just as failures can destroy it, especially in a country like France where foreign policy is so closely tied to the personality of a single individual. Conversely where coalition government is the norm, in states like Italy, any high-profile policy dispute has the potential to change the balance of power between competing parties. Kosovo did not become an issue in the 2001 Italian election because of the support of the official Opposition for Massimo D'Alema's decision to participate in the air war, but it probably weakened the coherence of his own centre–left coalition given the left's unhappiness over both the use of force and cooperation with NATO. As Paul Ginsborg has said, 'at the heart of the centre–right's victory was its capacity to unite its forces, whereas the centre–left entered the fray much more divided than in the previous election'.[65] In Germany governments are similarly vulnerable, even if the 2002 Federal election saw the unpopular 'Red–Green' coalition benefit from its opposition to the coming invasion of Iraq, so that it survived against all expectations.[66] George W. Bush clearly believed that Gerhard Schroeder had opposed the war purely for cynical domestic reasons, and even if that was a misreading the electoral factor had clearly played a part in the Chancellor's decision, which turned out to be shrewd in electoral terms.[67]

In the case of both Britain and Spain, the two countries which suffered mass casualties through terrorism, elections have also been implicated. As we saw in Chapter 4, the outcome of the Spanish election of March 2004 was not decided by the bombs which exploded in Madrid three days before the vote, but that was clearly the intention of the perpetrators. And both major parties had to face huge political and moral dilemmas as to how to respond to the outrage in the context of sharp party competition. The charges and counter-charges which followed are still affecting Spanish politics. In Britain, the 2005 general election took place just over two months before the 7/7 attacks. Labour had won the election with a clear majority of sixty-four seats, but with a vote share which (at 35.2 per cent) was the lowest ever vote share recorded by a victorious

[64] Tony Blair, whose first attempt to get a seat in Parliament ended with him losing Labour's deposit at the Beaconsfield by-election of 27 May 1982 (i.e. towards the end of the Falklands campaign), is said to have concluded that a successful short war bestows a huge electoral advantage on a leader. Cited in the BBC2 Documentary, *The Falklands Legacy*, broadcast on 1 April 2012.

[65] Paul Ginsborg, *Italy and its Discontents, 1980–2001* (London: Allen Lane, the Penguin Press, 2001), p. 317. Also Jason W. Davidson, 'Italy at War: Explaining the Italian Contribution to the Kosovo war (1999)', in Giacomello and Verbeek (eds), *Italy's Foreign Policy in the Twenty-First Century*, pp. 155–73.

[66] Simon Green and William Paterson (eds), *Governance in Contemporary Germany: The Semisovereign State Revisited* (Cambridge: Cambridge University Press, 2005), p. 162.

[67] Peter Rudolf, 'The Transatlantic Relationship: A View from Germany', in Maull (ed.), *Germany's Uncertain Power*, pp. 143–7 and 150–1.

Table 7.5. European 'big five' interventions 1991–2012 *without* any significant domestic blowback

Case	Dates	States Intervening
FYROM	2001–3	All five (NATO, 2001); all five (EU, 2003)
Lebanon	2006–	France, Italy, Spain (and Germany off-shore)
Chad	2008–9	France, Italy
Somalia/Indian Ocean	2008–	All five, though numbers are small in the Somali training operation
Libya	2011	Britain, France, Italy, Spain

Note: To qualify as an intervention here a state has to have >50 troops on the ground (with the exception of the Somalia/Indian Ocean, where the risks of reprisals are notable despite the military activity taking place at sea).[68]

party in a UK general election.[69] This was partly due to abstentions, which in part can be ascribed to unhappiness with the Blair government's commitment to the Iraq War.[70] In the ten constituencies with the largest Muslim populations, Labour's share of the vote fell by between 7.2 and 21.4 per cent, compared to the national average fall of 5.8 per cent.[71] There seems little doubt that Labour's eventual defeat in 2010, though largely due to the normal party cycle, also reflected the continuing disillusion among party loyalists over the wars and in particular by then Afghanistan. Labour's vote share fell further, to 29.7 per cent.[72] As late as March 2012 the anti-war Respect party took the formerly safe Labour seat of Bradford West in a by-election, with a swing of 36.6 per cent. Bradford is heavily populated with Muslims of Pakistani origin, and it was generally agreed that feeling about Iraq still ran high there.[73]

Even in contemporary conditions there are cases where foreign involvement has *not* produced significant domestic blowbacks (see Table 7.5). The NATO

[68] In May 2012 EUNAVFOR launched its first attack (with the assent of Somalia) on the shore bases of the pirates, to destroy their high-speed launches, *The Guardian*, 16 May 2012. For the scale of the piracy problem and future risks see Commander Roberto Peruzzi, 'Piracy off the Horn of Africa: Bringing air and space power to the fight', in *The Journal of the JAPCC (Joint Air Power Competence Centre)*, 15 (Spring/Summer 2012), pp.11–15.

[69] *General Election 2005*, House of Commons Library Research Paper 05/33, 17 May 2005 (final edn, 10 March 2006), p. 13.

[70] The 2005 Nuffield general election study found that many Labour voters, especially Muslims, defected as a result of the Iraq War. Dennis Kavanagh and David Butler, *The British General Election of 2005* (Houndmills: Palgrave Macmillan, 2005), pp. 238–41.

[71] *General Election 2005* House of Commons Library, p. 78. Labour held nine of the ten seats, and lost one to the Respect party.

[72] Dennis Kavanagh and Philip Cowley, *The British General Election of 2010* (Houndmills: Palgrave Macmillan, 2010), pp. 391–2 and 31.

[73] George Galloway for Respect polled 18,341 votes (55.89 per cent of votes cast) compared to Labour's Imran Hussain at 8,301 (24.99 per cent). This compares to the Labour majority of 5,763 in the General Election of 2010. 'Galloway Takes Bradford West: In Quotes', <http://www.bbc.co.uk/news/uk-politics-17560158> accessed 6 December 2012.

Operation Essential Harvest in FYROM in 2001, to disarm warring parties, in which all the big five contributed some troops, proceeded without serious reverberations at home, because it was successful, cost-free in terms of lives, and (at ninety days) short.[74] The more enduring Franco-Italian-Spanish commitment to UN peacekeeping in the Lebanon from 2006 on has also been relatively uncontroversial.[75] This is largely because although the potential for major conflict—and therefore great danger for the European peacekeepers—still exists, violence has not broken out on a major scale, and their casualties have been light. If, however, war between Hizbollah and Israel were to erupt once more, sharp debates inside the three states, over casualties but also attitudes to Israel and the Arab world, would undoubtedly arise, exacerbated by antagonisms between the various minority communities. Somalia is also a potentially dangerous case, in itself and for its strong diaspora connections.[76]

One last way of looking at the domestic dimension of interventions is to consider the *demands for interventions* which governments did *not* respond to, and which therefore might have caused slow-burning resentments, particularly in interested minorities (see Table 7.6). The very absence of action makes study difficult, but one should at least ask the question. We have already seen how the failure of Britain, and perhaps of the major European powers in general, to do more for the Bosnians in the 1990s led to a disillusion among their Muslim populations which fuelled eventual support for jihadism. In contrast the failure to stop the massive loss of life in Algeria in the same decade seems not to have led France—as the key EU state involved, and implicated through its support for the military regime—to suffer any notable reaction from its own Maghrebian population. The humanitarian failures over Rwanda, Darfur, and the Congo did produce a boost in most European countries for the idea of future interventions to stop genocide, and for the concept of the Responsibility to Protect, which may have had an impact in Kosovo, and over the inhabitants of Benghazi in 2011, but these indirect effects are almost impossible to chart.[77] Individual diasporas are capable of exerting political pressure in the short term—as Zimbabwean and Tamil exiles have done in recent years in London—but without a broad base of social support and a compelling case they cannot maintain their campaigns, let

[74] Eva Gross, *The Europeanization of National Foreign Policy: Continuity and Change in European Crisis Management* (Houndmills: Palgrave Macmillan, 2009), pp. 35–6 and 68–9.

[75] Germany also participates, but only off-shore through its Navy.

[76] Laura Hammond, 'The Absent but Active Constituency: The Role of the Somaliland UK Community in Election Politics', in Terrence Lyons and Peter Mandaville (eds), *Politics from Afar: Transnational Diasporas and Networks* (London: Hurst, 2012), pp. 157–80. Hammond's title is misleading; she deals mostly with diaspora involvement in Somali politics.

[77] The key words here are 'idea' and 'concept', as actual intervention is constrained by many more pragmatic considerations. See Karen E. Smith, *Genocide and the Europeans* (Cambridge: Cambridge University Press, 2010), pp. 250–1.

Table 7.6. Sites of potential military interventions either not undertaken by European states, or attempted but seen as inadequate by interested parties, 1991–2012

Sites	Dates
Bosnia	1991–5
Algeria	1992–9
Rwanda	1994
Democratic Republic of Congo	1996–
Zimbabwe	2000–8
Darfur, Sudan	2003–9
Sri Lanka	2009
Syria	2011–12

alone persuade governments to act. The angst and indecision over Syria in 2012 shows what happens when the arguments—and the advocates—are divided, and the perceived risks high.

CONCLUSIONS

The new interventionism has been largely discussed as a phenomenon of international relations. But the evidence presented in this chapter makes it clear that in different ways and to differing degrees European societies have felt the impact of their foreign interventions on their own interests and values. These 'blowbacks' have been to a large extent unanticipated because they come from the interplay between external relations and a domestic environment which is in a state of flux, partly through increased ethnocultural diversity. Clearly any active, high-profile foreign policy will draw some fire, especially when intervention turns sour. But diversity has added another particularly complicated dimension, whereby minorities may become antagonized over an issue which does not move the majority, leading to demands for action or changes in policy which, being then unmet, create new resentments. Such responses are more likely where the philosophy of multiculturalism has encouraged groups to feel distinctive and to see themselves in a wider, international context. In this respect Britain and the Netherlands have proved particularly vulnerable, but the examples of Spain and Germany show that sheer change and increasing *multiculturality* are to a degree making all societies vulnerable to foreign policy-related disturbances. Governments across Europe are all too aware of the possibilities.

Even where the majority is indifferent, and therefore seemingly permissive over a particular group's concerns, the latter is unlikely to be able to hitch official foreign policy to its cause. Indeed, at times competition between minorities will have a self-cancelling effect and heighten the sense that the 'national' interest lies precisely above all parochial preoccupations. Yet the result has not been to make things easier for decision-makers. Instead of a lofty certainty about the conduct of foreign policy, whether based on rationalist realism or a presumed unity of national identity and purpose, there has been a heightened confusion over the ends foreign policy is supposed to serve—and over its relationship with democracy. Britain, for example, seems ever more torn between, on the one hand, feelings of obligation to (certain) suffering peoples abroad, and on the other a diminished degree of confidence about whether the British people—whatever that now means—will still support costly foreign policy ventures.[78] Germany has moved in the opposite direction, with its slowly more assertive diplomacy still hobbled by a domestic culture which oscillates between humanitarianism and pacifism, while (like Greece) its emerging multiculturality has stimulated reactions which have serious implications for the country's image abroad.

It is hardly surprising that much national foreign policy in Europe is susceptible to political uncertainty and some erratic decision-making, being blown by unpredictable cross-winds from inside and out. In a democracy it is difficult at the best of times to identify a clear national interest amidst the endless debates over values, aims, and circumstance. How much more so when foreign policy not only no longer commands a passive consensus, but itself opens up fracture-lines in society—through alienating minorities—even to the point where some take up arms, and right-wing nationalists predictably mobilize in response? When a country's involvement in international politics polarizes its people and heightens internal security measures on an enduring basis, there is something wrong either with foreign policy, or with civil society.

All this should not be exaggerated: not every intervention leads to a significant blowback. What is more, the developments described here are in one sense progressive. More people are now drawn into the discussion of international affairs, with the profile of the debate accordingly higher, and there is a growing awareness that foreign policy is an inherently political as well as a strategic matter. Unfortunately the foreign policy concerns of minorities have not yet produced the modern equivalent of A. J. P. Taylor's 'troublemakers'—articulate dissidents over British foreign policy.[79] British Muslims are more organized than those in other European societies, but the

[78] Linda Colley has shown how war, the anti-slavery movement, and Catholic emancipation came together to forge a sense of Britishness in the first place. It would be a twist of fate if war, ethnicity, and conflict over religion were now to be instrumental in the disintegration of that identity, but a deeper factor in both periods is the unresolved relationships between England, Scotland, Wales, and Ireland. Linda Colley, *Britons: Forging the Nation 1707–1837* (London: BCA by arrangement with Yale University Press, 1992), pp. 361–75.

[79] A. J. P. Taylor, *The Trouble Makers: Dissent over Foreign Policy, 1792–1939* (London: Hamish Hamilton, 1957). Taylor wrote of such figures as Tom Paine, Richard Cobden, and E. D. Morel.

articulation of their foreign policy worries relies on the charisma of the Scottish showman George Galloway. It will take time for minorities to find their own consistent voices—or alternatively not to need one, because of full integration. In the meantime, the new interventionism, together with the new social diversity, requires us to work out revised terms of trade for foreign policy-making in a democracy.

8

The EU dimension

This book takes a comparative view of the relationship between society and international relations, and thus of how nation-states conduct themselves. But since the states in focus are European, the regional context in which they operate is of particular importance. The European Union represents a major element in the domestic life of all its Member States, even those like Britain which hold it at arm's length, and has become over the last forty years also a significant component of—if not a substitute for—national diplomacy.[1] The EU's role—or potential role—in shaping responses to the problem of foreign policy and multiculturalism now needs addressing more directly.

The European Union is an historical project of major proportions, with its original aims being the creation of a zone of peace in a previously war-torn and divided continent, together with the promotion of economic growth and prosperity. These aims were followed by others relating to social change, redistribution, enlargement, and security. Underlying them all has been the belief of the founding fathers and their descendants in the integration of Europe and the possible emergence of a federal union. The twenty-first century has seen a gradual decline in this kind of belief, culminating in the damage done to the EU by the unfolding Eurozone crisis. But as with any crisis the latter also precipitated major choices, in this case over the possible leap forward by a group of states into closer economic and political union, leaving the rest in an outer circle.

The EU project has entailed the promotion of certain basic values, notably peace, the rule of law, democracy, human rights, and freedom of movement. They in turn have been haphazardly related to external relations through what Ian Manners has labelled 'normative power', but they mostly relate to the kind of societies Europeans wish to live in themselves and to the notion of a shared

[1] For various surveys of the evolving relationship between national and collective foreign policies in the EU, see Christopher Hill (ed.), *The Actors in Europe's Foreign Policy* (London: Routledge, 1996); Ian Manners and Richard Whitman, *The Foreign Policies of European Union Member States* (Manchester: Manchester University Press, 2000); Reuben Wong and Christopher Hill (eds), *National and European Foreign Policies: Towards Europeanization?* (London: Routledge, 2011).

form of civility within the geographical space of the EU.[2] Given this it is inevitable that when new social debates arise, as over multiculturalism, the EU is potentially both an important point of reference and a participant actor. Potential becomes reality when social issues become entangled with international affairs, as they do inherently through the Single Market and the Schengen Area, and have done in a more inflammatory way through the heightened concern with terrorism. The questions which arise from this entanglement are: does the EU have the capacity—and the competence—to take a position on matters of ethnocultural diversity? What can it contribute to the resolution of the conflicts which can arise in this area? How is European foreign policy affected by its changing 'domestic' context, and by the dual levels of diversity—between and within Member States? In order to suggest some answers to these questions this chapter begins by looking at the general relationship between the EU and multiculturalism/multiculturality, then moves on to consider the associated issue of a European *demos*, or sense of common citizenship, before tackling the specific areas where foreign policy and social diversity meet most directly: immigration and asylum; homeland security and counter-terrorism; foreign and defence policy.

THE EUROPEAN UNION AND MULTICULTURALISM

It is plainly true that the EU has no legal competence in religion, or in the ways in which its Member States decide to handle the problem of diversity—that is, on the spectrum from assimilationism to full-blown multiculturalism. Insofar as actions at either extreme might call into question some human rights it would be the Council of Europe, and its Court of Human Rights, which would act as a means of adjudication and constraint. Indeed the latter has come into play in disputes over such matters as the display of crucifixes in the classroom.[3] Since 2009 the Member States have been committed to their own 'Charter of Fundamental Rights', but this does little more than ensure that their existing obligations to the Council of Europe are incorporated in

[2] Ian Manners, 'Normative Power Europe: A Contradiction in Terms?', *Journal of Common Market Studies*, 40/2 (2002), pp. 235–58.

[3] The so-called 'Lautsi affair' in Italy (named after the Finnish-born woman who first protested) over the place of the crucifix in the classroom, went to the European Court of Human Rights, which held that the crucifix was a violation of the rights of non-Christians. This caused uproar inside Italy, until the Court diametrically reversed its position on appeal. See Joseph Weiler, 'State, Faith and Nation—The European Conundrum', the 33rd Corbishley Lecture given at the House of Commons, London 14 September 2011, available online <http://www.wpct.org/lectures.htm>.

European Union law.[4] Moreover, the principle of national sovereignty is still predominant over decisions on cultural matters like the *burka* or faith schools, as it is over the 'high' political issues of counter-terrorism and (as it has become) immigration. It can be argued that there is a socialization effect by virtue of shared EU membership on moral issues like divorce and gay rights, but it is impossible to distinguish this from the broader impact of modernity.

All this is not to say that those who speak for the EU's institutions are silent on this relatively new and controversial set of issues. In their public as well as private capacities Commissioners, representatives of the Presidency, and even officials from the Council Secretariat, to say nothing of the party politicians in the European Parliament, have spoken out on the 'clash of civilizations', the impact of 9/11, immigration, relations with the Islamic world, and the politics of enlargement. Events like the Danish Cartoon Crisis or the actions and motives of Anders Breivik in Norway inevitably resonate across the continent. But just as the lack of legal competence means there can be no 'official' EU line on multiculturalism, so the cacophony of voices means that even informal consensus is unachievable, let alone the explicit coordination of policy. On occasions a chorus of general disapproval will be heard if the limits of what is deemed acceptable liberal conduct are breached. This occurs when violence replaces politics, as with calculated acts of terrorism or the racist attacks on individual members of minority communities. Europe also came together in 2000 to condemn the participation in the coalition government in Austria of Jörg Haider's Freedom Party, to the extent of agreeing some formal measures of ostracism.[5] The prospect of the rise to power anywhere in Europe of the extreme right—as with the success of Jean-Marie Le Pen in the first round of the French presidential elections of 2002—automatically raises the ghost of Nazism, producing a surge of solidarity across the continent. But such instances tend to be ephemeral and with little concrete product.

The lack of common action is partly because there is always the potential for the perception of interference in national affairs. This was the case over the issue of the Roma in France during 2010. A generally fevered atmosphere inside France over immigration (and recession), together with specific tensions between French 'travellers', the police, and some local communities, led to President Sarkozy demanding the clearing of Roma camps. This move required identifying them as a foreign ethnic group (who, as it happened, had the right of

[4] Paul Craig and Gráinne de Búrca, *EU Law: Text, Cases and Materials* (5th edn, Oxford: Oxford University Press, 2011), pp. 394–8.

[5] For the details of this episode, see Lee Miles, 'Developments in the Member States', in Geoffrey Edwards and Georg Wiessala (eds), *Journal of Common Market Studies: The European Union—Annual Review of the EU 1999–2000*, pp. 148–50, and also Lee Miles, 'Developments in the Member States', in Geoffrey Edwards and Georg Wiessala (eds), *Journal of Common Market Studies: The European Union—Annual Review of the EU 2000–2001*, pp. 143–4.

free movement under European law) while blurring the difference between them and French citizens 'of foreign origin'.[6] In so doing he succeeded at the same time in contradicting the whole ethos of France's approach to citizenship, which does not recognize ethnic groups, and in reminding the public of the shame of Vichy, when French Jews were interned and then deported to death camps.[7] Not surprisingly this aggressive move produced a storm of protest both inside and outside France. The European Commissioner for Fundamental Rights, Viviane Reding, quickly drew the analogy with the Second World War, thus further inflaming matters, but also in the end leading Paris to retreat, if only on procedural matters.[8] The issue mostly served to draw attention to the strong feelings that exist about the Roma on both liberal and conservative wings in Europe, and to illustrate that while the Commission could take a stand even against a major Member State on the basis of EU law, it could not go so far as to engineer a common position on the substance of the issue. In this respect the case of the Roma is typical of the debates about multiculturality which range across the Member States.

While the European Council and the various institutions which sit beneath it regularly intone homilies about the virtues of social cohesion, religious tolerance, and political participation, as well as the evils of terrorism, they usually skirt the underlying moral and political choices on such tricky issues as citizenship, group rights, lifestyles, and even migration. Cultural diversity, like foreign policy, is an issue which affects all Member States, transnationally and at times inter-governmentally. Indeed the two issues frequently become entangled. But whereas in foreign policy common positions are at least feasible, and regularly proposed, this is not so for multiculturalism. Controversy and debate quickly flash across European frontiers, but just as quickly fall back into national contexts for political settlement. This issue is the prerogative of the Member States, even if it also represents a major challenge for them.

Language can stand as an example of the bind in which the Union is caught on cultural issues: on the one hand, it wishes to promote integration, to which linguistic diversity is an obstacle. On the other hand, it is committed to the right of its Member States to use and preserve their own national languages—indeed the translation service needed to validate this principle is a significant factor in EU finances.[9] Furthermore, it now finds itself faced with the reality not just of

[6] For a full account, which sees this as the 'securitizing' of the Roma problem, see Owen Parker, 'Roma and the Politics of EU Citizenship in France: Everyday Security and Resistance', *Journal of Common Market Studies*, 50/3 (2012), pp. 475–91.

[7] See Chapter 3, p. 71.

[8] Parker, 'Roma and the Politics of EU Citizenship in France', pp. 479–81.

[9] According to the official EU website the annual cost of translation for all EU institutions in 2006 was *c.* €800 million per annum, which would be around two thirds of 1 per cent of the total budget of €147 billion in 2012, if costs have not increased through enlargement, as claimed. 'Translation—DG providing high-quality written translations and linguistic advice—our daily

ancient regional languages, like Basque or Gaelic, which have a claim to sustenance, but also of the burgeoning number of minority languages now spoken within European states as the result of global labour mobility. To rub salt in the wound at Brussels, the bottom-up solution to the problem of communication has turned out to be the increasing use of English—the language associated with euroscepticism and Americanization—as the business and educational language in Europe.[10] Even French universities are now requiring students to take some courses in English. Thus to some extent the Member States, no less than the EU, find themselves the victim of social movements beyond their control.

There have been some desultory attempts to create solidarity across faiths and nationalities in the face of post-9/11 tensions, so that the political agenda is not wholly occupied by security and counter-terrorism. Rallying calls have issued from both the EU and from individual states. Indeed attempts to head off tensions between the Arab world and its northern neighbours date back as far as 1973 to the Euro–Arab Dialogue set up to end the presumption of hostility between the two groups after the dangerous war of that year between Israel and Egypt.[11] More focused on the importance of intercultural ties was the Barcelona Process initiated two decades later. The Declaration agreed on 28 November 1995 by the EC-15 and twelve other members of the Euro-Mediterranean Conference (including the Palestinians, by that time being weaned off terrorism) talked a great deal about both human rights and diversity, with the aim of squaring that circle through the promotion of 'tolerance between different groups in society'. The signatories, 'aware that the new political, economic and social issues on both sides of the Mediterranean constitute common challenges . . . resolved to establish to that end a multilateral and lasting framework of relations based on a spirit of partnership, with due regard to the characteristics, values and distinguishing features peculiar to each of the participants'. They noted that turning the region into 'an area of dialogue, exchange and cooperation' would require, *inter alia*, poverty-reduction and the 'promotion of greater understanding between cultures'.[12]

mission', MEMO/08/579 [online press release] (23 September 2008), Europa, <http://europa.eu/rapid/press-release_MEMO-08-579_en.htm?locale=en> accessed 15 December 2012. Also 'How much does DG Translation cost?', 'Frequently asked questions about DG Translation' [webpage] (last updated 08 August 2012), European Commission, <http://ec.europa.eu/dgs/translation/faq/index_en.htm#faq_2> accessed 26 June 2012. It is still a sizeable sum.

[10] Brendan Simms optimistically advocates making this increasing trend a formality, in order to foster greater union in the current crisis. Brendan Simms, 'Towards a Mighty Union: How to Create a Democratic European Superpower', *International Affairs*, 88/1 (2012), p. 62.

[11] The Dialogue concentrated on economic and technical cooperation, although it had a political sub-text on both sides. See David Allen, 'Political Cooperation and the Euro–Arab Dialogue', in David Allen, Reinhardt Rummel, and Wolfgang Wessels (eds), *European Political Cooperation* (London: Butterworth Scientific, 1982), pp. 69–82.

[12] Quotations are taken from the extracted 'Barcelona Declaration and Work Programme Adopted at the Euro-Mediterranean Conference, Barcelona, 27–28 November 1995', Document

This was not yet the discourse of multiculturalism and its problems, but it was starting to move beyond the Palestinian issue to anticipate some wider issues, albeit tentatively. As early as 2002 Richard Youngs wrote of the Barcelona Process that 'political Islam, [was] the essential driving force behind the EU's whole Mediterranean policy [although it] remained at the level of nebulous generality'.[13] The renewed conflict in Algeria during the 1990s, after the suppression of the electoral victory of the Islamic Salvation Front, together with the war in Bosnia-Herzegovina (BiH), was beginning to concentrate minds on religious and ethnic differences, well before 9/11.

In the event the Barcelona Process never fulfilled its high-minded hopes, although it might be argued that without the 'track two diplomacy' involving civil society which it encouraged, matters might have been even worse. As it was, in raising the stakes over immigration from the Maghreb, the Seville EU summit of 2002 drew attention to the failure of the inter-regional partnership to bridge the 'development gap', which in its turn was exacerbating the relationship between the two littorals. The EU's own Security Strategy drew attention to the need for 'more effective economic, security and cultural cooperation in the framework of the Barcelona Process'.[14] By 2005 only two southern leaders were turning up to the annual summit, and one of those was the desperate leader of the Palestinian Authority.[15] It took the terrorist attacks in Madrid and London, plus the drawn-out wars in Afghanistan and Iraq, to produce the next attempt at an overarching inter-cultural framework—Nicolas Sarkozy's 'Mediterranean Union' proposal of 2007, which initially sought to make these issues the preserve of the southern Member States.[16] Unfortunately this only reawakened East–South rivalries over EU priorities, producing the rival 'Eastern partnership' in 2009. As so often happens with

4b/54 in Christopher Hill and Karen E. Smith (eds), *European Foreign Policy: Key Documents* (London: Routledge, in association with the Secretariat of the European Parliament, 2000) pp. 350–4.

[13] Richard Youngs, 'The European Union and Democracy Promotion in the Mediterranean: A New or Disingenuous Strategy?', *Democratization*, 9/1 (2002), p. 60.

[14] *A Secure Europe in a Better World: European Security Strategy* (Paris: European Union Institute for Security Studies, 2003), document adopted at the Brussels European Council of 12 December 2003, <http://www.iss.europa.eu/uploads/media/solanae.pdf> accessed 16 January 2013. See also Sven Biscop, 'The EU and Euro-Mediterranean Security: A New Departure?', in Nicola Casarini and Costanza Musu (eds), *European Foreign Policy in an Evolving International System: The Road towards Convergence* (Houndmills: Palgrave Macmillan, 2007), pp. 195–208. Biscop concludes (p. 208) that the implementation of the grand Euro-Med. plans has 'indeed been disappointing', a view supported by Karen Smith who shows how a combination of bilateralism and the subsuming of the Mediterranean in the bigger concept of the European 'Neighbourhood' has inhibited genuine regional cooperation. Karen E. Smith, *European Union Foreign Policy in a Changing World* (2nd edn, Cambridge: Polity Press, 2008), pp. 86–90.

[15] Dimitar Bechev and Kalypso Nicolaïdis, 'The Union for the Mediterranean: A Genuine Breakthrough or More of the Same?', *The International Spectator*, 43/3 (2008), p. 14.

[16] Bechev and Nicolaïdis, 'The Union for the Mediterranean', pp. 14–16. The answer to the authors' question is now clear: it represents more of the same.

international regimes the Barcelona process was not abolished and replaced by something more fit for purpose. Instead, an unsuccessful makeover was attempted under new leadership—here that of Sarkozy and Hosni Mubarak—only to run out of steam soon after.[17]

As a supplement to these grandiose but ultimately ineffective ways of addressing Europe's relations with what it saw as other cultures (but which were increasingly part of its own make-up), came various initiatives trying to encourage 'inter-cultural dialogue', both between and within societies.[18] In 2003, for example, under the Italian presidency, EU Interior Ministers agreed a Declaration which recognized the contribution of faith communities to social cohesion, as part of the Union's balancing act between unity and diversity.[19] Two years later Spain linked up with would-be member Turkey to launch at the United Nations the 'Alliance of Civilizations' project—an explicit challenge to the 'clash of civilisations' hypothesis made famous by Samuel Huntington.[20] Such activities do little more than make it clear that the EU wishes to promote harmony between religious groups globally, as it does internally, thus disassociating itself from the militancy of both US neo-conservatism and home-grown xenophobia. This is necessary and not insignificant, but it cannot conceal the fact that, as Sara Silvestri says and the three models identified in this book indicate, there are divergent attitudes towards Islam (and indeed multiculturality more generally) within the EU.[21]

Amidst this divergence there is both goodwill and hostility, but the very conceptualization of a dialogue between separate civilizations reveals the shared assumption underlying the different positions—namely, to paraphrase de Gaulle on France, that Europe has a certain idea of itself. This idea depends on a definition of those who are not Europeans, and is rooted in a sense of Europe's distinctive past. Thus however much willingness there is to adapt to the changing nature of society, it is inevitable that there will be attachment in many parts of the EU to what is often called the Judaeo-Christian heritage. This label is not at all accurate, partly because it excludes the influence of Islam, geographically in Spain and the Balkans, and intellectually across the board, but also because it neglects the powerful influence of the classical world mediated through the Renaissance. In 1924 Paul Valéry articulated what was

[17] Michael Emerson, 'Just Good Friends? The European Union's Multiple Neighbourhood Policies', *The International Spectator*, 46/4 (2011), pp. 45–62. The renaming gave birth to the 'Barcelona Process—Union for the Mediterranean'!

[18] Sara Silvestri, *Islam and the EU: The Merits and Risks of Inter-Cultural Dialogue* (Policy Brief for the European Policy Centre, Brussels, June 2007).

[19] Silvestri, *Islam and the EU.*

[20] See Chapter 4, p. 118.

[21] Sara Silvestri, 'Europe and Political Islam: Encounters of the Twentieth and Twenty-First Century', in Tahir Abbas (ed.), *Islamic Political Radicalism: A European Perspective* (Edinburgh, Edinburgh University Press, 2007), pp. 63, and 66–7.

to become the dominant conception among the Christian Democrats who were so influential in founding the European Community, '. . . toute race et toute terre qui a été successivement romanisée, christianisée et soumise, quant à l'esprit, à la discipline des Grecs, est absolument européenne'.[22]

In this context it was unsurprising, if paradoxical, that some wanted to see an acknowledgement of Christianity in the proposed European 'Constitution' of 2004.[23] A more generic reference simply to 'God' might have united all faith communities, but even that fell foul of the democratic arguments for the separation of church and state.[24] Thus, despite various authorities seeing Europe's identity as rooted in the fusion of the Enlightenment with the Christian tradition, it only proved possible in the event to make a brief reference in the Preamble to the Draft Constitution to the 'cultural, religious and humanist inheritance of Europe'.[25] Articles 1–2, dealing with the 'Values of the Union', refer to human rights, including minority rights, 'in a society in which pluralism, non-discrimination, tolerance, justice, solidarity and equality between men and women prevail', thus once again evading the fact that choices sometimes have to be made between these values.[26]

Thus while the EU as a geographical entity has changed to become multicultural in the sense of a visible cultural diversity which was not there in the 1960s, the Member States vary greatly in their reactions to this fact. We are not yet near what the one-time European Commissioner for Justice, Freedom, and Security, Franco Frattini, called 'an agreed integration approach' in which different communities and systems could agree upon certain lines not to cross.[27] Even if 'integration' might be subscribed to as a value by those from

[22] Cited by Marco Martiniello, in his 'La citoyenneté multiculturelle de l'Union européenne: une utopie post-nationale', in Mario Telò and Paul Magnette (eds), *Repenser l'Europe* (Brussels: Editions de l'Université de Bruxelles, 1996), p. 131.

[23] The countries in favour of such a reference were Italy, Poland, Lithuania, Malta, Portugal, the Czech Republic, and Slovakia, with the main objectors being Britain, France, Denmark, and Sweden, according to Madeleine Heyward, 'What Constitutes Europe? Religion, Law and Identity in the Draft Constitution for the European Union', *Hanse Law Review*, Vol. 1/2 (2005), footnotes 14–15, pp. 228–9.

[24] As Martiniello says, Europe's heritage is in fact a *mélange* of the Judaeo-Christian and the humanist/Enlightenment *acquis*. Martiniello, 'La citoyenneté multiculturelle de l'Union européenne', p. 131.

[25] Others who stress the mixed Christian/Enlightenment heritage are Mario Telò, *L'Europa Potenza civile* (Roma-Bari: Editori Laterza, 2004) pp. 123–6, and J. H. H. Weiler, *The Constitution of Europe: 'Do the New Clothes Have an Emperor?', And Other Essays on European Integration* (Cambridge: Cambridge University Press, 1999), pp. 252–5.

[26] *The Treaty Establishing a Constitution for Europe*, 29 October 2004 (Brussels: European Communities, 2005). The wording of the Preamble, at least, survived more or less unscathed to appear in the Treaty of Lisbon.

[27] 'Frattini. Da noi non'c'è la sharia' (we don't have sharia law), *La Repubblica*, 9 October 2006. Frattini cited a contract in Rotterdam that the local Muslim community had signed up to: 'this was a small example of cooperative integration which is the only way of avoiding the onset of extremism'.

competing political positions, there is sharp disagreement on the best way to achieve it. On the other hand, there is no need to go so far as a conference in Washington in 2012, which had as its theme the question 'The end of multiculturalism in Europe?'[28] Social systems, once initiated, do not fade rapidly away in adverse circumstances; they pose dilemmas. What is clear is that the handling of diversity, and its related issues of migration and religion, is not something the EU can be pro-active on. Although the Member States are well-used to the supremacy of European law in some areas, this, like foreign policy, is a *domaine réservé*, because of its centrality to citizenship, perceived national identity—and sovereignty.

DIVERSITY AND THE IDEA OF A EUROPEAN DEMOS

If there were to be general agreement that a European citizenry existed as more than a figment of Brussels' imagination, then the debate about multiculturalism would be pitched at the European level, in terms of how Europe as a whole should organize its social relations. It would also go hand-in-hand with arguments about whether European foreign policy exacerbated 'domestic' tensions, which would themselves be conceptualized as Europe-wide. It might even foster the development of a collective foreign policy, as a greater focus on diasporas by definition raises the profile of foreign policy. But the circularity here will be readily apparent: a European public opinion can only emerge if genuine policy dilemmas exist more at the EU than the national level, and on foreign policy only if European diplomacy already has a sufficiently high profile to provoke reactions right across the Union. Otherwise the notion of a European 'public sphere' amounts to little more than the fact that occasionally twenty-seven democratically elected ministers can agree on a position in the name of half a billion Europeans, and that the various EU presidents try to 'speak for Europe' and to set the agenda for the future. It is also true that the mass media across the continent reflect many common concerns, but there are no genuinely shared newspapers or television channels among the Member States to act as a sounding-board for transnational debate.

In effect there is general agreement among serious observers that a European *demos* is still only a dream among those with a certain view of the integration process.[29] The chicken and egg problem again raises its head, as

[28] At the Wilson Center, one of the US capital's major venues for intellectual life, on 24 May 2012.

[29] Of whom the most famous is of course Jürgen Habermas, with the development of his own concept of the 'public sphere', *The Structural Transformation of the Public Sphere: An Inquiry into a Category of Bourgeois Society*, trans. Thomas Burger (Cambridge, MA: MIT Press, 1989). See Habermas, 'Why Europe needs a Constitution', *New Left Review*, 11 (September–October,

it is not clear whether a European public opinion could only develop out of the existence of a shared 'communicative space', or whether common discourses are created by that opinion.[30] Either way, such transnational currents of debate as occur are not the cumulative processes which would be needed to move the sense of primary citizenship from the national to the European level. In a recent survey Cheneval and Schimmelfennig acknowledge that 'national *demoi* will persist for the foreseeable future rather than being replaced or superseded by a regional or even global *demos*'.[31] For as Eriksen has pointed out, not only are publics segmented, nationally and by issue-area, but there is an important distinction to be made between a possible space for 'deliberation' and the legitimacy deriving from *popular sovereignty* at the European level, which would enable collective actions through having the 'moral force needed to implement decisions [also] against opposition'.[32]

The Brussels world of officials, lobbyists, and associated commentators intermittently convinces itself that it represents the people of Europe, but this is at best an 'organised civil society' and one with limited scope at that.[33] Renaud Dehousse adds that it is neither possible nor automatically desirable to have issues 'politicised' at the European level. That would imply a raising of the level of decision to the Union level, and in a heterogeneous system national parties and publics would soon react against the idea, either paralysing EU decision-making or just going their own ways. It is what Dehousse calls 'la logique antimajoritaire du système', which has impeded the achievement of a consensual 'social model'—to go alongside the Single Market—which might conceivably have created a common feeling among the masses, and not just

2001) pp. 5–26. Habermas criticized the 'no-*demos*' thesis on conceptual and empirical grounds in the essay 'On the Relation between the Nation, Rule of Law and Democracy', in his *The Inclusion of the Other: Studies in Political Theory* (Cambridge, MA: The MIT Press, 1998), pp. 129–54.

[30] As Martiniello again points out, the EU's opinion surveys through *Eurobarometer* themselves do more towards constructing the idea of a European public opinion than symbols such as flags and hymns, even if the polls do give breakdowns by Member States, 'La citoyenneté multiculturelle de l'Union européenne', p. 132.

[31] Francis Cheneval and Frank Schimmelfennig, 'The Case for Democracy in the European Union', *Journal of Common Market Studies*, 51/2 (2013), p. 336.

[32] Erik O. Eriksen, 'An Emerging European Public Sphere', *European Journal of Social Theory*, 8/3 (2005), pp. 347–8. Even at the elite level this segmentation exists, as shown by Reiner Grundmann, Dennis Smith, and Sue Wright in their 'National Elites and Transnational Discourses in the Balkan War: A Comparison between the French, German and British Establishment Press', *European Journal of Communication*, 15/3 (2000), pp. 299–320. For this reference, and for her analysis in general I am indebted to Andra-Dina Pană, 'Models of the European Public Sphere' (2007), a paper arising from the EU Social Fund's support of doctoral students, <http://eucommunication.eu/documents/pana.pdf> accessed 1 July 2012.

[33] Debora Spini, 'The Double Face of Civil Society', in Furio Cerutti and Sonia Lucarelli (eds), *The Search for a European Identity: Values, Policies and Legitimacy of the European Union* (London: Routledge, 2008), pp. 142–56.

'the highly educated and well-to-do' who do tend to identify with Europe.[34] Habermas may hope for a 'constitutional patriotism' based on loyalty to Europe's civic and political project, rather than the 'community of fate shaped by common descent, language and history', but that too seems a long way off.[35] By the time of the debate on the abortive Constitution even 'the permissive consensus' whereby citizens allowed elites to build Europe (often in blissful ignorance of what was implied by issues like 'enlargement') had 'collapsed, resulting in a more complex pattern of social and political interaction'.[36]

Thus the most that can be said about the feeling of the citizens of the European Union (and its Member States) is that they may be embroiled in a slow process of adding European identity to the inner ring of their multiple selves together with gender, family, generation, locality, nationality, religion (perhaps), and political stance (intermittent). This cannot be called, what Joseph Weiler terms 'the affective crisis of European citizenship' for something has to exist before it can experience crisis.[37] On the other hand, crises like that engulfing the European currency in 2012 should not be assumed automatically to damage the process of identifying with Europe. They can be a catalyst. One of the attributes of this period has been the widespread assumption that 'we are all in this together', with the strange sight of British eurosceptics urging Eurozone members into further integration. And indeed few events in Europe's recent history more exemplify Benjamin Franklin's observation that 'we must, indeed, all hang together, or most assuredly we shall all hang separately'. Perhaps, too, younger people are becoming accustomed to Europe's open labour market and Erasmus-shaped education sector, to the point where their generation of voters may display a more obvious European 'we-feeling'.

The nature of debates that occur within Europe, especially in relation to the themes of this book, is revealing. Many issues are technical and involve only elites or at most the very attentive public. Others, such as that over the Danish cartoons, elicit significant reactions at both elite and popular levels—including in minority communities where strong views may be held. They do genuinely create some form of shared controversy, even if the players still mostly engage

[34] Renaud Dehousse, *La fin de l'Europe* (Paris: Flammarion, 2005), p. 183. See his analysis as a whole (pp. 176–84) of the democratic and civil society issues, on which Spini approves his scepticism, 'The Double Face of Civil Society', p. 142. On the barriers to the Social Model (including the asymmetries of the European monetary system) see Fritz W. Scharpf, 'The European Social Model: Coping with the Challenges of Diversity', *Journal of Common Market Studies*, 40/4 (2002), pp. 645–70. Cheneval and Schimmelfennig remark on identification with Europe as being a primary attribute of the educated and well-off, 'The Case for Demoicracy in the European Union', p. 4.

[35] Habermas, 'Why Europe needs a Constitution', p. 15.

[36] Simon Hix, *The Political System of the European Union* (2nd edn, Houndmills: Palgrave Macmillan, 2005), p. 173.

[37] Weiler, 'To be a European Citizen: Eros and Civilization', in his own *The Constitution of Europe*, pp. 324–57.

on the national stage for reasons of language and access. But such debates are far less common than what we might call the 'spill-out effect', whereby because an argument inside one state is deemed newsworthy elsewhere it soon gets known about across the continent, while remaining essentially a national concern, without producing the cross-border interactions which can change the nature of an issue. Examples here are the rows in France over the Roma (despite the Roma's transnational characteristics), in Switzerland over minarets, or even the various dramas over 'honour killings' which occur in most European countries but remain local and compartmentalized. Some reactive and emulative linkages always occur, but they are usually limited in scope and unable to generate a Europe-wide debate. One exception is that over the burka, over which argument has swirled across national frontiers. But even on this the law—and attitudes—vary greatly from state to state.

By definition minorities face obstacles in being able to identify with their country of residence. They are therefore more liable to pay attention to events across borders or to seek help from people like themselves living elsewhere. But equally they have their hands full in coping with the consequences of not being part of the majority in society. Those born abroad, and particularly those not possessing citizenship, will find participation in political life at all levels an uphill struggle.[38] Thus the extra dimension of the EU, indeed the whole notion of European citizenship, is barely relevant to those not fully part of a national community; if they need to call in the aid of the European Court of Human Rights, then immigrants/members of a minority may identify with what they see as European values, but for everyday life that is a remote last resort.

It might be argued that the principle of multiculturalism, and perhaps even the mere fact of diversity, weakens attachments to the nation-state by encouraging diaspora ties across the EU and beyond it. The first generation of immigrants may well be still plugged to some extent into the politics of their homeland, especially if refugees.[39] On the other hand, it is recognized that they are also keen to establish themselves in a new society, and to become accepted. They tend to be conservative, but generally do not wish to draw attention to themselves other than by living as traditional a life as is compatible with their new home.[40] This is especially true if they are only 'guest-workers', vulnerable to economic recession and political hostility.[41] Subsequent generations, however,

[38] Aida Just and Christopher J. Anderson, 'Immigrants, Citizenship and Political Action', *British Journal of Political Science*, 42/3 (2012), pp. 481–509.

[39] Eva Østergaard-Nielsen, *Transnational Politics: Turks and Kurds in Germany* (London: Routledge, 2003), p. 126.

[40] Paul Scheffer, *Immigrant Nations* (Cambridge: Polity, 2011), pp. 7–14.

[41] Stephan Lanz, 'The German Sonderweg: Multiculturalism as "Racism with a Distance"', in Alessandro Silj (ed.), *European Multiculturalism Revisited* (London: Zed Books, 2010), pp. 106–14. Wihtol de Wenden shows how it took the second generation of immigrants in France to engage in protests over discrimination. Catherine Withol de Wenden, 'Immigrants as Political Actors in

are subject to the difficult pulls between separate traditions which we have observed in various national contexts earlier in this book. They may be more politically frustrated, with some alienated groups unpredictable in their attitudes.

In sum, the idea of a European *demos* does not yet represent a helpful way to think about the issues arising from ethnocultural diversity, whether conceived of as a regional or a national phenomenon. It has little substantive content, and at best should be thought of as a slowly evolving and flimsy extra layer of identity, for both majority and minority members, at least outside the elites. There has been a certain amount of talk about 'multiple citizenship', or 'hyphenated-Europeans', along the lines of such familiar groups as Greek-Americans, or the Anglo-Irish, but these are for the moment just fantasy.[42] Any changes in identity are in any case complicated by the existence of sub-national minorities, usually geographically located, which leads to a complex pattern of interaction among the nation-state, the region, and immigrant communities. The European Union is nowhere near having the policies or instruments to be able to address the issues which then arise, and is reduced to promulgating such aspirations as 'united in diversity'.[43] It may, indeed, be the case that the new challenges and complexity over diversity and its interplay with the international realm have led to the nation-state reasserting its control over citizens. Faced not just with a lack of coincidence between *demos* and *ethnos*, but with an increasing number of *ethne* within a given *demos*, governments will have to tread carefully if they are to maintain the democratic achievement of post-1945 Europe.

SECURITY, FOREIGN POLICY, AND EUROPE'S DOMESTIC ENVIRONMENTS

The European Union can still claim, seven decades on from the Second World War, to be the foundation of peace in its region and the bulwark against the excesses of free market globalization.[44] But in recent decades many new issues have been added to this original agenda, with the result that it has lost

France', in Martin-Baldwin-Edwards and Martin A. Schain (eds), *The Politics of Immigration in Western Europe* (Ilford: Frank Cass, 1994), pp. 90–109.

42 Derek Heater, *Citizenship: The Civic Ideal in World History, Politics and Education* (3rd edn, Manchester University Press, 2004), pp. 321–54; Spini, 'The Double Face of Civil Society', p. 151, refers to 'hyphenated-Europeans'.

43 A phrase adopted as the official motto of the EU in 2000. See 'The Symbols of the EU', Europa, <http://europa.eu/abc/symbols/index_en.htm> accessed 18 December 2012. It is, of course, an echo of *E Pluribus Unum*, the phrase which is part of the United States' official seal.

44 Furio Cerutti, 'Why Political Identity and Legitimacy Matter in the European Union', in Furio Cerutti and Sonia Lucarelli (eds), *The Search for a European Identity: Values, Policies and Legitimacy of the European Union* (London: Routledge, 2008), p. 12.

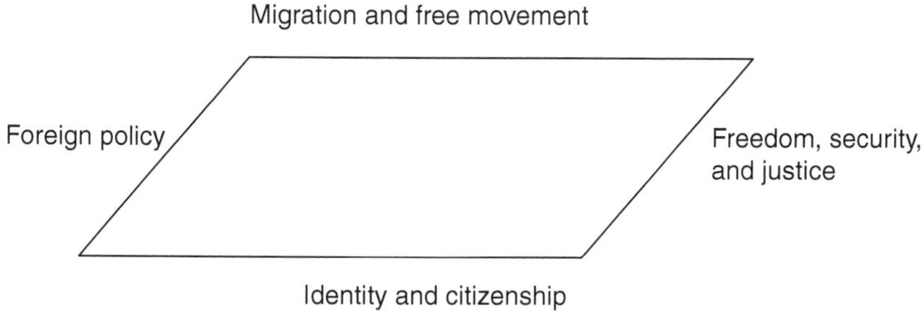

Figure 8.1. EU policies relating to diversity, migration and free movement

momentum. The free movement of money and labour have each produced difficult unforeseen effects, on top of which the return of terrorism after the relative lull of the 1990s has created new priorities for all governments. And the development of more diverse societies has impacted, albeit indirectly, on many debates from the proposed Constitution, through enlargement, to the war in Iraq. Figure 8.1 indicates the (overlapping and interacting) areas of EU policy in which diversity within the Member States is implicated.

For their part, while the Member States represent the sites where diversity manifests itself, their governments have come to rely on the European Union to help them cope with some of its consequences—whether through the development of a hard external frontier to limit illegal immigration, the attempt to create common policy on asylum, or the use of foreign policy cooperation to manage relations with countries which may be of particular concern to one or more minorities. Conversely the more heterogeneous nature of European societies has affected the EU's attempts to forge common policies, in particular over immigration, where states have been determined to retain national powers over arrivals from other countries, to the extent that the Schengen system has come under pressure through tensions among some of its signatories. Subnational demands for devolution inside Member States have added a further dimension to the differences which had already made the construction of a common European identity a distant prospect.

As a result of this interpenetration of national and EU concerns there now exists a set of supposedly interlocking institutional frameworks which provide some coordination capacity, but also complicate perceptions of agency and responsibility. On matters of serious crime, for example, Europol has been beefed up to enable the sharing of information over suspects, while Eurojust was set up in 2002 to bring together judges, prosecutors, and police to streamline procedures for the same purpose.[45] The European police college,

[45] The various bodies and competences are summarized in Sarah Wolff, Flora A. N. J. Goudappel, and Jaap W. de Zwaan (eds), *Freedom, Security and Justice after Lisbon and Stockholm* (The Hague: T. M. C. Asser Press, 2011), pp. 257–81.

CEPOL, was set up in 2005, in the same year the European Arrest Warrant came into force, whereby the twenty-seven Member States agreed that those wanted for criminal prosecution could be transferred across EU borders without having to rely on formal extradition procedures. All these instruments have increasingly been used to promote counter-terrorism cooperation, where there is the strongest incentive for collective action. Indeed, contrary to the EU's reputation for weakness on high political issues, such cooperation dates back to 1975 and the setting up of the TREVI working group of officials from police, interior ministries, and security services.[46] This was gradually taken over by the K4 Committee designed formally to oversee the workings of the third Pillar of the Treaty of Maastricht (1993) on Justice and Home Affairs (renamed Freedom, Justice, and Security in the Treaty of Amsterdam of 1999, with some parts moved to the *communautaire* first Pillar). Various Standing EU Committees, notably COSI (the Standing Committee on Internal Security) whose job is to promote operational cooperation on internal security, and the PSC (Political and Security Committee), which is the main agent of EU foreign and external security policy, oversee the institutional jungle, relying on a growing number of 'framework decisions' to guide national strategies.

Since 2010 the EU has also had its 'Internal Security Strategy' to match that launched for foreign policy in 2003. This document talks (briefly) about the need for 'security policies based on common values . . . including the rule of law and respect for fundamental rights'. It also says that 'we must . . . protect the privacy of individuals and their fundamental right to protection of personal data'.[47] Yet the great increase in activity in the area of 'Justice and Home Affairs' since the Tampere Summit of 1999 amounts to a notable strengthening of the powers of the state(s) vis-à-vis civil society, at the same time as it attempts to Europeanize what individual Member States do.[48] It is a

[46] Christopher Hill, 'The Political Dilemmas for Western Governments', in Lawrence Freedman et al., *Terrorism and International Order* (London: Routledge and Kegan Paul for the Royal Institute of International Affairs, 1986), pp. 77–100; Christopher Hill, 'European Preoccupations With Terrorism', in Alfred Pijpers, Elfriede Regelsberger, and Wolfgang Wessels (eds), *European Political Cooperation in the 1980s: A Common Foreign Policy for Western Europe?* (Dordrecht: Martinus Nijhoff, 1988), pp. 166–93; also Christopher Andrew, *The Defence of the Realm: The Authorised History of MI5* (London: Penguin, 2010).

[47] *The EU Internal Security Strategy in Action: Five steps towards a more secure Europe*, COM (2010) 673 Final, 22 November 2010 (Brussels: European Commission). The need for the Internal Security Strategy was agreed under the 'Stockholm Programme' launched in December 2009, and the Strategy itself agreed by the European Council in February 2010. The Commission thus found itself outflanked, before producing its own elaboration later in the year. See *The EU Internal Security Strategy*, European Union Committee of the House of Lords (London: The Stationery Office, 24 May 2011), pp. 7–9.

[48] For a useful summary of the literature which these developments have spawned, and especially the critiques, see Christina Boswell, 'Justice and Home Affairs', in Michelle Egan, Neill Nugent, and William E. Paterson (eds), *Research Agendas in EU Studies: Stalking the Elephant* (Houndmills: Palgrave Macmillan, 2010) pp. 278–304.

serious matter for minorities whose members, particularly those of the Islamic faith, find themselves disproportionately singled out in an atmosphere of suspicion over terrorism. The Union's push for a sense of common identity among Europeans is hardly helped by the resulting intercommunal tensions.

This is especially true in the area of asylum and immigration, although here non-Muslims are also significantly affected. The Member States have found themselves disadvantaged by their own commitment to the free movement of people within the EU. With global pressures of migration into Europe they have had little choice but to attempt to create a 'hard external border' through visa regimes, physical controls, and bilateral deals with third countries. These have created tensions, some rough justice in individual cases, and great difficulties for all the Mediterranean littoral states given their importance as either jumping-off points or vulnerable sites of entry to the EU. Furthermore, cooperation at the European level has not necessarily increased the efficiency or clarity of decision-making. The drivers of change may be evident—as markets, poverty, and mobility—but since the location of responsibility and the best means of action are not clear even to specialists, the lack of transparency and accountability to individual citizens is striking—and demoralizing to those directly affected.

Take the case of Frontex, the agency created in 2004 to monitor the external frontier of the EU and to facilitate the ability of the Member States of Schengen to enforce it.[49] Its tasks include surveillance, technical assistance, and the coordination of deportation flights. It is supplemented by Eurosur, the attempt to integrate national surveillance systems launched in 2008.[50] But Frontex has limited resources and political leverage over governments, with the result that actual cases can fall in the gaps between competences, while expectations of its impact have so far been disappointed. Indeed, some desperate people trying to enter Malta or Italy illegally by boat who have lost their lives, who could, in some instances, have been saved had there not been buck-passing between Frontex patrols, the national authorities, and (during the 2011 war in Libya) NATO. On another front, even the presence in 2011–12 of around two hundred Frontex staff (operating under Greek command) on Greece's land border with Turkey has not prevented thousands from entering the country, where they then become marooned in dire camp conditions to no one's benefit.[51]

[49] Frontex is the abbreviation of *Frontières Extérieures*. See Sarah Wolff and Ricard Zapata-Barrero, 'Border Management: Impacting on the Construction of the EU as a Polity', in Wolff, Goudappel, and de Zwaan, *Freedom, Security and Justice after Lisbon and Stockholm*, especially pp. 121–8. The UK and Ireland participate in the Frontex Management Board without voting rights—unlike the non-EU members Norway, Iceland, and Switzerland which do have some limited voting rights!

[50] Wolff and Zapata-Barrero, 'Border Management: Impacting on the Construction of the EU as a Polity', p. 128.

[51] For a detailed and authoritative discussion of the problems of would-be migrants and the countries they are heading for, see Anna Triandafyllidou and Thanos Maroukis, *Migrant Smuggling: Irregular Migration from Asia and Africa to Europe* (Basingstoke: Palgrave

In this context confident talk of 'multi-level governance' is exposed as a cynical charade. Neither efficiency nor transparency is being served. Andrew Geddes makes the best case for the development of an EU migration policy, but he only argues that habits of coordination now 'amount to the consolidation of networks of transgovernmental action on migration and asylum', with security agencies being the dominant players, even if liberal NGOs have made themselves heard on the human rights dimensions.[52] Another scholarly study stresses that the role of national executives over migration policy has actually been strengthened, and that 'there has been little EU impact on the national *politics* of immigration [in the six EU states studied]'.[53]

In part this is because of the inherent intractability of the issues. When a country refuses to accept deportees from Europe, as Iraq began to do in 2012, little can be done by either the EU or frustrated Member States.[54] Indeed, the issue has the potential to escalate, as when President Chavez of Venezuela threatened to disrupt oil supplies to Europe because of the 'Return Directive' of 2008 which he saw as criminalizing immigrants and violating human rights.[55] Pressures from individual states in immigration disputes can produce developments at the Union level which in turn lead to reactions in the external environment. In a further feedback loop, these then rebound inside European societies. The vicious circle is completed by the tendency of national governments to defect from the very cooperation they have set in train, through sensitivities over sovereignty and pressures from their own domestic environments. Bilateral readmission agreements, for example, are still more common—and

Macmillan, 2012). For Frontex in Greece, see pp. 69–70. For a powerful indictment of the problems of coordination and responsibility regarding a particularly tragic case in 2011, see 'Lives lost in the Mediterranean: Who is Responsible?', Report of the Committee of the Parliamentary Assembly of the Council of Europe on Migration, Refugees, and Displaced Persons, Doc. 12895 (Council of Europe, 5 April 2012), <http://assembly.coe.int/ASP/Doc/XrefViewHTML.asp?FileId=18095&lang=en> accessed 19 January 2013. Also Martin Scheinen, Ciaran Burke, and Alexandre Skander Galand, 'Rescue at Sea—Human Rights Obligations of States and Private Actors, with a Focus on the EU's External Borders', RCAS Policy Paper 2012/5 (Fiesole: Robert Schuman Centre of Advanced Studies, 2012).

52 Andrew Geddes, *Immigration and European Integration: Beyond Fortress Europe* (2nd edn, Manchester: Manchester University Press, 2008), pp. 187–91.

53 Peter Kivisto and Thomas Faist, *Beyond a Border: The Causes and Consequences of Contemporary Immigration* (Los Angeles: Pine Forge Press, 2010), p. 219 (my italics). The six states were: Germany, Greece, Poland, Spain, Sweden, and the United Kingdom. The full study is contained in Thomas Faist and Andreas Ette (eds), *The Europeanization of National Policies and Politics of Immigration: Between Autonomy and the European Union* (Houndmills: Palgrave Macmillan, 2007).

54 *The Guardian*, 3 July 2012. Until this point European states had varied in their policy over returning refugees to Iraq. Norway and Denmark had been in the van, with Sweden, the UK, and the Netherlands considering moves which are now blocked.

55 Sarah Wolff and Florian Trauner, 'A European Migration Policy Fit for Future Challenges', p. 69, footnote 29, in Wolff, Goudappel, and de Zwaan, *Freedom, Security and Justice after Lisbon and Stockholm*.

wide-ranging—than those the EU has concluded since it acquired the right to do so in the Treaty of Amsterdam.[56]

If security has been a key driver of migration policy it has been largely because of the spur from counter-terrorism policy. It has been said that the United States' Department of Homeland Security has become the most powerful source of pressure for European integration in the area of security.[57] This is a complete turnaround from the situation in the 1980s and 1990s when Washington was deeply suspicious of European aspirations to a common security policy.[58] And although the US has become steadily more relaxed about the EU's CSDP and JHA, its change of view has been largely conditioned by 9/11 and the fact that Mohamed Atta and his accomplices lived and trained in Europe. Some American Muslims have suffered through the increased surveillance imposed on them since then, but American officials are ultimately much more concerned about the larger numbers of disaffected Muslims living in Europe, where the level of alienation from US foreign policy is already high, and where terrorist plots have been common.[59] Accordingly Washington presses European governments hard to cooperate in providing surveillance, confidential information, and effective joint actions. It sees the territory of the EU as representing a single domestic environment, in which terrorists may move all too freely.[60]

Unfortunately the trauma of 9/11 also led the United States under President Bush into some extra-legal activity—Guantánamo, renditions, and the use of torture—in which it has implicated some of its allies, thus sharpening their own internal tensions. As Wetzling has pointed out, this creates a dilemma for the EU and its Member States:

> On the one hand, the EU benefits tremendously from its extensive counter-terrorism cooperation with the US . . . On the other hand, it has committed itself to a robust defence of the rule of law and knows that its power stems largely from the credibility of this defence. The latter is not merely a legal obligation, it also ensures vital support from domestic and international partners and helps to erode the ideological foundation of terrorist networks.[61]

[56] Marion Panizzon, 'Readmission Agreements of EU Member States: A Case for EU Subsidiarity or Dualism?', *Refugee Survey Quarterly*, 31/4 (2012) pp. 101–33. The EU has so far concluded 13 such agreements. France and Spain are in the forefront of the bilateral deals.

[57] By Dr Fraser Cameron, personal communication. See also Fraser Cameron, *An Introduction to European Foreign Policy* (London: Routledge, 2012), pp. 230–2.

[58] For example in its opposition to the revival of the WEU in 1984, and suspicions of the St Malo agreement in 1998.

[59] For US nervousness about the situation in Germany see Robert Leiken, *Europe's Angry Muslims: The Revolt of the Second Generation* (Oxford: Oxford University Press, 2012), pp. 256–7.

[60] John D. Occhipinti, 'Parallel Paths and Productive Partners: The EU and US on Counter-terrorism', in Frédéric Lemieux (ed.), *International Police Cooperation: Emerging Issues, Theory and Practice* (Portland: Willan, 2010), pp. 167–85.

[61] Thorsten Wetzling, 'What Role for What Rule of Law in EU–US Counterterrorism Cooperation?', in Patryk Pawlak (ed.), *The EU–US Security and Justice Agenda in Action*, Chaillot Paper 127 (European Union Institute for Security Studies, Paris, December 2011), pp. 39–40.

From the starting-point of its own experience with Federal agencies and the States of the Union, Washington has little patience with national divisions inside the EU, although it routinely threatens to go down the bilateral route if the EU as a whole will not cooperate. But as Jörg Monar says, 'it is simply much more efficient for the United States to seek an agreement with the EU as a whole rather than with individual Member States whose different legal frameworks and interests might require different deals and lengthy ratification procedures'.[62] In any case, all European governments remain, to a greater or lesser degree, timid about standing up to Washington, which has been surprisingly successful in persuading Europe to make concessions on civil liberties in such matters as the sharing of data on airline passenger names, or financial transactions, despite the furore, particularly in the European Parliament.[63] Thus the US represents a powerful force for EU-level decisions on counter-terrorism and counter-crime policy, whose benefits from the functional point of view need balancing against the price paid in terms of damage done to the fabric of civil society—and in particular to the attitudes of those most likely to be suspected of subversive activity. Olivier Roy has shown convincingly how important it is to define the field of terrorists in the narrowest possible way 'in order not to over-react and impose undue constraints and pressures on a too large segment of population'.[64]

Turning to foreign policy more directly, the familiar dualism at the heart of this enquiry immediately re-presents itself: on the one hand, is European foreign policy significantly affected by the issues of social diversity associated with the term 'multiculturalism'? And on the other, does the EU's international activity have an impact on the internal affairs of the Member States for whom it acts? These are difficult questions to answer, but they have rarely been addressed and are potentially important.

Some might wish to challenge the very premise that there is such a thing as a European foreign policy, as opposed to a loose bundle of national positions. After all, the CFSP is still an intergovernmental mechanism despite the formal abolition of the Pillars by the Treaty of Lisbon, while the Member States retain—and in some cases have developed—their own diplomacies and

[62] Jörg Monar, 'The Rejection of the EU–US SWIFT Interim Agreement by the European Parliament: A Historic Vote and Its Implications', *European Foreign Affairs Review*, 15/2 (2010), p. 150.

[63] Elaine Fahey, 'Challenging EU–US PNR and SWIFT law before the Court of Justice of the European Union', in Pawlak (ed.), *The EU–US Security and Justice Agenda in Action*. It should be noted that the EU has persuaded the US to take into account some of its concerns.

[64] Olivier Roy, 'Defining the Target: Al Qaeda as a "Narrative" for a Rebel Youth Without a Cause', in Martin Scheinen (ed.), 'European and United States Counter-terrorism Policies, the Rule of Law and Human Rights', RCAS Policy Paper 2011/3 (Fiesole: Robert Schuman Centre of Advanced Studies, 2011), p. 28.

networks of embassies.[65] Furthermore, the formidable literature which has grown up around the concept of a European foreign policy has all too often been stimulated by normative commitments to a European position in international politics and to using foreign policy as a driver of integration more generally.[66] These positions are supported by the widely held belief that a common foreign policy has the support of public opinion across the EU.[67] Yet most specialists in the subject are sceptical both of the strongest claims for Europe's world role and of the most dismissive accounts.[68] For even Britain and France, the most internationally active of the Member States, would not wish to have to go it alone in international relations, or to be wholly reliant on NATO for support. Furthermore, as this chapter has tried to show, it is no longer possible to make a strict separation between the *communautaire* internal policies of the Union, and its merely coordinating functions in external affairs. The Single Market has always had external implications, even if those for the mobility of people have become rather more evident in recent years. Similarly the development of internal security policy has not been possible without cooperation from third countries.[69] On the other side of the coin, foreign policy often has major internal reverberations. Relations with Russia or Middle Eastern states may affect the supply and price of energy, while decisions about sanctions against China or Iran have run into concerns about the consequences for trade and thus employment at home.

What we can say, therefore, is that a collective foreign policy dimension exists alongside that of the Member States, sometimes encouraging solidarity

[65] For example, the emergence of more confident national policies in such states as Germany, Italy, Ireland, Finland, and the CEECS, have been made possible by their location within the safe place of EU membership. The embassy networks thrive despite the emergence of the External Action Service in which so many hopes have been vested. David Rijks and Geoffrey Edwards, 'Boundary Problems in EU External Representation', in Lisbeth Aggestam et al., *Institutional Competences in the EU External Action: Actors and Boundaries in CFSP and ESDP* (Stockholm: Swedish Institute for European and Policy Studies, 2008), pp. 66–71. See also Rosa Balfour, with Alyson Bailes and Megan Kenna, 'The European External Action Service at Work: How to Improve EU Foreign Policy', EPC Issue Paper 67 (Brussels: The European Policy Centre, January 2012).

[66] European diplomacy itself is often reflexive, if not always integration-driven. See Gorm Rye Olsen, 'The EU and Military Conflict Management in Africa: For the Good of Africa or Europe?', *International Peacekeeping*, 16/2 (2009), pp. 245–60. For the concept of reflexivity (which he calls 'self-styled'), see Roy H. Ginsberg, *Foreign Policy Actions and the European Community: The Politics of Scale* (Boulder: Lynne Reinner, 1989), pp. 34–6.

[67] Rooted in Eurobarometer polls which indicate this in principle, but which do not address the issues of what costs people are willing to bear in support of a European foreign policy. See Roy H. Ginsberg and Susan E. Penska, *The European Union in Global Security: The Politics of Impact* (Houndmills: Palgrave Macmillan, 2012), pp. 158–60.

[68] For a good recent example, see Asle Toje, *The European Union as a Small Power: After the Post-Cold War* (Houndmills: Palgrave Macmillan, 2010).

[69] For instance, the EU opened its first immigration centre beyond its own borders in Mali in 2008: 'Reaching out to Migrants' [online news story] (last updated 19 November 2012), European Commission, <http://ec.europa.eu/news/justice/081002_1_en.htm> accessed 18 December 2012. I am grateful to Catherine Gegout for this example.

and adding value, but sometimes stalling because of the very inability of the Member States to agree, and/or to back up their rhetoric with action and the commitment of resources. Over more than four decades of coordination an element of variable geometry has grown up, which means that this rather stiff process of *engrenage* never grinds fully to a halt. Since the Treaty of Amsterdam a 'constructive abstention' clause has allowed states to opt out of a common position or joint action on the basis of a vital national interest. Although rarely used, its existence reduces tensions over apparent 'defections' from the common cause as well as helping to save face globally. For intermittent divisions over foreign policy are inevitable given the intimate relationship of sovereignty to foreign policy, embodied in the kind of formal opt-out over defence insisted on by Denmark, and the privileged positions of Britain and France in the UN Security Council.

On this basis the next move is to ask what the 'domestic sources' of European foreign policy might be—indeed what meaning that concept might have. A liberal intergovernmentalist (LI) view deriving from the work of Andrew Moravcsik might see Europe's domestic environment as consisting of little more than the sum of the national parts, with interests and opinion within the Member States influencing the positions of governments which are then negotiated at the level of the European Council.[70] Even this probably goes beyond the original LI argument, which stresses the unitary nature of governments-as-actors, and the primary influence on them of *economic* interest-groups. Neither assumption is regarded as appropriate here when thinking about the broad ambit of foreign policy. Although there is some weight to Moravcsik's view that there is little change in European states' foreign policy goals—'it is the continuity and stability of preferences, not their instability, that stands out'—it is perverse to ignore such important changes as the emergence of human rights thinking in foreign policy, or the gradual change in the balance of sympathies between Israel and the Palestinians.[71] What is more, despite the strengths of the executive in the conduct of foreign policy, governments have more to concern them at home than the brokering of powerful economic interests. If the latter were the main thing at stake domestically Britain would probably not have sent a Task Force to regain

[70] Andrew Moravcsik, *The Choice for Europe: Social Purpose and State Power from Messina to Maastricht* (Ithaca, NY: Cornell University Press, 1998); see also Catherine Gegout, *European Foreign and Security Policy: States, Power, Institutions and American Hegemony* (Toronto: University of Toronto Press, 2010), especially pp. 11–14 and 23–9. Moravcsik seems to accept that on foreign policy, changing geopolitical and security factors enter in as well as preformed national preferences, while Gegout stresses the importance of the USA, the European Commission, and path dependency. She is even more strictly intergovernmentalist in her belief that it is not worth opening the black box of intra-state politics and civil society.

[71] Moravcsik, *The Choice for Europe*, p. 493.

the Falkland Islands, and Greece would not have worsened its debts by excessive defence expenditure.[72]

The domestic sources of European diplomacy thus involve both national and transnational pressures and currents of opinion, which cut across and confuse each other as within any democratic process, allowing politicians to play them off, and also to ignore them to the extent that there are few penalties to be paid by doing so on foreign policy. Given this, what space might there be for ethnocultural minorities to exert influence, or for the more general issues of social diversity to feed through into European foreign policy?

Such impact as there is, is bound to be indirect. Member States vary according to how far their foreign policy is contested, and also how far their policy-making process is open to inputs from domestic society. Of the EU-15, Denmark and Germany are at one end of the spectrum, with relatively lively debates arising out of the particular parliamentary structures. At the other end lie France, together with Belgium, Italy, and Portugal, which have occasional outbreaks of domestic concern over foreign policy, but where argument tends to be confined to the political and intellectual elites. The remainder fall between the two ends of this rough continuum, displaying quite extensive levels of domestic interest in external policy but with decision-making systems which have still to adapt.[73] This variable pattern means that when governments are debating in the Foreign Affairs Council ('negotiating' is not the usual format for such classical foreign policy issues as Kosovo, or the Arab Spring), their awareness of pressure-groups, let alone 'the European street', is generally not high. Yet since European foreign policy is remote from normal political processes, ministers are all too conscious of it lacking both legitimacy and credibility inside the Member States. They hold back from attempting anything too dramatic at the EU level for this reason as well through the sheer difficulty of reaching agreement among so many sovereign states.

At the transnational level linkages between different societies occasionally affect foreign policy. The demonstrations over the Danish cartoons, which led

[72] There has been a vigorous debate on whether the Falkland Islands victory helped Mrs Thatcher to win the 1983 General Election as well as she did. See for example Helmut Norpoth, 'The Popularity of the Thatcher Government: A Matter of War and Economy', and David Sanders, Hugh Ward, and David Marsh, 'Macro-economics, the Falklands War and the Popularity of the Thatcher government: A Contrary View', both in Helmut Norpoth, Michael S. Lewis-Beck, and Jean-Dominque Lafay (eds), *Economics and Politics: The Calculus of Support* (Michigan: University of Michigan Press, 1991) pp. 141–60, and 161–84. But regardless of the votes cast, the decision to send a Task Force was not rooted in electoral calculation—rather it was seen as a matter of honour, sovereignty, and prestige, albeit at home as well as abroad.

[73] Vivien Schmidt also focuses on the variable ability of Member States to adapt, but more in relation to the impact of EU mechanisms on their national systems. She distinguishes between the relatively 'simple polities' of Britain and France, and the more 'compound' systems of Germany and Italy. Vivien Schmidt, *Democracy in Europe: The EU and National Polities* (Oxford: Oxford University Press, 2006), pp. 33–6.

indirectly to the resignation of the Swedish foreign minister, are an example of such linkages.[74] The networks of al-Qaeda sympathizers cutting across state borders are another. Yet since the days of the First and Second Internationals we have known how difficult it is for political movements to mobilize in defiance of state and national pressures.[75] Despite the huge changes in the European international system over the last century it has not become much easier to create effective transnational movements. The failure of the attempts at trade union solidarity, and the inability to foster genuine European political parties, both testify to the formidable barriers facing such integration.

The European Parliament should be the main site for debate on collective foreign policy activity, and indeed it has become a significant source of expertise on the subject, while steadily increasing its formal role in the policy-making process to the point where external agreements now require its agreement under the Co-Decision procedure.[76]

Yet the European Parliament is not well-placed to give voice to the views of ethnocultural minorities on external relations, whether transnationally or via national representatives. Of 785 MEPs in 2007, representing 492 million EU citizens, only 13 had origins from outside Europe, coming respectively from the UK (5), Germany (3), France (3), the Netherlands (1), and Belgium (1). Of the 27 Member States, twenty-one had no 'non-white' MEPs at all.[77] The contrast between the ethnically diverse city of Brussels and the white composition of the parliamentary chamber is striking, especially, as Patrick Barkham has pointed out, given the hyper-sensitivity of the European Parliament on threatened languages, and to a lesser extent on gender. The result is that minorities feel excluded. The only Asian female MEP (a British Sikh) says 'she receives "almost weekly" calls from Sikh groups in Italy and France who are attacked because of "the turban issue" '.[78] In principle, minorities' interests may be represented by MEPs not from their group, while there seems no possibility of a consociationalism or formal multiculturalism at the European level based on ethnic quotas. But as the French Socialist Kader Arif has said, '. . . if

[74] See Chapter 3, p. 81.

[75] See James Joll, *The Second International: 1889–1914* (London: Weidenfeld and Nicolson, 1955).

[76] For the EP's powers over agreements (excluding the CFSP), see Article 218 of the Lisbon Treaty, available online <http://www.lisbon-treaty.org/wcm/the-lisbon-treaty.html> accessed 17 January 2013. Also Christopher Lord, 'Legitimate and Democratic? The EU's International Role', in Christopher Hill and Michael Smith (eds), *International Relations and the European Union* (2nd edn, Oxford: Oxford University Press, 2011) pp. 138–45.

[77] Patrick Barkham, 'Minority Report', *The Guardian*, G2 Section, 14 February 2007. The calculations are not exact, as the article refers mostly to 'non-white' MEPs, a category which it identifies as referring to those 'with origins outside Europe'—including the Roma and people from Turkey. This begs the questions of how many generations it takes to eradicate extra-European origins, and of why 'white' should be a useful category. But it does give a basic indicator of the ethnic homogeneity of the European Parliament.

[78] Barkham, 'Minority Report'. Mrs Gill was a Labour MEP from 1999–2009.

you don't have institutions that represent the diversity of Europe you can't fight against racism properly', and the currently unrepresentative cohort of MEPs means that minority activists will inevitably seek other routes to express their political concerns.[79]

It is clear that professional lobbies are the most successful form of transnational mobilization in Europe, and that they have been stimulated, even funded, by the European institutions around which they swarm.[80] Businesses, consultancies, human rights and development groups have all flourished, together with important foreign policy think-tanks like the International Crisis Group and the European Council of Foreign Relations. But ethnocultural minorities have been so far much less successful, struggling to establish themselves first within their national contexts, and perhaps not even conceiving of the need to raise international issues at the European level. In a list of the nine categories of European-level groups encountered by MEPs in the year 2000, minorities did not figure at all.[81]

On the substance of foreign policy, the issues which matter most to minorities tend to have a diaspora dimension, but for the reasons given earlier the focus is more likely to be on national governments than on the CFSP. When that route seems blocked, there may be a turn to any international organization which seems able to exert pressure. The Russian minorities in the Baltic states have often looked to the OSCE, the Council of Europe, or the European Parliament to protest against what they see as discrimination, but since they can also find support in Moscow this is an extremely sensitive issue for European foreign policy, which has made little progress with a common policy towards Russia.[82] As a result, little has changed on the ground or at the level of the CFSP. Moreover, calculations of *realpolitik* aside, European foreign policy is unlikely to be captured by any particular civil society group because of the competitive nature of pluralist politics. In 1982, for example, Italians with connections in Argentina, and British supporters of the Falkland Islanders, both wanted EC support for their cause. The result was that after the pre-emptive

[79] Barkham, 'Minority Report'. Mr Arif is of Algerian extraction. Things had not changed by 2010, when the deputy Leader of the Socialist Group in the EP, Hannes Swoboda, called for quotas in selection processes to remedy the 'shameful' situation. Martin Banks, 'Socialist MEP Calls for EU Electoral Quotas for Ethnic Minorities' [online news story], *theparliament.com*, 2 June 2010, <http://www.theparliament.com/no_cache/latestnews/news-article/newsarticle/socialist-mep-calls-for-eu-electoral-quotas-for-ethnic-minorities-1/> accessed 12 July 2012.

[80] Hix, 'Chapter 7: Interest Representation', in *The Political System of the European Union*, pp. 208–31. For an analysis of the way economic lobbies move easily between Brussels and national capitals, see Jürgen Hartmann, 'Organized Interests and Foreign Policy', in Wolf-Dieter Eberwein and Karl Kaiser (eds), *Germany's New Foreign Policy: Decision-Making in an Interdependent World* (Houndmills: Palgrave, 2001), pp. 264–78.

[81] Hix, *The Political System of the European Union*, Table 7.3, p. 229.

[82] The *European Foreign Policy Scorecard 2010*, of the European Council of Foreign Relations (London: ECFR, 2011)—which is admittedly not to be taken wholly seriously—gave only a C+ to the performance of the EU in relation to Russia.

British move in the first days of the crisis, which succeeded in getting their European partners to impose sanctions on Argentina, the Community gradually retreated from any strong position, aware that Member States were coming under diverse pressures from their various domestic lobbies.[83]

One might have expected the same self-cancelling effect to have been visible over Cyprus, where Greek Cypriot lobbies in Athens and London could be balanced by Turks in Germany and Turkish Cypriots also in London. But it is difficult to find evidence of this, despite the highly contested nature of the issue. Cyprus barely figures among Germany's foreign policy concerns, and its Turkish minority seems to have other priorities. The British government is certainly aware of the domestic lobbying it would incur were it to upset the government in Nicosia, but the issue is mostly the preserve of high politics, involving major geopolitical interests.[84] For its part the EU's role has been limited to its potentially important leverage through the carrot of enlargement, but this was lost when Cyprus joined the Union in 2004 without a settlement having been insisted upon.

In this it is probably typical of the main concerns of European foreign policy. For example, while the dispute between Israel and the Palestinians provokes debate across Europe, the line which the EU takes (effectively in favour of a two-state solution) has barely changed since the Venice Declaration of 1980, and cannot be said to have been affected by a changing civil society at home—although it does indicate that European opinion is more divided on the conflict than that, say, of the US public. While Europe's Muslims are undoubtedly pro-Palestinian, many of their fellow-citizens also lean in that direction. The more critical tone evident towards Israel in the pronouncements of European politicians in recent years has more to do with the increasingly hard-line stance of Israel itself, and the visible plight of ordinary Palestinians—and it is in any case most cautiously expressed. Arguably some tensions inside European societies have been caused by the perceived passivity of European foreign policy-makers at both national and EU levels in the face of Israeli policies on settlements and on the West Bank.

On the related issue of change in the states of the Maghreb, so important a part of Europe's neighbourhood, the EU as much as the key Member States showed an unwillingness to challenge the autocratic governments holding sway there until blind-sided by the rapid turn of events during the Arab Spring of 2011. This despite the presence of large numbers of young Maghrebians living in France, Spain, and Italy, many of whom may be presumed to have been in sympathy with the opposition, Islamic or otherwise. Yet these same *émigrés* were not in a position to take part in organized lobbying, being

[83] Stelios Stavridis and Christopher Hill (eds), *Domestic Sources of Foreign Policy: West European Reactions to the Falklands Conflict* (Oxford: Berg, 1996), pp. 175–6.

[84] David Hannay, *Cyprus: The Search for a Solution* (London: I. B. Tauris, 2007).

poor, often on the wrong side of the law, and needing to maintain their links with home. What is more, although in principle the EU has tried to help North African societies through the Barcelona process, its effectiveness has been limited, and overshadowed by the hard-headed political deals done by France with the regime in Algiers, and both Britain and Italy with Ghaddafi in Libya. In this context the views of small groups of expatriates inside EU Member States counted for very little.

The same was not quite true over the two great issues of Iraq and Afghanistan. After all, Iraqi exiles like Ahmed Chalabi had influenced the UK government with their (dis)information about weapons of mass destruction. And the many Afghan exiles arriving in Europe after the US-led invasion of late 2001 had strengthened the human rights arguments for continuing the war against the Taliban. Yet as time passed a groundswell of opinion arose inside European societies against first the very prospect of a war with Iraq, and then the agonizing prolongation of the campaign in Afghanistan. In both movements the presence of Muslim opinion was an important factor, and more than counter-balanced the views of the exiles wanting regime change. But more important was the sheer weight of numbers from across the social spectrum of those opposing official policy, to the point that it became clear that some governments might pay an electoral price. As a 'domestic' constraint on European foreign policy this can be seen to have inhibited, indeed paralysed, the EU level of decision-making during the attempt to reconstruct Iraq, once the initial split over going to war had healed over. On Afghanistan it fostered a level of caution which meant that NATO took the lead, with the EU mainly involved at the level of nation-building and reconstruction. But the 'Muslim factor' only entered in indirectly, via the Member States and as part of a generalized anxiety about worsening intercommunity relations in Europe.

The two areas where it is plausible to argue that the European Union's international positions have been shaped by developments in civil society are counter-terrorism on the one hand, and the approach to global Islam on the other. It is undeniable that counter-terrorism has shot to the top of the EU's agenda, as well as those of Member States, over the last decade. Cooperation on the issue had begun, as we have seen, with the TREVI process in 1975, but the attack on the United States in 2001 had a transformative effect, shaking out any complacency which had built up.[85] The proof that some Europeans were capable of the kind of atrocity seen in Madrid in 2004 and London in 2005 then stepped things up to a new level of urgency. Whatever the justice of the profiling of potential terrorists that then began, with Muslim citizens the most obvious target, it is clear (*1*) that this has been an area where EU policy,

[85] On the connections between TREVI and later developments in Justice and Home Affairs, see Valsamis Mitsilegas, Jörg Monar, and Wyn Rees, *The European Union and Internal Security: Guardian of the People?* (Houndmills: Palgrave Macmillan, 2003), pp. 23–5.

internal and external, has been of substantive importance; and (*2*) that it has both responded to and affected the dynamics of civil society in many Member States, even if in the event only a minority of Member States have actually been attacked.

In terms of relations with the Muslim world, the EU and national governments have followed the same path. Through a concern to minimize threats both at home and abroad there has been a consensus on being on good terms with Islamic states, from the Near East, through the Gulf, to Malaysia, and Indonesia. This was seen as vital to counter-balance the harm done to the image of the West, and by extension that of Europe, through the endless images of Muslim civilians being killed in Iraq and Afghanistan. The transnational connection between antagonisms abroad and disaffection at home was readily understood after 2004, as it had not been during the Bosnia conflict of 1991–5. Yet the implementation of this need to convince the Muslim world of the EU's wish for an 'alliance of civilizations' has not been straightforward. The rise of prejudice, suspicion, and discrimination in some parts of European society has been all too evident to outsiders, and therefore difficult to smooth over diplomatically. Moreover, the wish of some states to see Turkey enter the EU as a way of cementing relations with 'moderate' Islam has been countered by the rise of opposition, especially in the key states of France and Germany, to the arrival of a population of 70 million Muslims in a Union which they (and many of their voters) see as already sufficiently cosmopolitan. The resultant stalemate over Turkish accession is hardly optimal from any viewpoint, although it has so far not created any major problem for the EU.

It is the division between state and society, central to this book's theme, which plagues foreign policy at the EU level as much as at that of the nation-state. Just as the EU consists of governments whose foreign policy decisions may not be appreciated by elements within their own societies, so the EU and its members must deal with Muslim states through the governments in power, in the full knowledge that they may not represent the views of the masses—who may ultimately overthrow them. When that stops being a hypothetical scenario, and actually begins to happen, as in the Arab world during 2011, Europeans can easily find themselves associated with hated regimes, unless they have been able to keep channels open to the opposition. The dilemma is sharpened by the divisions within the Arab world, and within Islam. Such complexity inevitably pushes the fragile construction of European foreign policy further towards caution, as can be seen over Iran. Not only does the EU wish to avoid a potentially catastrophic war in the Middle East, but it wishes to encourage the reform movement inside Iran without driving the regime even further into a siege mentality. Many exiled Iranians in Europe would like to see pressure put on Tehran; equally a military conflict between Iran and the West could well lead to terrorism on European streets which would stir up social tensions unpredictably. In this and many other cases the wary interplay between governments and civil societies (on both sides of a negotiation) represents a permanent background to any act of foreign policy. It also erects yet another obstacle to the achievement of a meaningful collective diplomacy.

CONCLUSION

The European Union does not represent a means of addressing the problems arising from ethnocultural diversity. It has no competence over the social models states choose to handle such issues or the solutions they find for disputes over such matters as dress or faith schools. Together with the Council of Europe the EU does stand for a set of values and principles to which individuals threatened by excessive state power may appeal, but neither organization has the right or power to instruct states on how their citizens should live together. Nor is there any real sign of a European *demos* emerging which would justify approaching the issues of diversity on a Union-wide basis.

This plain fact has not prevented the EU from developing some policies and institutions which have considerable impact on civil society. Measures on crime and justice, extended significantly by the anti-terrorism and counter-terrorism drives of the first decade of the twenty-first century, have probably had the desired effect of protecting citizens from acts of violence (although it is impossible to prove a negative), while at the same time they have increased the feelings of vulnerability among targeted minorities, and erected new barriers to integration.[86] The measures have been intergovernmental because they derive from states' needs and rely on them for implementation. The same is true of migration, where governments are desperate for help in managing the consequences of labour mobility and an external frontier which is 'hard' only in theory, but where they will not surrender sufficient powers to make a common migration policy feasible. Yet the multiculturality of their societies, which has generated so many dilemmas, is intimately tied to decisions on migration. The control of irregular immigration is particularly critical and this in turn involves relations with key third states—foreign policy in all but name.

Despite the fact that the Union has had major aspirations to a common foreign policy for more than forty years, it has not managed to progress much beyond a refined form of coordination, although that is itself an achievement given the gradual enlargement of the players from six in 1970 to twenty-seven in 2007. In principle, the Member States have strong shared interests in dealing collectively with the external factors which impact upon their societies. They need to calm relations with the Islamic world to stabilize the European

[86] Anti-terrorism refers to measures taken to protect society from terrorism, as opposed to counter-terrorism which attempts to apprehend terrorists.

Neighbourhood, and thus reduce the pressure from refugees and asylum-seekers, as well as helping partner-countries to interdict terrorists. But these things are not easy to do even with the unity of purpose which has so often eluded the CFSP, whose standard problems have been compounded by the increasing vulnerability of relations between governments to the transnational interplay between civil societies. Common foreign policy has traditionally been used as a form of 'cover' by individual states not wanting to be exposed internationally on a given policy. But it is equally true that if the EU were to punch its weight by taking high-profile stances, it could attract odium not only from third parties, but increasingly from inside its own states—depending on the content of its policy.

The result has been a degree of passivity, even paralysis, on the part of EU foreign policy, allowing a return to bilateralism of the kind practised by Britain and France over Libya.[87] Where European Political Cooperation (1970–93) faced mainly the problem of states' tendency to associate foreign policy closely with sovereignty, EU external relations since 1993 have been alternately boosted by the need for new policies at the level of the interaction of society and international politics (such as human rights, or conflict resolution), and hamstrung by fears over transnational forces beyond their control. Whereas the CFSP was founded on the presumption that its single 'domestic environment' consisted of Member States behaving as unitary actors, it is now evident that it also operates in the midst of twenty-seven overlapping and more active domestic constituencies. A greater element of democratic participation has thus been introduced into European foreign policy, but in a haphazard manner which does not bode well either for effectiveness or for legitimacy.

[87] As predicted by Jan Zielonka in his *Explaining Euro-Paralysis: Why Europe is Unable to Act in International Politics* (Houndmills: Macmillan, 1998). Zielonka was one of the first to raise the issues of legitimacy, identity, and indeed civil society (pp. 123–8) underlying European foreign policy.

9

The state, multiculturality, and foreign policy

Europe as we know it is the product of historical forces working through from ancient Greece, Rome's imperial unification, and the long and ambivalent encounter with Islam. Its societies have always been accustomed to the inflow of goods, ideas, and to a lesser extent people, even if most such transactions were limited to narrow elites. For those living on the southern and eastern flanks of mediaeval Christendom, the idea of change through the encounter with difference had a more tangible meaning, given the possibilities of invasion, slavery, and persecution, but also trade and cultural exchange. When the Europeans began their global voyages of discovery in the fifteenth century it led to further change in their own societies, through the import of precious metals and new foodstuffs, but more dramatically through the widening of horizons—literally and intellectually. On the other hand, the terms of cultural trade at this time were unequal, with Europe having a much greater (and often damaging) effect on other continents than vice versa.[1] The degree and pace of externally induced change, however, sharpened notably from the mid-nineteenth century onwards with the new phase of European imperialism, as the development of new colonies began to lead to population movements in the reverse direction, partly for military reasons (as with the regular use of conscripted troops from overseas) and partly through the increasing importation of labour from overseas to fuel industrialization.

Despite these precedents, it was only in the period after 1960 that ethnocultural diversity came to have a significant effect on European societies, through both the arrival of immigrants in greater numbers and the increasing liberalism and prosperity of the post-war period. Even so, the impact was differentiated, with Britain, Belgium, France, and the Netherlands affected first, Germany importing many guest-workers but not wanting to recognize itself as 'a country

[1] For Europe's formation and encounter with other civilizations see John Darwin, *After Tamerlane: The Rise and Fall of Global Empires 1400–2000* (London: Penguin Books, 2008), especially pp. 4–39. For the constant interplay between the diverse societies living on the shores of the Mediterranean in the centuries before Christian Europe began to look further afield, see David Abulafia, *The Great Sea: A Human History of the Mediterranean* (London: Allen Lane, 2011), especially pp. 241–410.

of immigration', and the southern European countries not attracting significant numbers of immigrants until the last years of the twentieth century. Yet as things stand now none of the members of the EU-15 can hide from the world in the sense that economic globalization, migration, and transnational communications are bringing international affairs inside their own borders whether they like it or not. As part of this process the European states confront new issues arising from ethnocultural diversity, with groups facing both ways—inside and out—in their search for identity. This is also just beginning to be the case for the twelve states which joined the EU in 2004 and 2007, but apart from the micro-states of Malta and Cyprus, they have not yet encountered the same pressures.

It is the argument of this book that European governments have been increasingly unable to keep their foreign relations behind a glass wall, unaffected by the changing nature of society. This is the more so for those countries with an active foreign policy touching on the concerns of special interests or minorities at home. A further important catalyst is the changing nature of international relations themselves. The unfreezing of diplomatic alignments since 1991 has allowed individual states much more latitude in their pattern of external political relationships, just when many supposed that national freedom of action, if not the very independence of the state, was becoming fatally compromised. It is true that the Europeans have responded to changing external conditions by seeking to create a common foreign and security policy, to build on the common commercial policy and common currency. But they have not had notable success in this venture, while collective action has proved to be even less of an option in relation to the challenges of multiculturality.

States have followed their own national paths in relation to diversity, less by conscious decision than through the power of long-established patterns of state–society relationships. They have coordinated their policies towards some of the phenomena *associated* with it, as over migration or counter-terrorism. But the EU lacks any competence over this dimension of internal affairs. Multiculturality touches on the deepest issues of national identity and social relations, while diversity is not susceptible to being 'managed' in any case. Thus states pursue their varied approaches, if in the full glare of pan-European and indeed global attention. At the same time they have only slowly woken up to the implications which diversity has for their external relations.

These societies are in a condition of flux. The natural process of change has been accentuated not only by the number of incomers, but by the sheer variety of the groups and value-systems which they now face. While all states are affected to some degree by the challenge of integrating sizeable numbers into societies which are often unwelcoming, governments are diverse in their starting-points, rhetoric, and the strategies which they employ. Yet all have to recognize that the long process of trying to make the 'nation-state' less of an oxymoron has now become problematic in new ways. Domestic society is ever more multi-faceted, indeed cosmopolitan—particularly in the cities—which means that national consensus can be less often assumed, even in a specialist area like foreign policy. The concept of the national interest seems threadbare, and claims to be pursuing it are more likely to be met with scepticism by special interests, among which diasporas are prominent.

Against such a background, this concluding chapter draws together the themes which have run through this book. That means both generalizing about how foreign policy and social diversity interact, and mapping the variations to be observed among the ten EU Member States on which the analysis has been primarily focused. In particular it attempts to establish the importance for this relationship of, on the one hand the approach a state takes to multiculturality, and on the other the type of foreign policy pursued. These issues were set out in Chapter 1 in the form of five questions:

1. To what extent does ethnocultural diversity within a European society affect the conduct of a country's foreign policy?
2. Conversely, in what ways, and with what significant consequences, have foreign policy actions and events impacted upon civil society in the multicultural societies of western Europe?
3. What difference does the particular approach taken by a society towards multiculturality make to the interaction between the domestic environment and foreign policy?
4. What difference is made to the interaction between the internal and the external by the nature and scope of the foreign policy which a government pursues?
5. How do the various developments entailed in the interplay between civil society and foreign policy affect the concept of the national interest, and its use as the fundamental criterion for states' external actions?

THE IMPACT OF DIVERSITY ON FOREIGN POLICY

Diversity is not in itself a driver of foreign policy, which is primarily concerned with the constraints and opportunities presented to a state by its external environment. But in a transnational age even the notion of accommodation to the outside world opens up the possibility of different parts of a society relating to it in different ways, and/or engaging directly with third parties. Thus the mosaic nature of multicultural societies must be regarded as a significant factor for foreign policy-makers to take into account. Depending on the degree and the nature of diversity it will complicate the conduct of diplomacy, with the capacity to generate new and challenging issues, or even crises. It may exert a degree of centrifugal force on foreign policy, as can be seen in the USA where the attempt to keep ethnocultural groups happy sometimes undermines the cohesion to which foreign policy aspires.[2] In the EU, states now accept that their foreign relations are at least indirectly affected by the nature of their immigrant communities, in terms of negotiations over contentious practical matters such as visas, work permits, family unification, readmissions, and the like, but also through the unpredictable linkages between internal politics and the reactions of those outside the state claiming rights of involvement.

Such complications do not derive from diversity alone, but from its playing into a pre-existing trend—that of the gradual awakening of public opinion to the importance of foreign policy to everyday life and to its own capacity to exert influence. This should not be exaggerated; the executive still holds most of the cards in the conduct of external policy. But the growth of a more educated and widely travelled generation in the Member States, a significant proportion of which has studied and/or practised aspects of international relations, development, European integration, and global business, means that governments not only cannot ignore their domestic environment, but may have to accept the need to form partnerships with certain groups within it. The proliferation of ethnocultural minorities reinforces the trend by increasing the numbers of people alert to the world beyond a state's borders.

On the other hand, it may be argued that the very differences inherent in *multi*-culturalism create a space which a government can exploit so as to steer its own course. Furthermore, no minority group has yet been able to capture even a particular strand of the foreign policy of a European state. More plausible is the argument that the collective impact of ethnocultural groups, and their orientation outwards, will tend to focus more public attention on foreign policy, encouraging its politicization and thus more vigorous debate than has been usual outside periods of high crisis—by when it is usually too late to change the course of official decisions. Their very existence also reminds officialdom that the society on whose behalf it is acting cannot be assumed to be either quiescent or consensual. The UK government, for example, has to engage in a delicate balancing-act not only on the substance of its relations with India and Pakistan, but also with regard to the sensitivities of the domestic minorities which identify with the two countries, with each quick to suspect the British government of leaning towards the other. This is a difficult task, not best handled through crude divide and rule tactics.

This picture does not apply uniformly to the states examined here. In some, minorities are still below the radar. In most, some groups are more active and

[2] Tony Smith, *Foreign Attachments: The Power of Ethnic Groups in the Making of US Foreign Policy* (Cambridge, MA: Harvard University Press, 2000); Martin A. Schain, *The Politics of Immigration in France, Britain and the United States: A Comparative Study* (Houndmills: Palgrave Macmillan, 2008); John J. Mearsheimer and Stephen M. Walt, *The Israel Lobby and US Foreign Policy* (London: Penguin Books, 2008).

effective than others. Paradoxically, where one minority is particularly sizeable and established, as with the Turks in Germany and the Albanians in Greece, their influence on foreign policy may be less than one might expect, perhaps because of nervousness over pressing for too high a profile on highly sensitive issues, but also because they have simply not achieved full rights of citizenship and thus access to political participation. Conversely, the ghost of a lost minority may have a notable effect in shaping or constraining a country's foreign policy, where it is associated with historical memory. This is true for Germany, Italy, and the Netherlands, whose small Jewish communities evoke a huge weight of guilt over how their predecessors were treated during the Second World War.[3] Accordingly these countries have been cautious over any criticism of Israel, despite the growing numbers of Muslims in their societies, who may be presumed to have minimal sympathy for the Jewish state.

In general European policy-makers are now more attentive than in the past to the domestic effects of their international actions. Foreign policy has become a matter for prudence on all fronts. Although minorities mostly come to the fore through reactions to external events, as with Kurds across Europe in their protests against Turkey's abduction of Abdullah Ocalan in 1999, they are naturally sensitive to the attitudes of their 'host' government to what they see as their 'home' country.[4] What is more, European governments have learned that a single *cause célèbre* can all too easily ripple down the years, as with the Rushdie affair and the controversy over the Danish cartoons. Atrocities in war are even less likely to be laid to rest, as with the events in a Basra prison after the Iraq War, which particularly damaged the British Army's reputation among Muslims. They have also had to cope with the disputes of others being fought out in their cosmopolitan cities, as with the Litvinenko assassination in London in 2006, or the attempt to assassinate a retired Indian General living in the same city, because of his role in the killing of Sikhs at the Amritsar Golden Temple in India nearly three decades earlier.[5] Here the British government was left to face the consequences for policing and for foreign relations.

The conclusion cannot be avoided that one factor in particular has intensified these interactions—that of Islam. Over the last twenty years or so the number of occasions on which issues arising from the place of Islam in European societies have produced fall-out for foreign policy has gradually increased. This is not to point the finger at Muslims themselves; if on the surface religion might seem the issue, it also conceals social divisions and antagonisms. Even when this is not the case Islam always suffers collateral

[3] For a subtle exploration of the way the Jewish question has played into post-war Italian life see Robert Gordon, *The Holocaust in Italian Culture, 1944–2010* (Stanford, CA: Stanford University Press, 2012).

[4] On the Ocalan case, see Chapter 3, footnote 105.

[5] 'Murder Attempt on Golden Temple Raid's General Brar', BBC News, 2 October 2012, <http://www.bbc.co.uk/news/world-asia-india-19796418> accessed 12 October 2012.

damage from acts of terrorism, and from apocalyptic debates over the supposed 'clash of civilisations' or the 'Islamisation' of Europe.[6] It is also the case that the processes identified in this book would exist even without large Muslim minorities. 'Diversity' means just that—a wide range of groups with distinctive concerns and diaspora ties, not a single homogeneous minority.

At the same time, few would deny that the large number of devout Muslims now living in European societies, identifying with a global community of belief, and often at odds with the foreign policy of the country in which they live, has generated serious political dilemmas—particularly since 9/11 and the heightening of fear on all sides. Foreign and domestic issues get caught in a vicious circle which only heightens the barriers to social cohesion, already considerable because of the prejudice and hostility which Muslims encounter from sections of their host populations.

Apart from immigration and the random crises caused by these structural interconnections, there are two main ways in which states' foreign policies are affected by multiculturality. The first is the dilemmas which crop up when considering intervention in a country to which a significant number of its own citizens feels attached. If the target is poor and Muslim, as it usually has been, then the problems are greater. It has become ever more apparent that governments have to consider the possibility of a violent blowback inside their society from such actions. More likely is simple political unrest, possibly with electoral costs, which they would have been much less likely to have to factor in three decades before. All European states have had to face that issue as one dimension of their decisions over involvement in Afghanistan, as that war has dragged on. Moreover, the DRC, Sudan, Somalia, and Zimbabwe have all had difficult domestic reverberations for various states at various times, while events in north Africa, Israel/Palestine, Syria, and the Gulf have also exposed some awkward transnational linkages.

The second way in which multiculturality affects foreign policy is through states' increasing concern to project a positive image of themselves abroad.[7] Cultural diplomacy has become an increasingly important arm of democratic states' foreign policies, and if diversity can be turned to advantage by becoming a symbol of international understanding and relaxed cosmopolitanism, there may be long-term advantages in terms of the ability to communicate across cultures, short-circuiting the formalities of diplomacy.[8] If outsiders can

[6] Fred Halliday persistently emphasized the need for the disaggregation of abstract political entities, whether the 'state', the 'West', or 'Islam'. See for example Fred Halliday, *Two Hours that Shook the World. September 11 2001: Causes and Consequences* (London: Saqi Books, 2002), p. 197.

[7] Simon Anholt, *Places: Identity, Image and Reputation* (Houndmills: Palgrave Macmillan, 2010).

[8] Joseph S. Nye, Jr, *Soft Power: The Means to Success in World Politics* (New York: Public Affairs, 2004); Raymond C. Cohen, *Negotiating across Cultures: International Communication in an Interdependent World* (Washington, DC: United States Institute of Peace Press, 1997).

have direct and positive experiences when encountering diversity, as occurred during the London Olympics, this in itself may assist in conducting external relations, especially outside the European family, but to have more than an ephemeral effect it needs not to be countered by evidence of intercommunal tensions or discrimination (as were commonly thought to have characterized the London riots of summer 2011).

Years of patient work in projecting a country's image can be undercut by a single incident involving the treatment of minorities, as with the case of mistaken identity in which the Brazilian Jean-Charles de Menezes was tragically killed by counter-terror police in London in July 2005, or with that of the caricature of the Prophet Mohammed printed in the French satirical paper *Charlie Hebdo* in September 2012.[9] European societies have made progress since the dark days of colonial racism, but their images are still tainted by the past. Thus it is well known that the fate of French Jews under Vichy was hushed up for decades, while French Algerians have unmet grievances from the days of the struggle for independence. This has produced what are termed 'memory wars'.[10]

A prime example is the French state's inability to face up to the 1961 massacre in Paris by police of Algerian demonstrators—'the bloodiest repression in Paris since the Paris Commune of 1871' even in the view of a conservative historian.[11] Such denials produce and prolong an 'evoked set'

[9] 'Qui sont les Salafistes Français?', *Libération,* 22–23 September 2012. It should be noted that the provocations of *Charlie Hebdo* were resisted by most French Muslims, who remained calm despite the panic-stricken governmental reaction in banning their demonstrations. 'Face aux caricatures, les musalmans appelés a "l'indifference"', *Le Monde,* 22 September 2012. The government was even more nervous about international reactions, closing embassies and cultural centres in twenty countries on a temporary basis. In the event, demonstrations in Afghanistan and Iran aside, the international reaction was limited, although the UN High Commissioner for Human Rights was quick to comment on France's internal affairs. See 'Charlie Hebdo cartoons doubly irresponsible: UN', *The Nation* (Lahore), 22 September 2012.

[10] Séverine Labat, 'Les binationaux franco-algériens. Un nouveau rapport entre nationalité et territorialité', *Critique Internationale,* 56 (Juillet–Septembre 2012), p. 81. The importance of memory to both European politics and scholarship is mapped in Richard Ned Lebow, Wulf Kansteiner, and Claudio Fogu (eds), *The Politics of Memory in Postwar Europe* (Durham, NC: Duke University Press, 2006).

[11] See Jean-Paul Brunet, 'Police Violence in Paris, October 1961: Historical Sources, Methods and Conclusions', *The Historical Journal,* 51/1 (2008), pp. 195–204. The actual numbers are hotly disputed, with the lower limit being Brunet's (30–50) and the upper the estimate of Jean-Luc Einaudi (*c.*250). Most convincing are House and MacMaster who say between 108 and 121 deaths are attributable to police action on this single occasion. See Jim House and Neil MacMaster, 'Time to Move On: A Reply to Jean-Paul Brunet', *The Historical Journal,* 51/1 (2008), pp. 205–14. Also Jean-Luc Einaudi, *Octobre à Paris: Un massacre à Paris* (Paris: Fayard, 2001); Jean-Paul Brunet, *Police contre FLN. Le drame d'octobre 1961* (Paris, Flammarion, 1999); and Jim House and Neil Macmaster, *Paris 1961: Algerians, State Terror and Memory* (Oxford: Oxford University Press, 2006). The massacre is strangely understated even in the later editions of Alistair Horne's compendious *A Savage War of Peace: Algeria 1954–1962* (3rd edn, New York: New York Review of Books, 2006), p. 501, reflecting the tacit silence there has been on the issue in French political life until recently. In late 2012 François Hollande became the first president to

of hostile attitudes all too easily awakened in both ex-colonial countries and minorities within Europe—attitudes which were hardly undermined by the counter-terrorist and restrictive immigration policies stimulated by the Algerian insurgency of the 1990s. The belated awareness of such difficulties is leading governments—not just in France—to begin to offer apologies for the sins of their predecessors, and to a new willingness to envisage returning artefacts to the countries from which they had been taken during the years of European predominance. The aggrieved abroad, and the aggrieved at home, are between them starting to put European governments onto the back foot.

THE IMPACT OF FOREIGN POLICY AND EXTERNAL RELATIONS ON SOCIETY

If we now look through the other end of the telescope, we see that in relatively few of the European states under review is it possible to identify the direct consequences for civil society of a specific foreign policy being pursued. Even where this seems to be the case, it is usually a matter of controversy as to whether the external action was the prime cause of the event at home, given the inherently multivariate nature of both sets of processes, and the difficulties over time-lags between one and the other. Yet in the most dramatic cases—the terrorist attacks in Madrid and London of 2004–5—neither objection has much force. It is clear that the bombs in Spain were timed to affect the campaign of the imminent general election in which the issue of the presence of Spanish troops in Iraq was a major debate. Only a few conspiracy theorists claim that any other motive was at stake. The London bombings are more controversial, in that the Prime Minister of the day Tony Blair has always argued that Britain was targeted simply because it stood for Western values, and not because of his foreign policy in Afghanistan and Iraq.[12] This has become an increasingly implausible position to hold, given the lack of equally significant attacks in countries which have not been so committed overseas—and not so aligned with the United States.

It is true that plots against other European countries have been discovered and foiled (as well as in Spain and Britain), after the withdrawal of their troops

acknowledge official responsibility for this atrocity, in a rare political opening towards French-Algerians. Fiachra Gibbons, 'Truth Hurts Less than Lies', *The Guardian*, 20 October 2012.

[12] It is notable that Tony Blair does not address in his memoirs the question of why Britain suffered terrorist attacks. He deals with the issue entirely in terms of facing a threat from fanatical enemies. Tony Blair, *A Journey* (London: Hutchinson, 2010), pp. 565–72 and 583. See also Anthony Seldon, *Blair Unbound* (London: Simon & Schuster, 2008), pp. 375–6. As Seldon points out (p. 458), had any of the other plots after 7/7 succeeded, the issue of the Iraq War would have had 'hugely destabilising consequences' for Blair and his government.

from Iraq. This may be less surprising in the case of the UK than in that of Spain, given the latter's retreat from Iraq and lower profile under the Zapatero government, but the continued alertness of all European governments over possible threats shows both that participation in the Iraq War of 2003 is not the only motivation for European jihadists, and that their quarrel with the West has become gradually more general and transnational in nature. Given the prolonged nature of the Afghan war in particular and the steady increase in counter-terrorist cooperation across Europe, revolutionaries are unlikely to bother with fine distinctions over which EU state is responsible and which not. Furthermore, the proclivity to intervene, however well-meaning the motivation, can produce blowbacks within European societies so long as they contain even small numbers of alienated people with links to those overseas resisting occupation.

The gradual diffusion of the conflict with al-Qaeda and other sources of anti-Western feeling should not be framed as a 'clash of civilizations'—the majorities on both sides are too silent and moderate for that. But the steady rise in tension since the mid-1990s, brought to a head by 9/11 and the War on Terror, has had indiscriminate effects across Europe in raising levels of fear and hostility. Populist parties have emerged in most countries, often with a racist impetus. They have blended anti-Islamic and anti-immigrant rhetoric to play on the anxieties created by acts of terror which, while powerful as spectacles and appalling for those affected, have inflicted little structural damage on European states. For their part minority groups, particularly Muslims, have responded by turning inwards, away from integration, as a defensive measure. In this atmosphere a single drama in one country can easily flash across the whole continent, with destabilizing effects, whether it is the murder by arson of a Turkish family in eastern Germany or an 'honour' killing in Italy. Thus the general climate of international relations, even if shaped by relatively few countries, and independent of the wisdom or otherwise of their actions, has hotted up Europe's multicultural societies, posing dilemmas for governments over cohesion, justice, and at times civil peace.

Some of these dilemmas, as we saw in Chapter 6, are specific and practical, as over the issue of recruitment into public service, notably the armed services, airport security, diplomacy, and intelligence. Distrust engendered by fear and concerns over security compound the existing barriers of discrimination or cultural introspection. Completely law-abiding citizens who happen to come from a minority group find that they have even more obstacles to surmount in applying for jobs, while officialdom faces difficulties over whether or not to employ ethnic profiling as a way of narrowing down the search for those who might represent a threat to public safety.

Just as significant are the indirect consequences for society caused by the backwash from foreign policy and from wider international relations. Of these immigration is the most important, being an issue-area which straddles the domestic–external divide, becoming literally visible at the frontiers of the state. It is therefore a moot point as to whether immigration has become part of foreign policy more through the demands of public opinion to pressurize the sending countries into imposing more restrictions, or through international factors such as refugee crises and EU enlargement. Either way, immigration represents the world impacting on a community, and precipitating change.[13] This may be positive, economically and culturally, but a rapid and/or large influx can be destabilizing in the period before integration can take place. In this context, diplomatic disputes can have tangible consequences for society, as at various phases of Italo–Libyan, Spanish–Moroccan, and Greek–Turkish relations, when the non-EU states have been either unable or unwilling to prevent the movement northwards of illegal immigrants. For its part the French Fifth Republic has been unable to ignore Algeria, despite trying for periods to do so, given that proximity makes it a second home to many Algerians.[14]

This last example illustrates how immigration is closely connected to the issue of identity, given specific attention in Chapter 5. Identity is also an inherently border-crossing phenomenon, with a people's sense of itself being closely tied to its understanding of its differences from friends and enemies, neighbours, and those more remote. Since identity is in constant evolution, a country experiencing increased social diversity may find it particularly difficult to maintain national consensus and cohesion if external events incite widely differing reactions—that is, degrees of *identification* and *dis-identification*—between majority and minorities, or across the range of ethnocultural groups. International relations naturally reverberate in a multicultural social mix, where diaspora members—by definition outwardly directed—may easily find themselves conflicted.

When states are internally fragile because of relative youth, traumatic collective memories, or strong regional pulls, they find it particularly difficult to deal with these challenges. The result is a tendency to avoid making choices, which does not mean that events stand still. In some states the interaction between civil society and foreign policy issues has called aspects of national identity explicitly into question. Depending on the state, identity may even be said to be in flux. The Netherlands, for example, is still a multiculturalist society, but has reacted strongly against some of its implications in recent

[13] As memorably summed up by Chad Alger with his phrase 'Your Community in the World; the World in Your Community', *Global Perspectives* (October 1979), pp. 3–6.

[14] Martin Evans, *Algeria: France's Undeclared War* (Oxford: Oxford University Press, 2012), pp. 348–70. But not all regions or groups are equally affected. As Morisse-Schilbach says of the war of independence itself, 'La plupart des Français n'étaient pas vraiment touchés par la guerre. En effet, celle-ci se déroulait dans une lontaine Algérie peu connue des métropolitains'. Melanie Morisse-Schilbach, *L'Europe et la question algérienne* (Paris: Presses Universitaires de France, 1999).

years. Germany has been deeply troubled over the balance between blood and soil as criteria for its citizenship, and in its moves towards the latter has been acutely sensitive to international opinion. France has had to accept that assimilation has not worked, and is falling back on the more egalitarian notion of 'integration'.

National identity becomes particularly complicated in times of war. European societies tend to be engaged in a perpetual balancing-act between their roles as representatives of the West in general, and as members of the EU pursuing liberal-progressive values which do not always coincide with those of the US. This sleight of hand may not convince all outsiders, but it becomes more problematic when European citizens themselves do not buy into the story. When minorities are passionately angry over the fate of their families or co-religionists in third countries, or simply complain over double standards, governments find them less easy to brush off than the critics of the traditional radical fringes. The social base for their foreign policy can therefore seem far from unified, with the result that war ceases to have its familiar unifying effect. Instead, it can call the very conception of national identity into question. This was the import of the 'not in my name' slogan of the large numbers of demonstrators against the Iraq War, and of the bitter divisions seen in Britain, Spain, and Italy. Ethnic diversity is not a necessary condition of such challenges, but it makes more of them possible.

Another way in which foreign policy impacts upon civil society relates to European integration. The EU has divisive effects on popular opinion in an increasing number of Member States, but ethnic diversity is not a factor in that. More relevant is the fact that the EU, despite its aspirations to promote European citizenship and common values across the continent, has few means of assisting with the problems which have arisen over multiculturality in the last decade. It has not been able to agree common policies on migration—legal or illegal.[15] Its foreign policy has proved incapable of holding the Member States together on two of the most important issues for European voters, namely Iraq and Afghanistan, and has been weak on the emotive Israel–Palestine question. It has, in contrast, managed to foster consensus over counter-terrorism strategy by trying to ensure that civil liberties and security are given equal weight, but it gets little public credit for this unspectacular work on process. So far as the wounds that have opened up inside societies like the Netherlands or Greece on diversity are concerned, the EU

[15] In a recent survey Members of the European Parliament expressed a wish for both a common EU policy on asylum burden-sharing (69 per cent either agreed or strongly agreed; 12.2 per cent disagreed or strongly disagreed), and a common policy on how to treat illegal migrants (76.6 per cent agreed or strongly agreed; 9.9 per cent disagreed or strongly disagreed). Simon Hix, Roger Scully, and David M. Farrell, *National or European Parliamentarians? Evidence from a New Survey* (London School of Economics and Political Science: European Parliament Research Group, 2011), p. 20. But neither policy is even close to being formulated.

simply has no competence to act. Insofar as it has any impact it has been negative, through the insistence since 2008 on policies of financial rectitude to save the euro, despite the severe social strains imposed, and in particular through its insouciant approach to the internal impact of enlargement.

The determination to open the Union up to new members has arguably worsened tensions within the societies of Member States by increasing the numbers of poor, mobile people seeking ever fewer jobs in times of recession. Labour markets and welfare systems already under significant pressure from the numbers of irregular migrants arriving from the Maghreb, sub-Saharan Africa, and Asia, found the situation exacerbated by the unpredicted inflows from central Europe and from the Balkans after the enlargements of 2004 and 2007. In this situation the revival of xenophobic populist parties, and thus the sense of alienation among ethnic minorities, was virtually inevitable. The feedback into external policy has been the stalling of negotiations on the possible accession of Turkey to the EU, to which a number of Member States had been committed. Changes in domestic societies and economies have put that into the deep-freeze.[16]

North African states are effectively excluded from EU membership.[17] But as the migration issue shows, their societies are intimately connected to those further north. The Arab Spring of 2011 demonstrated this vividly with rapid and dramatic effect. France discovered that its previously favoured regimes had overnight become anathema to public opinion on both sides of the Mediterranean. Britain was embarrassed by the fact that individuals it had stigmatized as extremists had been suddenly legitimized by their role in a successful revolution, and that the ties the Libyan regime had been fostering with British universities were suddenly a source of shame.[18]

[16] Nathalie Tocci and Dimitar Bechev, 'Will Turkey Find its Place in Post-crisis Europe?', Global Turkey in Europe, Policy Brief (Rome: Istituto degli Affari Internazionali, 5 December 2012). Canan-Sokullu shows, in a study of France, Germany, the Netherlands, and the UK between 2004 and 2008, that 'public opinion became more Turkosceptic, to the extent that large-scale immigration into Europe was perceived as an important threat'. See Ebru Canan-Sokullu, 'Islamophobia and Turcoscepticism in Europe? A Four-Nation Study', in Christopher Flood et al. (eds), *Political and Cultural Representations of Muslims: Islam in the Plural* (Leiden: Brill, 2012), pp. 109–11.

[17] Morocco applied in 1987, only to be quickly rebuffed, unlike all other applicants who have at least been put into a queue.

[18] France was embarrassed by the personal ties between members of the government and the Ben Ali regime when history suddenly moved against the Tunisian dictator. In Britain injunctions were issued against both former Foreign Secretary Jack Straw and MI6 officer Sir Mark Allen for their alleged part in 'rendering' enemies of Colonel Gadaffi to Libya, before the latter's overthrow. 'Jack Straw Accused of Misleading MPs Over Torture of Libyan Dissidents', *The Guardian*, 10 October 2012. On 13 December 2012 the Government settled out of court, tacitly admitting the claim. The British government had been pleased to see the Director of the LSE and the Vice Chancellor of Exeter University make high-level visits to the Gadaffi regime, after the latter appeared to wish to rejoin the society of states. *The Guardian*, 14 March 2011.

The EU's ambitious attempt to create a holistic Mediterranean policy from 1995 had represented an attempt precisely to forestall crises over such connections, by stressing the solidarity of the civil societies of the two littorals, one poor and exporting people, the other rich and importing diversity. Spain's idea of an 'alliance of civilizations' was also intended to promote understanding of the historical interpenetration of European and Arab cultures. Yet as the risings of 2011 indicated, these initiatives were ineffective, both in fostering reform and in slowing down emigration to the EU.[19] Such events illustrate how the feedback loops between actions in the domestic and foreign spheres are becoming ever clearer.

DIFFERING DOMESTIC APPROACHES TO MULTICULTURALITY

It is challenging to try to separate out the effects of a structural feature like that of a given national approach to state–society relations, whatever data or methodology are used. Any political analysis has to cope with a panoply of simultaneously moving targets. At the same time we have to address the big questions about change and power. Here I return to the three 'models' identified in Chapters 2–4 to see what conclusions may be drawn about the impact of different patterns of handling multiculturality on the interaction between civil society and external relations.

The first thing to be said is that many of the same dilemmas occur in all states, regardless of their distinctive approaches. For example, the Cartoon Crisis which engulfed Denmark could have happened in any European country, given the sensitivity of the issue and the speed of transnational developments. But the ways in which such issues were handled, and the effects they had, did vary according not only to the skill of those in charge, but also to a state's conformation and political culture. In this case the domestic upheaval might have been even greater in a state like Britain, where Muslims were both more numerous and more conscious of their group identity. In the *Charlie Hebdo* case of 2012, it was demonstrably less, through the determined, even ruthless, approach of the French authorities.

In relation to the integrationist approach to diversity, represented here by France, Denmark, and Greece, it seems clear that while its confident view of the state–society relationship just about remains intact in the face of increased immigration, it has come under some severe strains. Civic nationalism is still

[19] On the EU's approaches to Mediterranean strategy, see Federica Bicchi, *European Foreign Policy Making towards the Mediterranean* (Houndmills: Palgrave Macmillan, 2007). See also Chapter 4, footnote 77, on the Alliance of Civilizations.

resistant in principle to the recognition of group rights, meaning that a tight triangular bond still obtains between the conceptions of state, society, and nation (unlike in Spain, for example). On the face of it this makes for clarity over national identity, as well as a capacity to compartmentalize foreign policy on the basis of a presumed domestic consensus over external interests. France epitomizes this view. Its executive still manages to conduct foreign policy relatively untroubled by societal interference, while episodes of domestic turbulence are not easily ascribable to transnational linkages. Despite the economic hardship and social discrimination suffered by many of the country's large number of *maghrébins*, protests are focused more on their lack of the proper rights of Frenchmen and women than on any systemic cultural conflict.[20] During both the 2005 riots and the later *Charlie Hebdo* incident, French Muslim organizations were at pains to call for calm and respect for the law. Sympathizers abroad, concerned over the headscarf ban, found it surprisingly difficult to mobilize their French equivalents as the centre-point of an international campaign.

The republican tradition can be accused of selectivity over rights for ethnic groups. It has suited the French interest in resisting Turkey's wish to enter the EU to accede to the Armenian community's pressure for recognition of the 1915 genocide, to the extent of passing a law to that effect. A more important weakness of the French position, however, is that the theoretical commitment to integrate even post-migrants to the privileged status of being French is hardly lived up to. Minorities may not be recognized in France, but they are still discriminated against. The *embourgeoisement* of people from an immigrant background has been painfully slow by comparison to multiculturalist Britain. Even the many Algerian professionals who fled the bloodshed at home during the 1990s, and whose francophone culture made settling in the 'hexagon' easier, do not find progress easy. They are a standing reminder of 'une décolonialisme inachevée', partly because with modern communications they can cope with their frustrations inside France by remaining involved with their country of origin. Their brain drain poses problems for Algeria, just as their bi-national identity raises issues for a French society 'hantée par le spectre du communautarisme', thus complicating official foreign relations between the two countries.[21]

What of Denmark and Greece in this context? Both countries, like France, have a strong sense of their own national identity, linked to a stress on sovereign independence. In each case this has caused difficulties in relation to immigration-derived social change and some aspects of classical foreign policy. For example, Denmark's commitment to universal human rights, so

[20] Alec G. Hargreaves, *Multi-Ethnic France: Immigration, Politics, Culture and Society* (2nd edn, London: Routledge, 2007), pp. 8–10 and 108–9.

[21] Labat, 'Les binationaux franco-algériens', pp. 79–82 and 89–92.

evident in its development aid policy and in its willingness even to fall out with China, sits uneasily in practice with its unwillingness to be relaxed about changes to the 'Danish way of life' and with the rise of the anti-immigrant Danish People's Party to a prominent position in national politics. However, there have been some signs of wavering in these attitudes, and of a degree of convergence with Denmark's multiculturalist neighbour Sweden, indicating some uncertainty over how to handle these inherently transnational issues.[22]

Greece, by contrast, has shown little signs of doubt over the ethnic nationalism which underpins its sense of self. Its detente with Turkey, porous borders, and commitment to a European destiny, have led to a major influx of irregular migrants, received with increasing hostility in the Attica region where they mostly settle, all too predictably given the increasing economic desperation of the local population. A strongly nationalist, indeed neo-fascist, reaction has awakened memories of the deep internal divisions of the civil war and military Junta periods in recent history. Arguably the inward-looking nature of Greek society is particularly ill-suited to an era of 'human globalization', but the financial crisis, both endogenous and exogenous in its origins, has brought its fault-lines to the surface.

In sum, the integrationist countries have not made major efforts to adapt to the changing nature of their environments. They have clung to their view that their version of democracy and social cohesion entails a strong sense of national identity, not to be put at risk by the granting of rights to ethnocultural groups, especially if that risks the formation of cells of terrorist 'sleepers'. Indeed, it is arguable that the best explanation of France's relative freedom from major acts of terror over the last fifteen years lies in a combination of the state's effective security apparatus and its republican, integrationist, approach to identity.[23] On the other hand, these states may not be able to maintain their resistance to group rights indefinitely. The outside world is pressing in through migration, communications, the Single European Market, and through attitudinal shifts. Multiculturality is already a growing reality in all three, with some *de facto* elements of a multi-*ethnic* society emerging regardless of government hostility to multicultural*ism*. Given this, the more that those from immigrant backgrounds are denied the opportunity to enjoy citizenship, jobs, and housing on equal terms with the indigenous population (as they certainly still are in

[22] For an excellent summary of border-crossing issues, see Steven Vertovec, *Transnationalism* (London: Routledge, 2009). Vertovec draws our attention (pp. 86–90) to the idea of the triad between identities, borders, and orders, proposed in Mathias Albert, David Jacobson, and Yosef Lapid (eds), *Identities, Borders, Orders: Rethinking International Relations Theory* (Minneapolis: University of Minnesota Press, 2001).

[23] As concluded by Briquetti in her specific study of the issue. Sophie Briquetti, 'The "French Exception" in the Field of Islamist Terrorism Since the End of the Cold War', dissertation submitted for the degree of MPhil in International Relations, University of Cambridge, 2012. For further discussion of this issue, see Chapter 6.

France and Greece), the more they will find their identity through religion, ties with home countries, or political resistance—all of which have implications for foreign policy.[24] This trend is already evident in France with the rise of Salafism.[25] The existing order, then, has a choice between either adjusting to the new circumstances at the expense of tradition, or facing new tensions at home or abroad. History shows that there are other, more apocalyptic, possibilities, but it is to be hoped that European democracies have become robust enough to withstand them.

Multiculturalist systems are those which seem to have been caused the most problems by external factors. The whole rationale of this approach to society has been called into question over the last fifteen years, to the point where politicians barely use the word 'multiculturalism' except to deny its relevance—as with the synchronized announcements of Cameron, Merkel, and Sarkozy in 2011.[26] If this is disingenuous, most people would agree that multiculturalism has run into difficulties, some intrinsic to the project, but some exacerbated by the transnational and foreign policy dimensions. This is evident in all three of the projects we have looked at—the Netherlands, Sweden, and the UK—as well as in Spain, which often considers itself to be a multicultural country despite not giving groups the formal recognition such a system requires.[27] In each one there has been a reaction against the idea of pressing ahead with multiculturalism, and in some respects a rowing back from it. There have been moves in both the Netherlands and Britain to require of new immigrants better language skills and a familiarity with the country's past. There have also been sharper arguments over the benefits of faith schools and of the need for cultural 'exceptions' in matters of dress. In all these states there has been a new determination to restrict immigration, and to limit the freedom of fundamentalist preachers to influence Muslim youth. Nonetheless, the embedded sets of social practices, anchored in law, which exist in countries that have followed multiculturalism for decades, cannot simply be consigned to history even if rhetorically renounced. They may be rebalanced, and will evolve, but once the pattern has been established it creates expectations over

[24] Cesari distinguishes between diasporas, which are internationally dispersed communities, and bilateral transnational ties with a country of origin, which she says still characterize North African groups. Jocelyn Cesari, 'Global Multiculturalism: The Challenge of Heterogeneity', *Alternatives: Global, Local, Political*, 27/5, Special Issue (2002), p. 13.

[25] 'Qui sont les Salafistes Français?', *Libération*, 22–23 September 2012.

[26] Steven Vertovec and Susanne Wessendorf (eds), *The Multiculturalism Backlash: European Discourses, Policies and Practices* (London: Routledge, 2010). See also *The Guardian*, 5 February 2011, and footnote 31 in Chapter 4.

[27] Spain's ambiguous self-image occurs because both politicians and citizens at times conflate two things: Kymlicka notes how Spain is 'strongly multicultural' in attitudes towards 'territorially concentrated national minorities', but that it has not moved on policies towards 'immigrant multiculturalism'. See Will Kymlicka, *Multicultural Odysseys: Navigating the New International Politics of Diversity* (Oxford: Oxford University Press, 2007), pp. 69–77.

rights and separate identities which cannot be easily dispelled. Thus there have been no major reversals in these countries, at least of rights previously granted over dress, places of worship, and schooling.

To many there seems to be a straightforward link between terrorism and the multiculturalist model. Because the two major attacks by al-Qaeda in Europe have taken place in societies where groups have considerable autonomy, it might seem as if multiculturalism is a breeding-ground for jihadism. This is too simple a view, even if such societies are in certain respects particularly vulnerable to linkages with hostile external forces. For one thing, Britain is really the only case in point; as we have seen, Spain's multiculturalism mostly relates to the regions and their territorial nationalities. For another, the Madrid attacks were enabled more by the 'parallel society' of immigrants living on the margins of normal Spanish life, than by any granting of special privileges to the Moroccan community. Indeed, given that Spanish identity 'has been built in opposition to the picture of the Muslim in general and the Moroccan in particular', it is the very political invisibility of Spanish Muslims that builds up tension.[28]

It is also true that while the other two relevant European countries, the Netherlands and Sweden, have suffered disturbing incidents associated with multiculturalism, they have not experienced a serious terrorist attack. Finally, the bombs in Madrid and London were certainly not *caused* by the countries' social systems; the most that could be said is that the latter made attacks more likely given certain other conditions to do with foreign policy, geography, and belief-systems. In any case, as Joseph Nye pointed out in relation to the uproar over an anti-Islamist film in the US, 'There will always be provocateurs; a liberal society cannot prevent them', because 'today a smart phone is enough to make any madman who burns the *Qur'an* into a celebrity'.[29] Yet uproar is not the same as subversion. The American film, like the provocative French cartoons in *Charlie Hebdo* at the same time, did not lead to serious violence, which suggests that the specific national context does make a difference. Perhaps multicultural societies do find it more difficult to contain controversies like these. But there are long leads and lags in such matters. Other systems may yet turn out to be vulnerable.

Terrorism has done more than anything to blacken the name of multiculturalism in Europe, although some degree of backlash had been evident from the mid-1990s, rooted in the pace of social change, leading to growing problems of competition over housing and welfare, especially at the local level. After

[28] The quotation is from Ricard Zapata-Barrero, 'The Muslim Community and Spanish Tradition: Maurophobia as a Fact, and Impartiality as a Desideratum', in Tariq Modood, Anna Triandafyllidou, and Richard Zapata-Barrero (eds), *Multiculturalism, Muslims and Citizenship: A European Approach* (London: Routledge, 2006), p. 143.

[29] My translation from the Italian of an interview given by Joseph Nye to *La Repubblica*, 20 September 2012: 'I provocatori ci saranno sempre. Una società liberale non può prevenerli'.

9/11, debates over immigration, which had blurred into those on multiculturalism, became further distorted by association with terrorism, despite the fact that in the UK at least attacks had been carried out by individuals born in the country, for whom immigration controls were irrelevant. The UK is distinctive given the extent of its ethnocultural diversity, and the seriousness of the alienation of a small group of second and third generation migrants. But if there is an outlier in this context then Sweden is a better case. For it has not suffered, as Britain, the Netherlands, and Spain have, significant violence associated with multiculturalism. It also does not fall into their category of countries with a history of global empire, which has had consequences for current demography. Furthermore, their history and foreign policy profiles meant that jihadists emerged in these states as a particular threat. In dangerous times minorities often suffer, as with the paranoia about Jews and black marketeering during the London Blitz of 1940–1.[30] In the same war totally integrated Jews were forced into minority status in Italy and elsewhere by the Nazis as part of their psychotic campaign of persecution and war—group identity then proving the lethal opposite of the benign intentions of modern multiculturalism.[31] In the different circumstances of modern multiculturality the autonomy of ethnocultural groups has proved at times to have difficult consequences both for the groups themselves, and for society in general, through the arrival of terrorism.

The third category we have used, that of parallel societies, is difficult to link clearly to outcomes in terms of the internal/external interplay, given that it represents a negative—states which have *not* followed a particular path in relation to the issue of ethnocultural diversity. Rather, they have avoided the choice between civic nationalism and multiculturalism, while usually talking the language of integration. The tendency to duck the issue has led to inconsistency and some running social sores which could eventually become serious maladies. Equally, it could be seen as a rational strategy given the seriousness and sensitivity of the issues, which states based on territorial devolution find it difficult to confront on top of their existing divisions. The lack of a philosophy of diversity, or even a clear direction of travel, does ensure some flexibility and a relatively low profile internationally. Yet the 'foreign nationals' proportion of their populations is now sizeable, entailing actual and potential social change.[32] Given that there are evident divisions over the desirability of greater

[30] Juliet Gardiner, *The Blitz: The British under Attack* (London: Harper Press, 2010), p. 370.

[31] Enzo Tayar recounts how Jewish Florentines were forced to distinguish themselves from their neighbours, a tragic narrative applicable right across Nazi Europe. In Tuscany many non-Jews resisted this differentiation, hiding their fellow-citizens at great risk to themselves. Enzo Tayar, *1943: i giorni della pioggia* (Firenze: Edizioni Polistampa, 2001).

[32] Eurostat, 'Main Tables', <http://epp.eurostat.ec.europa.eu/portal/page/portal/population/data/main_tables> accessed 2 November 2012. The figures for 2011 were: for Germany, 8.8 per cent; for Italy, 7.5 per cent; and for Spain, 12.3 per cent.

cosmopolitanism, and that immigration has many lagged effects, the relative calm of these countries' situation is not guaranteed to last.[33] Moreover, if their foreign policy profiles rise, as they are doing, then the more they become hostages to the need for domestic consensus. This is already a factor, for specific reasons, in Germany and Italy, but could become more difficult for all, especially when linked to immigration and/or issues of perceived offence to Muslims. In states of this kind, with strong sub-national pressures, problems can also arise at the regional level, as over the *Lega Nord*'s prejudicial attitudes towards southern Italians, let alone immigrants, and its resistance to the very notion of an Italian national interest.[34]

WHAT DIFFERENCE IS MADE BY THE KIND OF FOREIGN POLICY CONDUCTED?

The issue of whether certain foreign policy stances cause particular difficulties for the diverse societies they serve is more accessible than that of the impact of different socio-political systems. If a state engages in conflict, especially war, with an entity which has strong links, ethnic or religious, to groups within the state in question, then some unrest is to be expected. On the other hand, it is unlikely that even a vociferous minority will be able to deflect a government convinced it is acting in the overall national interest. Yet the evidence surveyed in this book shows that matters are more complex than either of these two observations suggest. This is partly because it depends on how far members of a given minority are prepared to go with their protests, and in particular whether they are prepared to turn to violence. But it also depends on how a conflict actually evolves; a war once begun is inherently uncontrollable—it may turn out well, or it may drag on with unforeseen, possibly disastrous, consequences. More fundamentally, the difference made by foreign policy needs breaking down into two dimensions: first, the profile which a state has

[33] The difficulties, flowing back and forth across borders, are illustrated by the row in Italy over 'the Lautsi affair'. See note 3, Chapter 8, this volume.

[34] There is a literature on the foreign policy of federal states, but it only touches on the question of multiculturalism in relation to Quebec. See Hans J. Michelmann (ed.), *Foreign Relations in Federal Countries Global Dialogue on Federalism*, vol. 5 (Montreal/Kingston: McGill-Queen's University Press, 2009); also Brian Hocking (ed.), *Foreign Relations and Federal States* (London: Leicester University Press, 1993).

in international relations, including the degree of its activism; second, the substance of that foreign policy, and the extent to which it attracts antagonism.

In terms of profile it is clear that even European states which are relatively inactive in world affairs will suffer some complications through the interaction between external relations and social diversity. The impact of immigration and the growing presence of diaspora groups both generate the need for some careful diplomacy towards countries of origin, while—as Switzerland found out through its conflict with the Gadaffi family—a local dispute can all too suddenly place a country in the eye of an international storm. Less publicly, small states like Belgium and Sweden have been sites for terrorist plots, even if they have not come to serious fruition.[35] Jihadist groups have formed anywhere in Europe where alienated Muslim youth have encountered radical Imams or individuals with access to transnational networks, regardless of the type of state, or its foreign policy. They do not represent a security threat, let alone generate attacks, unless the conditions are particularly conducive—that is, the presence of sizeable numbers of the alienated, and persistent antagonism towards the foreign policy in question.

The other side of this coin is that larger states can avoid serious complications in terms of the interplay with diversity, if they are cautious in their foreign relations. Germany and Italy have followed this path. Both have been notably less troubled by international terrorism than in the 1970s and 1980s when the Palestinian Liberation Organisation was able to inflict violence on them, largely through the support provided by their ideological allies inside German and Italian society.[36] The Palestinians and the Red Brigades characterized both states at the time as puppets of US imperialism, and thus legitimate targets—although neither had much choice in the matter. Since then Rome and Berlin have quietly been able to develop more independent and indeed more active national foreign policies, but they have still been ultracautious about taking a leading role in any extra-European intervention. Those who talk up Europe's international 'responsibilities' do not like to acknowledge it, but the less militarily active a state is, the less likely it is to attract opprobrium abroad, now with accompanying echoes inside domestic society. Conversely the European states which continue to be highly active internationally, namely France and Britain as permanent members of the UN

[35] For details of how Belgium was affected, from as early as the 1980s, and in the 1990s by Algerian exiles looking more towards France, see Rik Coolsaet, 'The Rise and Demise of Jihadi Terrorism in Belgium', in Rik Coolsaet (ed.), *Jihadi Terrorism and the Radicalisation Challenge: European and American Experiences* (2nd edn, Farnham: Ashgate, 2011), pp. 161–70.

[36] See Lawrence Freedman et al., *Terrorism and International Order* (London: Routledge and Kegan Paul for the Royal Institute of International Affairs, 1986).

Security Council, but also Spain in Latin America and the Maghreb, inevitably risk blowbacks from their activity. The pretension to act as an 'agent of the international community' is unlikely to go uncontested.

But it is what a country does with its activism, namely the actual content of its foreign policy, which counts more than its profile. No ethnocultural minority is likely to differ from public opinion in general over abstractions like levels of defence spending or roles in international organizations. But if a government takes a distinctive line on a particular conflict or region of the world, in which a significant group at home has an emotional and political stake, then it can expect domestic consequences. This was true of the United Kingdom and Spain in relation to Iraq, where their military presence incited powerful opposition at home. Feelings ran strongly across social classes and ethnicities, but the occupation of an Islamic country, with nightly televised accounts of civilian casualties, was felt particularly keenly by local Muslims. This produced a more active and tense political atmosphere than is usually the case on foreign policy issues. Both states also contained, it transpired, cells—Moroccans in Spain and men of Pakistani origin in the UK—who saw themselves as warriors in a global conflict against the Western 'crusaders'. They struck with devastating effect with bomb attacks on the busy transport systems of both capital cities.

It is too simple to attribute such acts of terror to foreign policy alone. There have been plots in other states without major involvement in Iraq, while to the committed jihadist the West as a whole is the enemy. Moreover, most European states have participated in some form in the long-running war in Afghanistan, while not all have been attacked. On the other hand it is difficult to avoid the conclusion that the countries which have suffered most domestic turbulence have been characterized by both a large Muslim population and a foreign policy strongly associated with the United States' War on Terror. This drew fire from small and completely alienated groups hidden among the law-abiding mass of their ethno-religious group, itself deeply unhappy about the role of the government to which they paid taxes in the occupation of 'Muslim lands'.

From this point of view the 'new interventionism', supported to varying degrees by many European states, has been naïve in its belief that the old empires could re-emerge in international politics as a 'force for good' without tapping the well of resentment over the past, and outrage over double standards, that exists in the developing world. If all the Europeans had steered clear of interventions such as those in Afghanistan and Iraq, thus differentiating themselves from the United States on issues like rendition and the Israel/Palestine conflict, they might have attracted less attention from al-Qaeda and its loose network of sympathizers, while also finding it easier to build consensus on foreign policy in their increasingly cosmopolitan societies. Their support for Bosnia and Kosovo might also have been given more credit by the governments of Muslim states. But the deep breach this would have caused with the Bush administration was seen as too risky a strategy by the foreign policy establishments in London, Madrid, and Rome, for a different set of reasons altogether.

On this logic the winding-down of the painful conflicts in Iraq and Afghanistan, which caused divisions partly through their very length and seemingly unattainable aims, should lead to a calming of tensions within European societies and to the possibility of pressing on with the integration of minorities, undisturbed by external relations. Yet here too the picture is more complicated than it seems. As the Arab Spring has demonstrated, Muslims and Arab minority groups in Europe are divided over what they hope for from their 'host' countries' foreign policies. Some are opposed root and branch to external interventions, particularly military. But others press for support to be given to the forces of reform, especially where that might lead to the replacement of authoritarian regimes backed historically by the West. Thus reactions among diaspora groups to the allied role in Libya were ambivalent, while events in both Bahrain and Syria have brought forth calls for Britain and France, given their historical roles in the two countries, to take action. But the demands have been muffled by ambivalence about relations with the West, to say nothing of divisions between Sunni and Shia, Muslim and Christian, the secular and the religious.

It will be difficult, at least for the major EU Member States, to withdraw from a role in the Mediterranean and Middle East, and indeed in Africa and West Asia, for reasons of geography, economic interest, association with the United States, and domestic society. What policies the European states will pursue is impossible to predict, dependent as they are on a changing constellation of forces. But dilemmas will continue to present themselves, with regular implications for domestic politics, through debates about immigration, human rights in the Arab world, Palestine, and Iran, or more broadly about the encounter between modernity and traditional cultures. In these debates ethnocultural groups may act as lobbies, but their role will be affected by state foreign policy—which can at times put them into the position of either drawing attention to themselves through opposition, or passively accepting actions which implicate their very sense of identity. In such circumstances, perceptions of divided loyalties all too easily arise on both sides. Yet the forces of transnationalism and differentiation within society are to a great degree irresistible, and need to be seen as providing opportunity more than danger.

Thus the nature and scope of a European state's foreign policy does impact on its domestic environment, and by extension on the relationship between society and the outside world. It is not a straightforward matter, let alone one which is predictable. The particular state, and the policy conducted, are crucial determinants of outcomes, while both interact with the dynamics of the wider international political system. But it no longer makes sense to ignore the role which in certain circumstances foreign policy can play in stirring up domestic tensions, especially within multicultural societies, or the feedback loops which exist between the two sets of factors. Because some states are more affected than others in this respect, they may draw fire away from others, but all have the potential to be embroiled in a chain of transnational interactions. For its part, however, the EU remains on the sidelines, having neither the competence to act on ethnocultural divisions nor the foreign policy drive to divert attention from national capitals. It is the Member States and their individual actions which will continue to preoccupy public opinion, in all its variety, for the foreseeable future.

WHAT IS LEFT OF THE NATIONAL INTEREST?

If, as I have argued, the evolution of multiculturality and of civil peace within a society will be affected strongly by the particular approach taken within a country towards its diversity, and by the nature of its engagement with the outside world (both official and unofficial), this returns the nation-state to a position of prime political importance. Should this then lead us to rehabilitate the notion of the 'national interest', traditionally central to the conduct of foreign policy and still employed by politicians of all stripes?

On the one hand, states are evidently not withering away, while civil societies still vary profoundly in their characteristics, notwithstanding the visual similarities created by economic globalization. Each society retains a sharp sense of its own distinctiveness. On the other, the increased diversity within each society, which has met varying degrees of acknowledgement, acceptance, and resistance, undermines the assumption of consensus on the things which bind a community together, especially in relation to outsiders. Any given territorial unit (which we call a nation-state) will always have some common interests vis-à-vis other such units. Yet whether these extend beyond the basic goals of survival, welfare, and prosperity, or numerical calculations of such things as the balance of trade or inflation, depends on the degree to which the population shares certain fundamental values, memories, and priorities. In principle this has always been open to doubt, but the dominance of elites in foreign policy-making has obscured it. In conditions of multiculturality the issue rises to the surface.

European states are embedded in a range of multilateral activity, rarely considering actions which do not involve some form of international cooperation. At the same time their domestic base is less coherent, through the pace of demographic change and the emergence of a *de facto* cosmopolitanism, especially in the cities. Both trends undermine the notion of a coherent national interest as the guide to foreign policy. In modern conditions governments are necessarily engaged in a constant process of reconciling diverse inputs into foreign policy (and reactions to them), just as they routinely do elsewhere in public policy. The process is hastened by the now extensive transnational links between civil societies, and the associated blurring of domestic and international issues. On another axis, public opinion has become more differentiated as society has become more diverse, which poses its own set of new problems for policy-makers.

This means that the concept of the national interest, already devoid of content from the analytical point of view, is also losing utility at the level of public discourse—which does not, of course, imply that we should expect it to fade from use soon. The 'national' half of the equation, which many thought to be losing definition under the impact of globalization, turns out to be at least as much challenged by internal fault-lines, some regional and long-standing, but some new and the result of ethnocultural diversity. 'Interest', on the other hand, while a powerful and ubiquitous criterion for political action, is always more difficult when pitched at the collective rather than the individual level. It is also now diluted by the existence not only of semi-autonomous groups within society, but by the possibility that they might see their interests as being shared with outsiders, in their 'home' state or elsewhere, as much as with the society in which they reside.

How, then, are we to think about the difficult issue of a government acting on behalf of a whole society—as it must—while acknowledging the diversity and elements of transnationalism which now characterize it? To begin with, it would be helpful if politicians could avoid talking about the national interest in the singular, as if it were always homogeneous and self-evident. On any given problem, any democracy will have not only a wide variety of opinions, but also a range of competing interests which it is the government's job to broker—and for which there is not always an acceptable common denominator. In other words, accepting the fact of diversity from the outset is necessary both intellectually and practically. Foreign policy is an inherently multipurpose and multivalue activity. Decision-makers may find it politically difficult to own up to compromises and fudges, but they should not behave as if engaged in a strategic game, with consensual aims and a clear set of rules. When they do, they lay themselves open to the charge that the national interest they are supposedly pursuing is in fact imposed from the top, and defined wholly by a self-interested elite.

Because foreign policy cannot be separated from issues of domestic society, civil peace, and identity, it needs to take into account the competing values arising from social diversity—which the traditional dichotomies of left/right and realist/idealist do not do justice to. Citizens define their interests in terms of who they conceive themselves to be, and with whom they feel connected, not just in material terms—a point so blindingly obvious that it is a wonder so much political science still proceeds as if in denial of it.

Abandoning our addiction to the idea of the national interest does not, however, mean that any given group can expect to have a veto over state policy, or to have their concerns privileged. Rather, it entails being sensitive to the disproportionate impact which foreign policies, as much as domestic, may have on particular parts of the community. In this context the idea of a '*vital* interest', also important traditionally and associated with *raison d'état*, needs to be expanded so that it allows for the possibility that different sections of society will have their own red lines, or what we might call 'critical concerns'. This is particularly important when contemplating acts of war. All citizens have a powerful interest in the expenditure of blood and treasure, while the destructive and mediatized nature of modern conflict means that the risks are very high, at home and abroad. Yet in multicultural societies there is the extra problem that a particular group can find itself agonizingly conflicted by a given decision. Thus, to adapt the metaphor of the British Chief of Staff at the time of the Iraq War, General Dannatt, at the very least you should not 'kick the door in' of a house belonging to some of your relatives without the most careful thought and consultation.[37]

Governments must ensure that they engage with those passionate about and particularly affected by foreign policy issues, as they have to do over petrol prices or the health service. This could encourage a more extensive and effective debate about foreign policy issues *across* society—not just with a multicultural dimension—which is long overdue in most European societies. For too long, foreign policy-making has been the preserve of a metropolitan elite, which co-opts various like-minded pressure-groups. A healthy society should provide opportunities for people to participate in such debates as citizens, and not only as members of a diaspora, faith group, or privileged NGO.

This is not to argue for or against multiculturalism as a model for society; the issues arise under conditions of multi*culturality* and need addressing whatever a country's political culture. The general portfolio of a national foreign policy should reflect the full range of domestic concerns if not opinions. Whatever the lines of policy which emerge from the democratic political process, there should be at least an engagement with the issues important to significant minorities while the latter remain a significant social fact—in other words before full integration, if it is even imaginable, is achieved. The neglect of their concerns, as with Muslims over Bosnia in the early 1990s, can have disastrous results, but there are also positive gains to be made by engaging with the sources of knowledge and empathy which reside in minority communities. 'Engaging'

[37] 'We Must Not "Break" Army, Warns Top General after Triggering Iraq Storm', *The Guardian*, 14 October 2006. General Dannatt actually said in his original interview in the *Daily Mail*, 12 October 2006, that 'we are in a Muslim country and Muslims' views of foreigners in their country are quite clear. As a foreigner you can be welcomed by being invited in a country, but we weren't invited certainly by those in Iraq at the time. The military campaign we fought in 2003 effectively kicked the door in'.

means being willing to react to a group's concerns and at a minimum justifying why they should not be met. At best, it means reflecting the pluralism of society so as, paradoxically, to maintain its cohesiveness. At the same time the resilience of foreign policy will be improved by more thorough debate at both parliamentary and public levels over broad national priorities.

This book has sought to throw light on how the facts of multiculturality, the varying ways of dealing with them in European societies, and the international political environment constantly modify each other. States act externally in a wide range of ways, which they loosely summarize as their 'foreign policy'. In order to do so they require conceptions of the public interest, which are becoming more difficult to formulate in conditions of ethnocultural diversity. In the past, the two debates—about multiculturalism on the one hand and foreign policy on the other—have been kept in separate compartments, producing feelings of bewildered impotence when events led them to collide, as over the Rushdie Fatwa, the Madrid bombings, or the Danish cartoons. We should move on from such compartmentalization to the task—difficult but indispensable—of attempting to reconcile their two logics.

States have always existed in a milieu of international diversity, finding ways both to defend themselves and to promote their preferred values. Since the Treaty of Versailles, with its hopes for national self-determination, they have tended to assume that they could at least operate on the basis of domestic homogeneity. After the Cold War this was extended by some, optimistically, to the idea of a homogeneous international civil society. More recently, however, states have run into new realities, even in the zone of civility represented by the European Union, of increased diversity and fragmentation. That has manifested itself in a retreat from European integration, in the flourishing of subnational identities, and—as we have seen—in the emergence of a notable degree of multiculturality in most EU Member States. These are major new challenges.

In the three key theatres, of intergovernmental relations, devolution, and the handling of ethnocultural diversity, politicians will need to show respect for difference, and to cope with its implications for co-existence. Paradoxically, that seems a more natural activity in relation to strangers than it does in relation to minorities residing inside the state. But since society now not only interacts with the outside world but to some extent also contains it, the problem has become more complicated. Writers on international relations have long talked about 'the domestic analogy', meaning the possibility of international society being constructed on the model of a state, with its aim of fostering the good life.[38] Perhaps we should now turn to the 'international analogy', to help us understand how we may adapt our domestic systems so as the better to manage diversity.

[38] See Hidemi Suganami, *The Domestic Analogy and World Order Proposals* (Cambridge: Cambridge University Press, 1989). The comparison between the two kinds of order can arguably be traced back to the contrasts drawn by Thomas Hobbes.

Primary Sources

This being a work of contemporary political analysis it has not had the benefit of the archival material used by historians. Yet apart from a very wide range of secondary materials I have drawn on a range of different sources which can still be classified as primary sources. These include official documents from national governments and from the European Union, speeches, statistical data-sets on population and migration, and reports from newspapers and other media. Many of the latter I have collected personally over the last decade. I have been able to read materials in English, French, Italian, Spanish, and (with more difficulty) German. I have also had the benefit of about twenty interviews with experts and practitioners. These have been informal, and used for the purposes of alerting me to dimensions I might have missed, and for triangulation.

Newspapers

Many ad hoc references, with the following used on a regular basis:

Britain

Financial Times
The Guardian
The Observer

France

Le Figaro
Libération
Le Monde

Italy

Corriere della Sera
La Repubblica

Spain

El País

United States

New York Times

Online material:

'Area and population' [online database] (Statistische Ämter: Des Bundes und der Länder), <http://www.statistik-portal.de/Statistik-Portal/en/en_inhalt01.asp> accessed 16 December 2012.

'Article 5: The Right to Liberty and Security', *Human Rights Review 2012*, pp. 169 (UK's Equality and Human Rights Commission, 2012), available online <http://www.equalityhumanrights.com/uploaded_files/humanrights/hrr_article_5.pdf> accessed 9 December 2012.

BBC News website.

Bildt, C., Minister of Foreign Affairs, *Statement of Government Policy in the Parliamentary Debate on Foreign Affairs* (Stockholm: Ministry of Foreign Affairs, 16 February 2011), <http://www.government.se/content/1/c6/16/11/48/dc78c337.pdf> accessed 21 November 2012.

'Constitution of October 4, 1958', Assemblée Nationale, <http://www.assemblee-nationale.fr/english/8ab.asp#Warning!> accessed 19 December 2012.

Council of Europe Parliamentary Assembly, Committee on Legal Affairs and Human Rights, 'Alleged Secret Detentions and Unlawful Inter-state Transfers Involving Council of Europe Member States', Draft report—Part II (Explanatory memorandum) (7 June 2006), available online <http://assembly.coe.int/committeedocs/2006/20060606_ejdoc 162006partii-final.pdf> accessed 14 January 2013.

Encuesta Nacional de Inmigrantes (Boletin Informativo del Instituto nacional de Estadistica, Madrid, 1/2009), <http://www.ine.es/revistas/cifraine/0109.pdf> accessed 19 August 2011.

Eurobarometer, 'Attitudes towards European Union Enlargement', Special Eurobarometer 255, fieldwork conducted March–May 2006 (for the European Commission, July 2006), p. 71, <http://ec.europa.eu/enlargement/pdf/reportsp255enlargement20060612_en.pdf> accessed 19 December 2012.

Eurobarometer, 'Public Opinion in the European Union', Standard Eurobarometer 71, fieldwork conducted June–July 2009, p. 74, <http://ec.europa.eu/public_opinion/archives/eb/eb71/eb713_annexes.pdf> accessed 19 December 2012.

Eurostat, 'Main Tables', <http://epp.eurostat.ec.europa.eu/portal/page/portal/population/data/main_tables> accessed 2 November 2012.

European Council Conclusions, Brussels ECO23/11, 23–24 June 2011, <http://register.consilium.europa.eu/pdf/en/11/st00/st00023.en11.pdf> accessed 20 December 2012.

European Defence Agency database, <http://www.eda.europa.eu/DefenceData/> accessed 14 December 2012.

'Extraordinary Rendition: Text Adopted 6 July 2006, P6_TA(2006)0316', available online, <http://www.europarl.europa.eu/sides/getDoc.do?pubRef=-//EP//TEXT+TA+P6–TA–2006–0316+0+DOC+XML+V0//EN&language=EN> accessed 27 December 2011.

Federal Statistical Office, and the Statistical Offices of the Länder, 31 December 2010, <https://www.destatis.de/EN/FactsFigures/SocietyState/Population/CurrentPopulation/Tables/PopulationBysexCitizenship.html> accessed 31 July 2012.

'Fertility Statistics', Eurostat, <http://epp.eurostat.ec.europa.eu/statistics_explained/index.php/Fertility_statistics> accessed 1 August 2012.

Foreign and Commonwealth Office internal communication, Sir Michael Jay to Sir Andrew Turnbull (18 May 2004), available online at *The Guardian* website, <http://politics.guardian.co.uk/foi/images/0,9069,1558170,00.html> accessed 9 February 2007.

German Marshall Fund, *Transatlantic Trends: Immigration 2009* (German Marshall Fund and Partners, 2009), <http://trends.gmfus.org/files/archived/immigration/doc/TTI2010_English_Key.pdf> accessed 31 March 2013.

German Marshall Fund, Transatlantic Trends poll conducted in June 2010, <http://trends.gmfus.org/doc/2010_English_Top.pdf>.

'HMG FLOATS PROPOSAL FOR MARINE RESERVE COVERING THE CHAGOS ARCHIPELAGO (BRITISH INDIAN OCEAN TERRITORY)', leaked cable passed to the *Telegraph*, 4 February 2011, available online, <http://www.telegraph.co.uk/news/wikileaks-files/london-wikileaks/8305246/HMG-FLOATS-PROPOSAL-FOR-MARINE-RESERVE-COVERING-THE-CHAGOS-ARCHIPELAGO-BRITISH-INDIAN-OCEAN-TERRITORY.html> accessed 19 December 2012.

'How much does DG Translation cost?', 'Frequently asked questions about DG Translation' [webpage] (last updated 8 August 2012), European Commission, <http://ec.europa.eu/dgs/translation/faq/index_en.htm#faq_2> accessed 26 June 2012.

India Pakistan Trade Unit [website], 'Pakistani relations with the UK', <http://www.iptu.co.uk/content/pakistan_economy.asp#7> accessed 27 December 2011.

'International Migration Outlook 2011, OECD, <http://www.oecd.org/els/internationalmigrationpoliciesanddata/internationalmigrationoutlook2011.htm> accessed 18 December 2012.

ISTAT, (Istituto nazionale di statistica), <http://demo.istat.it>.

'The Kurdish Disapora', Institut Kurd de Paris, <http://www.institutkurde.org/en/kurdorama> accessed 23 July 2012.

'The International Terrorist Threat to the UK', speech by Dame Eliza Manningham-Buller at Queen Mary's College, London, 9 November 2006, available online, <https://www.mi5.gov.uk/home/about-us/who-we-are/staff-and-management/director-general/speeches-by-the-director-general/the-international-terrorist-threat-to-the-uk.html> accessed 9 December 2012.

La Lega dei Ticinesi [organization's website], <http://www.legaticinesi.ch/> accessed 20 December 2012.

'Language Distribution', Federal Statistical Office of Switzerland, 2002, <http://www.swissworld.org/en/people/language/language_distribution/> accessed 18 December 2012.

Lisbon Treaty, available online <http://www.lisbon-treaty.org/wcm/the-lisbon-treaty.html> accessed 17 January 2013.

'Lives Lost in the Mediterranean: Who is Responsible?', Report of the Committee of the Parliamentary Assembly of the Council of Europe on Migration, Refugees, and Displaced Persons, Doc. 12895 (Council of Europe, 5 April 2012), <http://www.assembly.coe.int/ASP/Doc/XrefViewHTML.asp?FileID=11316&Language=EN> accessed 30 March 2013.

Lord Russell-Johnston's Report of the Committee on Culture, Science, and Education of the Council of Europe's Parliamentary Assembly, 'The Cultural Situation of the Kurds' (7 July 2006), <http://assembly.coe.int/main.asp?Link=/documents/workingdocs/doc06/edoc11006.htm>

'Migrant Integration Policy Index', 'MIPEX' [online tool and reference guide] (British Council and Migration Policy Group), <http://www.mipex.eu/> accessed 16 December 2012.

'Millennium Development Goals Indicators' [online database], UN Stats, <http://unstats.un.org/unsd/mdg/SeriesDetail.aspx?srid=568> accessed 26 June 2011.

'Multiculturalism Policy Index' [online index] (Queen's University, Canada), <http://www.queensu.ca/mcp/index.html> accessed 16 December 2012.

OECD International Migration Outlook 2012 'Stocks of Foreign-Born Population', <http://www.oecd.org/els/internationalmigrationpoliciesanddata/internationalmigrationoutlook2011.htm> accessed 18 December 2012.

Pew Research, Global Attitudes Project [multiple surveys and reports cited, available online], <http://www.pewglobal.org>.

Rapport Commissie-Davids: Conclusions (English summary), 12 January 2010, para 7. Available online, <http://netherlandsmission.org/article.asp?articleref=AR00000874EN> accessed 30 March 2013.

'Reaching Out to Migrants' [online news story] (last updated 19 November 2012), European Commission, <http://ec.europa.eu/news/justice/081002_1_en.htm> accessed 18 December 2012.

'Reforming Diplomacy: Clear Choices, New Emphases', Announcement by Foreign Minister Uri Rosenthal, 8 April 2011 (Ministry of Foreign Affairs, the Netherlands), <http://www.government.nl/ministries/bz/about-the-ministry/missions-abroad/reforming-diplomacy-clear-choices-new-emphases> accessed 30 March 2013.

Return Migration and Development Platform (RDP) of the Robert Schumann Centre for Advanced Studies at the European University Institute in Fiesole: <http://rsc.eui.eu/RDP/registration> (registration required), accessed 30 March 2013.

Speech by Foreign Minister Guido Westerwelle, at the opening of the new Turkish Embassy in Berlin, 30 October 2012, <http://www.auswaertiges-amt.de/EN/Infoservice/Presse/Reden/2012/121030-BM_TUR_Botschaft.html> accessed 18 December 2012.

SpiegelOnline International, <http://www.spiegel.de/international/>.

A Secure Europe in a Better World: European Security Strategy (Paris: European Union Institute for Security Studies, 2003), document adopted at the Brussels European Council of 12 December 2003, <http://www.iss.europa.eu/uploads/media/solanae.pdf> accessed 16 January 2013.

Sky News poll of UK Muslims, fieldwork on 20–21 July 2005, conducted by Communicate Research, <http://www.comres.co.uk/polls/Sky_News_Poll.pdf> accessed 14 January 2013.

Statistics Netherlands, 'Figures', <http://www.cbs.nl/en-GB/menu/cijfers/default.htm> accessed 19 December 2012.

Statistisches Jahrbuch 2010 (Wiesbaden: Statistisches Bundesamt, September 2010), Table 2.20: 'Ausländische Bevölkerung in Deutschland', <https://www.destatis.de/DE/Publikationen/StatistischesJahrbuch/StatistischesJahrbuch2010.pdf?__blob=publicationFile> accessed 3 August 2010.

Sweden: Tables on 'Foreign-born persons by country of citizenship', <http://www.scb.se/Pages/SSD/SSD_SelectVariables____340507.aspx?px_tableid=ssd_extern%3aUtrikesFoddaR&rxid=40a5d53a-524b-43e1-9d18-87d64503edfd> accessed 30 March 2013.

Swissinfo.ch, <http://www.swissinfo.ch/>.

'The symbols of the EU', Europa, <http://europa.eu/abc/symbols/index_en.htm> accessed 18 December 2012.

Transatlantic Trends: Immigration 2009 (German Marshall Fund and Partners, 2009), available online, <http://trends.gmfus.org/archives/immigration-archive/transatlantic-trends-immigration-2009/> accessed 31 March 2013.

Transcript of Evidence given by Baroness Manningham-Buller, 20 July 2010, <http://www.iraqinquiry.org.uk/media/48331/20100720am-manningham-buller.pdf> accessed 9 December 2012.

'Translation—DG Providing High-quality Written Translations and Linguistic Advice —Our Daily Mission', MEMO/08/579 [online press release] (23 September 2008), Europa, <http://europa.eu/rapid/press-release_MEMO-08-579_en.htm?locale=en> accessed 15 December 2012.

'Twentieth Edition of the Barometer of the Elcano Royal Institute', March–April 2009, available online, <http://www.realinstitutoelcano.org/wps/portal/rielcano_eng/Content?WCM_GLOBAL_CONTEXT=/elcano/elcano_in/barometer/barometer20> accessed 30 March 2013.

UK Defence Statistics 2010, Chapter 2—Personnel, 'Table 2.10 Strength of UK Regular Forces by Service, Ethnic Origin and Rank, at 1 April 2010' [webpage], <http://www.dasa.mod.uk/modintranet/UKDS/UKDS2010/c2/table210.php> accessed 28 December 2011. United Nations Alliance of Civilizations [organization's website], <www.unaoc.org> accessed 20 December 2012.

'The World Factbook', CIA, <https://www.cia.gov/library/publications/the-world-factbook/> accessed 22 January 2013.

Other sources:

Alliance of Civilisations (Dirección General de Comunicación Exterior, Ministerio de Asuntos exteriores y de Cooperación, Madrid, November 2005).

Annual Report on Statistics on Migration, Asylum and Return in Greece (Reference Year 2004) (Athens: Centre of Planning and Economic Research, KEPE, January 2008).

'Bilateral Relations between Switzerland and Libya', 12 July 2010 (the actual date given is 2011, but the content suggests this to be a typographical error), Federal Department of Foreign Affairs, Switzerland.

Commons Foreign Affairs Committee, 2nd Report, 3 February 1999 on Sierra Leone, and response by the Secretary of State for Foreign Affairs, April 1999, Cmd 4325.

The EU Internal Security Strategy, European Union Committee of the House of Lords (London: The Stationery Office, 24 May 2011).

The EU Internal Security Strategy in Action: Five steps towards a more secure Europe, COM (2010) 673 Final, 22 November 2010 (Brussels: European Commission).

EU Terrorism Situation and Trend Report, Europol TE-SAT 2011, Annex 4: Data Convictions and Penalties (EUROJUST).

General Election 2005, House of Commons Library Research Paper 05/33, 17 May 2005 (final edn, 10 March 2006).

Hansard.

Hix, S., Scully, R., and Farrell, D. M., *National or European Parliamentarians? Evidence from a New Survey* (London School of Economics and Political Science: European Parliament Research Group, 2011).

'Immigrazione e presenza straniera in Italia 2009–10', Rapporto Sopemi Italia 2010 (Roma: Censis, November 2010), <http://www.censis.it> accessed 30 August 2011.

Law 3838/2010, *Provisions on the Greek Citizenship and the Political Participation of People of Greek Descent and Legally Residing Migrants and Other Provisions* (Athens; Office of the President of the Hellenic Republic, English translation). The 'Statement of Reasons' accompanying the original draft legislation (Ministry of Foreign Affairs Translation Service, 16 April 2010).

Legg, T. Sir and Ibbs, R. Sir, *Report of the Sierra Leone Arms Investigation*, ordered to be printed by the House of Commons, 27 July 1998 (London: The Stationery Office).

The Military Balance, Annual Issues (London: International Institute of Strategic Studies).

Piqué i Camps, J., 'Spanish Foreign Policy at the Turn of the Century' (lecture at the London School of Economics and Political Science, 24 January 2001), text released by Spanish Embassy, London.

The Treaty Establishing a Constitution for Europe, 29 October 2004 (Brussels: European Communities, 2005).

'Yiannis Kranidiotis: Interview with Gerassimos Zarkadis, *Hermes* (Athens News Agency, now ANA–MPA, October 1998).

Zapatero, J. L. R., 'In Spain's Interest: A Committed Foreign Policy', speech given at the Prado Museum (16 June 2008), for the Elcano Royal Institute and other foundations.

References

Abbas, T. (ed.), *Islamic Political Radicalism: A European Perspective* (Edinburgh, Edinburgh University Press, 2007).

Abulafia, D., *The Great Sea: A Human History of the Mediterranean* (London: Allen Lane, 2011).

Alcock, A., 'The South Tyrol Autonomy: A Short Introduction' (Londonderry: University of Ulster, 2001), available at <http://www.geography.ryerson.ca/wayne/geo773-f2011/South-Tyrol-Autonomy.pdf> accessed 30 March 2013.

Adler, E., 'Constructivism and International Relations', in Carlsnaes, W., Risse, T., and Simmons, B. A. (eds), *Handbook of International Relations* (London: Sage, 2005), pp. 95–118.

Aggestam, L., 'The European Internationalist: Sweden and European Security Cooperation', *Nação Difesa* (Lisbon), 118 (2007), pp. 203–18.

Aggestam, L., Anesi, F., Edwards, G., Hill, C., and Rijks, D., *Institutional Competences in the EU External Action: Actors and Boundaries in CFSP and ESDP* (Stockholm: Swedish Institute for European and Policy Studies, 2008).

Aggestam, L. and Hill, C., 'The Challenge of Multiculturalism in European Foreign Policy', *International Affairs*, 84/1 (2008), pp. 97–114.

Aixalà, A., 'The Parliamentary Session of Dissent', in Barbé, E. (ed.), *Spain in Europe 2004–2008*, Monograph of the Observatory of European Foreign Policy, 4 (Bellaterra, Barcelona: Institut d'Estudis Europeus, February 2008), pp. 1–5, available at <http://www.iuee.eu/pdf-publicacio/129/aGxqDe5YcIjtGdMGaKAu.PDF> accessed 31 March 2013.

Albert, M., Jacobson, D., and Lapid, Y. (eds), *Identities, Borders, Orders: Rethinking International Relations Theory* (Minneapolis: University of Minnesota Press, 2001).

Alden, C. and Aran, A., *Foreign Policy Analysis: New Approaches* (Abingdon: Routledge, 2012).

Alger, C., 'Your Community in the World; the World in Your Community', *Global Perspectives* (October 1979), pp. 3–6.

Allam, Magdi, 'Se i musulmani democratici sono estremisti', *Corriere della Sera*, 20 January 2007.

Allen, D., 'Political Cooperation and the Euro–Arab Dialogue', in Allen, D., Rummel, R., and Wessels, W. (eds), *European Political Cooperation* (London: Butterworth Scientific, 1982), pp. 69–82.

Allen, D., Rummel, R., and Wessels, W. (eds), *European Political Cooperation* (London: Butterworth Scientific, 1982).

Allison, G. T., and Zelikow, P., *Essence of Decision: Explaining the Cuban Missile Crisis* (2nd edn, Harlow: Longman, 1999).

Alonso, R., 'Jihadist Terrorism and the Radicalization Process of Muslim Immigrants in Spain', in Finkelstein, M. and Dent-Brown, K. (eds), *Psychosocial Stress in Immigrants and in Members of Minority Groups as a Factor of Terrorist Behavior* (Kiryat Shimona, Israel: IOS Press, NATO Science for Peace and Security Series, 2008), pp. 109–21.

D'Amato, G., 'Switzerland: A Multicultural Country Without Multicultural Policies', in Vertovec, S. and Wessendorf, S. (eds), *The Multiculturalism Backlash: European Discourses, Policies and Practices* (London: Routledge, 2010), pp. 130–51.

Amersfoort, H. van, *How the Dutch Government Stimulated the Unwanted Immigration from Suriname*, IMI Working Paper 47 (Oxford: Oxford University International Migration Institute, 2011), <http://www.imi.ox.ac.uk/pdfs/imi-working-papers/wp-11-47-how-the-dutch-government-stimulated-the-unwanted-immigration-from-suriname> accessed 11 December 2012.

Amiraux, V., 'Crisis and New Challenges? French Republicanism Featuring Multiculturalism', in Silj, A. (ed.), *European Multiculturalism Revisited* (London: Zed Books, 2010), pp. 65–104.

Amnå, E., 'Associational Life, Youth, and Political Capital Formation in Sweden: Historical Legacies and Contemporary Trends', in Trägårdh, L. (ed.), *State and Civil Society in Northern Europe: The Swedish Model Reconsidered* (Oxford: Berghahn Books, 2007), pp. 165–204.

Anderson, B., *Imagined Communities: Reflections on the origins and spread of nationalism* (London: Verso, 1983).

Andrew, C., *The Defence of the Realm: The Authorised History of MI5* (London: Penguin, 2010).

Anholt, S., *Places: Identity, Image and Reputation* (Houndmills: Palgrave Macmillan, 2010).

Archer, T., 'Welcome to the Umma: The British State and its Muslim Citizens since 9/11', *Cooperation and Conflict*, 44/3 (2009), pp. 329–47.

Archibugi, D., *The Global Commonwealth of Citizens: Towards Cosmopolitan Democracy* (Princeton: Princeton University Press, 2008).

Arendt, H., *The Human Condition* (Chicago: University of Chicago Press, 1958).

Armbruster, H. and Meinhof, U. H., *Negotiating Multicultural Europe: Borders, Networks, Neighbourhoods* (Houndmills: Palgrave Macmillan, 2011).

Art, B., Math Noortmann, and Bob Reinalda (eds), *Non-State Actors in International Relations* (Farnham: Ashgate, 2001).

Aspenia, L'interesse dell'Italia: Chi siamo, cosa vogliamo (Special Issue), 34 (2006).

Bach, J. P. G., *Between Sovereignty and Integration: German Foreign Policy and National Identity after 1989* (New York: St. Martin's Press, 1999).

Badarjí, R. L. and Cosidó, I., 'Spain: From 9/11 to 3/11 and Beyond', in Schmitt, G. J. (ed.), *Safety, Liberty and Islamist Terrorism: American and European Approaches to Domestic Counter-Terrorism* (Washington, DC: American Enterprise Institute, 2010), pp. 48–61.

Baldwin-Edwards, M. and Schain, M. A. (eds), *The Politics of Immigration in Western Europe* (Ilford: Frank Cass, 1994).

Baldwin-Edwards, M., Kyriakou, G., Kakalika, P., and Katsios, G., *Statistical Data on Immigrants in Greece: An Analytic Study of Available Data and Recommendations for Conformity with European Union Standards* (Athens: Hellenic Migration Policy Institute, 2004).

Balfour, R., Bailes, A., and Kenna, M., '*The European External Action Service at Work: How to Improve EU Foreign Policy*', EPC Issue Paper 67 (Brussels: The European Policy Centre, January 2012).

Banting, K. and Kymlicka, W. (eds), *Multiculturalism and the Welfare State: Recognition and Redistribution in Contemporary Democracies* (Oxford: Oxford University Press, 2006).

Barbagli, M. and Colombo, A. (eds), *Rapporto sulla criminalità e la sicurezza in Italia 2010* (Milan: Gruppo 24 Ore and the Fondazione Intelligence, Culture and Strategic Analysis, for the Ministero dell'Interno, 2011).

Barbé, E. (ed.), *Spain in Europe 2004–2008*, Monograph of the Observatory of European Foreign Policy, 4 (Bellaterra, Barcelona: Institut d'Estudis Europeus, February 2008).

Barbé, E., 'Spain and Europe: Mutual Reinforcement in Foreign Policy', in Wong, R. and Hill, C. (eds), *National and European Foreign Policies: Towards Europeanization* (London: Routledge, 2011), pp. 131–48.

Barber, B., 'Democracy and Terror in the Era of Jihad vs. McWorld', in Booth, K. and Dunne, T. (eds), *Worlds in Collision: Terror and the Future of Global Order* (Houndmills: Palgrave Macmillan, 2002), pp. 245–62.

Barkawi, T., 'On the Pedagogy of "Small Wars"', *International Affairs*, 80/1 (January 2004), pp. 19–37.

Barkawi, T., 'How Multiculturalism Can Save UK Grand Strategy', (London: Royal United Services Institution, 2011), available online <http://www.rusi.org/analysis/commentary/ref:C4E316C8388D65/> accessed 19 December 2012.

Baron, I. Z., 'The Problem of Dual Loyalty', *Canadian Journal of Political Science*, 42/4 (2009), pp. 1025–44.

Barry, B., *Culture and Equality: An Egalitarian Critique of Multiculturalism* (Cambridge: Polity, 2001).

Barry, B., 'Second Thoughts: Some First Thoughts Revived', in Kelly, P. (ed.), *Multiculturalism Reconsidered* (Cambridge: Polity, 2002), pp. 204–38.

Bass, G., *Freedom's Battle* (New York: Vintage Books, 2008).

Bauböck, R. (ed.), *Diasporas and Transnationalism: Concepts, Theories and Methods* (Amsterdam: University of Amsterdam Press, 2012).

Bauböck, R. and Rundell, J. (eds), *Blurred Boundaries: Migration, Ethnicity, Citizenship* (Aldershot: Ashgate, 1998).

Baylis, J., Smith, S., and Owens, P. (eds), *The Globalization of World Politics* (4th edn, Oxford: Oxford University Press, 2008).

Bechev, D. and Nicolaïdis, K., 'The Union for the Mediterranean: A Genuine Breakthrough Or More Of The Same?', *The International Spectator*, 43/3 (2008), pp. 13–20.

Bell, D. (ed.), *Ethics and World Politics* (Oxford: Oxford University Press, 2010).

Belloni, R., 'Italy in the Balkans: An Emerging Actor in its Neighbourhood', in Carbone, M. (ed.), *Italy in the Post-Cold War Order: Adaptation, Bipartisanship, Visibility* (Lanham, MD: Lexington, 2011), pp. 215–37.

Benedict, R., *The Chrysanthemum and the Sword* (London: Secker & Warburg, 1947).

Berger, T., 'The Power of Memory and Memories of Power: The Cultural Parameters of German Foreign Policy-making since 1945', in Müller, J-W. (ed.), *Memory and Power in Post-war Europe: Studies in the Presence of the Past* (Cambridge: Cambridge University Press, 2002), pp. 76–99.

Betts, R. K., 'Should Strategic Studies Survive?, *World Politics*, 50/1 (1997), pp. 7–33.

Bicchi, F., *European Foreign Policy Making Toward the Mediterranean* (Houndmills: Palgrave Macmillan, 2007).

Bigo, D., 'Security and Immigration: Toward a Critique of the Governmentality of Unease', *Alternatives*, 27/1, Supplement (2002), pp. 63–92.

Bigo, D. and Tsoukala, A. (eds), *Terror, Insecurity and Liberty: Illiberal Practices of Liberal Regimes after 9/11* (Abingdon and New York: Routledge, 2008).

Biscop, S., 'The EU and Euro-Mediterranean Security: A New Departure?', in Casarini, N. and Musu, C. (eds), *European Foreign Policy in an Evolving International System: The Road towards Convergence* (Houndmills: Palgrave Macmillan, 2007), pp. 195–208.

Blair, T., *A Journey* (London: Hutchinson, 2010).

Boardman, R. and Groom, A. J. R. (eds), *The Management of Britain's External Relations* (London: Macmillan, 1973).

Booth, K. and Dunne, T. (eds), *Worlds in Collision: Terror and the Future of Global Order* (Houndmills: Palgrave Macmillan, 2002).

Borcio, R., *La rivincita del Nord. La Lega dalla contestazione al governo* (Rome-Bari: Editori Laterza, 2010).

Bosman, F., 'Dutch Muslim Soldiers in the Dutch Armed Forces', in Menke, I. and Langer, P. C. (eds), *Muslim Service Members in Non-Muslim Countries: Experiences of Difference in the Armed Forces in Austria, Germany and The Netherlands, FORUM International* 29 (Strausberg, Germany: Sozialwissenschaftliches Institut der Bundeswehr, 2011), pp. 43–62.

Boswell, C., 'Justice and Home Affairs', in Egan, M., Nugent, N., and Paterson, W. E., *Research Agendas in EU Studies: Stalking the Elephant* (Houndmills: Palgrave Macmillan, 2010), pp. 278–304.

Boulding, K., *The Image: Knowledge in Life and Society* (Ann Arbor: University of Michigan Press, 1956).

Bousetta, H. and Jacobs, D., 'Multiculturalism, Citizenship and Islam in Problematic Encounters in Belgium', in Modood, T., Triandafyllidou, A., and Zapata-Barrero, R. (eds), *Multiculturalism, Muslims and Citizenship: A European Approach* (London: Routledge, 2006), pp. 23–36.

Braudel, F., *The Identity of France* (London: Collins, 1988).

Brighi, E., 'How to Change Your Foreign Policy in 100 Days: A New Course with the Prodi Government?', *The International Spectator*, 42/1 (March 2007), pp. 129–40.

Brighi, E., 'Resisting Europe? The Case of Italy's Foreign Policy', in Wong, R. and Hill, C. (eds), *National and European Foreign Policies: Towards Europeanization* (London: Routledge, 2011), pp. 57–71.

Brighi, E., *Foreign Policy, Domestic Politics and International Relations: The Case of Italy* (London: Routledge, 2013).

Brighton, S., 'British Muslims, Multiculturalism and UK Foreign Policy: "Integration" and "Cohesion" in and Beyond the State', *International Affairs*, 83/1 (2007), pp. 1–17.

Briquetti, S., 'The "French Exception" in the Field of Islamist Terrorism Since the End of the Cold War', thesis submitted for the degree of MPhil in International Relations, University of Cambridge (2012).

Bromesson, D., 'Normative Europeanization: The Case of Swedish Foreign Policy Reorientation', *Cooperation and Conflict*, 45/2 (2010), pp. 224–44.

Bronitsky, J., *British Foreign Policy and Bosnia: The rise of Islamism in Britain, 1992–1995* (London: King's College, International Centre for the Study of Radicalisation and Political Violence, 2010).

Brown, C., *International Relations Theory: New Normative Approaches* (Hemel Hempstead: Harvester Wheatsheaf, 1992).

Brown, C., *Sovereignty, Rights and Justice: International Political Theory Today* (Cambridge: Polity, 2002).

Brown, F., *For the Soul of France: Culture Wars in the Age of Dreyfus* (New York: Knopf, 2010).

Brunet, J-P., *Police contre FLN. Le drame d'octobre 1961* (Paris, Flammarion, 1999).

Brunet, J-P., 'Police Violence in Paris, October 1961: Historical Sources, Methods and Conclusions', *The Historical Journal*, 51/1 (March 2008), pp. 195–204.

Brusis, M., 'Enlargement and Inter-ethnic Power-sharing Arrangements', in Weller, M., Blacklock, D., and Nobbs, K. (eds), *The Protection of Minorities in the Wider Europe* (Houndmills: Palgrave Macmillan, 2008), pp. 232–50.

Bull, A. C. and Gilbert, M., *The Lega Nord and the Politics of Secession* (Houndmills: Palgrave, 2001).

Burke, E., *Spain's war in Afghanistan*, FRIDE Policy Brief 23 (Madrid, Fundación para las Relaciones Internacionales y el Diálogo Exterior [FRIDE], January 2010).

Burke, E., 'Why France is Leaving Afghanistan', blog entry (London, Centre for European Reform, 2 February 2012), <http://centreforeuropeanreform.blogspot.co.uk/2012/02/why-france-is-leaving-afghanistan.html> accessed 14 December 2012.

Buruma, I., *Murder in Amsterdam: The Death of Theo van Gogh and the Limits of Tolerance* (London: Penguin Books, 2006).

Calder, G. and Ceva, E. (eds), *Diversity in Europe: Dilemmas of Differential Treatment in Theory and Practice* (London: Routledge, 2011).

Cameron, F., *An Introduction to European Foreign Policy* (London: Routledge, 2012).

Campbell, D., *Writing Security: United States Foreign Policy and the Politics of Identity* (rev. edn, Manchester: Manchester University Press, 1998).

Canan-Sokullu, E., 'Islamophobia and Turcoscepticism in Europe? A Four-Nation Study', in Flood, C. et al. (eds), *Political and Cultural Representations of Muslims: Islam in the Plural* (Leiden: Brill, 2012), pp. 97–112.

Caplan, R., *Europe and the Recognition of New States in Yugoslavia* (Cambridge: Cambridge University Press, 2005).

Carbone, M. (ed.), *Italy in the Post-Cold War Order: Adaptation, Bipartisanship, Visibility*, (Lanham, MD: Lexington, 2011).

Carlsnaes, W., Sjursen, H., and White, B. (eds), *Contemporary European Foreign Policy* (London: Sage, 2004).

Carlsnaes, W., Risse, T., and Simmons, B. A. (eds), *Handbook of International Relations* (London: Sage, 2005).

Carr, G., *The Angry Brigade: A History of Britain's First Urban Guerrilla Group* (London: Gollancz, 1975).

Carstensen-Egwuon, I. and Holly, W., 'Integration, Post-Holocaust Identities and No-go Areas: Public Discourse and the Everyday Experience of Exclusion in a German Region', in Armbruster, H. and Meinhof, U. H., *Negotiating Multicultural Europe: Borders, Networks, Neighbourhoods* (Houndmills: Palgrave Macmillan, 2011), pp. 94–118.

Casarini, N. and Musu, C. (eds), *European Foreign Policy in an Evolving International System: The Road towards Convergence* (Houndmills: Palgrave Macmillan, 2007).

Cassarino, J-P., 'Informalising Readmission Agreements in the EU Neighbourhood', *The International Spectator*, 42/2 (June 2007), pp. 179–96.

Castiglione, D., 'Political Identity in a Community of Strangers', in Checkel, J. T. and Katzenstein, P. J. (eds), *European Identity* (Cambridge: Cambridge University Press, 2009), pp. 29–51.

Ceadel, M., *Thinking about Peace and War* (Oxford: Oxford University Press, 1987).

Cerutti, F., 'Why Political Identity and Legitimacy Matter in the European Union', in Cerutti, F. and Lucarelli, S. (eds), *The Search for a European Identity: Values, Policies and Legitimacy of the European Union* (London: Routledge, 2008), pp. 3–22.

Cerutti, F. and Lucarelli, S. (eds), *The Search for a European identity: Values, Policies and Legitimacy of the European Union* (London: Routledge, 2008).

Cesari, J., 'Global Multiculturalism: The Challenge of Heterogeneity', *Alternatives: Global, Local, Political*, 27/1 (special supplement), pp. 5–19.

Cesari, J. and McLoughlin, S. (eds), *European Muslims and the Secular State* (Aldershot: Ashgate, 2005).

Chabal, P. and Daloz, J-P., *Culture Troubles: Politics and the Interpretation of Meaning* (London: Hurst, 2006).

Chandler, D., *From Kosovo to Kabul and Beyond: Human Rights and International Intervention* (London: Pluto, 2005).

Checkel, J. T. and Katzenstein, P. J. (eds), *European Identity* (Cambridge: Cambridge University Press, 2009).

Cheneval, F. and Schimmelfennig, F., 'The Case for Demoicracy in the European Union', *Journal of Common Market Studies*, 51/2 (2013), pp. 334–50.

Chong, A. and Valenčič, J. (eds), '*The Image, the State and International Relations: Conference Proceedings*', EFPU Working Paper No 2001/2 (London: London School of Economics and Political Science, 2001).

Clark, I., *Globalization and International Relations Theory* (Oxford: Oxford University Press, 1999).

Clogg, R., *Modern Greece: A Short History* (2nd edn, Oxford: Oxford University Press, 1992).

Cobban, A., *A History of Modern France. Volume III: 1871–1962* (Harmondsworth: Penguin, 1965).

Cohen, B. C., *The Public's Impact on Foreign Policy* (Boston: Little Brown, 1973).

Cohen, R. (ed.), *Cambridge Survey of World Migration* (Cambridge: Cambridge University Press, 1995).

Cohen, R. C., *Negotiating across Cultures: International Communication in an Interdependent World* (Washington, DC: United States Institute of Peace Press, 1997).

Coker, C., *War in an Age of Risk* (Cambridge: Polity, 2009).

Colley, L., *Britons: Forging the Nation, 1707–1837* (London: BCA by arrangement with Yale University Press, 1992).

Coolsaet, R. (ed.), *Jihadi Terrorism and the Radicalisation Challenge: European and American Experiences* (2nd edn, Aldershot: Ashgate, 2011).

Coolsaet, R. and de Swielande, T. S., *Belgium and Counterterrorism Policy in the Jihadi Era (1986–2007)*, Egmont Paper 15 (Brussels: Royal Institute for International Relations, 2007).

Cooper, R., *The Breaking of Nations: Order and Chaos in the Twenty-First Century* (London: Atlantic Books, 2003).

Coppetiers, B., 'Political Loyalty and Military Disobedience: Militarism, Pacifism, Realism and Just-war Theory Compared', in Waller, M. and Linklater, A. (eds), *Political Loyalty and the Nation-State* (London: Routledge, 2003), pp. 74–88.

Coppi, A. and Spreafico, A., 'The Long Path from Recognition to Representation of Muslims in Italy', *The International Spectator*, 43/3 (2008), pp. 101–15.

Coticchia, F. and Giacomello, G., 'All Together Now! Military Operations Abroad as "Bipartisan" Instrument of Italian Foreign Policy', in Giacomello, G. and Verbeek, B. (eds), *Italy's Foreign Policy in the Twenty-First Century: The New Assertiveness of an Aspiring Middle Power* (Plymouth: Lexington, 2011), pp. 135–54.

Craig, P. and de Búrca, G., *EU Law: Text, Cases and Materials* (5th edn, Oxford: Oxford University Press, 2011).

Curtis, M., *Web of Deceit: Britain's Real Role in the World* (London: Vintage, 2003).

Dancygier, R. M., *Immigration and Conflict in Europe* (Cambridge: Cambridge University Press, 2010).

Dandeker, C. and Mason, D., 'Diversifying the Uniform? The Participation of Minority Ethnic Personnel in the British Armed Services', *Armed Forces and Society*, 29/4 (2003), pp. 481–507.

Darwin, J., *After Tamerlane: The Rise and Fall of Global Empires 1400–2000* (London: Penguin Books, 2008).

Dassù, M., *Mondo privato e altre storie* (Torino: Bollati Boringhieri, 2009).

Davidson, J. W., 'Italy at War: Explaining the Italian Contribution to the Kosovo war (1999)', in Giacomello, G. and Verbeek, B. (eds), *Italy's Foreign Policy in the Twenty-First Century: The New Assertiveness of an Aspiring Middle Power* (Plymouth: Lexington Books, 2011), pp. 155–73.

Debord, G., *La Société du Spectacle* (Paris: Buchet-Chastel, 1967).

Dehousse, R., *La Fin de l'Europe* (Paris: Flammarion, 2005).

Doe, N. and Sandberg, R., 'The Changing Criminal Law on Religion', *Law and Justice*, vol. 161 (2008), pp. 88–97.

Donelan, M., *Elements of International Political Theory* (Oxford: The Clarendon Press, 1990).

Dorman, A. M., *Blair's Successful War: British Military Intervention in Sierra Leone* (Aldershot: Ashgate, 2009).

Dunn, J., *Setting the People Free: The Story of Democracy* (London: Atlantic Books, 2005).

Dyson, K., *The State Tradition in Western Europe* (Oxford: Martin Robertson, 1980).

Eberwein, W-D. and Kaiser, K. (eds), *Germany's New Foreign Policy: Decision-making in an Interdependent World* (Houndmills: Palgrave, 2001).

Economides, S., 'The Europeanisation of Greek foreign policy', *West European Politics*, 28/2 (2005), pp. 471–91.

Edwards, G. and Meyer, C. O. (eds), *Journal of Common Market Studies*, 46/1, Special Issue (2008), pp. 1–218.

Egan, M., Nugent, N., and Paterson, W. E., *Research Agendas in EU Studies: Stalking the Elephant* (Houndmills: Palgrave Macmillan, 2010).

Eilstrup-Sangiovanni, M., 'The Future of the CSDP' (forthcoming).

Einaudi, J-L., *Octobre à Paris. Un massacre à Paris* (Paris: Fayard, 2001).

Einaudi, L., *Le politiche dell'immigrazione in Italia dall'Unità a oggi* (Roma-Bari: Editori Laterza, 2007).

Ekengren, M., 'National Foreign Policy Coordination: The Swedish EU Presidency', in Carlsnaes, W., Sjursen, H., and White, B. (eds), *Contemporary European Foreign Policy* (London: Sage, 2004), pp. 211–26.

Elliott, J. H., *Imperial Spain, 1469–1716* (London: Edward Arnold, 1963).

Elliott, J. H., *Europe Divided 1559–1598* (London: Collins, The Fontana History of Europe, 1968).

Emerson, M., 'Just Good Friends? The European Union's Multiple Neighbourhood Policies', *The International Spectator*, 46/4 (2011), pp. 45–62.

Eriksen, E. O., 'An Emerging European Public Sphere', *European Journal of Social Theory*, 8/3 (2005), pp. 341–63.

European Foreign Policy Scorecard 2010 (London: European Council of Foreign Relations, 2011).

Evans, M., *Algeria: France's Undeclared War* (Oxford: Oxford University Press, 2012).

Evans, R., *The Third Reich in Power* (London: Allen Lane, 2005).

Evans, R., *The Third Reich at War* (London: Allen Lane, 2008).

Everts, P. and Isernia, P. (eds), *Public Opinion and the International Use of Force* (London: Routledge, 2001).

Everts, P., *Democracy and Military Force* (Houndmills: Palgrave Macmillan, 2002).

Fahey, E., 'Challenging EU–US PNR and SWIFT Law before the Court of Justice of the European Union', in Pawlak, P. (ed.), *The EU–US Security and Justice Agenda in Action*, Chaillot Paper 127 (European Union Institute for Security Studies, Paris, December 2011), pp. 55–66.

Faist, T., 'How to Define a Foreigner? The Symbolic Politics of Immigration in German Partisan Discourse, 1978–1992', in Baldwin-Edwards, M. and Schain, M. A. (eds), *The Politics of Immigration in Western Europe* (Ilford: Frank Cass, 1994), pp. 50–71.

Faist, T. and Ette, A. (eds), *The Europeanization of National Policies and Politics of Immigration: Between Autonomy and the European Union* (Houndmills: Palgrave Macmillan, 2007).

Fallaci, O., *La rabbia e L'orgoglio* (Milan: Rizzoli, 2001).

Faurby, I., 'Foreign Policy-Making in Scandinavia', in Paterson, W. and Wallace, W. (eds), *Foreign Policy-making in Western Europe: A Comparative Approach* (London: Saxon House, 1978), pp. 106–34.

Favell, A., 'Immigration, Migration, and Free Movement', in Checkel, J. T. and Katzenstein, P. J. (eds), *European Identity* (Cambridge: Cambridge University Press, 2009), pp. 176–89.

Fearon, J. and Wendt, A., 'Rationalism v. Constructivism: A Skeptical View', in Carlsnaes, W., Risse, T., and Simmons, B. A. (eds), *Handbook of International Relations* (London: Sage, 2005), pp. 52–72.

Ferraris, L. (ed.), *Manuale della politica estera italiana, 1947–1993* (Roma-Bari: Editori Laterza, 1996).

Finkelstein, M. and Dent-Brown, K. (eds), *Psychosocial Stress in Immigrants and in Members of Minority Groups as a Factor of Terrorist Behavior* (Kiryat Shimona, Israel: IOS Press, NATO Science for Peace and Security Series, 2008).

Finnemore, M., *National Interests in International Society* (Ithaca, NY: Cornell University Press, 1996).

Flood, C., Hutchings, S., Miazhevich, G., and Nickels, H. (eds), *Political and Cultural Representations of Muslims: Islam in the Plural* (Leiden: Brill, 2012).

Forsyth, M., *Unions of States: The Theory and Practice of Confederation* (New York: Holmes & Meier, 1981).

Freedman, L., Hill, C., Roberts, A., Vincent, R. J., Wilkinson, P., and Windsor, P., *Terrorism and International Order* (London: Routledge and Kegan Paul for the Royal Institute of International Affairs, 1986).

Freedman, L., *Superterrorism: Policy Responses* (Oxford: Blackwell, 2002).

Freedman, L., *The Official History of the Falklands Campaign: Volume I. The Origins of the Falklands War* (London: Routledge, 2005).

Frisch, H., *Israel's Security and its Arab Citizens* (Cambridge: Cambridge University Press, 2011).

Gabaccia, D. R., *Italy's Many Diasporas* (London: UCL Press, 2000).

Gamble, A., 'The Meaning of the Third Way', in Anthony Seldon (ed.), *The Blair Effect 2001–5* (Cambridge: Cambridge University Press, 2005), pp. 430–8.

Gardiner, J., *The Blitz: The British under Attack* (London: Harper Press, 2010).

Gartner, S. S. and Segura, G. M., 'War, Casualties and Public Opinion', *Journal of Conflict Resolution*, 42/3 (1998), pp. 278–300.

Garton Ash, T., *Free World: Why a Crisis of the West Reveals the Opportunity of Our Time* (London: Penguin, 2004).

Geddes, A., *The Politics of Migration and Immigration in Europe* (London: Sage, 2003).

Geddes, A., *Immigration and European Integration: Beyond Fortress Europe* (2nd edn, Manchester: Manchester University Press, 2008).

Gegout, C., *European Foreign and Security Policy: States, Power, Institutions and American Hegemony* (Toronto: University of Toronto Press, 2010).

Gegout, C., *Why Europe Intervenes in Africa* (2013, forthcoming).

Giacomello, G. and Verbeek, B. (eds), *Italy's Foreign Policy in the Twenty-First Century: The New Assertiveness of an Aspiring Middle Power* (Plymouth: Lexington, 2011).

Giegerich, B. and Nicoll, A. (eds), *European Military Capabilities: Building Armed Forces for Modern Operations* (London: International Institute for Strategic Studies, 2008).

Gil, M. M., 'Spain's Foreign Policy in Africa: Time to Reassess the Vision', *FRIDE Policy Brief*, 59 (Madrid, November 2010).

Gildea, R., 'Myth, Memory and Policy in France Since 1945', in Müller, J-W. (ed.), *Memory and Power in Post-War Europe: Studies in the Presence of the Past* (Cambridge: Cambridge University Press, 2002), pp. 59–75.

Ginsberg, R. H., *Foreign Policy Actions and the European Community: The Politics of Scale* (Boulder: Lynne Reinner, 1989).

Ginsberg, R. H., *The European Union in International Politics: Baptism by Fire* (Lanham, MD: Rowman & Littlefield, 2001).

Ginsberg, R. H. and Penska, S. E., *The European Union in Global Security: The Politics of Impact* (Houndmills: Palgrave Macmillan, 2012).

Ginsborg, P., *Italy and its Discontents, 1980–2001* (London: Allen Lane, 2001).

Glaurdić, J., *The Hour of Europe: Western Powers and the Breakup of Yugoslavia* (New Haven: Yale University Press, 2011).

Golson, R. J., 'The Legacy of World War II in France: Mapping the Discourses of Memory', in Lebow, R. N., Kansteiner, W., and Fogu, C. (eds), *The Politics of Memory in Postwar Europe* (Durham, NC: Duke University Press, 2006), pp. 73–101.

Gordon, R., *The Holocaust in Italian Culture, 1944–2010* (Stanford, CA: Stanford University Press, 2012).

Green, S., 'Immigration and Integration Policy: Between Incrementalism and Non-decisions', in Green, S. and Paterson, W. E. (eds), *Governance in Contemporary Germany: The Semisovereign State Revisited* (Cambridge: Cambridge University Press, 2005), pp. 190–211.

Green, S., and Paterson, W. E. (eds), *Governance in Contemporary Germany: The Semisovereign State Revisited* (Cambridge: Cambridge University Press, 2005).

Grigoriadis, I. N., 'Seeking Opportunities in Crisis Times: Greek Foreign Policy in the Middle East', *Eliamep Thesis* (Athens: Eliamep, March 2012).

Gross, E., *The Europeanization of National Foreign Policy: Continuity and Change in European Crisis Management* (Houndmills: Palgrave Macmillan, 2009).

Grundmann, R., Smith, D., and Wright, S., 'National Elites and Transnational Discourses in the Balkan War: A Comparison between the French, German and British Establishment Press', *European Journal of Communication*, 15/3 (2000), pp. 299–320.

Guarneri, A., 'Muslim Diversity in Italy: An Unacknowledged Reality', *The International Spectator*, 43/3 (2008), pp. 117–35.

Guelke, A., 'The United States, Irish Americans and the Northern Ireland Peace Process', *International Affairs*, 72/3 (1996), pp. 521–36.

Guibernau, M. and Rex, J. (eds), *The Ethnicity Reader: Nationalism, Multiculturalism and Migration* (Cambridge: Polity Press, 1997).

Habermas, J., *The Theory of Communicative Action* (London: Heinemann, 1984).

Habermas, J., *The Structural Transformation of the Public Sphere: An Inquiry into a Category of Bourgeois Society*, trans. Thomas Burger (Cambridge, MA: MIT Press, 1989).

Habermas, J., *The Inclusion of the Other: Studies in Political Theory* (Cambridge, MA: The MIT Press, 1998).

Habermas, J., 'Why Europe Needs a Constitution?', *New Left Review*, 11 (September–October, 2001), pp. 5–26.

Halliday, F., *Two Hours that Shook the World: September 11, 2001: Causes and Consequences* (London: Saqi Books, 2002).

Halliday, F., *The Middle East in International Relations: Power, Politics and Ideology* (Cambridge: Cambridge University Press, 2005).

Hammond, L., 'The Absent but Active Constituency: The Role of the Somaliland UK Community in Election Politics', in Lyons, T. and Mandaville, P. (eds), *Politics from Afar: Transnational Diasporas and Networks* (London: Hurst, 2012), pp. 157–80.

Hannay, D., *Cyprus: The Search for a Solution* (London: I. B. Tauris, 2007).

Hansen, L., 'Sustaining Sovereignty: The Danish Approach to Europe', in Hansen, L. and Wæver, O. (eds), *European Integration and National Identity: The Challenge of the Nordic States* (London: Routledge, 2002), pp. 50–87.

Hansen, L. and Wæver, O. (eds), *European Integration and National Identity: The Challenge of the Nordic States* (London: Routledge, 2002).

Hargreaves, A. G., *Multi-Ethnic France: Immigration, Politics, Culture and Society* (2nd edn, London: Routledge, 2007).

Hartmann, F. H., *The Relations of Nations* (6th edn, New York: Macmillan, 1983).

Hartmann, J., 'Organized Interests and Foreign Policy', in Eberwein, W-D. and Kaiser, K. (eds), *Germany's New Foreign Policy: Decision-making in an Interdependent World* (Houndmills: Palgrave, 2001), pp. 264–78.

Harvey, M., 'Forged in the Crucible of Austerity', *The World Today*, 67/4 (2011), pp. 15–17.

Haslam, J., *No Virtue like Necessity: Realist thought in International Relations since Machiavelli* (New Haven: Yale University Press, 2001).

Heater, D., *Citizenship: The Civic Ideal in World History, Politics and Education* (3rd edn, Manchester: Manchester University Press, 2004).

Hedetoft, U., *Multiculturalism in Denmark and Sweden*, DIIS Brief (Copenhagen: Danish Institute for International Studies, December 2006).

Hedetoft, U., 'Denmark versus Multiculturalism', in Vertovec, S. and Wessendorf, S. (eds), *The Multiculturalism Backlash: European Discourses, Policies and Practices* (London: Routledge, 2010), pp. 111–29.

Heisbourg, F. and Marret, J-L., *Le terrorisme en France aujourd'hui* (Sainte-Marguerite-sur-Mer: Éditions des Équateurs, 2006).

Heitmeyer, W., 'Für turkische Jurgendliche in Deutschland spielt der Islam eine wichtige Rolle', *Die Zeit*, Nr. 35, 23 August 1996.

Held, D., *Democracy and Global Order: From the Modern State to Cosmopolitan Governance* (Cambridge: Polity, 1995).

Hellema, D., 'The Netherlands', in Hocking, B. and Spence, D. (eds), *Foreign Ministries in the European Union: Integrating Diplomats* (revd. edn, Houndmills: Palgrave Macmillan, 2005), pp. 177–90.

Herf, J., 'The Emergence and Legacies of Divided Memory: Germany and the Holocaust since 1945', in Müller, J-W. (ed.), *Memory and Power in Post-war Europe: Studies in the Presence of the Past* (Cambridge: Cambridge University Press, 2002), pp. 184–205.

Hewitt, V. and Wickham-Jones, M., 'New Labour and the Politics of Kashmir', in R. Little and M. Wickham-Jones (eds.), *New Labour's Foreign Policy: A New Moral Crusade* (Manchester: Manchester University Press, 2000), pp. 201–17.

Heyward, M., 'What Constitutes Europe? Religion, Law and Identity in the Draft Constitution for the European Union', *Hanse Law Review*, Vol. 1/2 (2005), pp. 227–35.

Hill, C., 'Britain's Elusive role in World Politics', *British Journal of International Studies*, 5/3 (October 1979), pp. 248–59.

Hill, C. (ed.), *National Foreign Policies and European Political Cooperation* (London: Allen & Unwin for the Royal Institute of International Affairs, 1983).

Hill, C., 'The Political Dilemmas for Western Governments', in Freedman, L. et al., *Terrorism and International Order* (London: Routledge and Kegan Paul for the Royal Institute of International Affairs, 1986), pp. 77–100.

Hill, C., 'European Preoccupations with Terrorism', in Pijpers, A., Regelsberger, E., and Wessels, W. (eds), *European Political Cooperation in the 1980s: A Common Foreign Policy for Western Europe?* (Dordrecht: Martinus Nijhoff, 1988), pp. 166–93.

Hill, C. (ed.), *The Actors in Europe's Foreign Policy* (London: Routledge, 1996).

Hill, C., 'The EU's Capacity for Conflict Prevention', *European Foreign Affairs Review*, 6/3 (2001), pp. 315–33.

Hill, C., 'Foreign Policy', in Seldon, A. (ed.), *The Blair Effect: The Blair Government 1997–2001* (London: Little Brown, 2001), pp. 331–53.

Hill, C., *The Changing Politics of Foreign Policy* (Houndmills: Palgrave Macmillan, 2003).

Hill, C., 'Putting the World to Rights: The Foreign Policy Mission of Tony Blair', in Seldon, A. and Kavanagh, D. (eds), *The Blair Effect, 2001–5* (Cambridge: Cambridge University Press, 2005), pp. 384–409.

Hill, C., 'Bringing War Home: Foreign Policy-making in Multicultural Societies', *International Relations*, 21/3 (2007), pp. 259–83.

Hill, C., 'The European Union and Soft Power', in Parmar, I. and Cox, M. (eds), *Soft Power and Hegemony in US Foreign Affairs: Theoretical, Historical and Contemporary Perspectives* (Abingdon, Routledge, 2010), pp. 182–98.

Hill, C. and Andreatta, F., 'Struggling to Change: The Italian State and the New Order', in Niblett, R. and Wallace, W. (eds), *Rethinking European Order: West European Responses, 1989–1997* (Basingstoke: Palgrave, 2001), pp. 242–67.

Hill, C. and Smith, K. E. (eds), *European Foreign Policy: Key Documents* (London: Routledge, in association with the Secretariat of the European Parliament, 2000).

Hill, C. and Smith, M. (eds), *International Relations and the European Union* (2nd edn, Oxford: Oxford University Press, 2011).

Hippel, K. von (ed.), *Europe Confronts Terrorism* (Houndmills: Palgrave, 2005).

Hiscott, A., '"Parallel Societies"—A Neologism Gone Bad' (Prague: Multicultural Center, July 2005), <www.migration.cz> accessed 14 August 2012.

Hix, S., *The Political System of the European Union* (2nd edn, Houndmills: Palgrave Macmillan, 2005).

Hobolt, S. B. and Brouard, S., 'Contesting the European Union? Why the Dutch and the French rejected the European Constitution', *Political Research Quarterly*, 64/2 (2011), pp. 309–22.

Hockenos, P., *Homeland Calling: Exile Patriotism and the Balkan Wars* (Ithaca, New York: Cornell University Press, 2003).

Hocking, B. (ed.), *Foreign Relations and Federal States* (London: Leicester University Press, 1993).

Hocking, B. and Spence, D. (eds), *Foreign Ministries in the European Union: Integrating Diplomats* (revd. edn, Houndmills: Palgrave Macmillan, 2005).

Hoffman, B., *Inside Terrorism* (New York: Columbia University Press, 2006).

Horne, A., *A Savage War of Peace: Algeria 1954–1962* (3rd edn, New York: New York Review of Books, 2006).

House, J. and MacMaster, N., *Paris 1961: Algerians, State Terror and Memory* (Oxford: Oxford University Press, 2006).

House, J. and Macmaster, N., 'Time to Move On: A Reply to Jean-Paul Brunet', *The Historical Journal*, 51/1 (2008), pp. 205–14.

Howorth, J., 'The EU's Security and Defence Policy: Towards a Strategic Approach', in Hill, C. and Smith, M. (eds), *International Relations and the European Union* (2nd edn, Oxford: Oxford University Press, 2011), pp. 197–225.

Hudson, V. M., *Foreign Policy Analysis: Classic and Contemporary Theory* (Lanham, MD: Rowman & Littlefield, 2007).

Human Rights Watch, 'Setting an Example? Counter-terrorism Measures in Spain', 17/1, D (January 2005).

Huntington, S. P., 'The Clash of Civilisations?', *Foreign Affairs*, 72/3 (Summer 1993), pp. 22–49.

Huntington, S. P., *The Clash of Civilizations and the Remaking of World Order* (New York: Simon & Schuster, 1996).

Huntington, S. P., *Who Are We? America's Great Debate* (London: Simon & Schuster, 2004).

Hussain, A. and Ishaq, M., 'British Pakistani Muslims' Perceptions of the Armed Forces', *Armed Forces and Society*, 28/4 (2002), pp. 601–18.

Huysmans, J., *The Politics of Insecurity: Fear, Migration and Asylum in the EU* (Abingdon: Routledge, 2006).

Huysman, J. and Buonfino, A., 'Politics of Exception and Unease: Immigration, Asylum and Terrorism in the Parliamentary Debates in the UK', *Political Studies*, 56/4 (2008), pp. 766–88.

Hvidt, N. and Mouritzen, H. (eds), *Danish Foreign Policy Yearbook 2007* (Copenhagen: Danish Institute for International Studies, 2007).

Hvidt, N. and Mouritzen, H. (eds), *Danish Foreign Policy Yearbook 2012* (Copenhagen: Danish Institute for International Studies, 2012).

Institut Kurd de Paris, 'The Kurdish Diaspora', <www.institutkurde.org/en/kurdorama> accessed 23 July 2012.

Isernia, P., 'Italian Public Opinion and the International Use of Force', in Everts, P. and Isernia, P. (eds), *Public Opinion and the International Use of Force* (London: Routledge, 2001), pp. 86–115.

Ishaq, M. and Hussain, A., 'British Ethnic Minority Communities and the Armed Forces', *Personnel Review*, 31, 5/6 (2002), pp. 722–39.

Jackson, R., *Writing the War on Terrorism: Language, Politics and Counter-Terrorism* (Manchester: Manchester University Press, 2005).

Jans, M. T. and Stouthuysen, P., 'Federal Regions and External Relations: The Belgian Case', *International Spectator*, 42/2 (2007), pp. 209–20.

Jeffrey, C., 'Federalism: The New Territorialism', in Green, S. and Paterson, W. E. (eds), *Governance in Contemporary Germany: The Semisovereign State Revisited* (Cambridge: Cambridge University Press, 2005), pp. 78–93.

Jensen, T. G., '"Making Room": Encompassing Diversity in Denmark', in Silj, A. (ed.), *European Multiculturalism Revisited* (London: Zed Books, 2010), pp. 181–213.

Jervis, R., *Perception and Misperception in International Politics* (Princeton, NJ: Princeton University Press, 1976).

Jessop, B., *State Power* (Cambridge: Polity, 2007).

Joffé, G., *Islamist Radicalization in North Africa: Politics and Process* (Abingdon: Routledge, 2011).

Johnstone, D., *Politics of Euromissiles: Europe's Role in America's World* (London: Verso, 1984).

Joll, J., *The Second International: 1889–1914* (London: Weidenfeld and Nicolson, 1955).

Jones, P., 'The Ethics of International Society', in Bell, D. (ed.), *Ethics and World Politics* (Oxford: Oxford University Press, 2010), pp. 111–29.

Joppke, C., *Veil: Mirror of Identity* (Cambridge: Polity, 2009).

Josselin, D. and Wallace, W. (eds), *Non-State Actors in World Politics* (Houndmills: Palgrave Macmillan, 2001).

Judt, T., 'The Past is Another Country: Myth and Memory in Post-war Europe', in Müller, J-W. (ed.), *Memory and Power in Post-War Europe: Studies in the Presence of the Past* (Cambridge: Cambridge University Press, 2002), pp. 157–83.

Just, A. and Anderson, C. J., 'Immigrants, Citizenship and Political Action', *British Journal of Political Science*, 42/3 (2012), pp. 481–509.

Kagan, R., *Of Paradise and Power: America and Europe in the New World Order* (London: Atlantic, 2003).

Kahler, M., *Decolonization in Britain and France: The Domestic Consequences of International Relations* (Princeton, NJ: Princeton University Press, 1984).

Kaldor, M., *New and Old Wars: Organized Violence in a Globalized Era* (Cambridge: Polity Press, 1999).

Kampfner, J., *Blair's Wars* (London: The Free Press, 2003).

Katzenstein, P. J., *Policy and Politics in Germany: The Growth of a Semisovereign State* (Philadelphia: Temple University Press, 1987).

Katzenstein, P. J. (ed.), *The Culture of National Security: Norms and Identity in World Politics* (New York: Columbia University Press, 1996).

Katzenstein, P. J. (ed.), *Tamed Power: Germany in Europe* (Ithaca, NY: Cornell University Press, 1997).

Katzenstein, P. J., 'Conclusion: Semi-sovereignty in United Germany', Green, S. and Paterson, W. E. (eds), *Governance in Contemporary Germany: The Semisovereign State Revisited* (Cambridge: Cambridge University Press, 2005), pp. 283–306.

Kavanagh, D. and Butler, D., *The British General Election of 2005* (Houndmills: Palgrave Macmillan, 2005).

Kavanagh, D. and Cowley, P., *The British General Election of 2010* (Houndmills: Palgrave Macmillan, 2010).

Kaya, A., *Islam, Migration and Integration: The Age of Securitization* (Houndmills: Palgrave Macmillan, 2009).

Keating, M., *Federalism and the Balance of Power in European States* (Paris: OECD SIGMA Programme, 2006).

Kelly, P. (ed.), *Multiculturalism Reconsidered* (Cambridge: Polity, 2002).

Kennedy, P., 'Spain', in Manners, I. and Whitman, R. (eds), *The Foreign Policies of European Union Member States* (Manchester: Manchester University Press, 2000), pp. 105–27.

Keohane, R. O. and Nye, J. S. (eds), *Transnational Relations and World Politics* (Cambridge MA: Harvard University Press, 1973).

Kepel, G., *Allah in the West: Islamic Movements in America and Europe* (Cambridge: Polity Press, 1997).

Kepel, G., 'Europe's answer to Londonistan' [online article], *Opendemocracy*, 24 August 2005, <www.opendemocracy.net> accessed 18 December 2012.

Kepel, G., with the collaboration of Arslan, L. and Zouheir, S., *Banlieue de la République: Résumé* (Paris: Institut Montaigne, October 2011), p. 2, <http://www.institutmontaigne.org/medias/documents/banlieue_republique_resume_institut_montaigne.pdf> accessed 6 April 2012.

Keukeleire, S. and MacNaughtan, J., *The Foreign Policy of the European Union* (Houndmills: Palgrave Macmillan, 2008).

Kiras, J. D., 'Terrorism and Globalization', in Baylis, J., Smith, S., and Owens, P. (eds), *The Globalization of World Politics* (4th edn, Oxford: Oxford University Press, 2008), pp. 370–85.

Kitroeff, A., *War-time Jews: The Case of Athens* (Athens: Eliamep, 1995).

Kivisto, P. and Faist, T., *Beyond a Border: The Causes and Consequences of Contemporary Immigration* (Los Angeles: Pine Forge Press, 2010).

Knodt, M., 'External Representation of German Länder Interests', in Eberwein, W-D. and Kaiser, K. (eds), *Germany's New Foreign Policy: Decision-making in an Interdependent World* (Houndmills: Palgrave, 2001), pp. 173–88.

Koliopoulos, J. S. and Veremis, T. M., *Modern Greece: A History since 1821* (Chichester: Wiley-Blackwell, 2010).

Kreisi, H. and Trechsel, A. H., *The Politics of Switzerland: Continuity and Change in a Consensus Democracy* (Cambridge: Cambridge University Press, 2008).

Kull, S. and Destler, I. M., *Misreading the Public: The Myth of a New Isolationism*, (Washington DC: Brookings Institution, 1999).

Kymlicka, W., *Liberalism, Community and Culture* (Oxford: The Clarendon Press, 1989).

Kymlicka, W., *Politics in the Vernacular: Nationalism, Multiculturalism and Citizenship* (Oxford: Oxford University Press, 2001).

Kymlicka, W., *Multicultural Odysseys: Navigating the New International Politics of Diversity* (Oxford: Oxford University Press, 2007).

Kymlicka, W., 'The Evolving Basis of European Norms of Minority Rights: Rights to Culture, Participation and Autonomy', in Weller, M., Blacklock, D., and Nobbs, K. (eds), *The Protection of Minorities in the Wider Europe* (Houndmills: Palgrave Macmillan, 2008), pp. 11–41.

Labat, S., 'Les binationaux franco-algériens. Un nouveau rapport entre nationalité et territorialité', *Critique Internationale*, 56 (Juillet–Septembre 2012).

Laborde, C., *Critical Republicanism: The Hijab Controversy and Political Philosophy* (Oxford: Oxford University Press, 2008).

Laden, A. S., and Owen, D. (eds), *Multiculturalism and Political Theory* (Cambridge: Cambridge University Press, 2007).

Lægaard, S., 'The Cartoon Controversy: Offence, Identity, Oppression?', *Political Studies*, 55/3 (2007), pp. 481–98.

Lagrange, H., *Le déni des cultures* (Paris: Seuil, 2010).

Lanz, S., 'The German Sonderweg: Multiculturalism as "Racism with a Distance"', in Silj, A. (ed.), *European Multiculturalism Revisited* (London: Zed Books, 2010), pp. 105–46.

Larsen, H., 'The Cartoons Crisis in Danish Foreign Policy: A New Balance between the EU and the US?', Hvidt, N. and Mouritzen, H. (eds), *Danish Foreign Policy Yearbook 2007* (Copenhagen: Danish Institute for International Studies, 2007), pp. 51–86.

Larsen, H., 'Danish Foreign Policy and the Balance between the EU and the US: The Choice between Brussels and Washington after 2001', *Cooperation and Conflict*, 44/2 (2009), pp. 209–30.

Larsen, H., 'Denmark: A Committed Member—with Opt-outs!', in Wong, R. and Hill, C. (eds), *National and European Foreign Policies: Towards Europeanization* (London: Routledge, 2011), pp. 93–110.

Laurence, J., 'Why Is It So Hard to Say "Sorry" in French?', *Foreign Policy*, 5 July 2012, <http://www.foreignpolicy.com/articles/2012/07/05/why_is_it_so_hard_to_say_sorry_in_french> accessed 29 July 2012.

Laurence, J. and Vaisse, J. (eds), *Integrating Islam: Political and Religious Challenges in Contemporary France* (Washington, DC: The Brookings Institution, 2006).

Lavenex, S., *The Europeanisation of Refugee Policies: Between Human Rights and Internal Security* (Aldershot: Ashgate, 2001).

Layton-Henry, Z. (ed.), *The Political Rights of Migrant Workers in Western Europe* (London: Sage, 1990).

Lebow, R. N., Kansteiner, W., and Fogu, C. (eds), *The Politics of Memory in Postwar Europe* (Durham, NC: Duke University Press, 2006).

Lechner, F. J., *The Netherlands: Globalization and National Identity* (London: Routledge, 2008).

Leiken, R. S., *Europe's Angry Muslims: The Revolt of the Second Generation* (Oxford: Oxford University Press, 2012).

Lemieux, F. (ed.), *International Police Cooperation: Emerging Issues, Theory and Practice* (Portland: Willan, 2010).

Leonardy, U., 'Federation and *Länder* in German Foreign Relations: Power-sharing in Treaty-making and European Affairs', in Hocking, B. (ed.), *Foreign Relations and Federal States* (London: Leicester University Press, 1993), pp. 236–51.

Levi, M., *Consent, Dissent and Patriotism* (Cambridge: Cambridge University Press, 1997).

Liang, C. S. (ed.), *Europe for the Europeans: The Foreign and Security Policy of the Populist Radical Right* (Aldershot: Ashgate, 2007).

Linklater, A., *The Transformation of Political Community: Ethical Foundations of the Post-Westphalian Era* (Cambridge: Polity Press, 1998).

Lord, C., 'Legitimate and Democratic? The EU's International Role', in Hill, C. and Smith, M. (eds), *International Relations and the European Union* (2nd edn, Oxford: Oxford University Press, 2011) pp. 128–48.

Lucarelli, S., 'European Political Identity, Foreign Policy and the Others' Image: An Underexplored Relationship', in Cerutti, F. and Lucarelli, S. (eds), *The Search for a European Identity: Values, Policies and Legitimacy of the European Union* (London: Routledge, 2008), pp. 23–37.

Lupton, R. and Power, A., *Minority Ethnic Groups in Britain* (London: London School of Economics and Political Science, November 2004).

Lyons, T. and Mandaville, P. (eds), *Politics from Afar: Transnational Diasporas and Networks* (London: Hurst, 2012).

McCourt, D. M., 'Role-playing and Identity Affirmation in International Politics: Britain's Reinvasion of the Falklands, 1982', *Review of International Studies*, 37/4 (2011), pp. 1599–621.

McLaren, L., 'Immigration and Trust in Politics in Britain', in *British Journal of Political Science*, 42/1 (2012), pp. 163–86.

MacMaster, N., 'Islamophobia in France and the "Algerian Problem"', in Qureshi, E. and Sells, M. A. (eds), *The New Crusades: Constructing the Muslim Enemy* (New York: Columbia University Press, 2003), pp. 288–313.

McNamara, R. S., *In Retrospect: The Tragedy and Lessons of Vietnam* (New York: Random House, 1996).

Maher, S., *Ties that Bind: How the Story of British Muslim Soldiers Can Forge a National Identity* (London: Policy Exchange, 2011), pp. 71–6, available online, <http://www.policyexchange.org.uk/publications/category/item/ties-that-bind-how-the-story-of-britain-s-muslim-soldiers-can-forge-a-national-identity> accessed 31 March 2013.

Majone, G., 'The Rise of the Regulatory State in Europe', *West European Politics* 17/3 (1994), pp. 77–101.

Mandler, P., *The English National Character: The History of an Idea from Edmund Burke to Tony Blair* (New Haven: Yale University Press, 2006).

Manners, I., 'Normative Power Europe: A Contradiction in Terms?', *Journal of Common Market Studies*, 40/2 (2002), pp. 235–58.

Manners, I. and Whitman, R. (eds), *The Foreign Policies of European Union Member States* (Manchester: Manchester University Press, 2000).

Martiniello, M., 'La citoyenneté multiculturelle de l'Union européenne. Une utopie post-nationale', in Telò, M. and Magnette, P. (eds), *Repenser l'Europe* (Brussels: Editions de l'Université de Bruxelles, 1996), pp. 127–38.

Maull, H. W. (ed.), *Germany's Uncertain Power: Foreign Policy of the Berlin Republic* (Houndmills: Palgrave Macmillan, 2006).

Mavrodi, G., 'Ulysses Turning European: The Different Faces of "Europeanization" of Greek Immigration Policy', in Faist, T. and Ette, A. (eds), *The Europeanization of National Policies and Politics of Immigration: Between Autonomy and the European Union* (Houndmills: Palgrave Macmillan, 2007), pp. 157–77.

May, E. R., *'Lessons' of the Past: The Use and Misuse of History in American Foreign Policy* (Oxford: Oxford University Press, 1973).

May, E. R., Rosecrance, R., and Steiner, Z. (eds), *History and Neorealism* (Cambridge: Cambridge University Press, 2010).

Mayall, J. and Economides, S. (eds), *The New Interventionism: United Nations Experience in Cambodia, former Yugoslavia and Somalia* (Cambridge: Cambridge University Press, 1996).

Mearsheimer, J. J., *Why Leaders Lie: The Truth about Lying in International Politics* (New York: Oxford University Press, 2011).

Mearsheimer, J. J. and Walt, S. M., *The Israel Lobby and US Foreign Policy* (London: Penguin Books, 2008).

Measuring Integration—The French Case: Regional Indices of Social and Labour Market Inclusion of Third Country Nationals. Final Report (Paris: Sciences Po—CERI, 2008).

Menke, I. and Langer, P. C. (eds), *Muslim Service Members in Non-Muslim Countries: Experiences of Difference in the Armed Forces in Austria, Germany and The Netherlands, FORUM International* 29 (Strausberg, Germany: Sozialwissenschaftliches Institut der Bundeswehr, 2011).

Mény, Y. with Knapp, A., *Government and Politics in Western Europe: Britain, France, Italy, Germany* (2nd edn, Oxford: Oxford University Press, 1993).

Merton, R. K., *Sociological Ambivalence and Other Essays* (New York: Free Press, 1976).

Michelmann, H. J. (ed.), *Foreign Relations in Federal Countries*, Global Dialogue on Federalism, vol. 5 (Montreal/Kingston: McGill-Queen's University Press, 2009).

Miles, L., 'Developments in the Member States', in Edwards, G. and Wiessala, G. (eds), *Journal of Common Market Studies: The European Union—Annual Review of the EU 1999–2000*, pp. 143–62.

Miles, L., 'Developments in the Member States', in Edwards, G. and Wiessala, G. (eds), *Journal of Common Market Studies: The European Union—Annual Review of the EU 2000–2001*, pp. 139–56.

Miles, L., 'Sweden and Finland', in Manners, I. and Whitman, R. G. (eds), *The Foreign Policies of European Union Member States* (Manchester: Manchester University Press, 2000), pp.181–203.

Mirza, M., Senthilkumaran, A., and Ja'far, Z., *Living Apart Together: British Muslims and the Paradox of Multiculturalism* (London: Policy Exchange, 2007), available online <http://www.policyexchange.org.uk/publications/category/item/living-apart-together-british-muslims-and-the-paradox-of-multiculturalism> accessed 31 March 2013.

Missiroli, A., 'Italy' in Manners, I. and Whitman, R. (eds), *The Foreign Policies of European Union Member States* (Manchester: Manchester University Press, 2000), pp. 87–104.

Mitsilegas, V., Monar, J., and Rees, W., *The European Union and Internal Security: Guardian of the People?* (Houndmills: Palgrave Macmillan, 2003).

Modelski, G., *A Theory of Foreign Policy* (New York: Praeger, 1962).

Modood, T., *Multiculturalism: A Civic Idea* (Cambridge: Polity, 2007).

Modood, T., Triandafyllidou, A., and Zapata-Barrero, R. (eds), *Multiculturalism, Muslims and Citizenship: A European Approach* (London: Routledge, 2006).

Monar, J., 'The Rejection of the EU–US SWIFT Interim Agreement by the European Parliament: A Historic Vote and Its Implications', *European Foreign Affairs Review*, 15/2 (2010), pp. 143–51.

Monar, J., *The External Dimension of The EU's Area of Freedom, Security and Justice: Progress, potential and limitations after the Treaty of Lisbon* (Stockholm: Swedish Institute for European Policy Studies, SIEPS, 2012), <http://www.sieps.se/sites/default/files/Rapport%202012_1_A5.pdf> accessed 16 December 2012.

Moravcsik, A., *The Choice for Europe: Social Purpose and State Power from Messina to Maastricht* (Ithaca, NY: Cornell University Press, 1998).

Morisse-Schilbach, M., *L'Europe et la question algérienne* (Paris: Presses Universitaires de France, 1999).

Mouzelis, N., 'Modes of National Identity in the Context of Globalisation', in Tsoukalis, L. (ed.), *Globalisation and Regionalism: A Double Challenge for Greece* (London: London School of Economics and Political Science, The Hellenic Observatory/Athens: Hellenic foundation for European and Foreign Policy, 2001), pp. 49–53.

Mudde, C., 'A Fortuynist Foreign Policy', in Liang, C. S. (ed.), *Europe for the Europeans: The Foreign and Security Policy of the Populist Radical Right* (Aldershot: Ashgate, 2007), pp. 209–21.

Mueller, J., *War and Ideas: Selected Essays* (Abingdon: Routledge, 2011).

Müller, J-W. (ed.), *Memory and Power in Post-War Europe: Studies in the Presence of the Past* (Cambridge: Cambridge University Press, 2002).

Musu, C., *European Union Policy Towards the Arab–Israeli Peace Process: The Quicksands of Politics* (Houndmills: Palgrave, 2010).

Nacos, B. L., Shapiro, R. Y., and Isernia, P. (eds), *Decisionmaking in a Glass House: Mass Media, Public Opinion and American and European Foreign Policy in the 21st Century* (Lanham: Rowman & Littlefield, 2000).

Neumann, I. B., *Russia and the Idea of Europe: A Study in Identity and International Relations* (London: Routledge, 1996).

Neumann, I. B., *Uses of the Other: The 'East' in European Identity Formation* (Manchester: Manchester University Press, 1999).

Neumann, I. B. and Welsh, J., 'The Other in European Self-definition: A Critical Addendum to the Literature on International Society', *Review of International* Studies, 17/4 (1991), pp. 327–48.

Niblett, R. and Wallace, W. (eds), *Rethinking European Order: West European Responses, 1989–1997* (Basingstoke: Palgrave, 2001).

Nincic, M., 'Elections and U.S. Foreign Policy', in Wittkopf, E. R. and McCormick, J. M. (eds), *The Domestic Sources of American Foreign Policy: Insights and Evidence* (4th edn, Oxford: Rowman & Littlefield, 2004), pp. 117–27.

Norpoth, H., 'The Popularity of the Thatcher Government: A Matter of War and Economy', in Norpoth, H., Lewis-Beck, M. S., and Lafay, J-D. (eds), *Economics and Politics: The Calculus of Suppor*t (Michigan: University of Michigan Press, 1991) pp. 141–60.

Norpoth, H., Lewis-Beck, M. S., and Lafay, J-D. (eds), *Economics and Politics: The Calculus of Suppor*t (Michigan: University of Michigan Press, 1991).

Nye, J. S. Jr, *Soft Power: The Means to Success in World Politics* (New York: Public Affairs, 2004).

Oakeshott, M., *Experience and its Modes* (Cambridge: Cambridge University Press, 1933; repr. 1966).

Oakeshott, M., *Rationalism in Politics and Other Essays* (London: Methuen, 1962).

Occhipinti, J. D., 'Parallel Paths and Productive Partners: The EU and US on Counter', in Lemieux, F. (ed.), *International Police Cooperation: Emerging Issues, Theory and Practice* (Portland: Willan, 2010), pp. 167–85.

Olsen, G. R., 'The EU and Military Conflict Management in Africa: For the Good of Africa or Europe?', *International Peacekeeping*, 16/2 (2009), pp. 245–60.

Omand, D., *Securing the State* (London: Hurst & Co., 2010).

Osiander, A., *The States System of Europe, 1640–1990: Peacemaking and the Conditions of International Stability* (Oxford: The Clarendon Press, 1994).

Østergaard-Nielsen, E., *Transnational Politics: Turks and Kurds in Germany* (London: Routledge, 2003).

Owen, D., *Balkan Odyssey* (London: Indigo/Gollancz, 1996).

Pace, M., 'Collective Identity: The Greek Case', in Carlsnaes, W., Sjursen, H., and White, B. (eds), *Contemporary European Foreign Policy* (London: Sage, 2004), pp. 227–38.

Palermo, F., 'The Foreign Policy of Italian Regions', *The International Spectator*, 42/2 (2007), pp. 197–208.

Pană, A-D., 'Models of the European Public Sphere' (2007), a paper arising from the EU Social Fund's support of doctoral students, <http://eucommunication.eu/documents/pana.pdf> accessed 1 July 2012.

Panizzon, M., 'Readmission Agreements of EU Member States: A Case for EU Subsidiarity or Dualism?', *Refugee Survey Quarterly*, 31/4 (2012), pp. 101–33.

Paoletti, E., *The Migration of Power and North–South Inequalities: The Case of Italy and Libya* (Houndmills: Palgrave Macmillan, 2010).

Parekh, B., 'The Concept of National Identity', *Journal of Ethnic and Migration Studies*, 21/2 (1995), pp. 255–68.

Parekh, B., 'Terrorism or Intercultural Dialogue', in Booth, K. and Dunne, T. (eds), *Worlds in Collision: Terror and the Future of Global Order* (Houndmills: Palgrave Macmillan, 2002), pp. 270–83.

Parekh, B., *A New Politics of Identity: Political Principles for an Interdependent World* (Houndmills: Palgrave Macmillan, 2008).

Parker, O., 'Roma and the Politics of EU Citizenship in France: Everyday Security and Resistance', *Journal of Common Market Studies*, 50/3 (2012), pp. 475–91.

Parmar, I. and Cox, M. (eds), *Soft Power and Hegemony in US Foreign Affairs: Theoretical, Historical and Contemporary Perspectives* (Abingdon and New York: Routledge, 2010).

Parsi, V. E., 'Conclusion: After the Cold War, A World of Opportunity and Greater Responsibility for Italy Too', in Carbone, M. (ed.), *Italy in the Post-Cold War Order: Adaptation, Bipartisanship, Visibility* (Lanham, Md: Lexington, 2011), pp. 255–70.

Paterson, W. and Wallace, W. (eds), *Foreign Policy-making in Western Europe: A Comparative Approach* (London: Saxon House, 1978).

Pawlak, P. (ed.), *The EU–US Security and Justice Agenda in Action*, Chaillot Paper 127 (European Union Institute for Security Studies, Paris, December 2011).

Pearson, F. S., 'Foreign Military Interventions and Domestic Disputes', *International Studies Quarterly*, 18/3 (1974), pp. 259–90.

Peled, A., *A Question of Loyalty: Military Manpower Policy in Multi-Ethnic States* (Ithaca: Cornell University Press, 1998).

Pelkmans, J. and Limonard, B., 'The Netherlands and the Future of Europe Convention', EPIN Briefing Note (European Policy Institutes Network, March 2003), available online, <http://www.epin.org/new/files/debate_netherlands.pdf> accessed 31 March 2013.

Peruzzi, R., 'Piracy off the Horn of Africa: Bringing Air and Space Power to the Fight', *The Journal of the JAPCC (Joint Air Power Competence Centre)*, 15 (Spring/Summer 2012), pp. 11–15.

Pettifer, J. and Vickers, M., *The Albanian Question: Reshaping the Balkans* (London: I. B. Tauris, 2007).

Pew Forum on Religion and Public Life, *Muslim Networks and Movements in Western Europe* (Washington, DC: Pew Research Center, September 2010), available online <http://www.pewforum.org/Muslim/Muslim-Networks-and-Movements-in-Western-Europe.aspx>.

Phillips, A., *Multiculturalism without Culture* (Princeton: Princeton University Press, 2007).

Pijpers, A., Regelsberger, E., and Wessels, W. (eds), *European Political Cooperation in the 1980s: A Common Foreign Policy for Western Europe?* (Dordrecht: Martinus Nijhoff, 1988).

Pinyol, G., 'Spain's Immigration Policy as a New Instrument of External Action', in Barbé, E. (ed.), *Spain in Europe 2004–2008*, Monograph of the Observatory of European Foreign Policy, 4 (Bellaterra, Barcelona: Institut d'Estudis Europeus, February 2008), pp. 1–6, available at <http://www.iuee.eu/pdf-publicacio/129/aGxqDe5YcIjtGdMGaKAu.PDF> accessed 31 March 2013.

Pipes, D., *The Rushdie Affair: The Novel, the Ayatollah, and the West* (2nd rev. edn, New Brunswick: Transaction Press, 2004).

Popper, K., *The Open Society and its Enemies* Vol. 2 (London: Routledge, 1966).

Powell, C., 'Dalla A(znar) alla Z(apatero)', *Aspenia*, 34 (Rome: Rivista of the Aspen Institute, Italy, 2006), pp. 200–8.

Prizel, I., *National Identity and Foreign Policy: Nationalism and Leadership in Poland, Russia, and Ukraine* (Cambridge: Cambridge University Press, 1998).

Putnam, R. D., Leonardi, R., and Nanetti, R. Y., *Making Democracy Work: Civic Traditions in Modern Italy* (Princeton, NJ: Princeton University Press, 1993).

Qureshi, E. and Sells, M. A. (eds), *The New Crusades: Constructing the Muslim Enemy* (New York: Columbia University Press, 2003).

Rabasa, A., Chalk, P., Cragin, K., Daly, S. A., Gregg, H. S., Karasik, T. W., O'Brien, K. A., and Rosenau, W., *Beyond al-Qaeda. Part 1: The Global Jihadist Movement* (Santa Monica, CA: RAND, 2006); e-book available at <http://www.rand.org/pubs/monographs/2006/RAND_MG429.pdf> accessed 16 December 2012.

Rath, J., Penninx, R., Groenendijk, K., and Meyer, A., *Western Europe and its Islam* (Leiden: Brill, 2001).

Rawls, J., *The Law of Peoples* (Cambridge, MA: Harvard University Press, 1999).

Rees, W., 'The External Face of Internal Security', in Hill, C. and Smith, M. (eds), *International Relations and the European Union* (2nd edn, Oxford: Oxford University Press, 2011), pp. 226–45.

Reher, D-S., Alcalá, L. C., Quiñones, F. G., Requena, M., Domínguez, M. I. S., Gimeno, A. S., and Stanek, M., *Informe encuesta nacional de inmigrantes (ENI-2007)* Documentos de Trabajo 2/2008 (Madrid, April 2008), <http://www.ine.es/daco/daco42/inmigrantes/informe/eni07_informe.pdf> accessed 20 January 2013.

Rex, J., 'The Concept of a Multicultural Society', *Occasional Papers in Ethnic Relations No. 3* (CRER, 1985), reprinted in Guibernau, M. and Rex, J. (eds), *The Ethnicity Reader: Nationalism, Multiculturalism and Migration* (Cambridge: Polity Press, 1997), pp. 205–19.

Riddervold, M. and Sjursen, H., 'The Importance of Solidarity: Denmark as a Promoter of Enlargement', in Sjursen, H. (ed.), *Questioning EU Enlargement: Europe in search of Identity* (London: Routledge, 2006), pp. 81–103.

Rijks, D. and Edwards, G., 'Boundary Problems in EU External Representation', in Aggestam, L., et al., *Institutional Competences in the EU External Action: Actors and Boundaries in CFSP and ESDP* (Stockholm: Swedish Institute for European and Policy Studies, 2008), pp. 15–96.

Risse, T., '"Let's Argue!": Communicative Action in World Politics', *International Organization*, 54/1 (2000), pp. 1–39.

Risse-Kappen, T., 'Public Opinion, Domestic Structure and Liberal Democracies', *World Politics*, 43/4 (1991), pp. 491–517.

Risse-Kappen, T. (ed.), *Bringing Transnational Relations Back In: Non-State Actors, Domestic Structures and International Institutions* (Cambridge: Cambridge University Press, 1995).

Roberts, J. M., *The Triumph of the West* (London: BBC, 1985).

Roma, G., *Italy: The Opportunities Represented by Confusion* (Washington, DC: Centre for Strategic and International Studies, 26 September 1996).

Rosenau, J. N., 'The National Interest', in Sills, D. L. (ed.), *International Encyclopedia of the Social Sciences* (New York: Macmillan and The Free Press, 1968), pp. 34–40.

Rosenau, J. N., *Linkage Politics* (New York: Free Press, 1969).

Rosenau, J. N., *The Scientific Study of Foreign Policy* (New York: Free Press, 1971).

Roy, O., *Secularism confronts Islam* (New York: Columbia University Press, 2007).

Roy, O., 'Defining the Target: Al Qaeda as a "Narrative" for a Rebel Youth Without a Cause', in Scheinen, M. (ed.), '*European and United States Counter-terrorism Policies, the Rule of Law and Human Rights,*' RCAS Policy Paper 2011/3 (Fiesole: Robert Schuman Centre of Advanced Studies, 2011), pp. 27–34.

Rudolf, P., 'The Transatlantic Relationship: A View from Germany', in Maull, H. W. (ed.), *Germany's Uncertain Power: Foreign Policy of the Berlin Republic* (Houndmills: Palgrave Macmillan, 2006), pp. 137–51.

Runblom, H., 'Swedish Multiculturalism in a Comparative European Perspective', *Sociological Forum*, 9/4 (1994), pp. 623–40.

Rytkønen, H., 'Drawing the Line: The Cartoons Controversy in Denmark and the US', in Hvidt, N. and Mouritzen, H. (eds), *Danish Foreign Policy Yearbook 2007* (Copenhagen: Danish Institute for International Studies, 2007), pp. 86–109.

Saha, L., *Du Quartier aux Étoiles. Le Safari du Footballeur* (Paris: Éditions Anne Carrière, with a foreword by Charles Biétry, 2012). Translated as, *Thinking Inside the Box: Reflections on life as a Premier League Footballer* (Kingston upon Thames: Vision Sports, 2012).

Saltarelli, S., Cova, R., and Risso, E., *Identities in Transition: Who Do We Want to Be? The Opinions of Italian and British Youth* (Trieste and Bologna: Publica ReS, 2008).

Sanders, D., Ward, H., and Marsh, D., 'Macro-economics, the Falklands War and the popularity of the Thatcher government: A Contrary View', in Norpoth, H., Lewis-Beck, M. S., and Lafay, J. D. (eds), *Economics and Politics: The Calculus of Support* (Michigan: University of Michigan Press, 1991), pp. 161–84.

Sarrazin, T., *Deutschland schafft sich ab: Wie wir unser Land aufs Spiel setzen* (Munich: Deutsche Verlags-Anstalt, 2010).

Schain, M. A., *The Politics of Immigration in France, Britain and the United States: A Comparative Study* (New York: Palgrave Macmillan, 2008).

Scharpf, F. W., 'The European Social Model: Coping with the Challenges of Diversity', *Journal of Common Market Studies*, 40/4 (2002), pp. 645–70.

Scheffer, P., *Immigrant Nations* (Cambridge: Polity, 2011).

Scheinen, M. (ed.), '*European and United States Counter-terrorism Policies, the Rule of Law and Human Rights*', RCAS Policy Paper 2011/3 (Fiesole: Robert Schuman Centre of Advanced Studies, 2011).

Scheinen, M., Burke, C., and Galand, A. S., *'Rescue at Sea—Human Rights Obligations of States and Private Actors, with a Focus on the EU's External Borders'*, RCAS Policy Paper 2012/5 (Fiesole: Robert Schuman Centre of Advanced Studies, 2012).

Scheppele, K. L., 'Bringing Security Services under the Rule of Law in the Global Anti-Terror Campaign', in Scheinin, M., organiser, *European and United States Counter-terrorism Policies, the Rule of Law and Human Rights*, RCSAS Policy Paper 2011/3 (Fiesole, European University Institute: Robert Schumann Centre for Advanced Studies, 2011), pp. 43–8.

Schindall, J., 'Switzerland's Non-EU Immigrants: Their Integration and Swiss Attitudes', June 2009, <http://www.migrationinformation.org> accessed 12 August 2011.

Schlesinger, A. M., Jr, *The Disuniting of America* (New York: Norton, 1992).

Schmidt, V., *Democracy in Europe: The EU and National Polities* (Oxford: Oxford University Press, 2006).

Schmitt, G. J. (ed.), *Safety, Liberty and Islamist Terrorism: American and European Approaches to Domestic Counter-Terrorism* (Washington DC: American Enterprise Institute, 2010).

Scholte, J. A., *International Relations of Social Change* (Milton Keynes: Open University Press, 1993).

Schönwalder, K., 'Germany: Integration Policy and Pluralism in a Self-conscious Country of Immigration', in Vertovec, S. and Wessendorf, S. (eds), *The Multiculturalism Backlash: European Discourses, Policies and Practices* (London: Routledge, 2010), pp.152–69.

Schroeder, P. W., *Systems, Stability, and Statecraft: Essays on the International History of Modern Europe* (New York: Palgrave Macmillan, 2004).

Schroeder, P. W., 'Not Even for the Seventeenth and Eighteenth Centuries: Power and Order in the Early Modern Era', in May, E. R., Rosecrance, R., and Steiner, Z. (eds), *History and Neorealism* (Cambridge: Cambridge University Press, 2010), pp. 78–102.

Schümer, T., *New Humanitarianism: Britain and Sierra Leone, 1997–2003* (Houndmills: Palgrave, 2008).

Schwarz, P. (ed.), *Die Sarrazin Debatte. Eine Provokation—alle Antworten* (Hamburg: Die Zeit, 2010).

Seldon, A. and Kavanagh, D. (eds), *The Blair Effect, 2001–5* (Cambridge: Cambridge University Press, 2005).

Seldon, A. and Kavanagh, D., *Blair* (London: The Free Press, 2005).

Seldon, A. and Kavanagh, D., *Blair Unbound* (London: Simon & Schuster, 2008).

Shain, Y., *Kinship and Diaspora in International Affairs* (Ann Arbor: University of Michigan Press, 2007).

Shute, S. and Hurley, S., *On Human Rights: The Oxford Amnesty Lectures* (New York: Basic Books, 1993).

Siegel, M. and Neubourg, C. de, '*A Historical Perspective on Immigration and Social Protection in the Netherlands*', UNU-MERIT Working Paper 2011-014 (Maastricht: Maastricht University and United Nations University, 2011), <http://www.merit.unu.edu/publications/wppdf/2011/wp2011-014.pdf> accessed 11 December 2012.

Silj, A. (ed.), *European Multiculturalism Revisited* (London: Zed Books, 2010).

Sills, D. L. (ed.), *International Encyclopedia of the Social Sciences* (New York: Macmillan and The Free Press, 1968).

Silvestri, S., *Islam and the EU: The Merits and Risks of Inter-Cultural Dialogue* (Policy Brief for the European Policy Centre, Brussels, June 2007).

Silvestri, S., 'Europe and Political Islam: Encounters of the Twentieth and Twenty-First Century', in Abbas, T. (ed.), *Islamic Political Radicalism: A European Perspective* (Edinburgh, Edinburgh University Press, 2007), pp. 57–70.

Silvestri, S., *Islam and the EU: The Merits and Risks of Inter-Cultural Dialogue* (Policy Brief for the European Policy Centre, Brussels, June 2007).

Simms, B., *Unfinest Hour: Britain and the Destruction of Bosnia* (London: Penguin Books, 2001).

Simms, B., *Three Victories and a Defeat: The Rise and Fall of the First British Empire, 1714–1783* (London: Allen Lane, 2007).

Simms, B., 'Towards a Mighty Union: How to Create a Democratic European Superpower', *International Affairs*, 88/1 (2012), pp. 49–62.

Simms, B. and Trim, D. J. B. (eds), *Humanitarian Intervention: A History* (Cambridge: Cambridge University Press, 2011).

Simon, P. and Sala Pala, V., '"We're Not Multiculturalists Yet": France Swings Between Hard Integration and Soft Anti-discrimination', in Vertovec, S. and Wessendorf, S. (eds), *The Multiculturalism Backlash: European Discourses, Policies and Practices* (London: Routledge, 2010), pp. 92–110.

Sjursen, H. (ed.), *Questioning EU Enlargement: Europe in Search of Identity* (London: Routledge, 2006).

Skidmore, D. and Hudson, V. M. (eds), *The Limits of State Autonomy: Society Groups and Foreign Policy* (Boulder, CO: Westview Press, 1992).

Smith, A. D., *National Identity* (London: Penguin Books, 1991).

Smith, K. E., *European Union Foreign Policy in a Changing World* (2nd edn, Cambridge: Polity Press, 2008).

Smith, K. E., *Genocide and the Europeans* (Cambridge: Cambridge University Press, 2010).

Smith, K. E. and Light, M. (eds), *Ethics of Foreign Policy* (Cambridge: Cambridge University Press, 2001).

Smith, M. and Steffenson, R., 'The EU and the United States', in Hill, C. and Smith, M. (eds), *International Relations and the European Union* (2nd edn, Oxford: Oxford University Press, 2011), pp. 404–31.

Smith, S., Hadfield, A., and Dunne, T. (eds), *Foreign Policy: Theories, Actors, Cases* (2nd edn, Oxford: Oxford University Press, 2012).

Smith, S. W., 'Nodding and Winking: The French Retreat from Africa', *London Review of Books*, 32/3 (11 February 2010).

Smith, T., *Foreign Attachments: The Power of Ethnic Groups in the Making of US Foreign Policy* (Cambridge, MA: Harvard University Press, 2000).

Snyder, J., *Myths of Empire: Domestic Politics and International Ambition* (Ithaca: Cornell University Press, 1991).

Solana, J., *A Secure Europe in a Better World: European Security Strategy* (Paris: European Union Institute for Security Studies, 2003).

Spång, M., 'Sweden: Europeanization of Policy, but not of Politics?', in Faist, T. and Ette, A. (eds), *The Europeanization of National Policies and Politics of Immigration: Between Autonomy and the European Union* (Houndmills: Palgrave Macmillan, 2007), pp. 116–35.

Spence, D. (ed.), *The European Union and Terrorism* (London: John Harper, 2007).

Spini, D., 'The Double Face of Civil Society', in Cerutti, F. and Lucarelli, S. (eds), *The Search for a European Identity: Values, Policies and Legitimacy of the European Union* (London: Routledge, 2008), pp. 142–56.

Sprout, H. and Sprout, M., *Foundations of International Politics* (Princeton, NJ: Van Nostrand Co., 1962).

Stavridis, S. and Hill, C. (eds), *Domestic Sources of Foreign Policy: Western European Reactions to the Falklands Conflict* (Oxford: Berg, 1996).

Suganami, H., *The Domestic Analogy and World Order Proposals* (Cambridge: Cambridge University Press, 1989).

Sunier, T., 'Assimilation by Conviction or Coercion? Integration Policies in the Netherlands', in Silj, A. (ed.), *European Multiculturalism Revisited* (London: Zed Books, 2010), pp. 214–34.

Talmon, J. L., *A History of Totalitarian Democracy* (London: Secker and Warburg, 1952).

Tarchi, M., 'Recalcitrant Allies: The Conflicting Foreign Policy Agenda of the *Alleanza Nazionale* and the *Lega Nord*', in Liang, C. S. (ed.), *Europe for the Europeans: The Foreign and Security Policy of the Populist Radical Right* (Aldershot: Ashgate, 2007), pp. 187–207.

Taspinar, O., 'Europe's Muslim Street', *Foreign Policy*, 135 (March/April 2003), pp. 76–7.

Tayar, E., *1943: i giorni della pioggia* (Firenze: Edizioni Polistampa, 2001).

Tayfur, M. F., *Semiperipheral Development and Foreign Policy: The Cases of Greece and Spain* (Aldershot: Ashgate, 2003).

Taylor, A. J. P., *The Trouble Makers: Dissent over Foreign Policy, 1792–1939* (London: Hamish Hamilton, 1957).

Telò, M., *L'Europa potenza civile* (Roma-Bari: Editori Laterza, 2004).

Telò, M. and Magnette, P. (eds), *Repenser l'Europe* (Brussels: Editions de l'Université de Bruxelles, 1996).

Tetlock, P. E., Lebow, R. N., and Parker, G. (eds), *Unmaking the West: 'What-if?' Scenarios that Rewrite World History* (Ann Arbor: University of Michigan Press, 2006).

Thatcher, M., *The Downing Street Years* (London: HarperCollins, 1993).

Tocci, N., 'The Europeanization of Minority–Majority Relations in the Greece–Turkey–Cyprus Triangle', in Weller, M., Blacklock, D., and Nobbs, K. (eds), *The Protection of Minorities in the Wider Europe* (Houndmills: Palgrave Macmillan, 2008), pp. 251–75.

Tocci, N. and Bechev, D., 'Will Turkey Find its Place in Post-crisis Europe?', Global Turkey in Europe, Policy Brief (Rome: Istituto degli Affari Internazionali, 5 December 2012).

Toje, A., *The European Union as a Small Power: After the Post-Cold War* (Houndmills: Palgrave Macmillan, 2010).

Tonra, B., 'Denmark and Ireland', in Manners, I. and Whitman, R. (eds), *The Foreign Policies of European Union Member States* (Manchester: Manchester University Press, 2000), pp. 224–42.

Tonra, B., *Global Citizen and European Republic: Irish Foreign Policy in Transition* (Manchester: Manchester University Press, 2006).

Townshend, C., *Terrorism: A Very Short Introduction* (Oxford: Oxford University Press, 2011).

Trägårdh, L., 'Sweden and the EU: Welfare State Nationalism and the Spectre of "Europe"', in Hansen, L. and Wæver, O. (eds), *European Integration and National Identity: The Challenge of the Nordic states* (London: Routledge, 2002), pp. 130–81.

Trägårdh, L. (ed.), *State and Civil Society in Northern Europe: The Swedish Model Reconsidered* (Oxford: Berghahn Books, 2007).

Triandafyllidou, A., *Immigrants and National Identity in Europe* (London: Routledge, 2001).

Triandafyllidou, A., 'Religious Diversity and Mutliculturalism in Southern Europe: The Italian Mosque Debate', in Modood, T., Triandafyllidou, A., and Zapata-Barrero, R. (eds), *Multiculturalism, Muslims and Citizenship: A European Approach* (London: Routledge, 2006), pp. 117–42.

Triandafyllidou, A., 'Greek Immigration at the Turn of the Twenty-First Century: Lack of Political Will or Purposeful Mismanagement?', *European Journal of Migration and Law*, 11/3 (2009), pp. 159–77.

Triandafyllidou, A. (ed.), *Irregular Migration in Europe: Myths and Realities* (Aldershot: Ashgate, 2010).

Triandafyllidou, A. and Gropas, R., 'Constructing Difference: The Mosque Debates in Greece', *Journal of Ethnic and Migration Studies*, 35/6 (2009), pp. 957–75.

Triandafyllidou, A. and Gropas, R., 'Migrants and Political Life in Greece: Between Political Patronage and the Search for Inclusion', *South European Society and Politics*, 17/1 (2012), pp. 45–63.

Triandafyllidou, A. and Maroukis, T., *Migrant Smuggling: Irregular Migration from Asia and Africa to Europe* (Basingstoke: Palgrave Macmillan, 2012).

Tripodi, P., 'Operation Alba: A Necessary and Successful Preventive Deployment', *International Peacekeeping*, 9/4 (2002), pp. 89–104.

Tsardanidis, C., 'Immigration and its Impact on Greek Foreign Policy', *Hellenic Studies* (Quebec), 15/1 (2007), pp. 133–60.

Tsardanidis, C. and Stavridis, S., 'Greece: From Special Case to Limited Europeanisation', in Wong, R. and Hill, C. (eds), *National and European Foreign Policy: Towards Europeanization* (London: Routledge, 2011), pp. 111–30.

Tsoukalis, L. (ed.), *Globalisation and Regionalism: A Double Challenge for Greece* (London: London School of Economics and Political Science, The Hellenic Observatory/Athens: Hellenic Foundation for European and Foreign Policy, 2001).

Verbeek, B. and van Ufford, P. Q., 'Non-State Actors in Foreign Policy-Making: A Policy Sub-System Approach', in Art, B., Noortmann, M., and Reinalda, B. (eds), *Non-State Actors in International Relations* (Farnham: Ashgate, 2001), pp. 127–44.

Vertovec, S. (ed.), *Migration*, 5 vols (Abingdon: Routledge, 2009).

Vertovec, S., *Transnationalism* (London: Routledge, 2009).

Vertovec, S. and Cohen, R. (eds), *Migration, Diasporas and Transnationalism* (Cheltenham: Edward Elgar, 1999).

Vertovec, S. and Wessendorf, S. (eds), *The Multiculturalism Backlash: European Discourses, Policies and Practices* (London: Routledge, 2010).

'*A Very Special Relationship: Why Turkey's EU Accession Process Will Continue*', Opinión Europa, No. 91 (Barcelona Centre for International Affairs, CIDOB, November 2010), <http://www.cidob.org/en/publications/opinion/europa/a_very_special_relationship_why_turkey_s_eu_accession_process_will_continue> accessed 19 December 2012.

Vince, N., LSE Blog, 19 July 2012, <http://www.blogs.lse.ac.uk/europpblog/category/authors/natalya-vince/> accessed 29 July 2012.

Vincent, J., *Human Rights and International Relations* (Cambridge: Cambridge University Press, 1986).

Vink, M. P., 'Dutch "Multiculturalism": Beyond the Pillarisation Myth', *Political Studies*, 5/3 (2007), pp. 337–50.

Vlcek, W., 'Hitting the Right Target: EU and Security Council Pursuit of Terrorist Financing', *Critical Studies on Terrorism*, 2/2 (2009), pp. 275–91.

Wæver, O., 'Identity, Communities and Foreign Policy', in Hansen, L. and Wæver, O. (eds), *European Integration and National Identity: The Challenge of the Nordic States* (London: Routledge, 2002), pp. 20–49.

Wæver, O., Buzan, B., Kelstrup, M., and Lemaitre, P., *Identity, Migration and the New Security Agenda in Europe* (London: Pinter, 1993).

Wagener, M., 'Normalization in Security Policy? Deployments of Bundeswehr Forces Abroad in the Era Schröder, 1998–2004', in Maull, H. W. (ed.), *Germany's Uncertain Power: Foreign Policy of the Berlin Republic* (Houndmills: Palgrave Macmillan, 2006), pp. 79–92.

Wallace, W., 'The Role of Interest-groups', in Boardman, R. and Groom, A. J. R. (eds), *The Management of Britain's External Relations* (London: Macmillan, 1973), pp. 263–88.

Wallace, W., 'Foreign Policy and National Identity in the United Kingdom', *International Affairs*, 67/1 (1991), pp. 65–80.

Waller, M. and Linklater, A. (eds), *Political Loyalty and the Nation-State* (London: Routledge, 2003).

Walzer, M., *Politics and Passion: Towards a More Egalitarian Liberalism* (New Haven, CT: Yale University Press, 2004).

Weil, P. and Crowley, J., 'Integration in Theory and Practice: A Comparison of France and Britain', in Baldwin-Edwards, M. and Schain, M. A. (eds), *The Politics of Immigration in Western Europe* (London: Frank Cass, 1994), pp. 110–26.

Weiler, J. H. H., 'State, Faith and Nation', the 33rd Corbishley Lecture given at the House of Commons, London 14 September 2011, available online <http://www.wpct.org/lectures.htm> accessed 31 March 2013.

Weiler, J. H. H., *The Constitution of Europe: 'Do the New Clothes Have an Emperor?', And Other Essays on European Integration* (Cambridge: Cambridge University Press, 1999).

Weinberg, G. L., *A World At Arms: A Global History of World War II* (Cambridge: Cambridge University Press, 1994).

Weller, M., Blacklock, D., and Nobbs, K. (eds), *The Protection of Minorities in the Wider Europe* (Houndsmill: Palgrave Macmillan, 2008).

Welsh, J. M. (ed.), *Humanitarian Intervention and International Relations* (Oxford: Oxford University Press, 2004).

Welsh, J. M., 'A Normative Case for Pluralism: Reassessing Vincent's Views on Humanitarian Intervention', *International Affairs*, 87/5 (September 2011), pp. 1196–9.

Wendt, A., 'Anarchy is What States Make of It: The Social Construction of Power Politics', *International Organization*, 46/2 (1992), pp. 391–425.

Wendt, A., *Social Theory of International Politics* (Cambridge: Cambridge University Press, 1999).

Westin, C., 'Temporal and Spatial Aspects of Multiculturality', in Bauböck, R. and Rundell, J. (eds), *Blurred Boundaries: Migration, Ethnicity, Citizenship* (Aldershot: Ashgate, 1998).

Wetzling, T., 'What Role for What Rule of Law in EU—US Counterterrorism Cooperation?', in Pawlak, P. (ed.), *The EU-US Security and Justice Agenda in Action*, Chaillot Paper 127 (European Union Institute for Security Studies, Paris, December 2011), pp. 29–40.

White, B., Little, R., and Smith, M. (eds), *Issues in World Politics* (Houndmills: Macmillan, 1997).

Whyte, G. R., *The Dreyfus Affair: A Chronological History* (Houndmills: Palgrave, 2005).

Wihtol de Wenden, C., *Les immigrés et la politique. Cent cinquante ans d'évolution* (Paris: Presses de la Fondation nationale des sciences politique, 1988).

Wilde, T. de, D'Estmael, 'La politique étrangère de la Belgique 2004–2006. Un essai d'évaluation', *Studia Diplomatica. The Brussels Journal of International Relations*, 60 (2007), pp. 73–83.

Williams, M. C., *The Realist Tradition and the Limits of International Relations* (Cambridge: Cambridge University Press, 2005).

Williams, M. C. (ed.), *Realism Reconsidered: The Legacy of Hans J. Morgenthau in International Relations* (Oxford: Oxford University Press, 2007).

Wind, M., 'The Blind, the Deaf and the Dumb! How Domestic Politics Turned the Danish Schengen Controversy into a Foreign Policy Crisis', in Hvidt, N. and Mouritzen, H. (eds), *Danish Foreign Policy Yearbook 2012* (Copenhagen: Danish Institute for International Studies, 2012), pp. 131–56.

Withol de Wenden, C., 'Immigrants as Political Actors in France', in Baldwin-Edwards, M. and Schain, M. A. (eds), *The Politics of Immigration in Western Europe* (London: Frank Cass, 1994), pp. 91–109.

Wittkopf, E. R. and McCormick, J. M. (eds), *The Domestic Sources of American Foreign Policy: Insights and Evidence* (4th edn, Oxford: Rowman & Littlefield, 2004).

Wolfers, A., *Discord and Collaboration: Essays on International Politics* (Baltimore: Johns Hopkins University Press, 1962).

Wolff, S., *The Mediterranean Dimension of the European Union's Internal Security* (Houndmills: Palgrave, 2012).

Wolff, S., Goudappel, F. A. N. J., and de Zwaan, J. W. (eds), *Freedom, Security and Justice after Lisbon and Stockholm* (The Hague: T. M. C. Asser Press, 2011).

Wolff, S. and Trauner, F., 'A Migration Policy Fit for Future Challenges', in Wolff, S., Goudappel, F. A. N. J., and de Zwaan, J. W. (eds), *Freedom, Security and Justice after Lisbon and Stockholm* (The Hague: T. M. C. Asser Press, 2011), pp. 63–78.

Wolff, S. and Zapata-Barrero, R., 'Border Management: Impacting on the Construction of the EU as a Polity', in Wolff, S., Goudappel, F. A. N. J., and de Zwaan, J. W. (eds), *Freedom, Security and Justice after Lisbon and Stockholm* (The Hague: T. M. C. Asser Press, 2011), pp. 117–34.

Wong, R. and Hill, C. (eds), *National and European Foreign Policies: Towards Europeanization* (London: Routledge, 2011).

Young, I. M., *Justice and the Politics of Difference* (Princeton: Princeton University Press, 1990).

Youngs, R., 'The European Union and Democracy Promotion in the Mediterranean: A New or Disingenuous Strategy?', *Democratization*, 9/1 (2002), pp. 40–62.

Zaotti, R., *Cultures of Border Control: Schengen and the Evolution of European Frontiers* (London: University of Chicago Press, 2011).

Zapata-Barrero, R., 'The Muslim Community and Spanish Tradition: Maurophobia as a Fact, and Impartiality as a Desideratum', in Modood, T., Triandafyllidou, A., and Zapata-Barrero, R. (eds), *Multiculturalism, Muslims and Citizenship: A European Approach* (London: Routledge, 2006), pp. 143–61.

Zapata-Barrero, R., 'Dynamics of Diversity in Spain: Old Questions, New Challenges', in Vertovec, S. and Wessendorf, S. (eds), *The Multiculturalism Backlash: European Discourses, Policies and Practices* (London: Routledge, 2010), pp. 170–89.

Zarakol, A., 'What Makes Terrorism Modern? Terrorism, Legitimacy, and the International System', *Review of International Studies*, 37/5 (2010), pp. 2311–36.

Zarakol, A., *After Defeat: How the East Learned to Live with the West* (Cambridge: Cambridge University Press, 2011).

Zielonka, J., *Explaining Euro-Paralysis: Why Europe is Unable to Act in International Politics* (Houndmills: Macmillan, 1998).

Zielonka, J., *Europe as Empire: The Nature of the Enlarged European Union* (Oxford: Oxford University Press, 2006).

Index

Printed and bound by CPI Group (UK) Ltd, Croydon, CR0 4YY